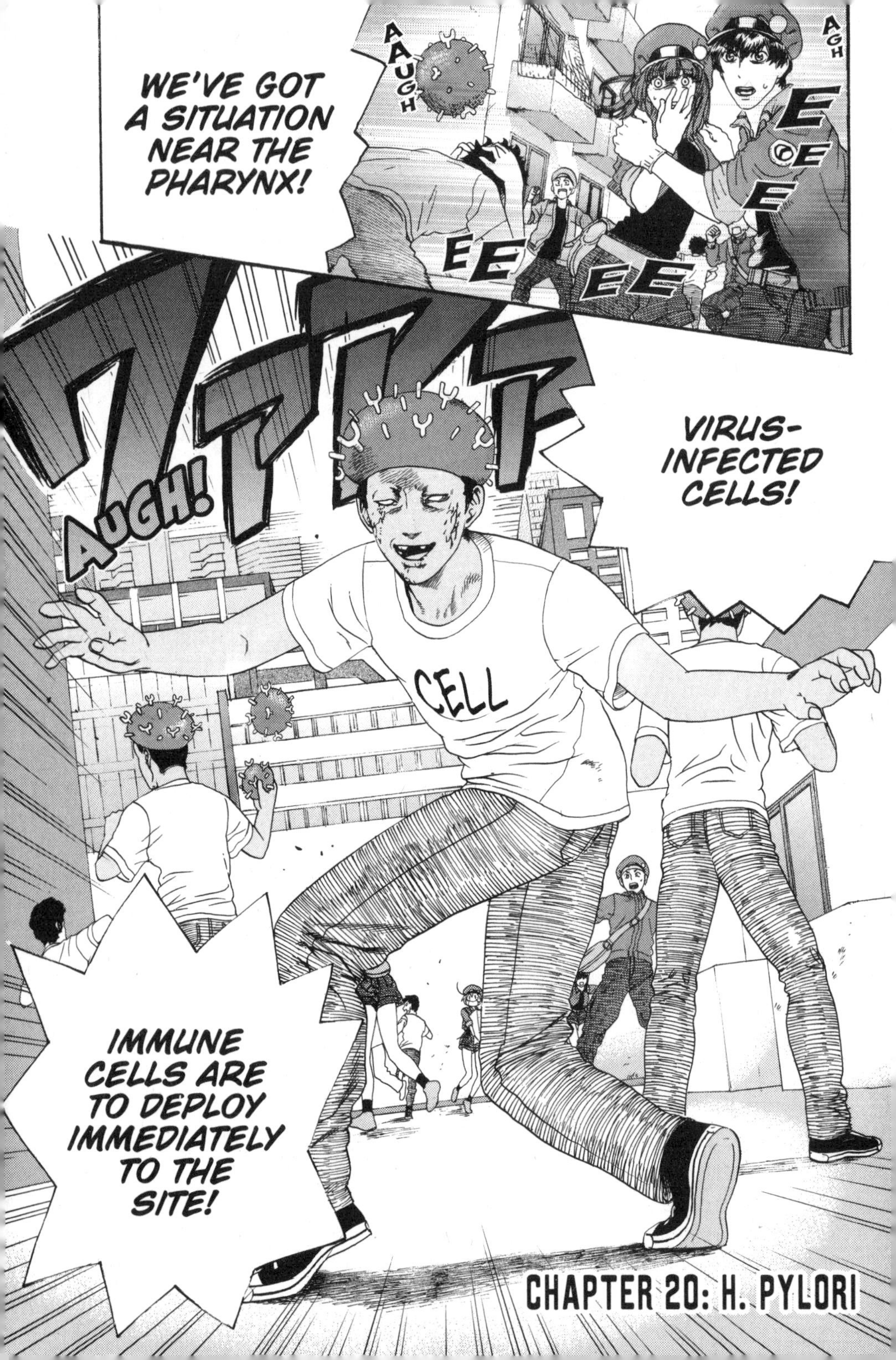
AGH
EEE
WE'VE GOT A SITUATION NEAR THE PHARYNX!
AAUGH
EEEE
VIRUS-INFECTED CELLS!
AUGH!
CELL
IMMUNE CELLS ARE TO DEPLOY IMMEDIATELY TO THE SITE!
CHAPTER 20: H. PYLORI

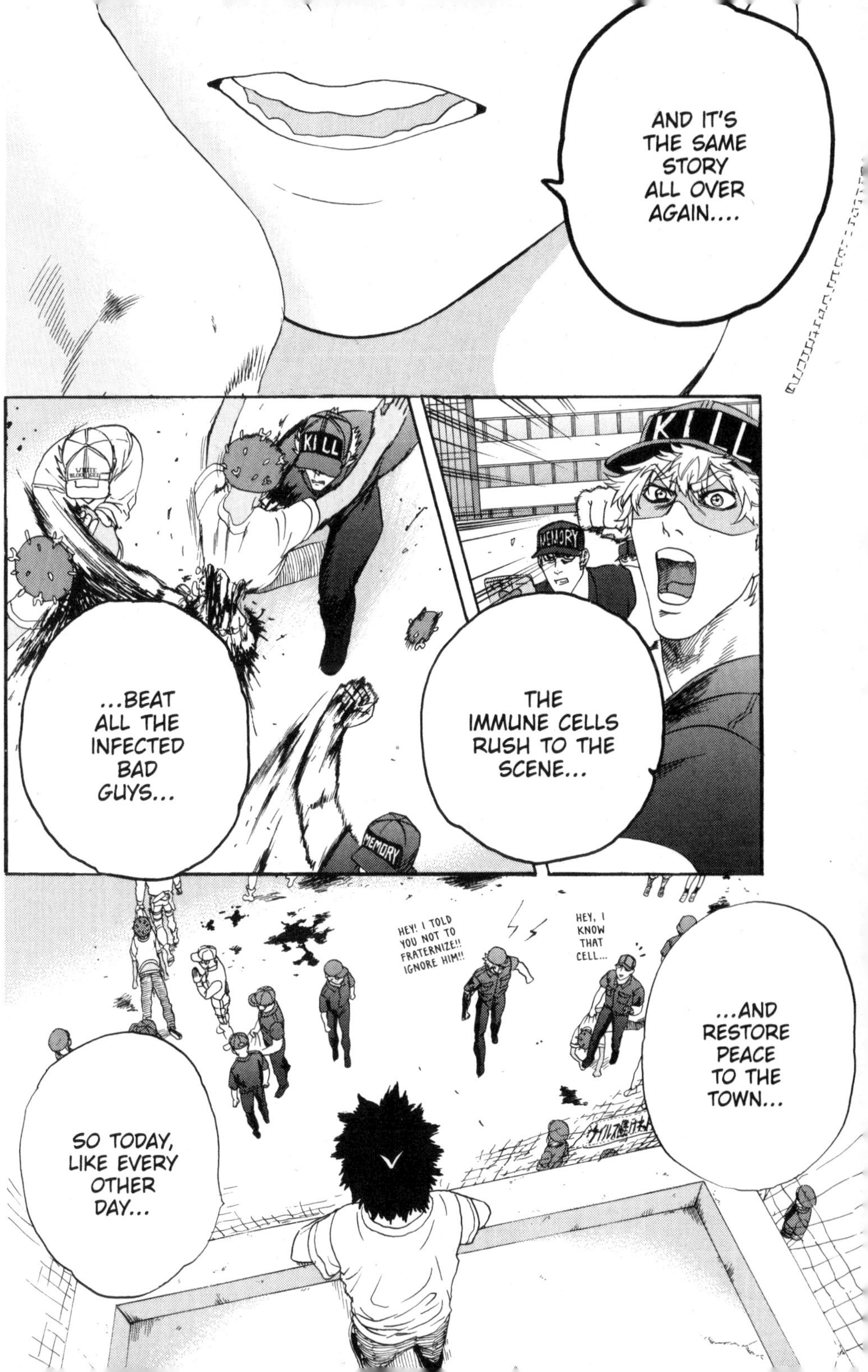
AND IT'S THE SAME STORY ALL OVER AGAIN....
THE IMMUNE CELLS RUSH TO THE SCENE...
...BEAT ALL THE INFECTED BAD GUYS...
...AND RESTORE PEACE TO THE TOWN...
HEY, I KNOW THAT CELL...
HEY! I TOLD YOU NOT TO FRATERNIZE!! IGNORE HIM!!
SO TODAY, LIKE EVERY OTHER DAY...

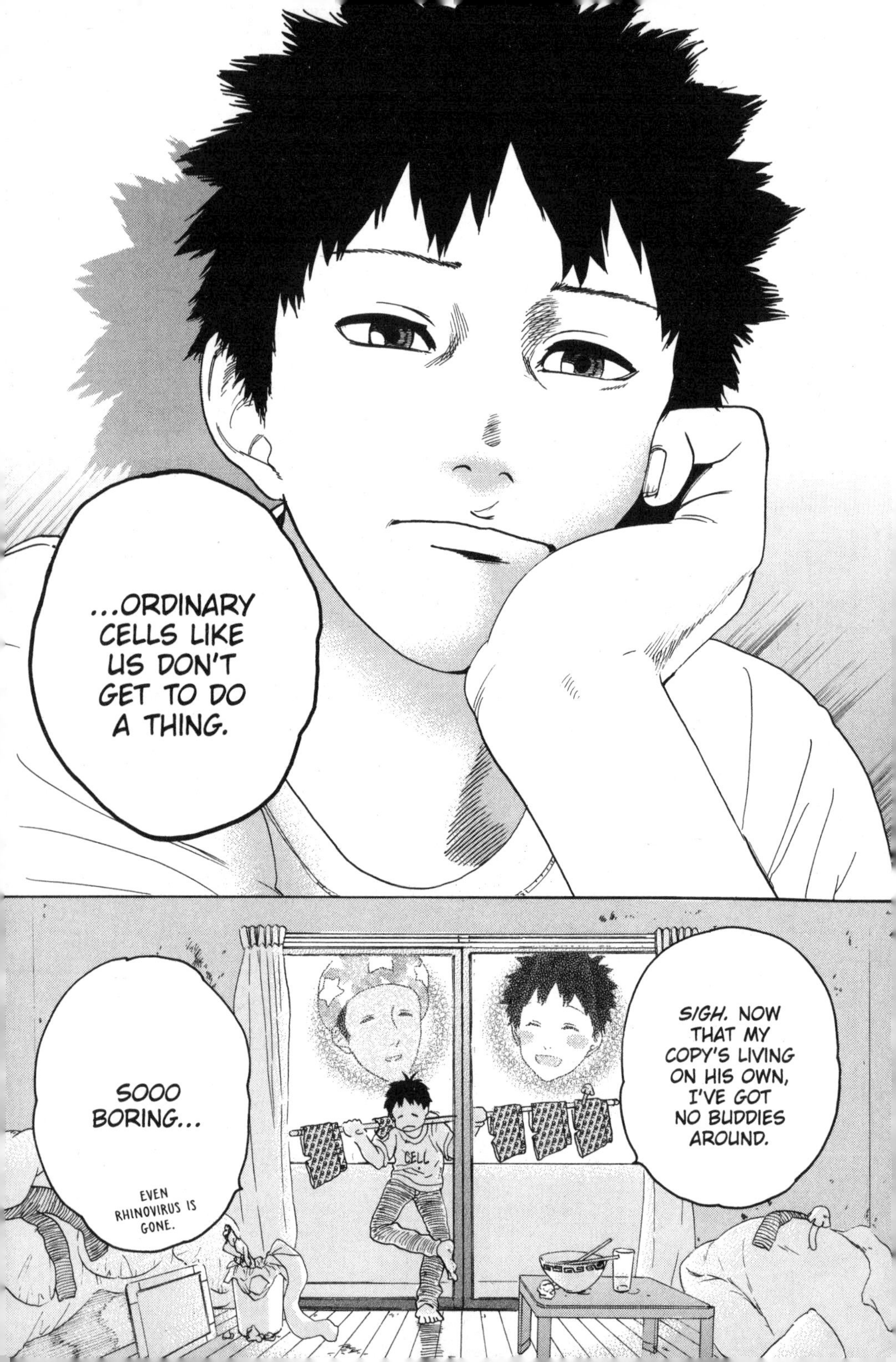
...ORDINARY CELLS LIKE US DON'T GET TO DO A THING.
SIGH. NOW THAT MY COPY'S LIVING ON HIS OWN, I'VE GOT NO BUDDIES AROUND.
SOOO BORING...
EVEN RHINOVIRUS IS GONE.

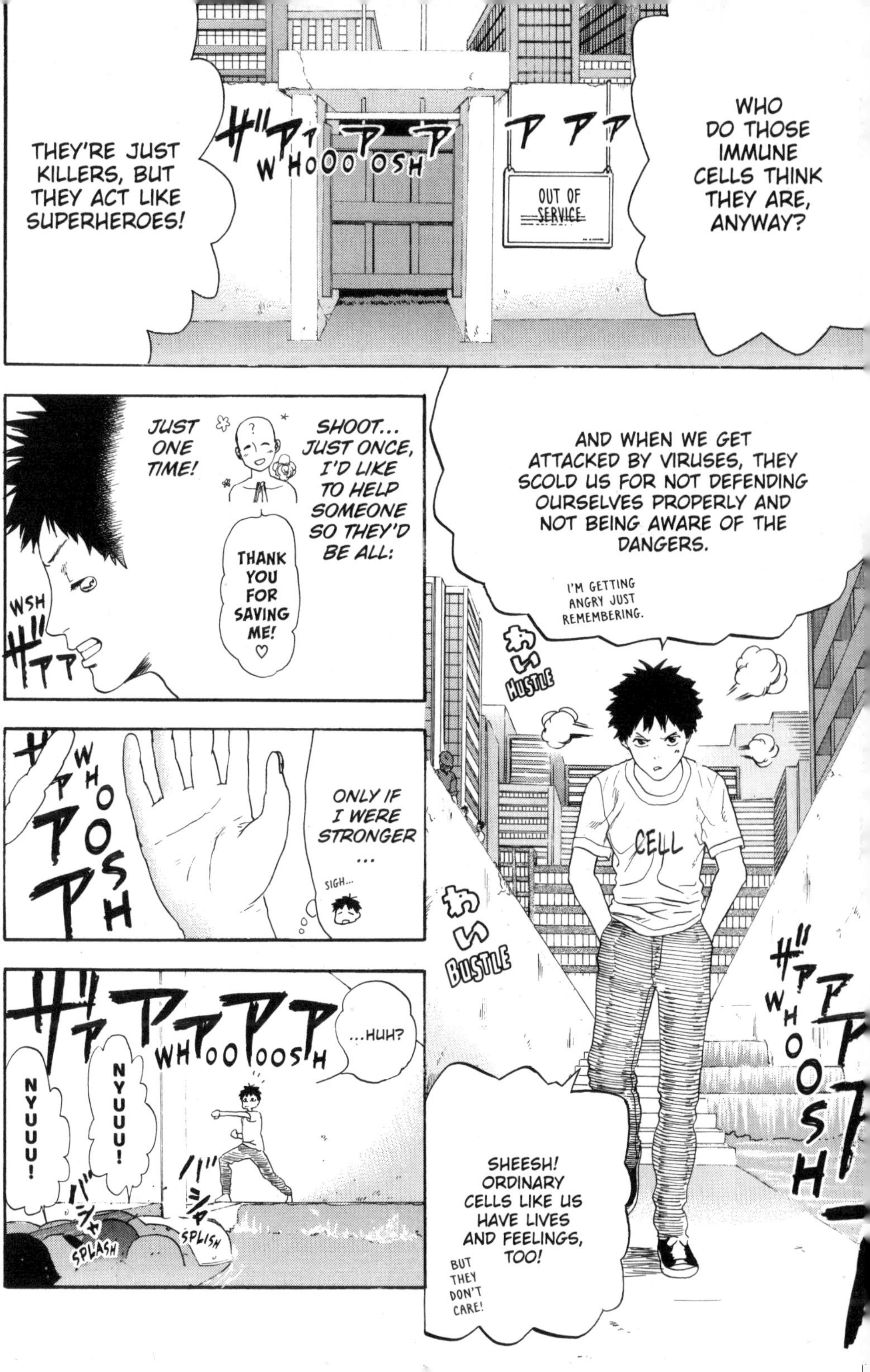
WHO DO THOSE IMMUNE CELLS THINK THEY ARE, ANYWAY?
WHOOOOSH
OUT OF SERVICE
THEY'RE JUST KILLERS, BUT THEY ACT LIKE SUPERHEROES!
AND WHEN WE GET ATTACKED BY VIRUSES, THEY SCOLD US FOR NOT DEFENDING OURSELVES PROPERLY AND NOT BEING AWARE OF THE DANGERS.
I'M GETTING ANGRY JUST REMEMBERING.
HUSTLE
CELL
WHOOOSH
BUSTLE
SHEESH! ORDINARY CELLS LIKE US HAVE LIVES AND FEELINGS, TOO!
BUT THEY DON'T CARE!
SHOOT... JUST ONCE, I'D LIKE TO HELP SOMEONE SO THEY'D BE ALL:
THANK YOU FOR SAVING ME! ♡
JUST ONE TIME!
WSH
ONLY IF I WERE STRONGER ...
SIGH...
WHOOSH
...HUH?
WHOOOOOSH
NYUUUU!
NYUUUU!
SPLISH
SPLASH

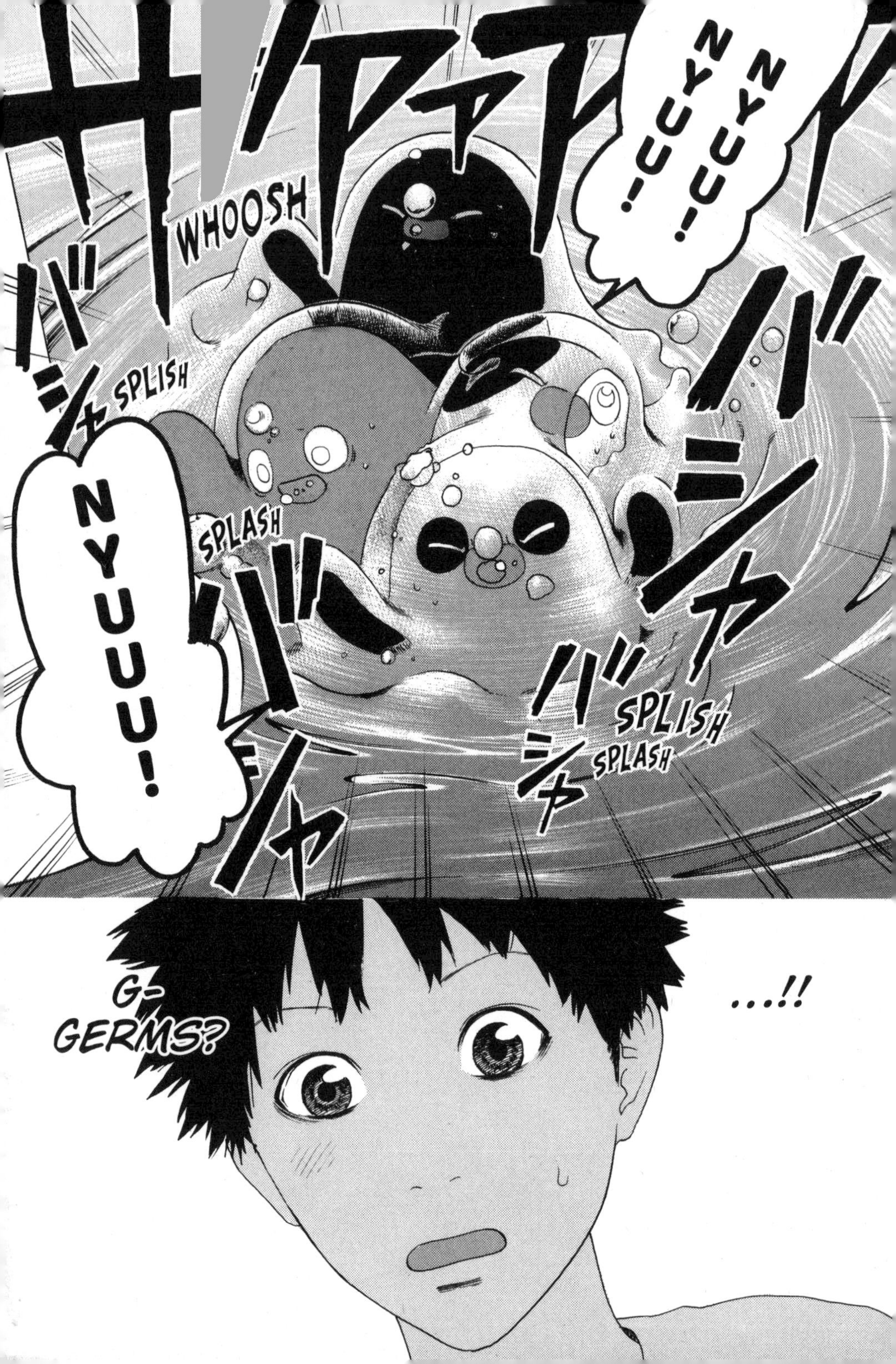
NYUUU! NYUUU!
WHOOSH
SPLISH
SPLASH
NYUUU!
SPLISH SPLASH
...!!
G- GERMS?

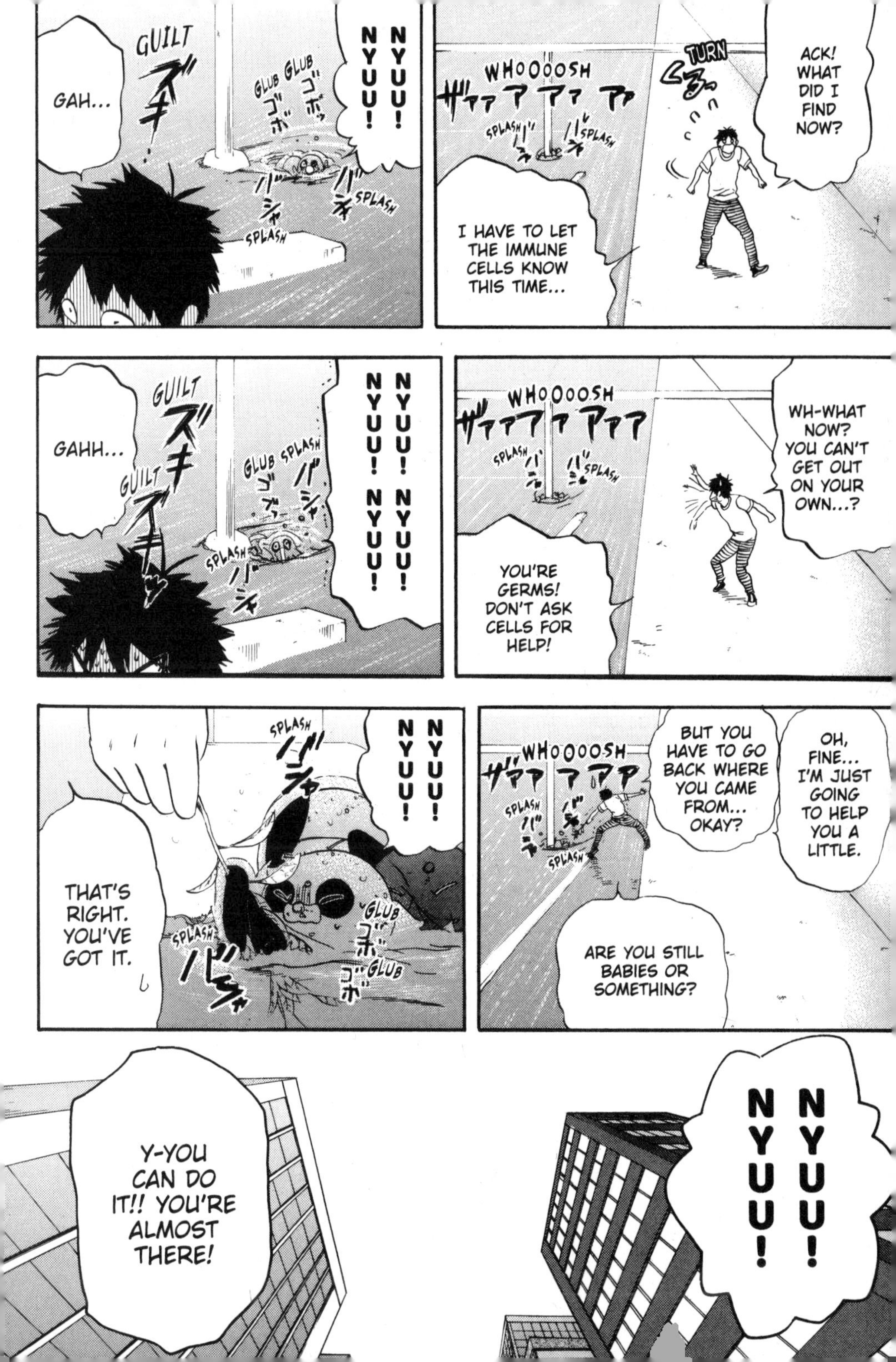
ACK! WHAT DID I FIND NOW?
TURN
WHOOOOSH
SPLASH
SPLASH
I HAVE TO LET THE IMMUNE CELLS KNOW THIS TIME...
NYUU! NYUU!
GUILT
GLUB GLUB
GAH...
SPLASH
SPLASH
WH-WHAT NOW? YOU CAN'T GET OUT ON YOUR OWN...?
WHOOOOSH
SPLASH
SPLASH
YOU'RE GERMS! DON'T ASK CELLS FOR HELP!
NYUU! NYUU! NYUU! NYUU!
GUILT
GAHH...
GLUB SPLASH
GUILT
SPLASH
OH, FINE... I'M JUST GOING TO HELP YOU A LITTLE.
BUT YOU HAVE TO GO BACK WHERE YOU CAME FROM... OKAY?
WHOOOOSH
SPLASH
SPLASH
ARE YOU STILL BABIES OR SOMETHING?
NYUU! NYUU!
SPLASH
THAT'S RIGHT. YOU'VE GOT IT.
SPLASH
GLUB
GLUB
NYUU! NYUU!
Y-YOU CAN DO IT!! YOU'RE ALMOST THERE!

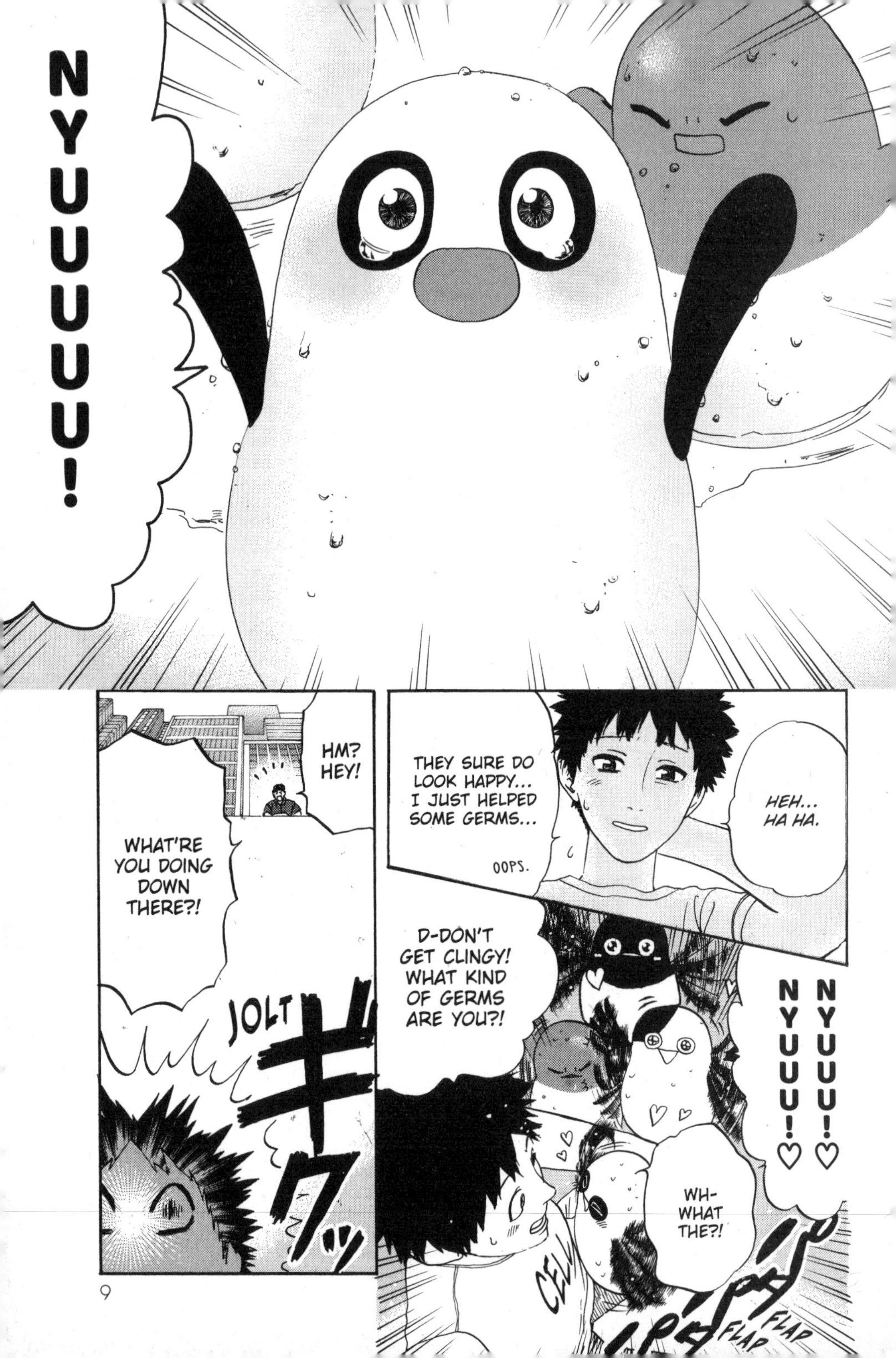
NYUUUUU!
HEH... HA HA.
THEY SURE DO LOOK HAPPY... I JUST HELPED SOME GERMS...
OOPS.
NYUUU!♡
NYUUU!♡
D-DON'T GET CLINGY! WHAT KIND OF GERMS ARE YOU?!
WH-WHAT THE?!
CELL
FLAP FLAP
HM? HEY!
WHAT'RE YOU DOING DOWN THERE?!
JOLT

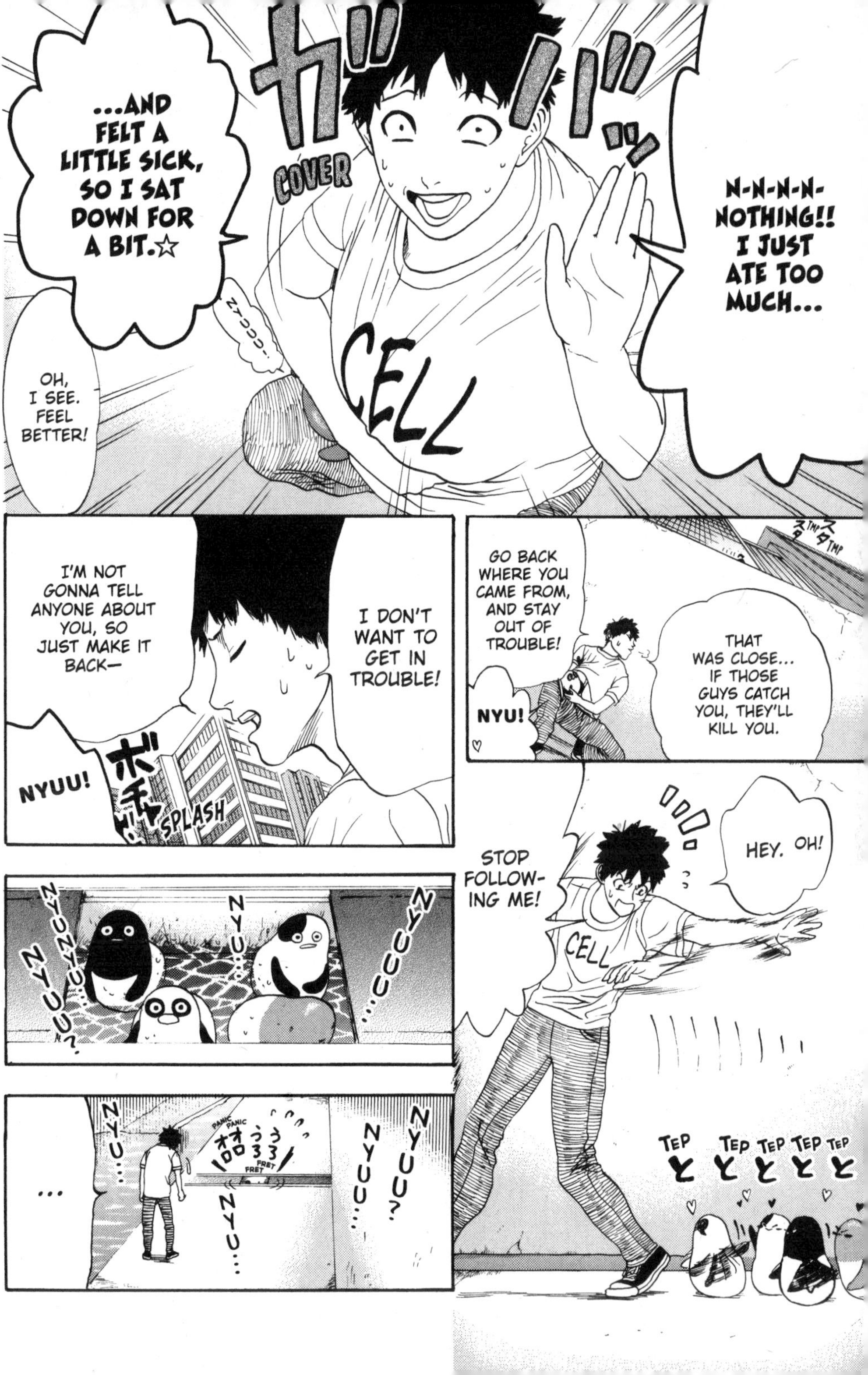

N-N-N-N-NOTHING!! I JUST ATE TOO MUCH...
...AND FELT A LITTLE SICK, SO I SAT DOWN FOR A BIT.☆
COVER
ZYUUU...
OH, I SEE. FEEL BETTER!
TMP TMP
THAT WAS CLOSE... IF THOSE GUYS CATCH YOU, THEY'LL KILL YOU.
GO BACK WHERE YOU CAME FROM, AND STAY OUT OF TROUBLE!
NYU!
I DON'T WANT TO GET IN TROUBLE!
I'M NOT GONNA TELL ANYONE ABOUT YOU, SO JUST MAKE IT BACK—
NYUU!
SPLASH
HEY. OH!
STOP FOLLOW-ING ME!
TEP TEP TEP TEP TEP
NYUUUU...
NYU...
NYUNYU...
NYUUU?
...
NYU...
PANIC PANIC
FRET FRET
NYUUU?
NYUU...
NYU...

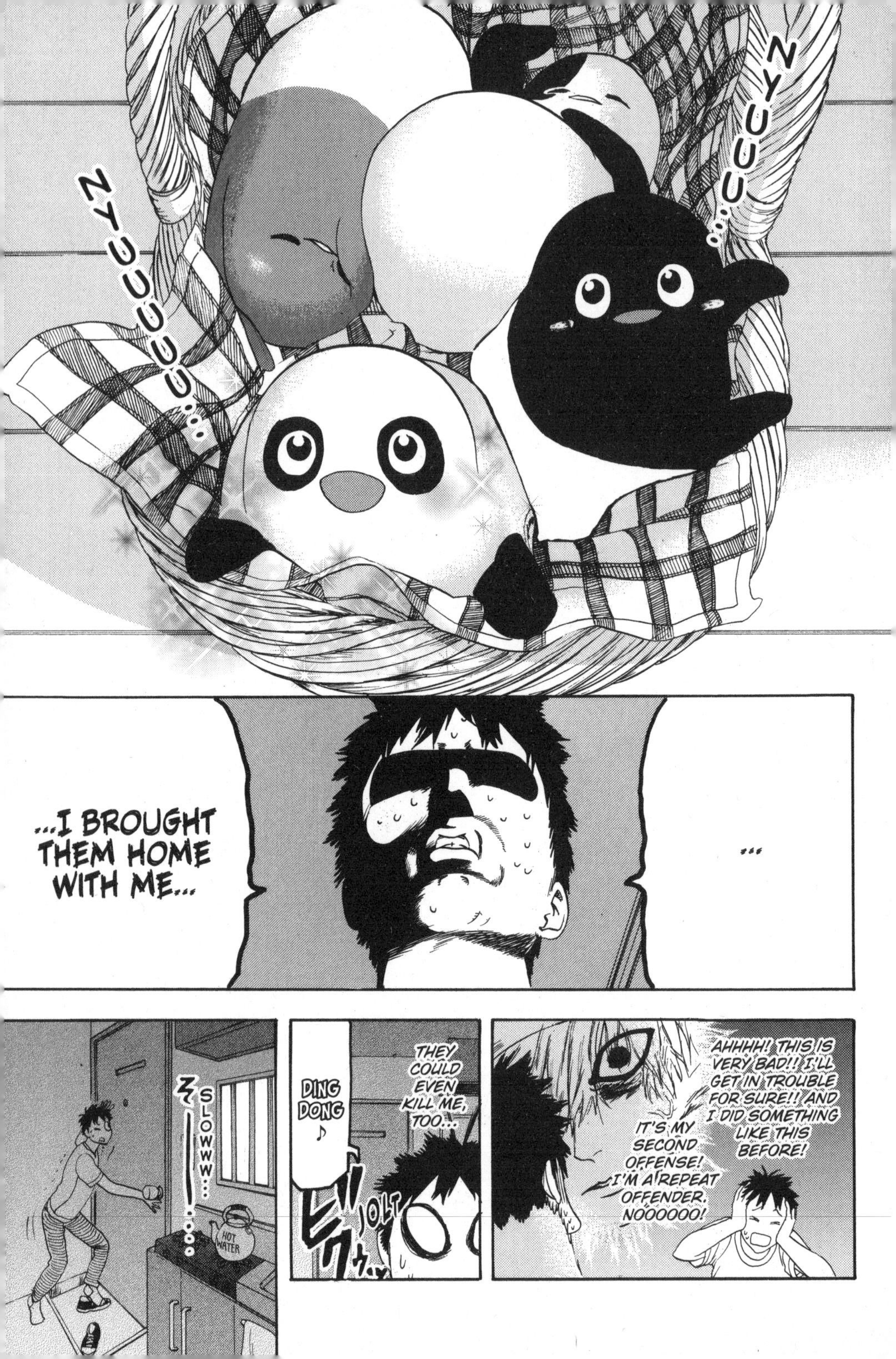
NYUUUU...
NYUUUUUU...
...
...I BROUGHT THEM HOME WITH ME...
AHHHH! THIS IS VERY BAD!! I'LL GET IN TROUBLE FOR SURE!! AND I DID SOMETHING LIKE THIS BEFORE!
IT'S MY SECOND OFFENSE! I'M A REPEAT OFFENDER. NOOOOOO!
THEY COULD EVEN KILL ME, TOO...
DING DONG ♪
JOLT
SLOWWW...
HOT WATER

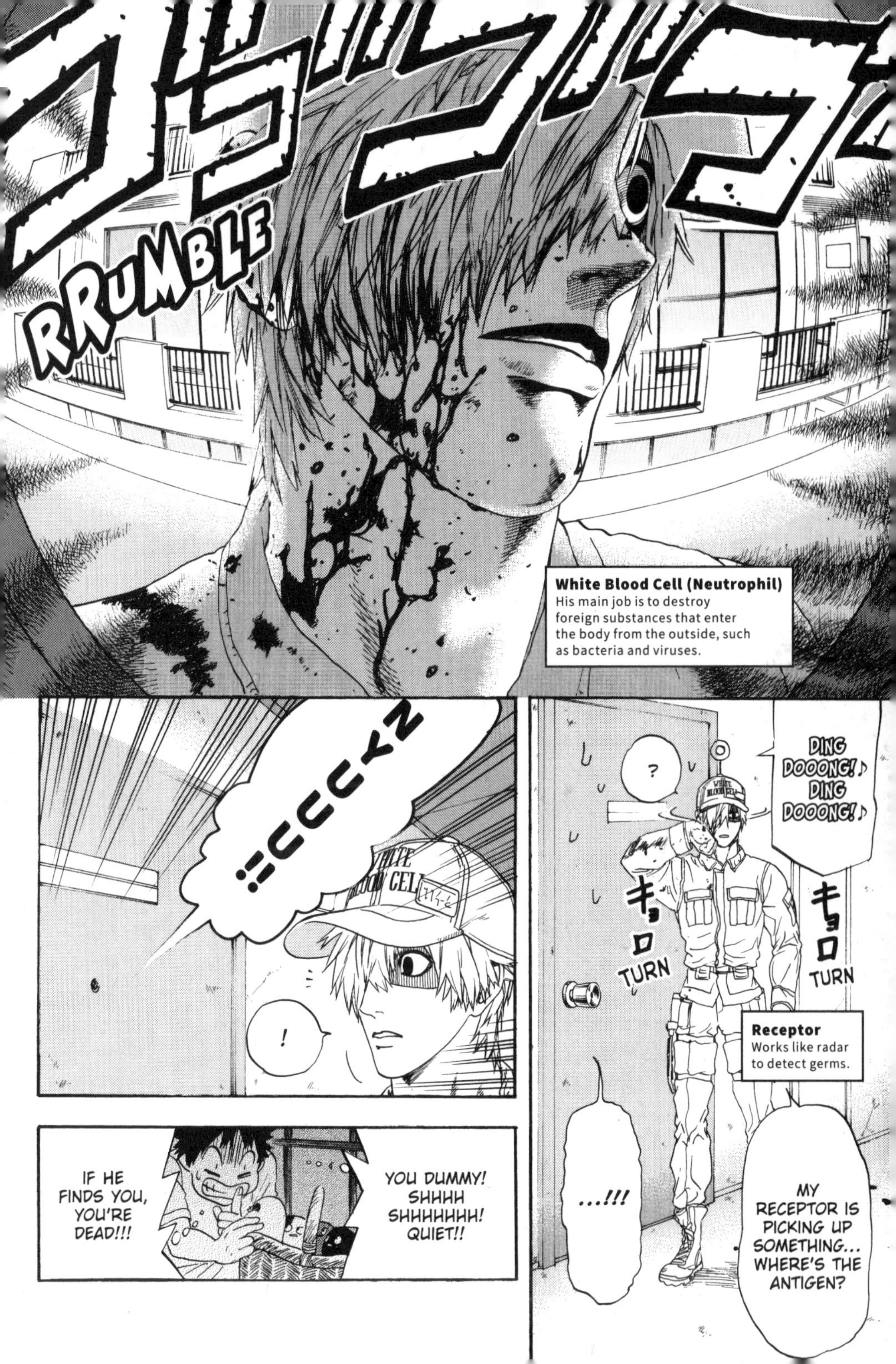

RRUMBLE
White Blood Cell (Neutrophil)
His main job is to destroy foreign substances that enter the body from the outside, such as bacteria and viruses.
DING DOOONG!♪ DING DOOONG!♪
?
キョロ TURN
キョロ TURN
Receptor
Works like radar to detect germs.
MY RECEPTOR IS PICKING UP SOMETHING... WHERE'S THE ANTIGEN?
...!!!
!
YOU DUMMY! SHHHH SHHHHHHH! QUIET!!
IF HE FINDS YOU, YOU'RE DEAD!!!

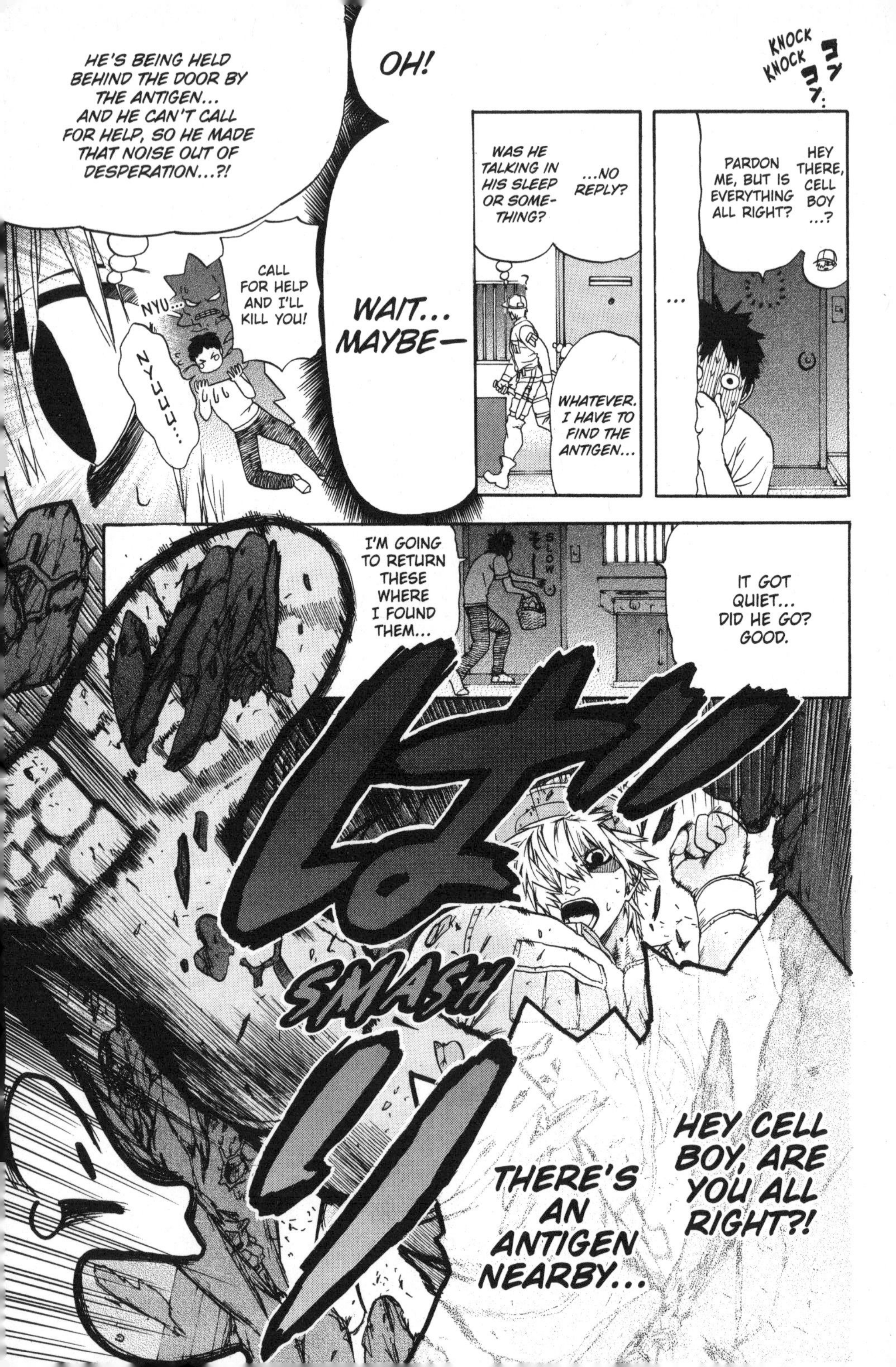
KNOCK KNOCK
HEY THERE, CELL BOY ...?
PARDON ME, BUT IS EVERYTHING ALL RIGHT?
...
...NO REPLY?
WAS HE TALKING IN HIS SLEEP OR SOME-THING?
WHATEVER. I HAVE TO FIND THE ANTIGEN...
OH!
WAIT... MAYBE—
HE'S BEING HELD BEHIND THE DOOR BY THE ANTIGEN... AND HE CAN'T CALL FOR HELP, SO HE MADE THAT NOISE OUT OF DESPERATION...?!
CALL FOR HELP AND I'LL KILL YOU!
NYU...
NYUUUU...
IT GOT QUIET... DID HE GO? GOOD.
I'M GOING TO RETURN THESE WHERE I FOUND THEM...
SLOW
HEY CELL BOY, ARE YOU ALL RIGHT?!
THERE'S AN ANTIGEN NEARBY...
SMASH

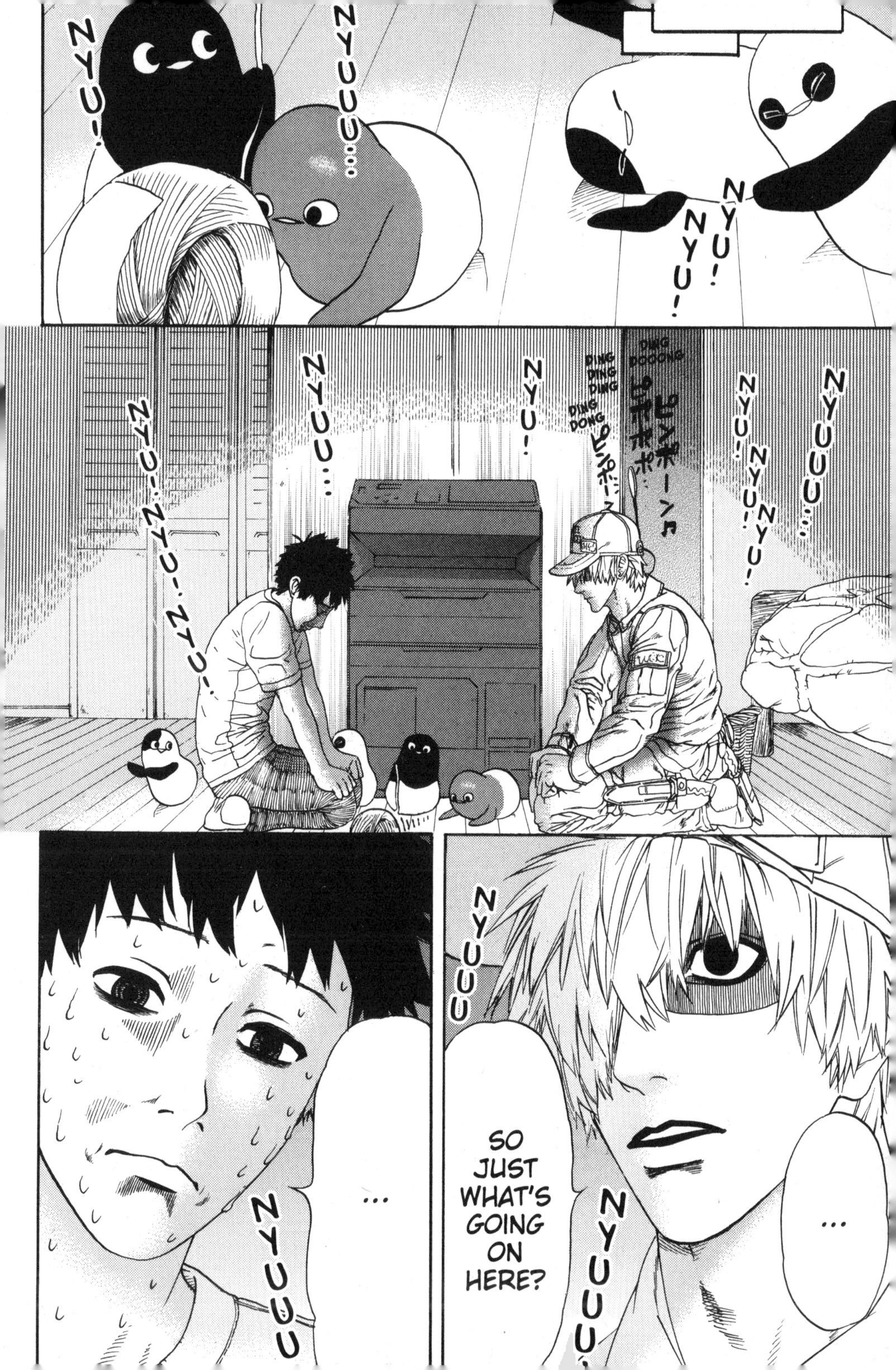

NYU-!
NYU-!
NYUUUU...
NYU-!
NYUUUU...
NYU-!
NYU-!
NYU-!
DING DOOONG
DING DING DING DING DONG
NYU-!
NYUUU...
NYU-NYU-NYU-NYU-!
...
NYUUU...
SO JUST WHAT'S GOING ON HERE?
NYUUUU
...
NYUUUU

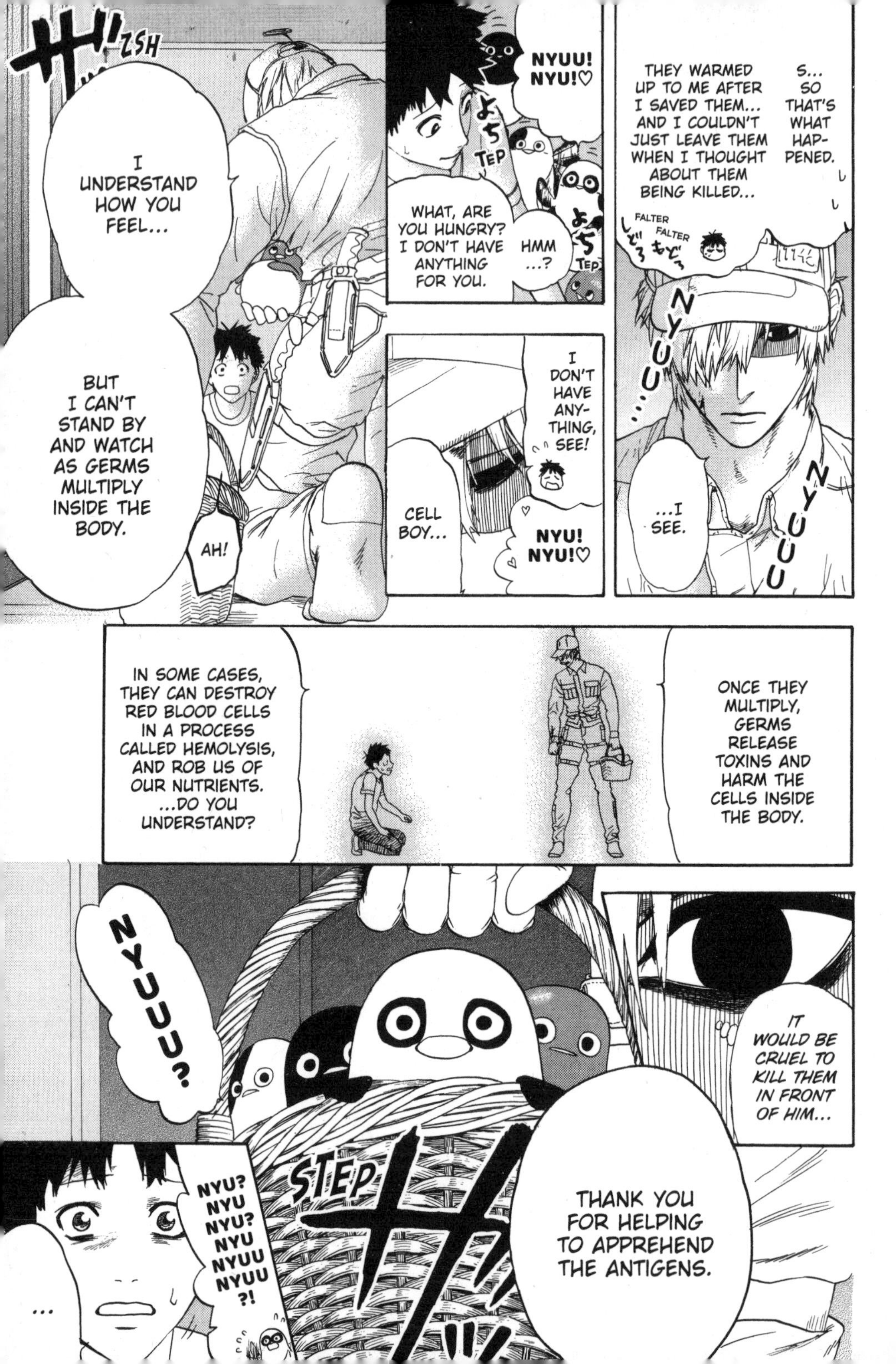
S... SO THAT'S WHAT HAP-PENED.
THEY WARMED UP TO ME AFTER I SAVED THEM... AND I COULDN'T JUST LEAVE THEM WHEN I THOUGHT ABOUT THEM BEING KILLED...
FALTER FALTER
NYUUU...
...I SEE.
NYUUUN
NYUU! NYU!♡
TEP
TEP
HMM ...?
WHAT, ARE YOU HUNGRY? I DON'T HAVE ANYTHING FOR YOU.
I DON'T HAVE ANY-THING, SEE!
NYU! NYU!♡
CELL BOY...
ZSH
I UNDERSTAND HOW YOU FEEL...
BUT I CAN'T STAND BY AND WATCH AS GERMS MULTIPLY INSIDE THE BODY.
AH!
ONCE THEY MULTIPLY, GERMS RELEASE TOXINS AND HARM THE CELLS INSIDE THE BODY.
IN SOME CASES, THEY CAN DESTROY RED BLOOD CELLS IN A PROCESS CALLED HEMOLYSIS, AND ROB US OF OUR NUTRIENTS. ...DO YOU UNDERSTAND?
IT WOULD BE CRUEL TO KILL THEM IN FRONT OF HIM...
THANK YOU FOR HELPING TO APPREHEND THE ANTIGENS.
STEP
NYUUU?
NYU? NYU NYU? NYU NYUU NYUU ?!
...

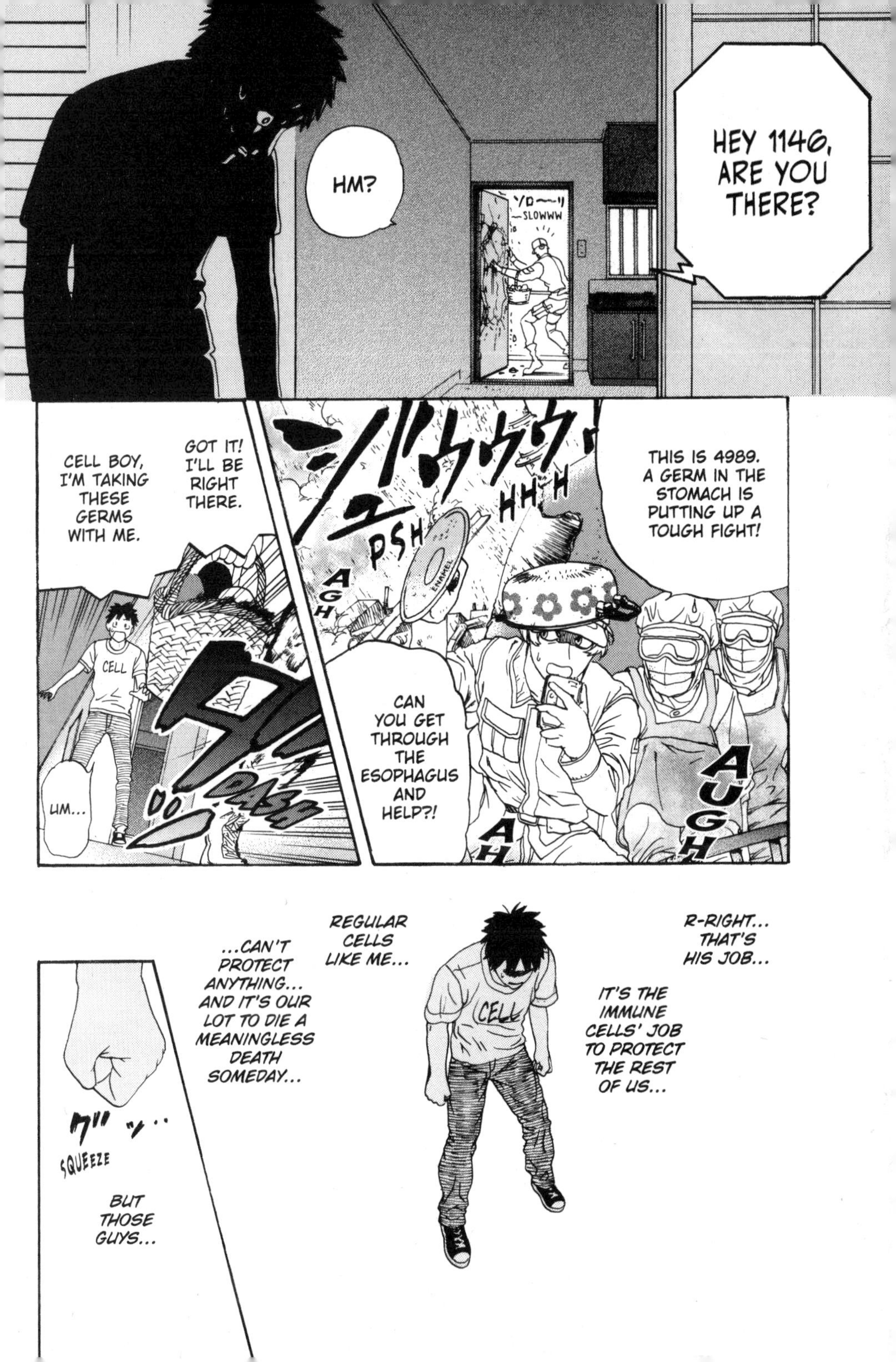
HEY 1146, ARE YOU THERE?
HM?
ソロ〜〜リ
—SLOWWW
THIS IS 4989. A GERM IN THE STOMACH IS PUTTING UP A TOUGH FIGHT!
HHH
PSH
ENAMEL
AGH
CAN YOU GET THROUGH THE ESOPHAGUS AND HELP?!
AUGH
AH
GOT IT! I'LL BE RIGHT THERE.
CELL BOY, I'M TAKING THESE GERMS WITH ME.
DASH
UM...
R-RIGHT... THAT'S HIS JOB...
IT'S THE IMMUNE CELLS' JOB TO PROTECT THE REST OF US...
REGULAR CELLS LIKE ME...
...CAN'T PROTECT ANYTHING... AND IT'S OUR LOT TO DIE A MEANINGLESS DEATH SOMEDAY...
SQUEEZE
BUT THOSE GUYS...

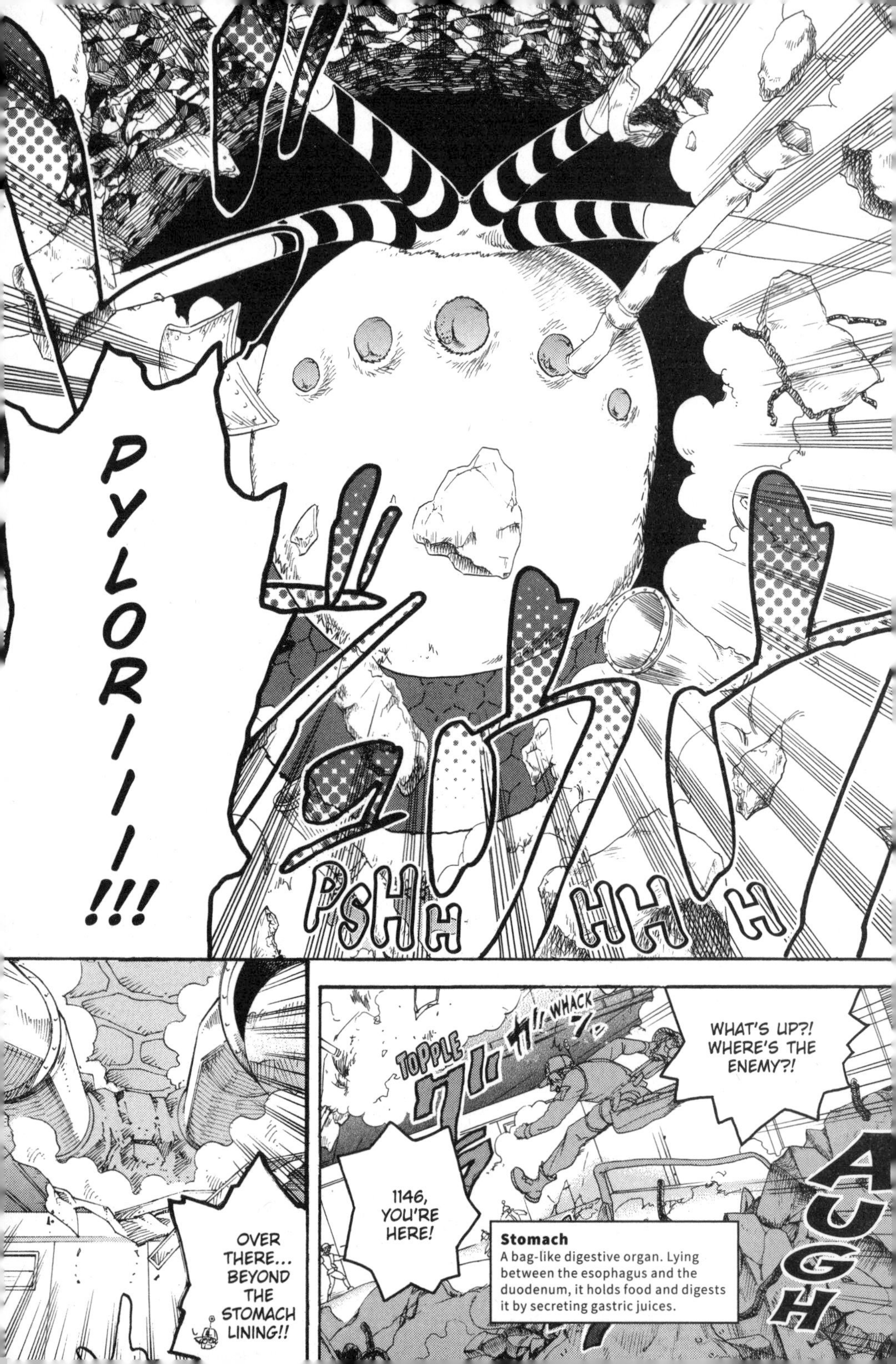
PYLORI!!!
PSHHHHHH
WHAT'S UP?! WHERE'S THE ENEMY?!
TOPPLE
WHACK
AUGH
1146, YOU'RE HERE!
Stomach
A bag-like digestive organ. Lying between the esophagus and the duodenum, it holds food and digests it by secreting gastric juices.
OVER THERE... BEYOND THE STOMACH LINING!!

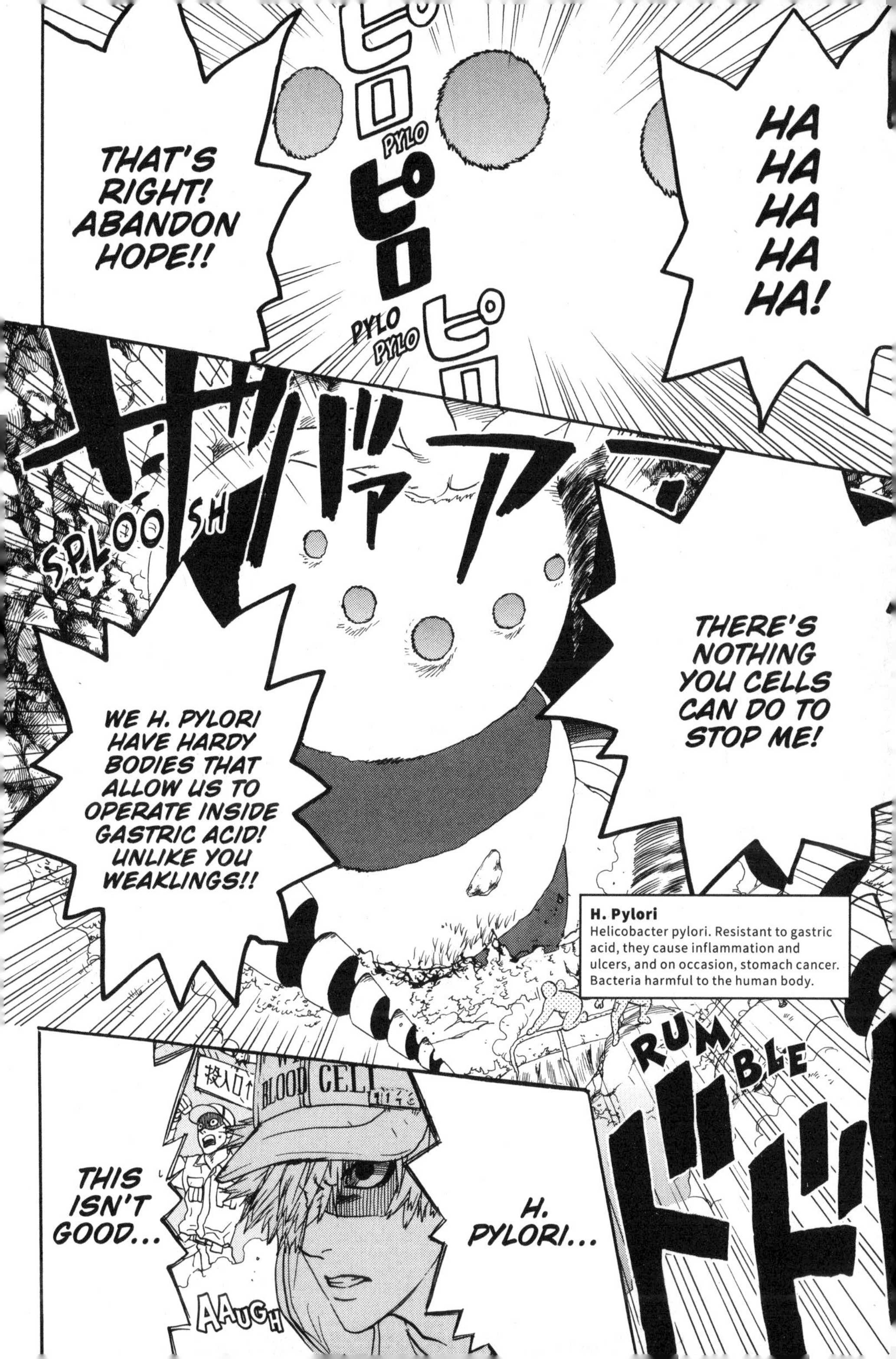
HA HA HA HA HA!
PYLO
PYLO PYLO
THAT'S RIGHT! ABANDON HOPE!!
SPLOOSH
THERE'S NOTHING YOU CELLS CAN DO TO STOP ME!
WE H. PYLORI HAVE HARDY BODIES THAT ALLOW US TO OPERATE INSIDE GASTRIC ACID! UNLIKE YOU WEAKLINGS!!
H. Pylori
Helicobacter pylori. Resistant to gastric acid, they cause inflammation and ulcers, and on occasion, stomach cancer. Bacteria harmful to the human body.
RUMBLE
H. PYLORI...
BLOOD CELL
投入口↑
THIS ISN'T GOOD...
AAUGH

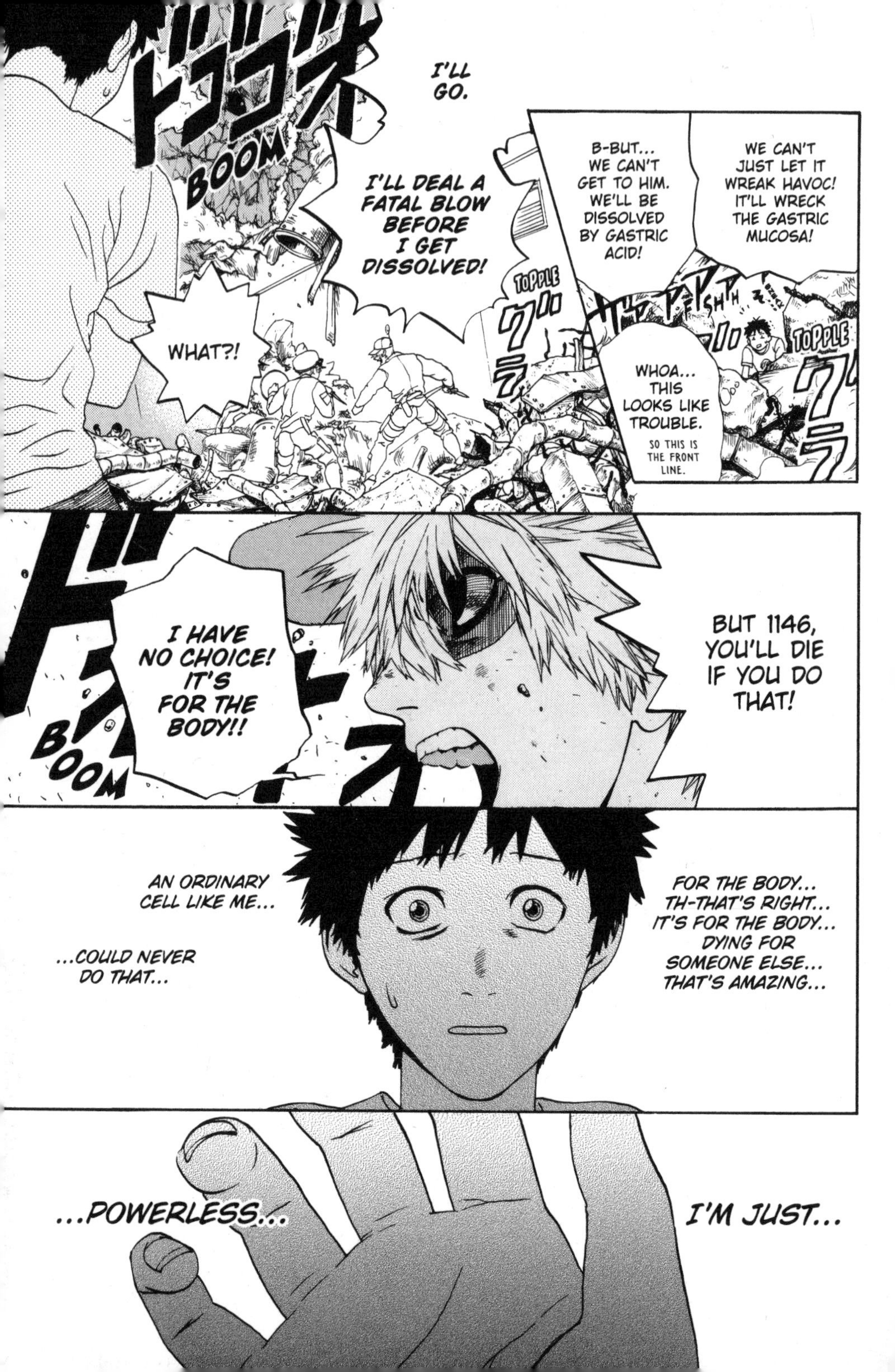
WE CAN'T JUST LET IT WREAK HAVOC! IT'LL WRECK THE GASTRIC MUCOSA!
B-BUT... WE CAN'T GET TO HIM. WE'LL BE DISSOLVED BY GASTRIC ACID!
TOPPLE
WHOA... THIS LOOKS LIKE TROUBLE.
SO THIS IS THE FRONT LINE.
I'LL GO.
I'LL DEAL A FATAL BLOW BEFORE I GET DISSOLVED!
BOOM
TOPPLE
WHAT?!
BUT 1146, YOU'LL DIE IF YOU DO THAT!
I HAVE NO CHOICE! IT'S FOR THE BODY!!
BOOM
FOR THE BODY... TH-THAT'S RIGHT... IT'S FOR THE BODY... DYING FOR SOMEONE ELSE... THAT'S AMAZING...
AN ORDINARY CELL LIKE ME...
...COULD NEVER DO THAT...
I'M JUST...
...POWERLESS...

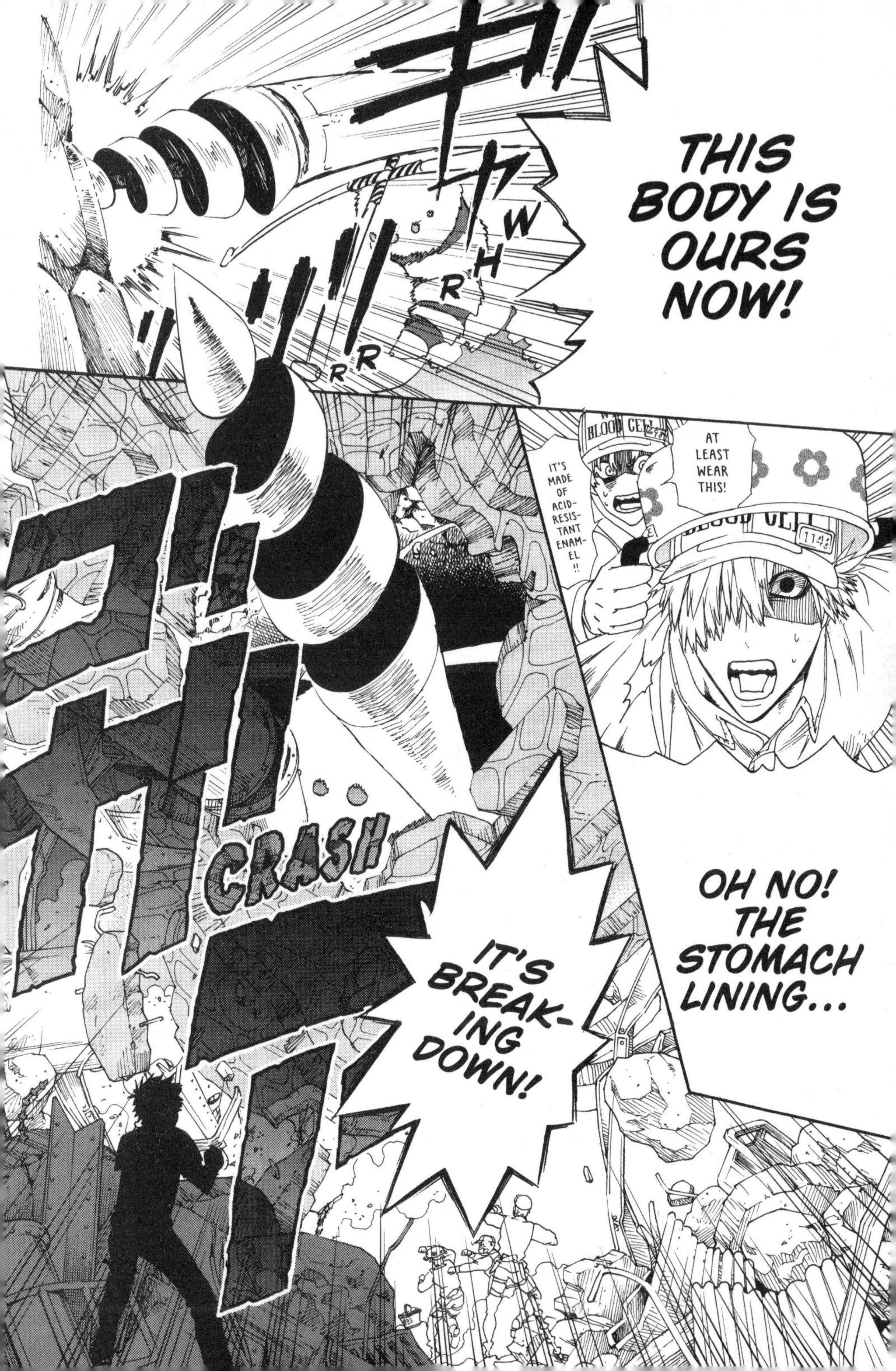
THIS BODY IS OURS NOW!
WHRRR
AT LEAST WEAR THIS!
IT'S MADE OF ACID-RESISTANT ENAMEL !!
OH NO! THE STOMACH LINING...
IT'S BREAKING DOWN!
CRASH

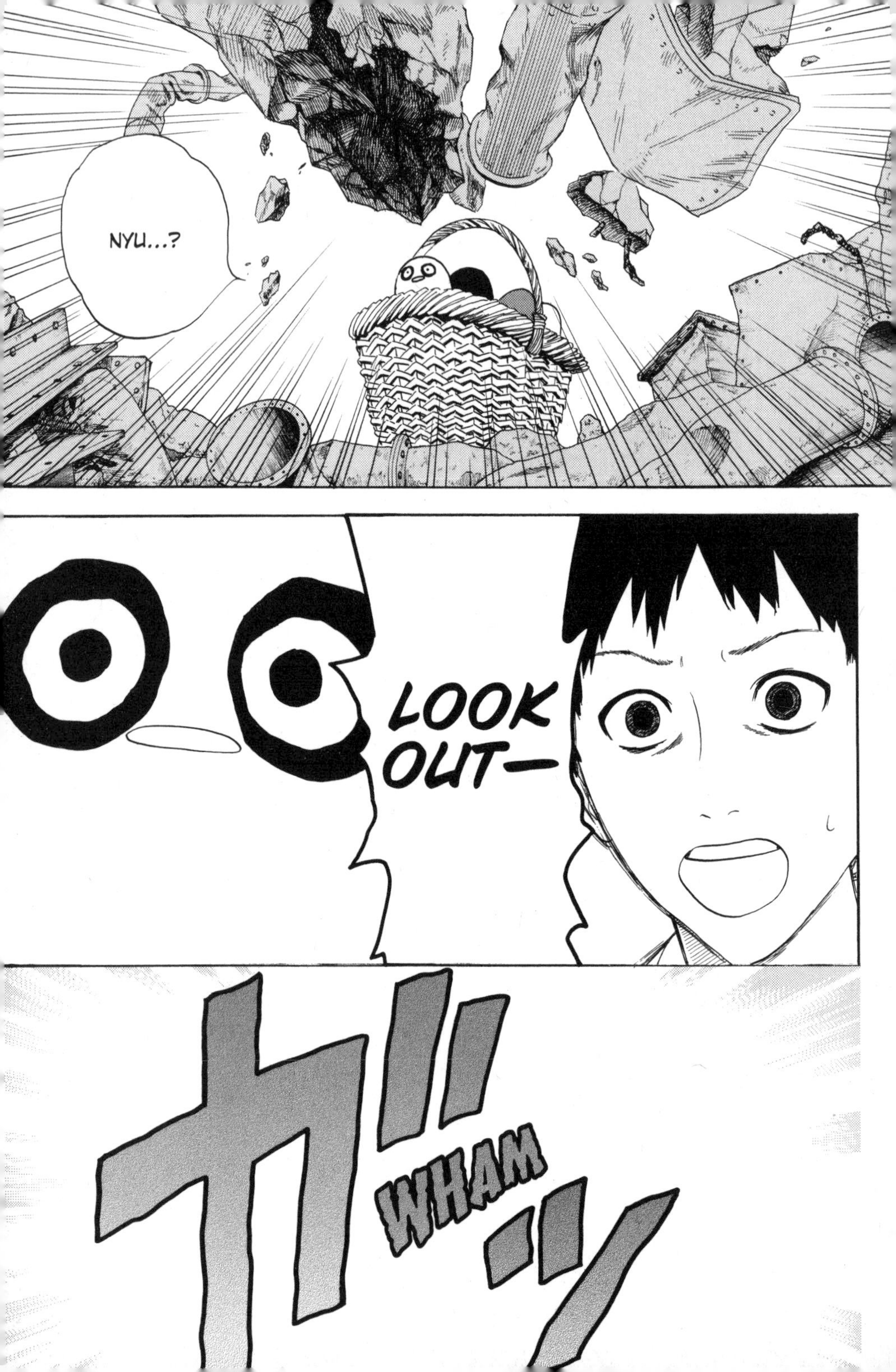
NYU...?
LOOK OUT—
ガッ
WHAM

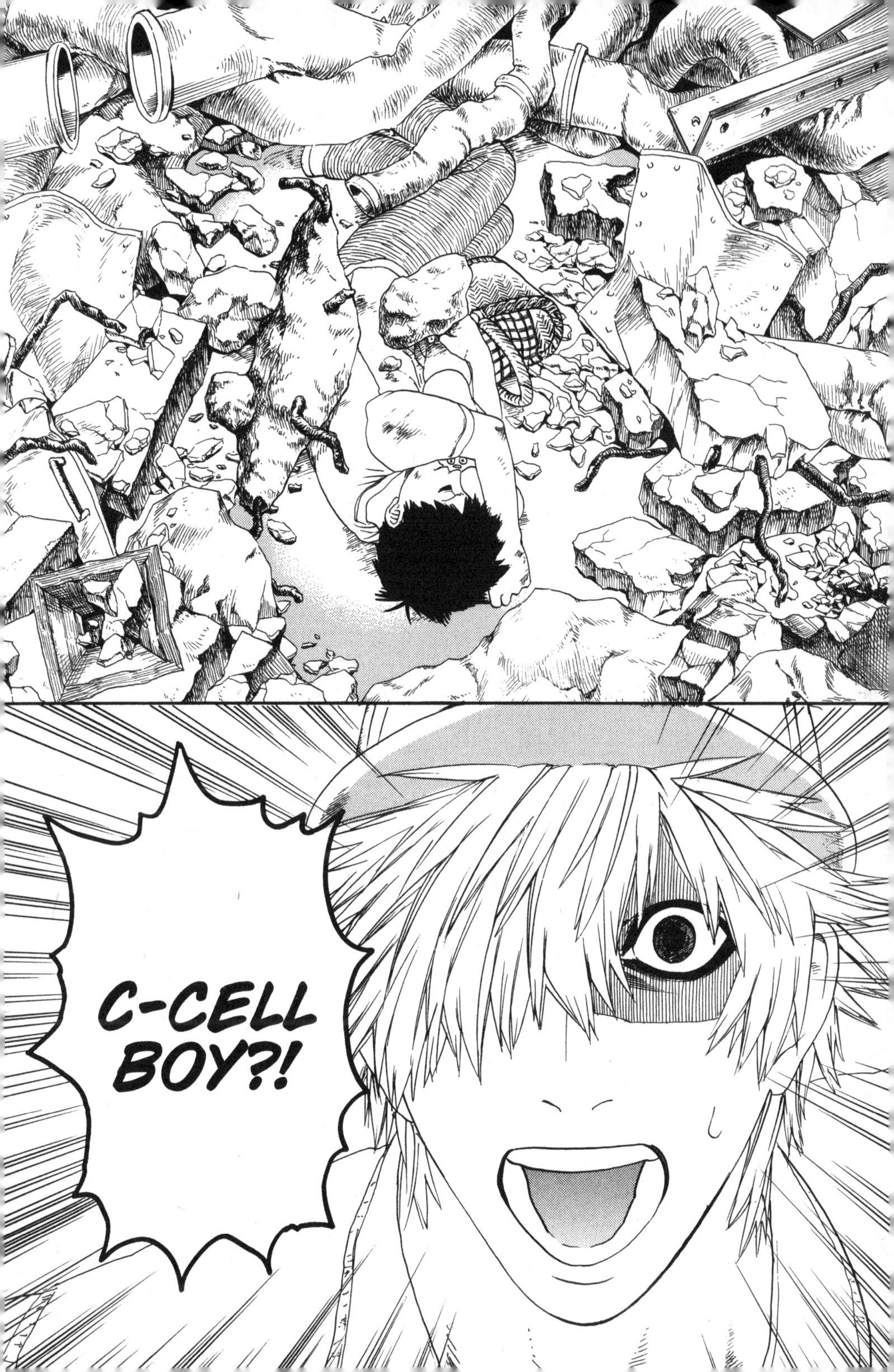
C-CELL BOY?!

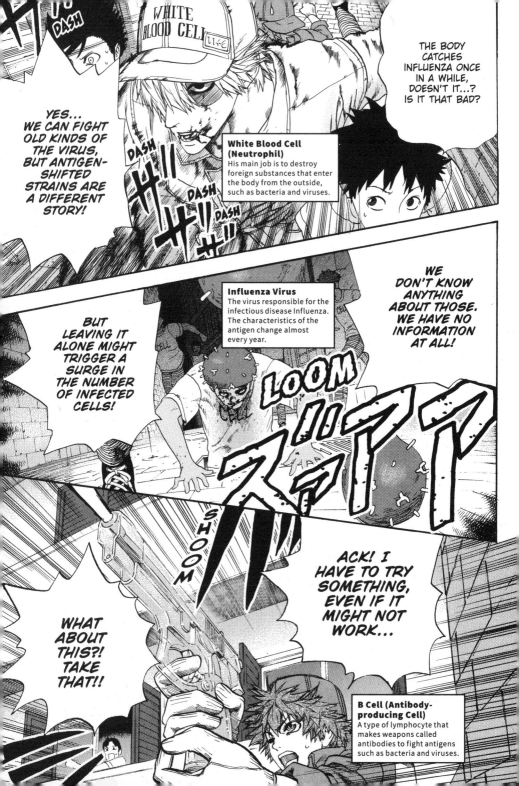

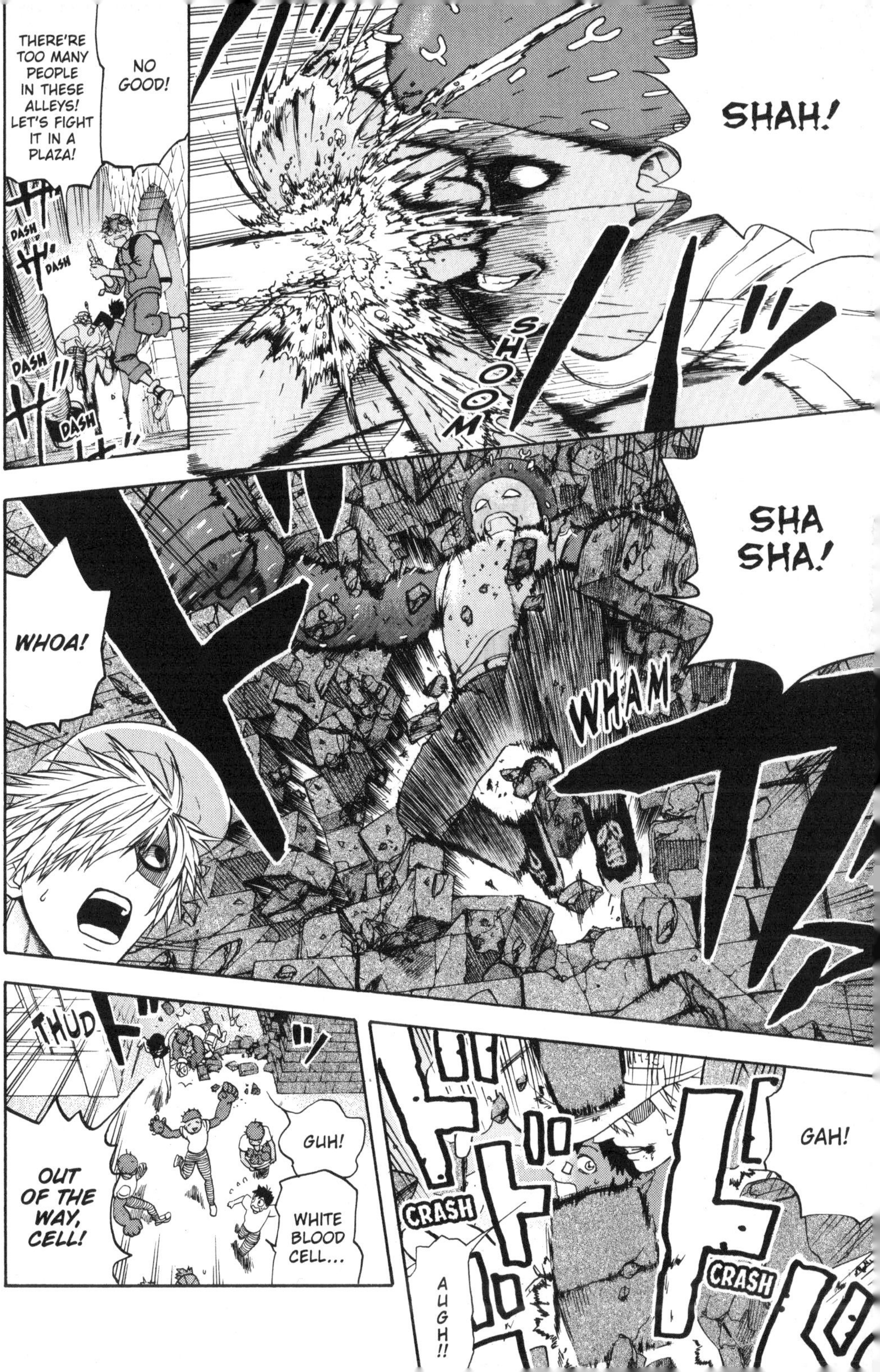
SHAH!
SHOOOM
NO GOOD!
THERE'RE TOO MANY PEOPLE IN THESE ALLEYS! LET'S FIGHT IT IN A PLAZA!
DASH
DASH
DASH
DASH
SHA SHA!
WHAM
WHOA!
GAH!
CRASH
CRASH
AUGH!!
THUD
GUH!
WHITE BLOOD CELL...
OUT OF THE WAY, CELL!

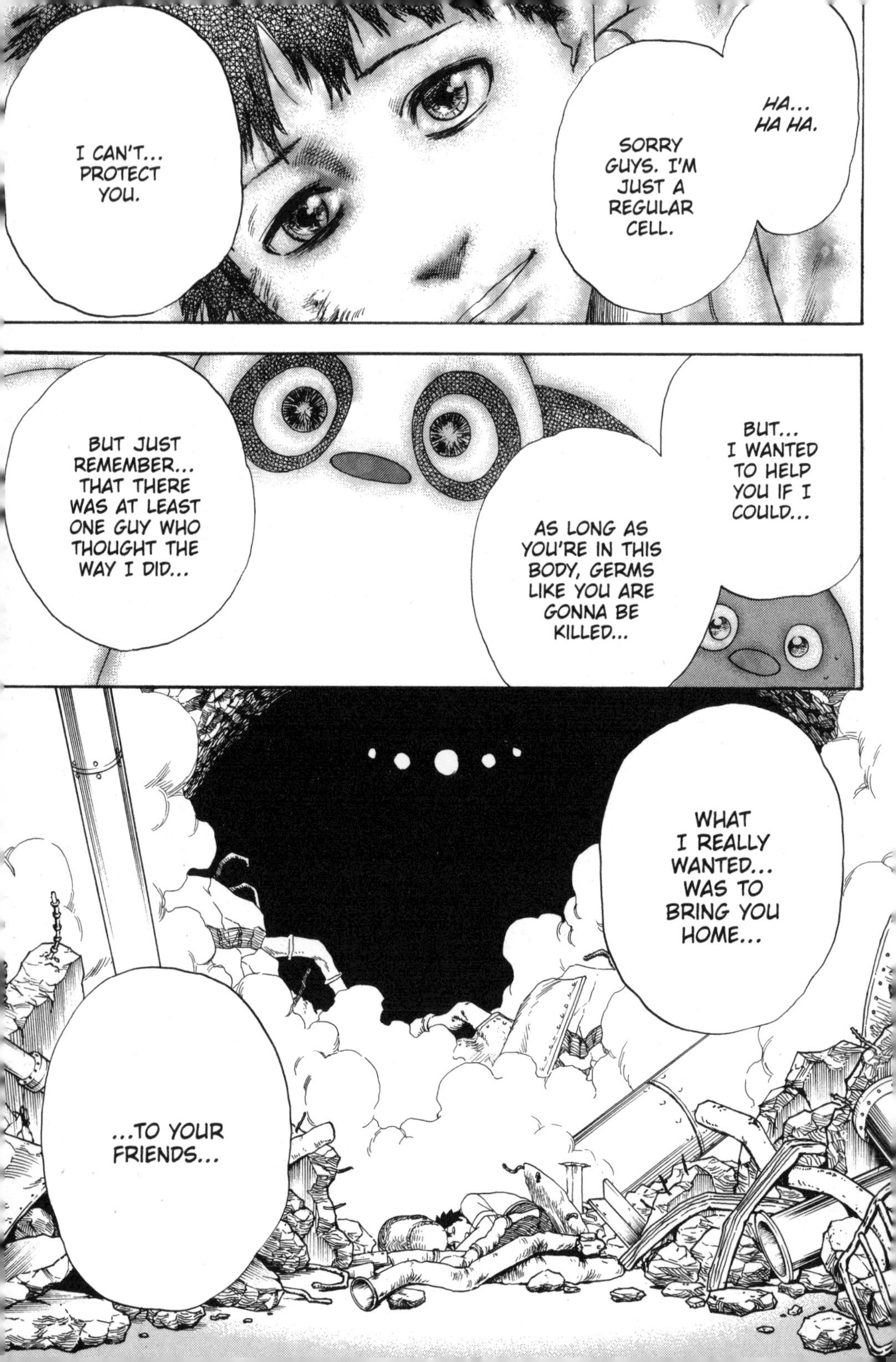
HA... HA HA.
SORRY GUYS. I'M JUST A REGULAR CELL.
I CAN'T... PROTECT YOU.
BUT... I WANTED TO HELP YOU IF I COULD...
AS LONG AS YOU'RE IN THIS BODY, GERMS LIKE YOU ARE GONNA BE KILLED...
BUT JUST REMEMBER... THAT THERE WAS AT LEAST ONE GUY WHO THOUGHT THE WAY I DID...
WHAT I REALLY WANTED... WAS TO BRING YOU HOME...
...TO YOUR FRIENDS...

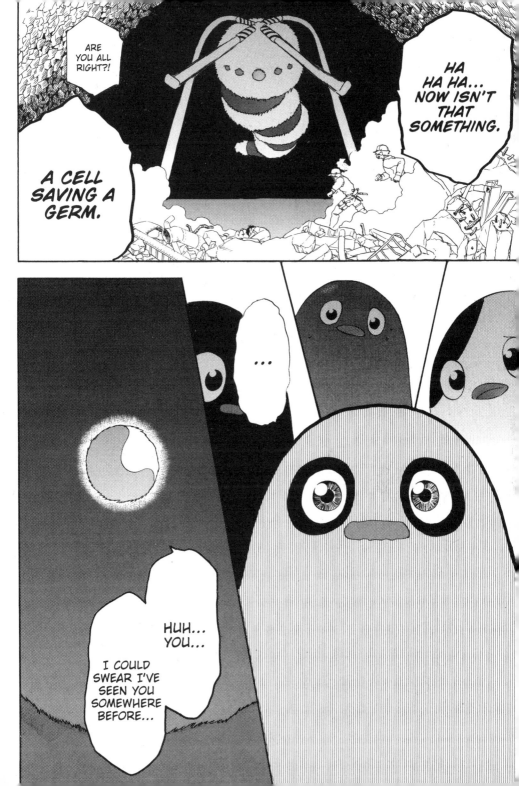

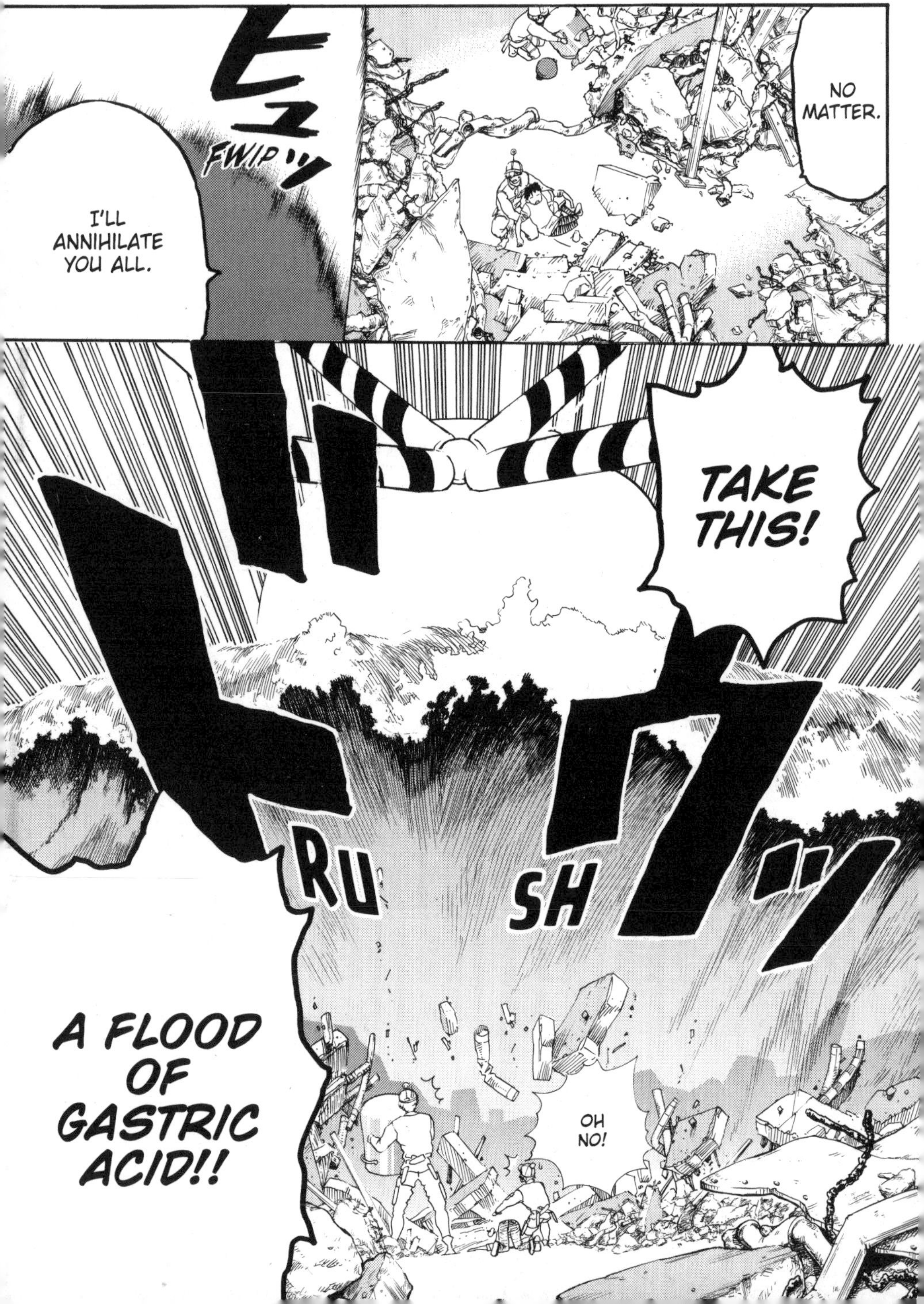
NO MATTER.
FWIP
I'LL ANNIHILATE YOU ALL.
TAKE THIS!
RUSH
A FLOOD OF GASTRIC ACID!!
OH NO!

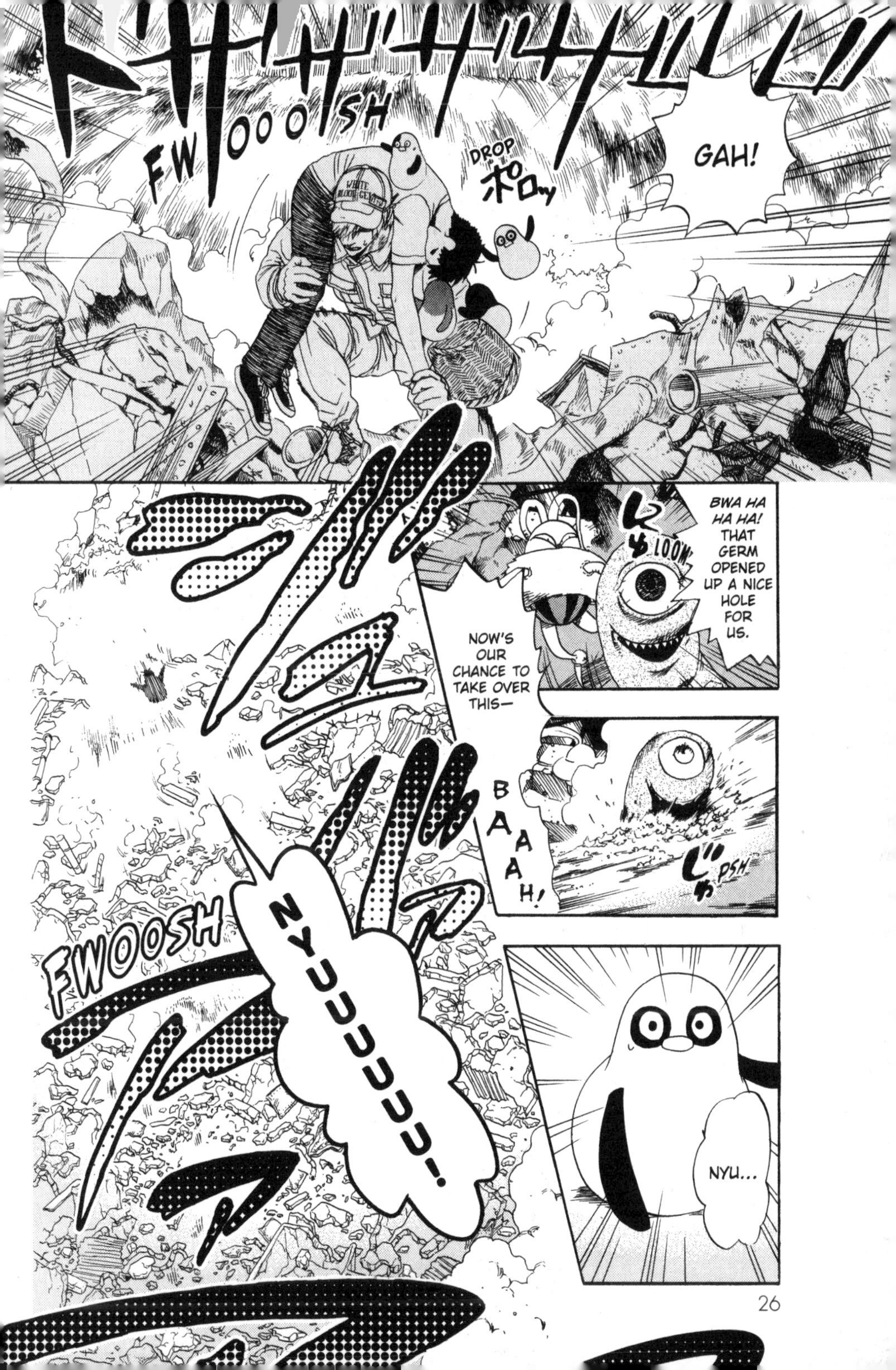

GAH!
DROP
FWOOOSH
BWA HA HA HA! THAT GERM OPENED UP A NICE HOLE FOR US.
LOOM
NOW'S OUR CHANCE TO TAKE OVER THIS—
PSH
BAAAH!
NYU...
NYUUUUUUU!
FWOOSH

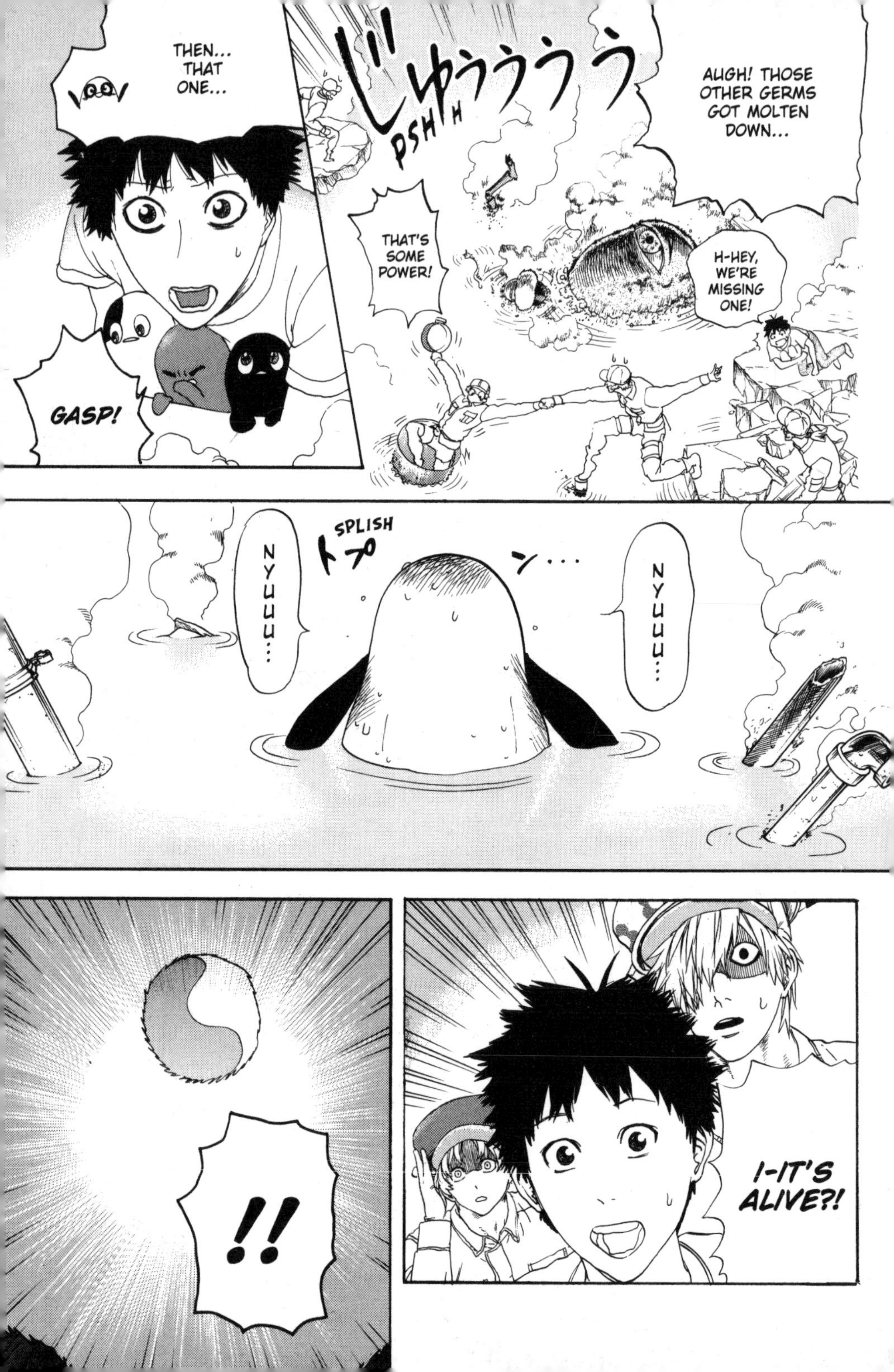
AUGH! THOSE OTHER GERMS GOT MOLTEN DOWN...
じゅうううう
PSH H
H-HEY, WE'RE MISSING ONE!
THAT'S SOME POWER!
THEN... THAT ONE...
GASP!
NYUUU...
ン...
トプ
SPLISH
NYUUU...
I-IT'S ALIVE?!
!!

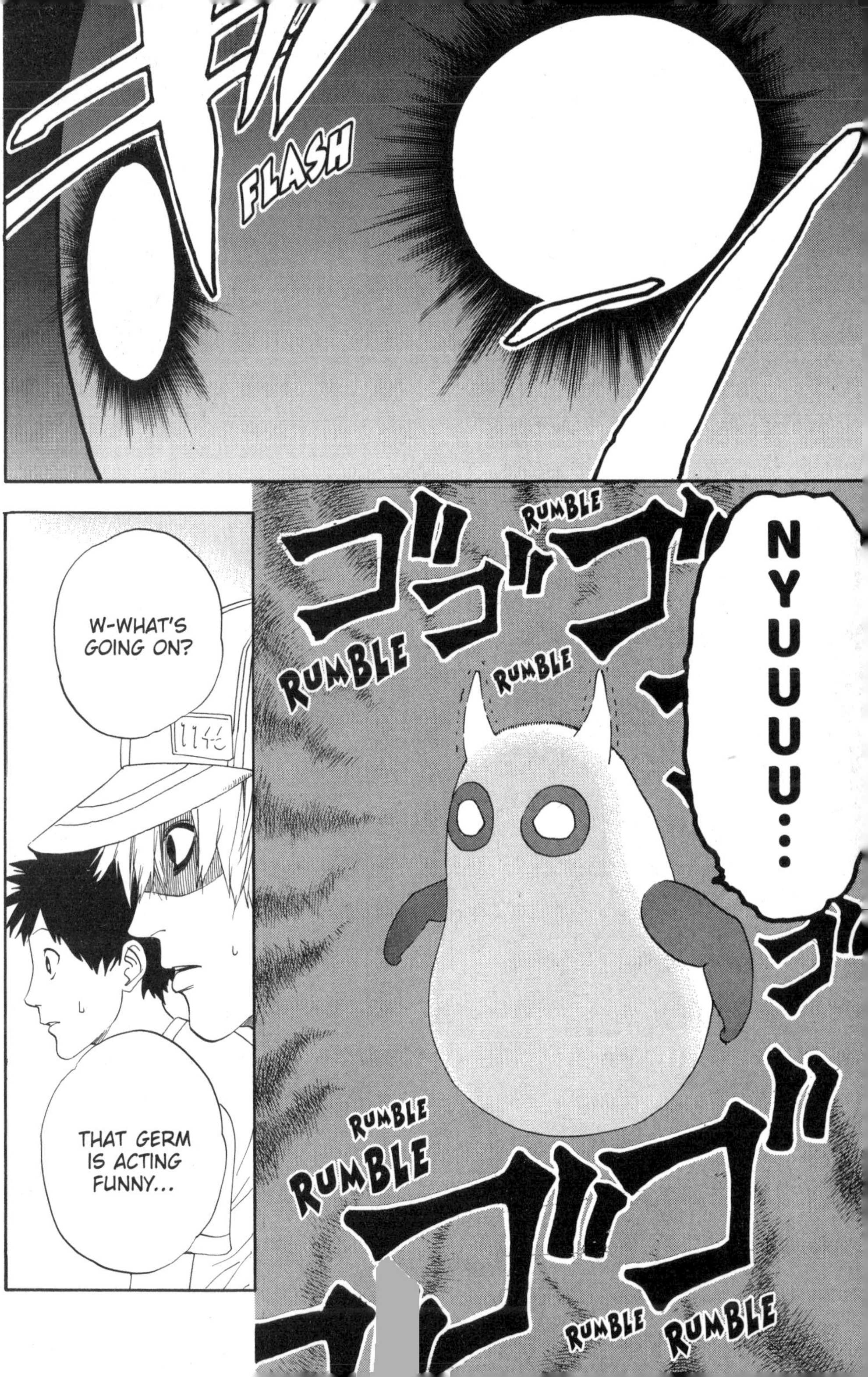
FLASH
RUMBLE
NYUUUU...
RUMBLE
RUMBLE
RUMBLE
RUMBLE
RUMBLE
RUMBLE
W-WHAT'S GOING ON?
THAT GERM IS ACTING FUNNY...

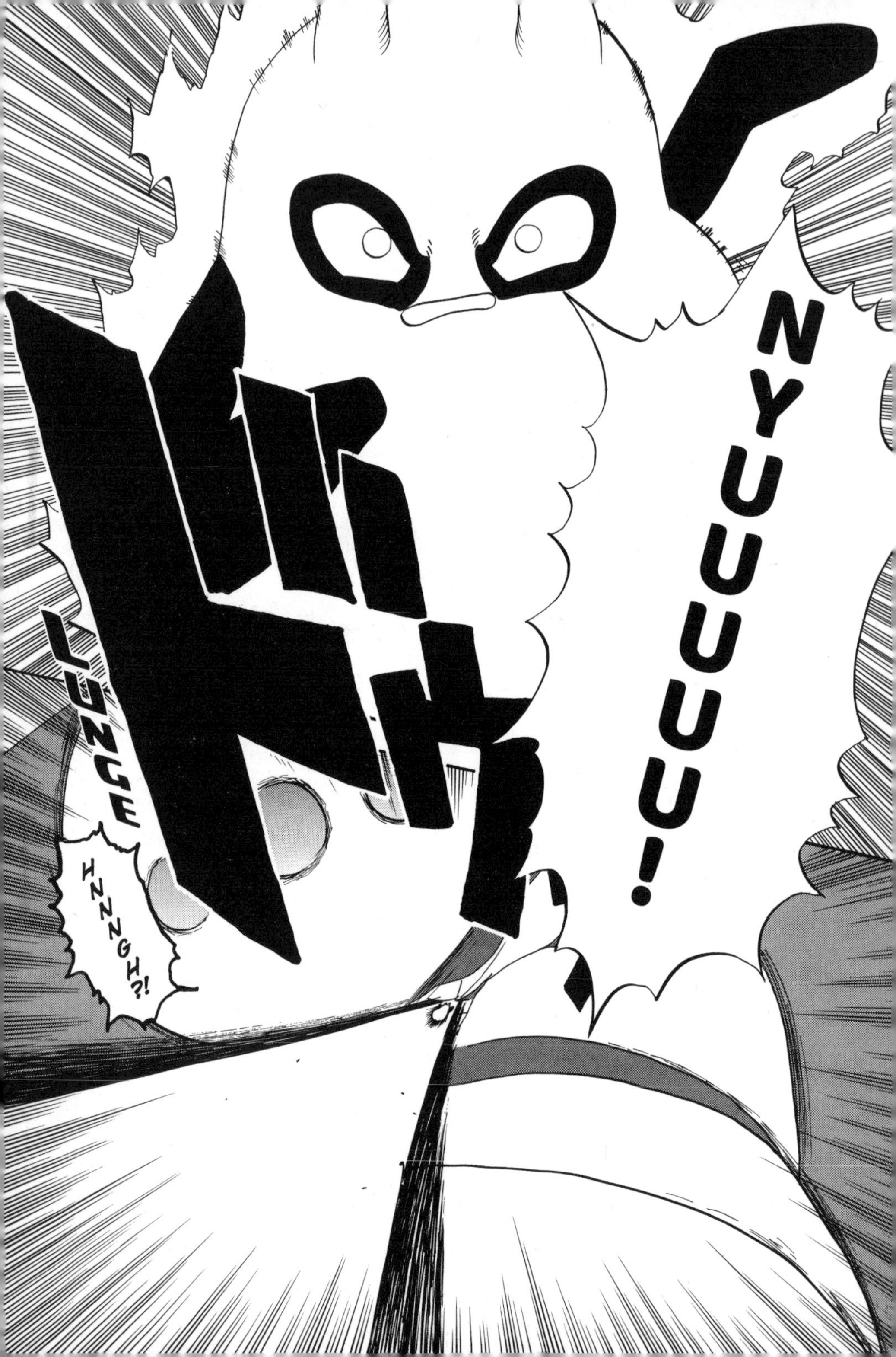
NYUUUUUU!
LUNGE
HNNNGH?!

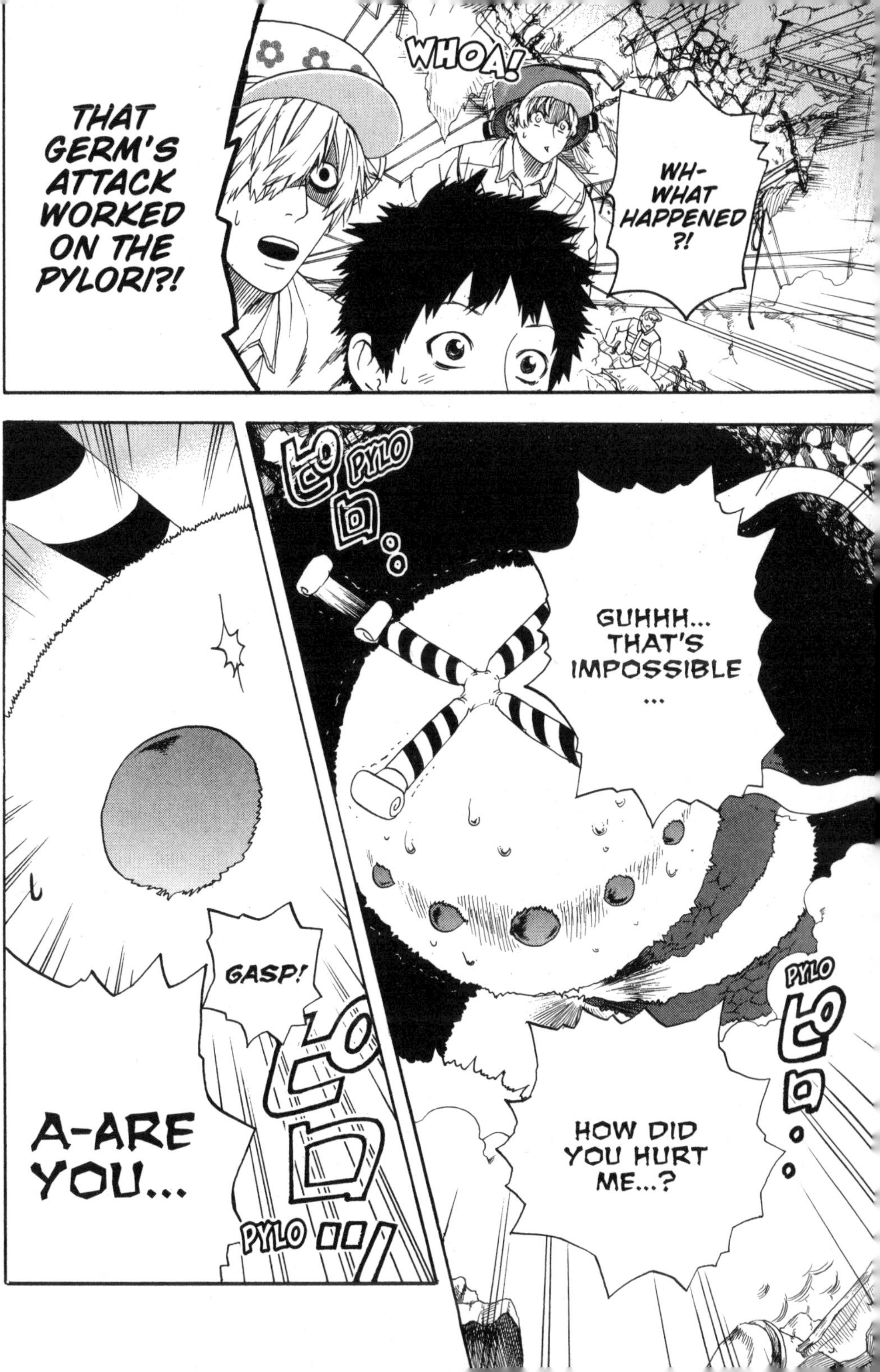

WHOA!
WH-WHAT HAPPENED?!
THAT GERM'S ATTACK WORKED ON THE PYLORI?!
PYLO
GUHHH... THAT'S IMPOSSIBLE...
PYLO
HOW DID YOU HURT ME...?
GASP!
PYLO
A-ARE YOU...

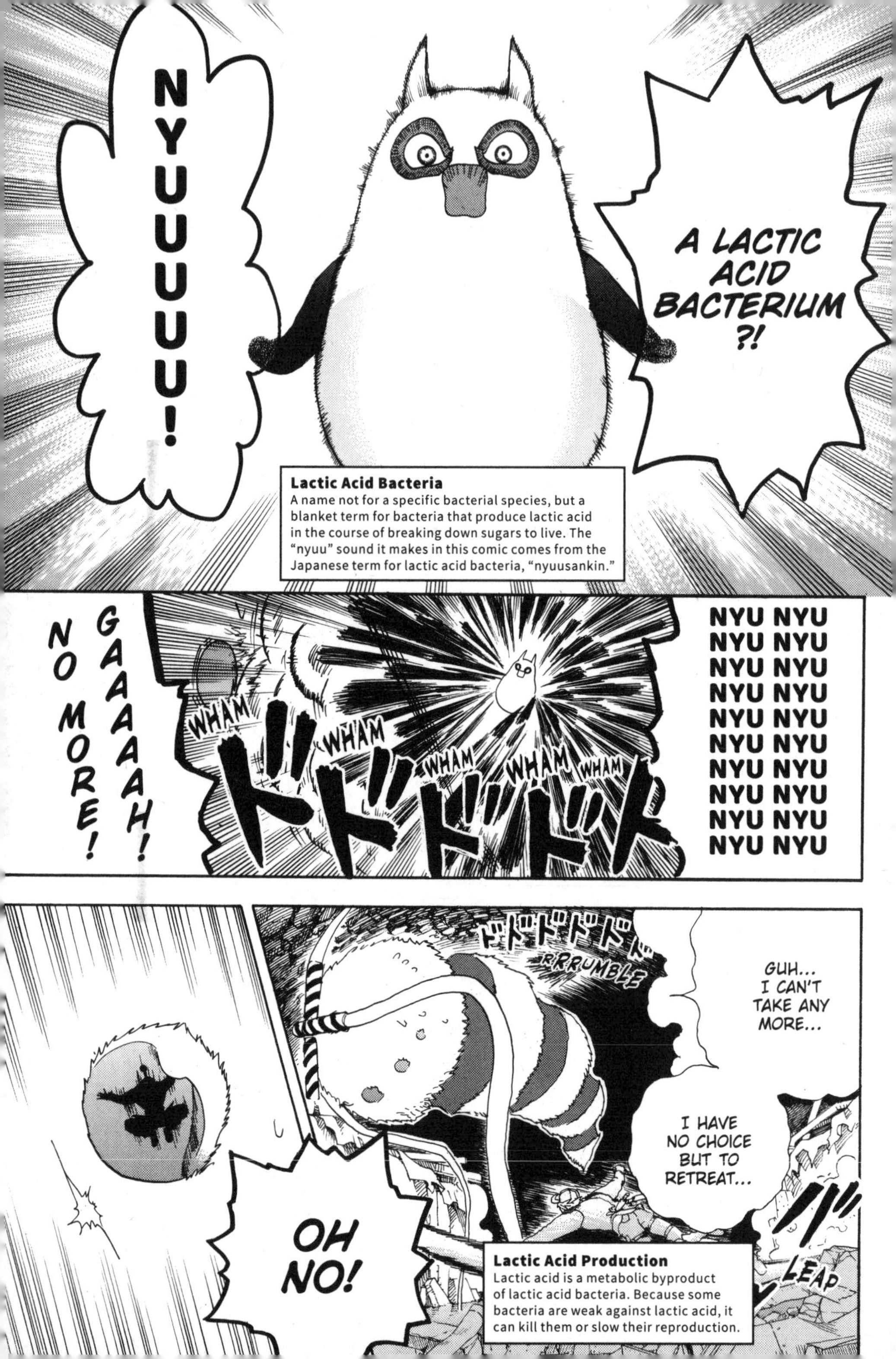
A LACTIC ACID BACTERIUM ?!
NYUUUUU!
Lactic Acid Bacteria
A name not for a specific bacterial species, but a blanket term for bacteria that produce lactic acid in the course of breaking down sugars to live. The “nyuu” sound it makes in this comic comes from the Japanese term for lactic acid bacteria, “nyuusankin.”
NYU NYU NYU NYU NYU NYU NYU NYU NYU NYU NYU NYU NYU NYU NYU NYU NYU NYU NYU NYU
WHAM WHAM WHAM WHAM WHAM
GAAAAAH!
NO MORE!
RRRUMBLE
GUH... I CAN'T TAKE ANY MORE...
I HAVE NO CHOICE BUT TO RETREAT...
LEAP
OH NO!
Lactic Acid Production
Lactic acid is a metabolic byproduct of lactic acid bacteria. Because some bacteria are weak against lactic acid, it can kill them or slow their reproduction.

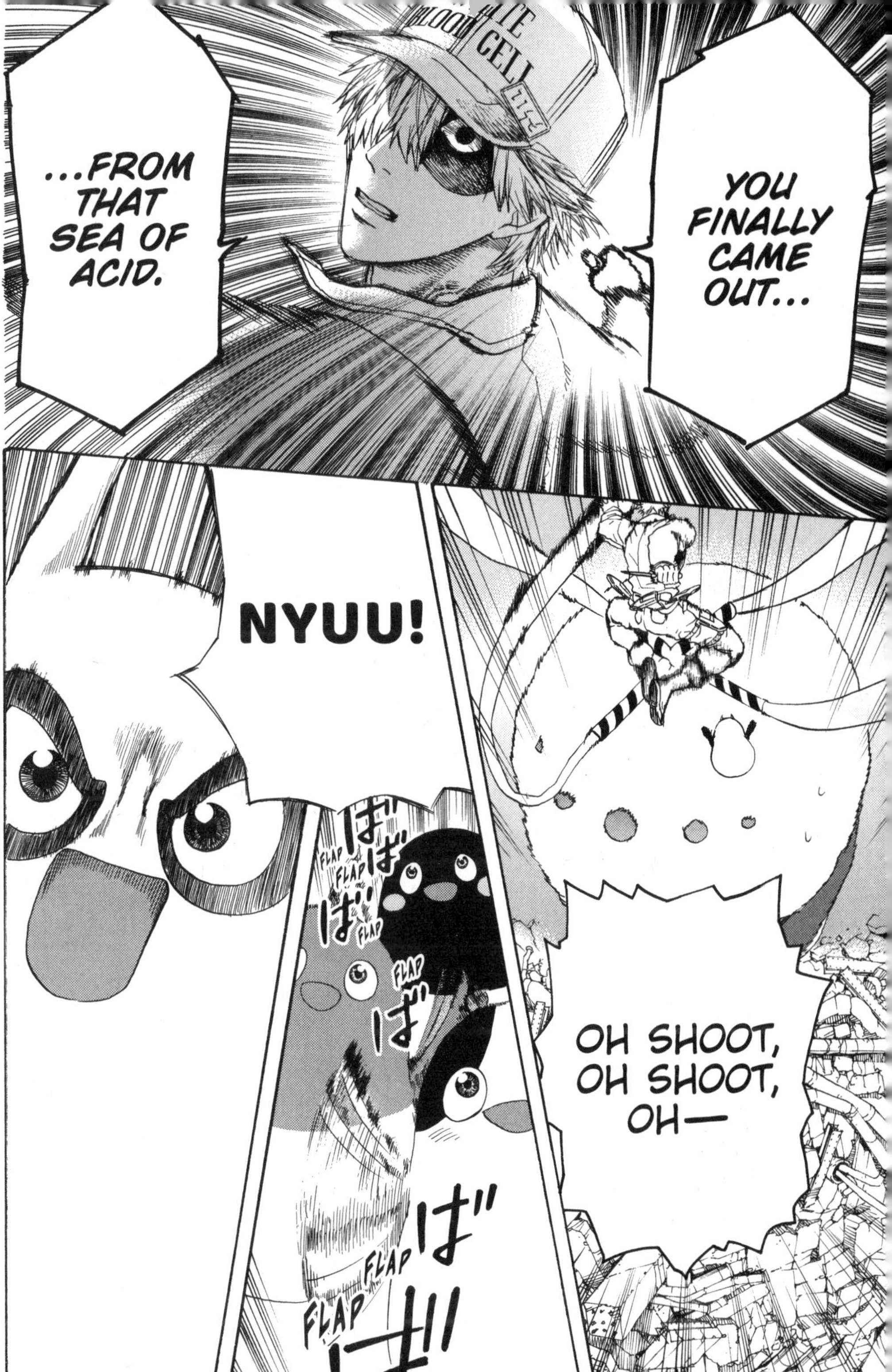
YOU FINALLY CAME OUT...
...FROM THAT SEA OF ACID.
OH SHOOT, OH SHOOT, OH—
FLAP FLAP FLAP FLAP
FLAP
FLAP FLAP
NYUU!

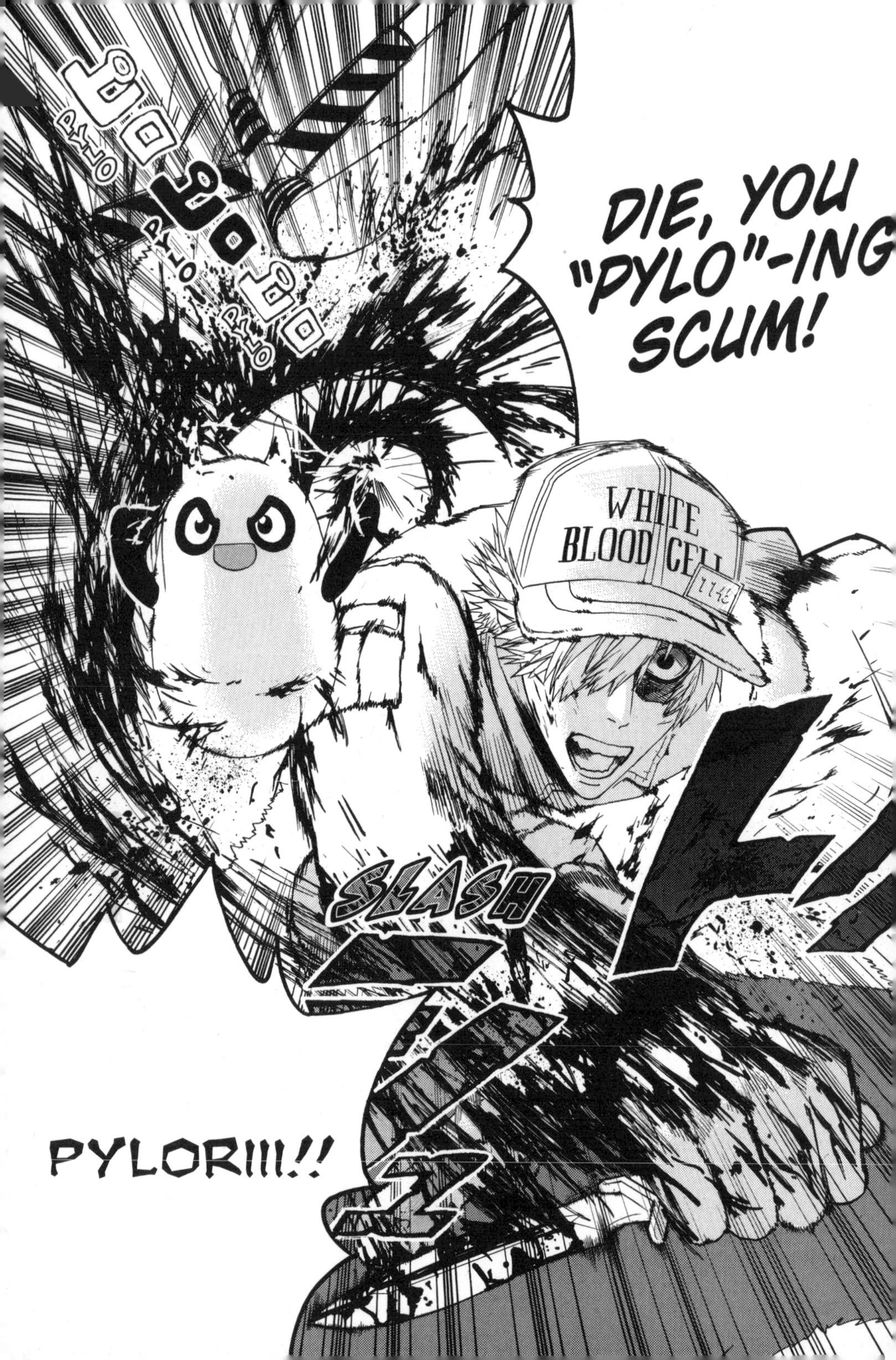
DIE, YOU "PYLO"-ING SCUM!
PYLO
PYLO
PYLO
WHITE BLOOD CELL
SLASH
PYLORIII!!

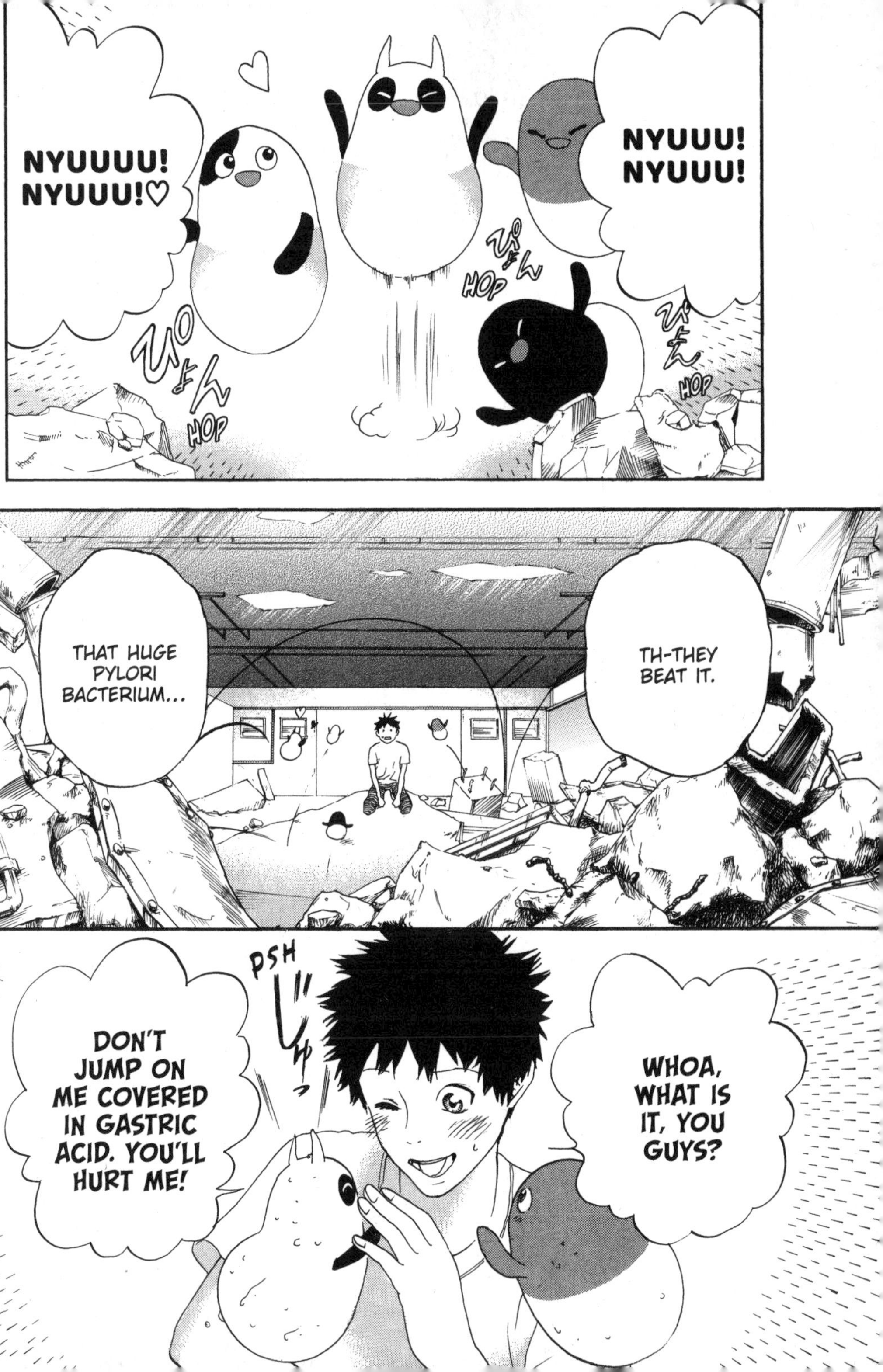
NYUUU! NYUUU!
ぴょん HOP
ぴょん HOP
NYUUUU! NYUUU!♡
ぴょん HOP
TH-THEY BEAT IT.
THAT HUGE PYLORI BACTERIUM...
WHOA, WHAT IS IT, YOU GUYS?
PSH じゅっ
DON'T JUMP ON ME COVERED IN GASTRIC ACID. YOU'LL HURT ME!

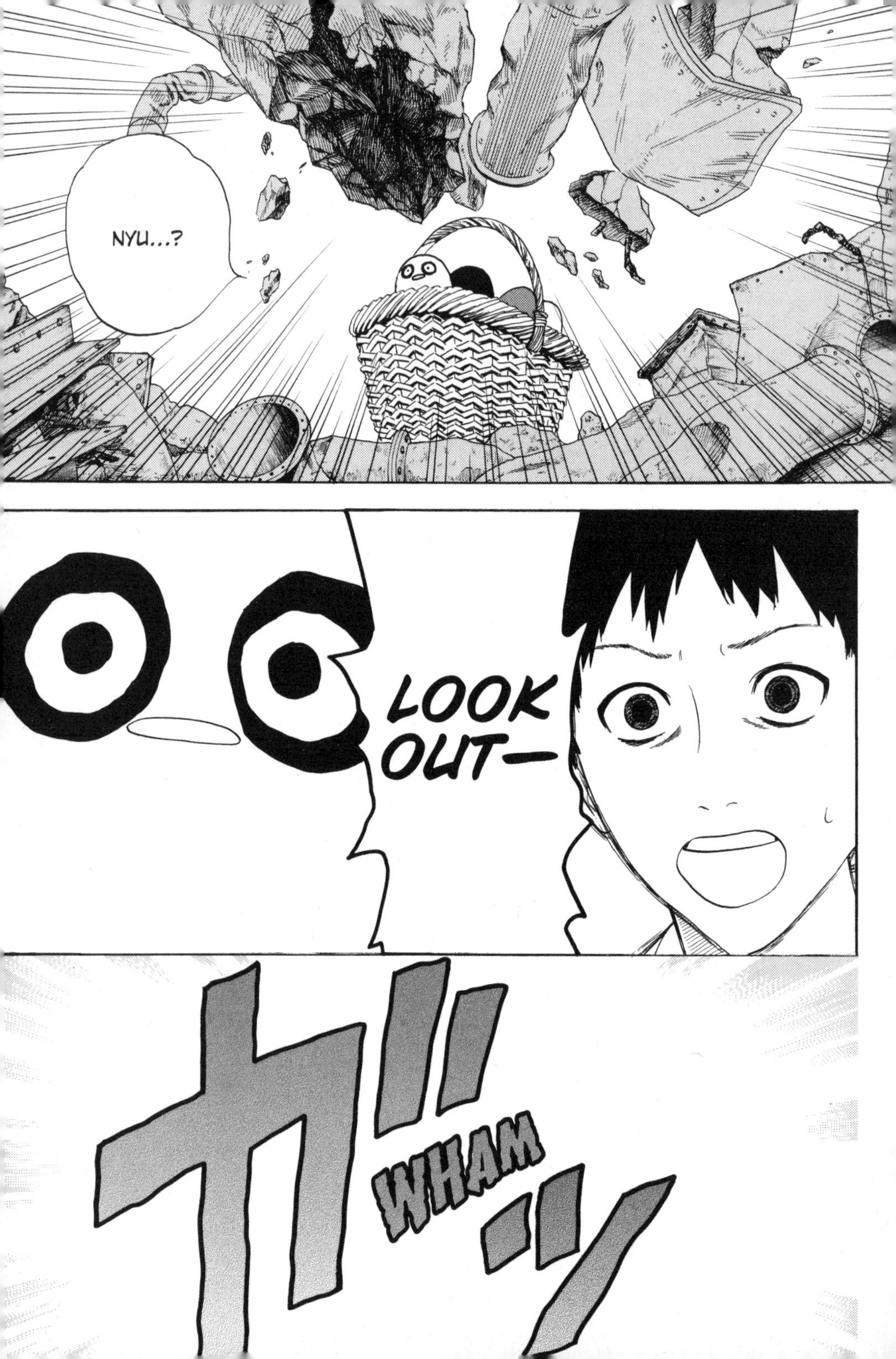
NYU...?
LOOK OUT—
ガッ
WHAM

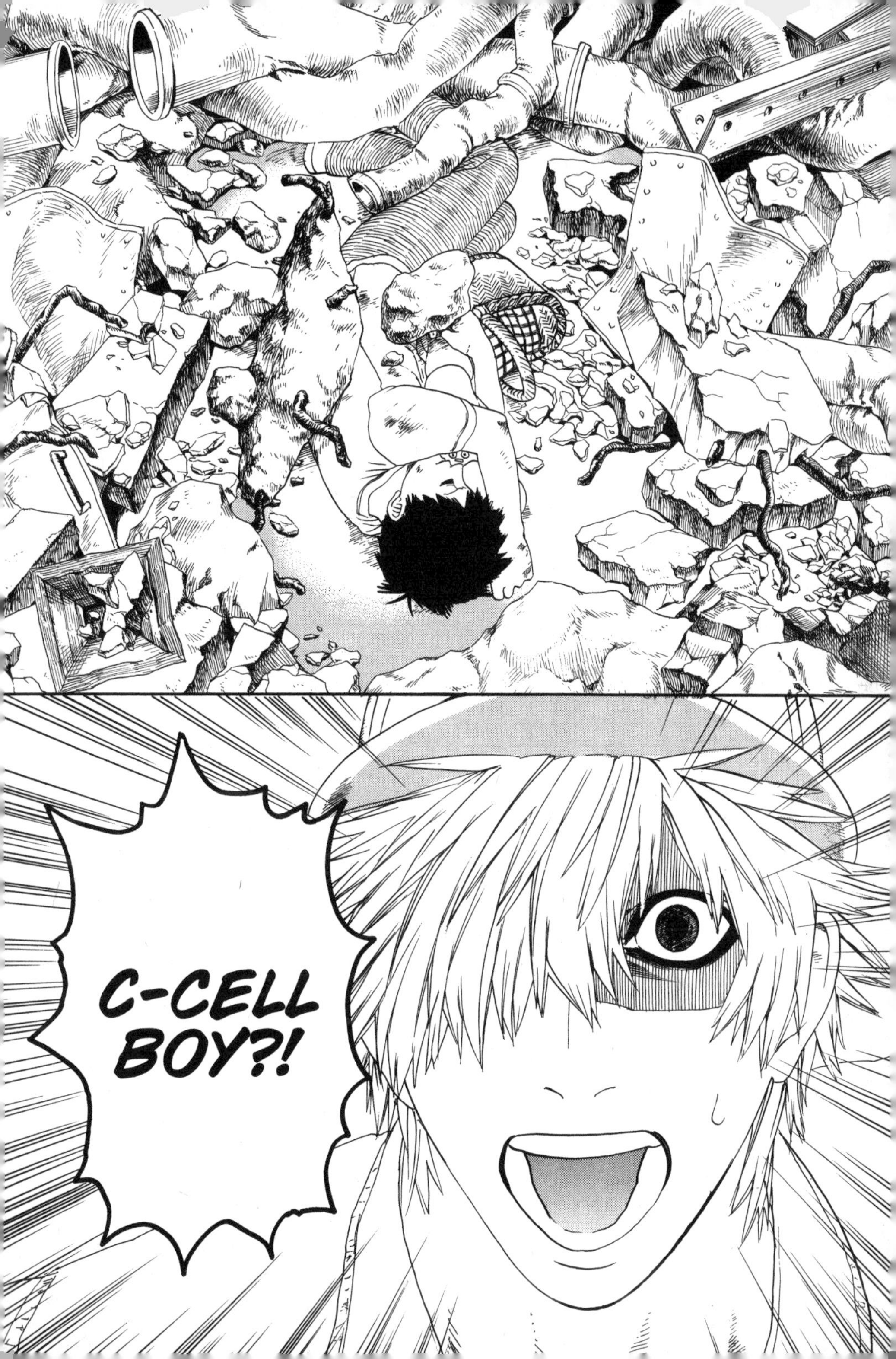
C-CELL BOY?!

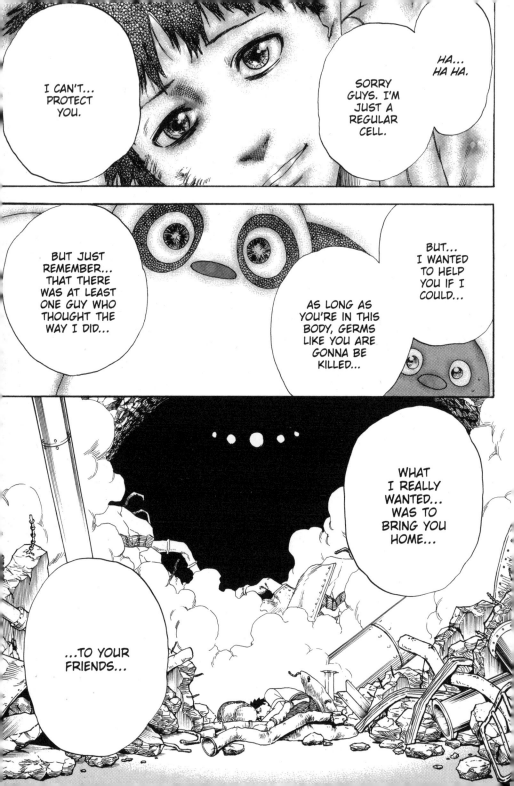

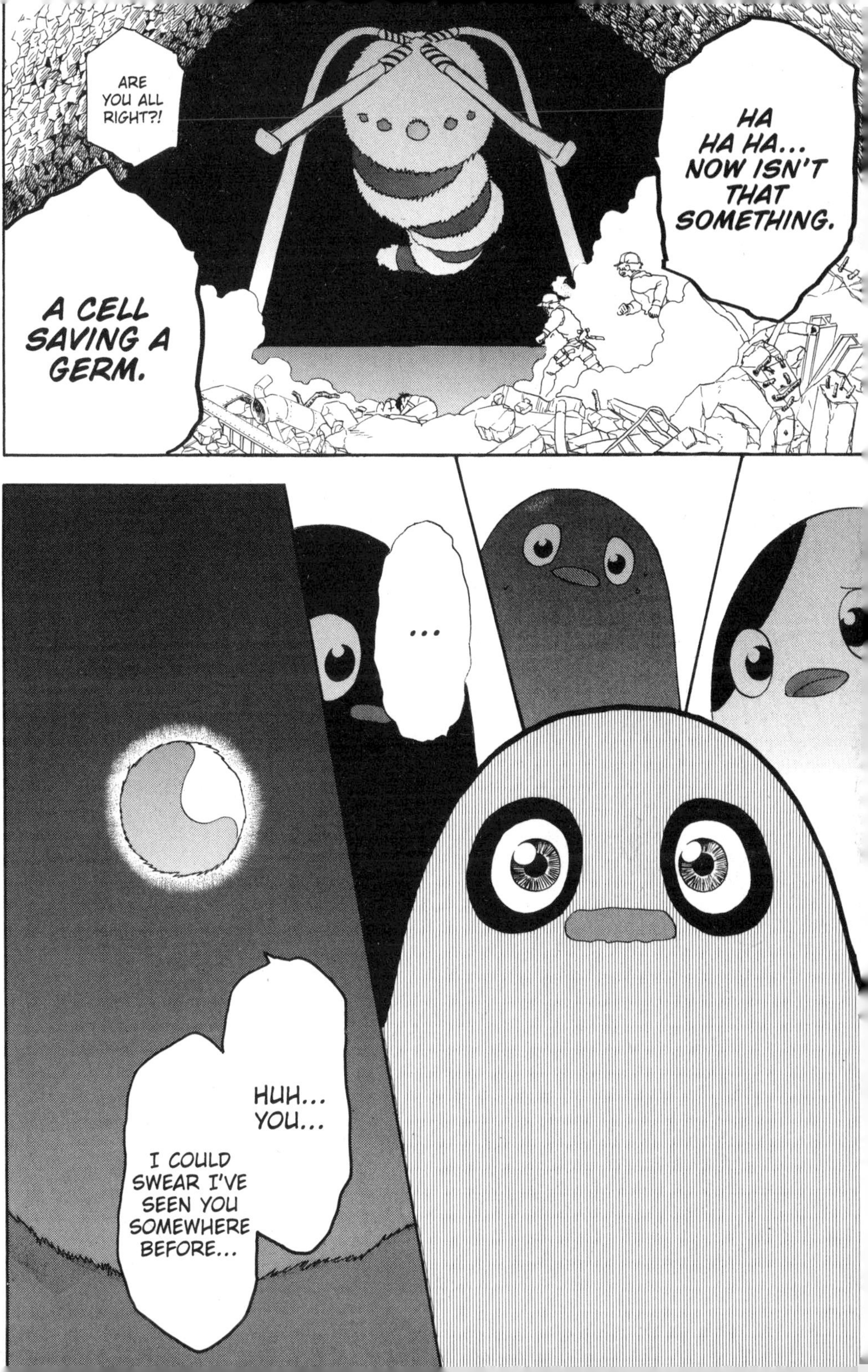
HA HA HA... NOW ISN'T THAT SOMETHING.
ARE YOU ALL RIGHT?!
A CELL SAVING A GERM.
...
HUH... YOU...
I COULD SWEAR I'VE SEEN YOU SOMEWHERE BEFORE...

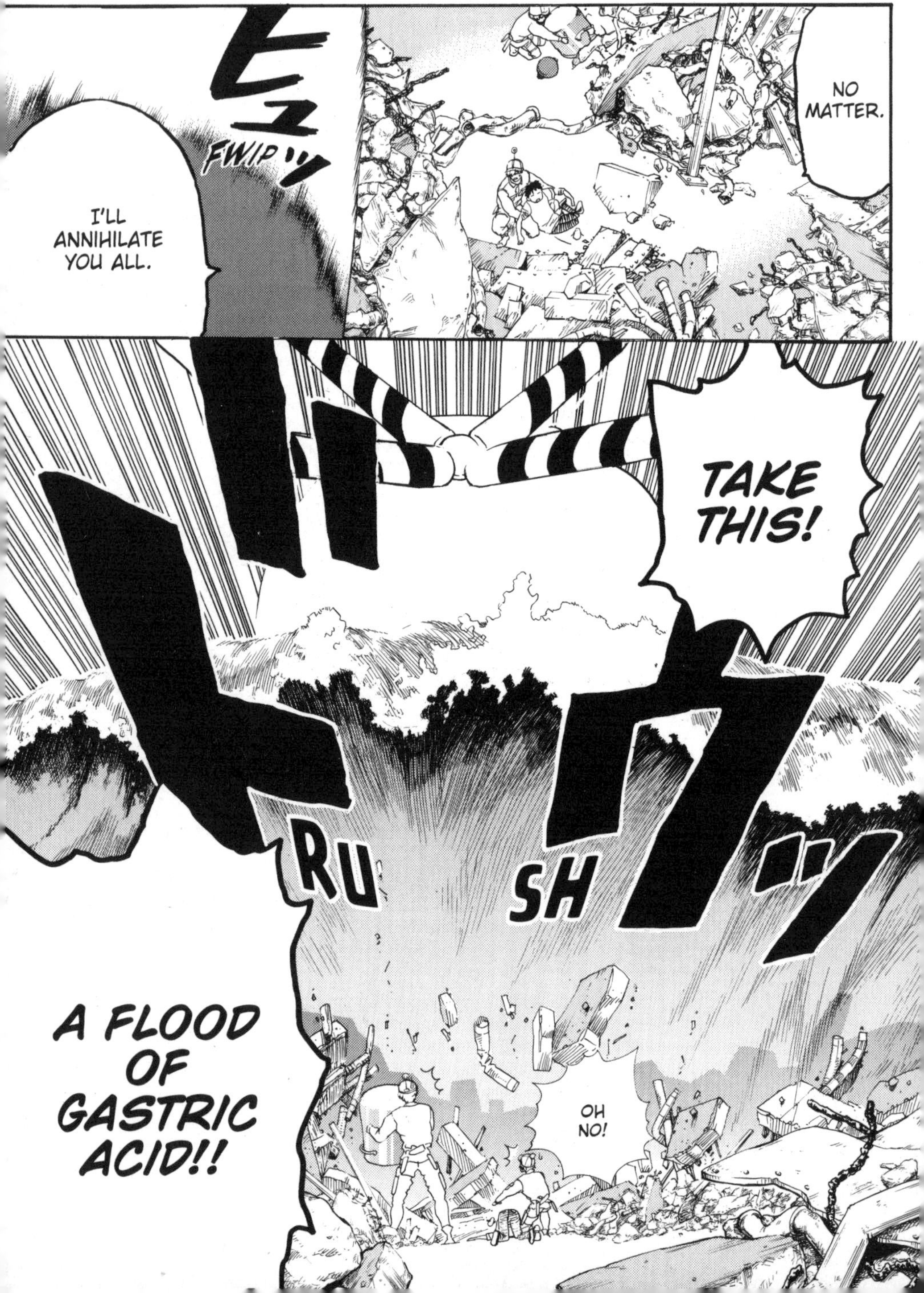
NO MATTER.
FWIP
I'LL ANNIHILATE YOU ALL.
TAKE THIS!
RUSH
OH NO!
A FLOOD OF GASTRIC ACID!!

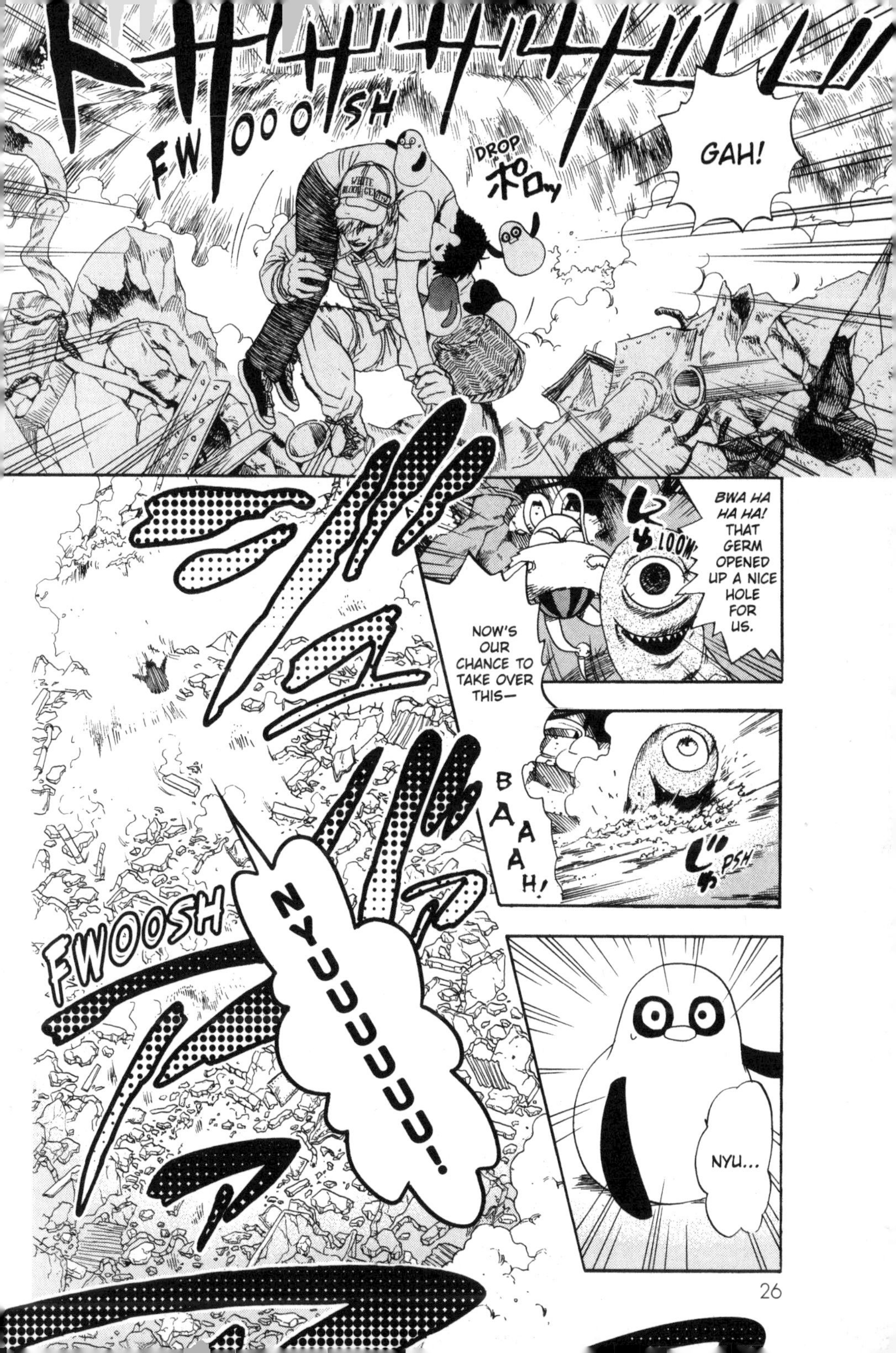
FWOOOSH
DROP
GAH!
BWA HA HA HA! THAT GERM OPENED UP A NICE HOLE FOR US.
LOOM
NOW'S OUR CHANCE TO TAKE OVER THIS—
BAAAH!
PSH
NYU...
NYUUUUUUU!
FWOOSH

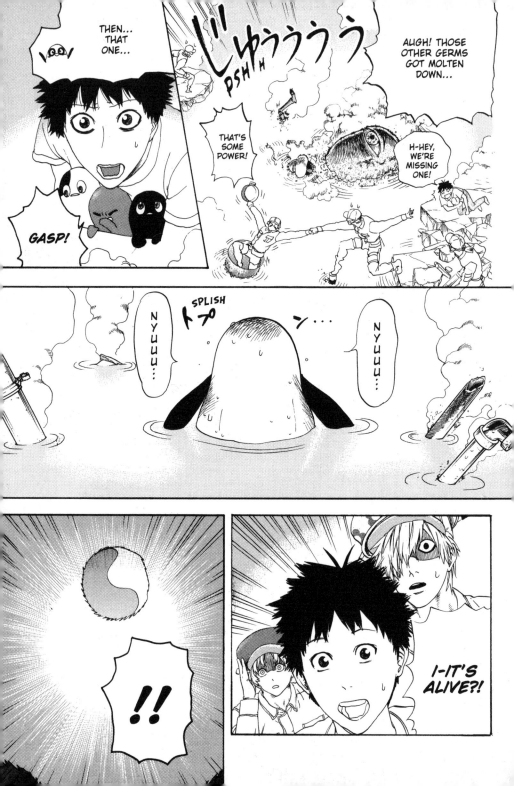

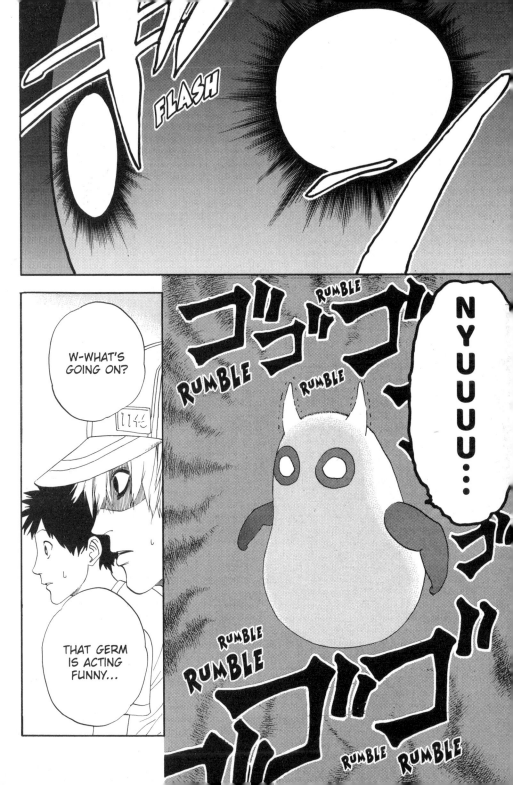

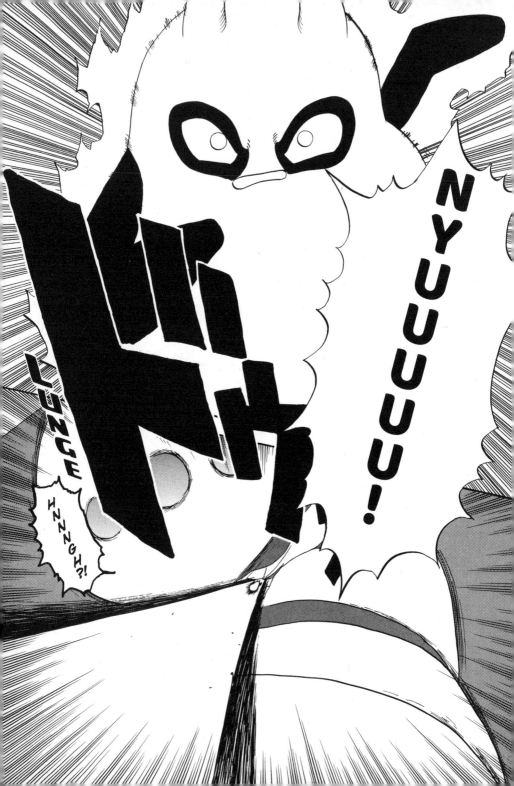

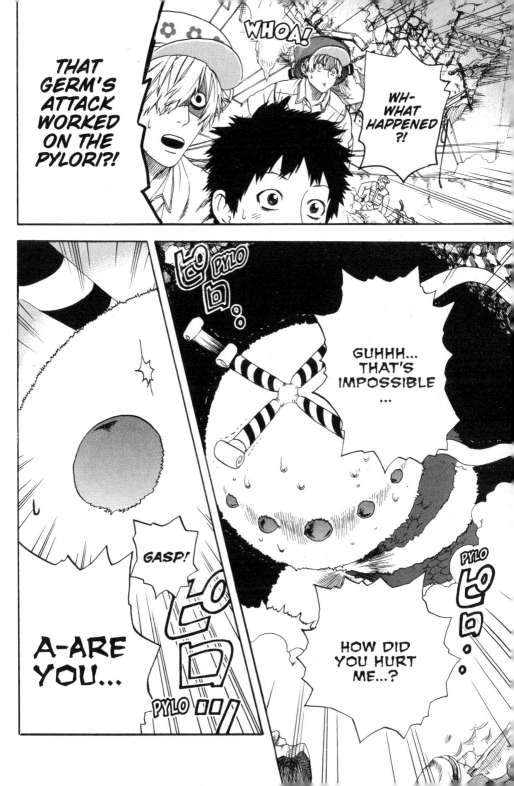

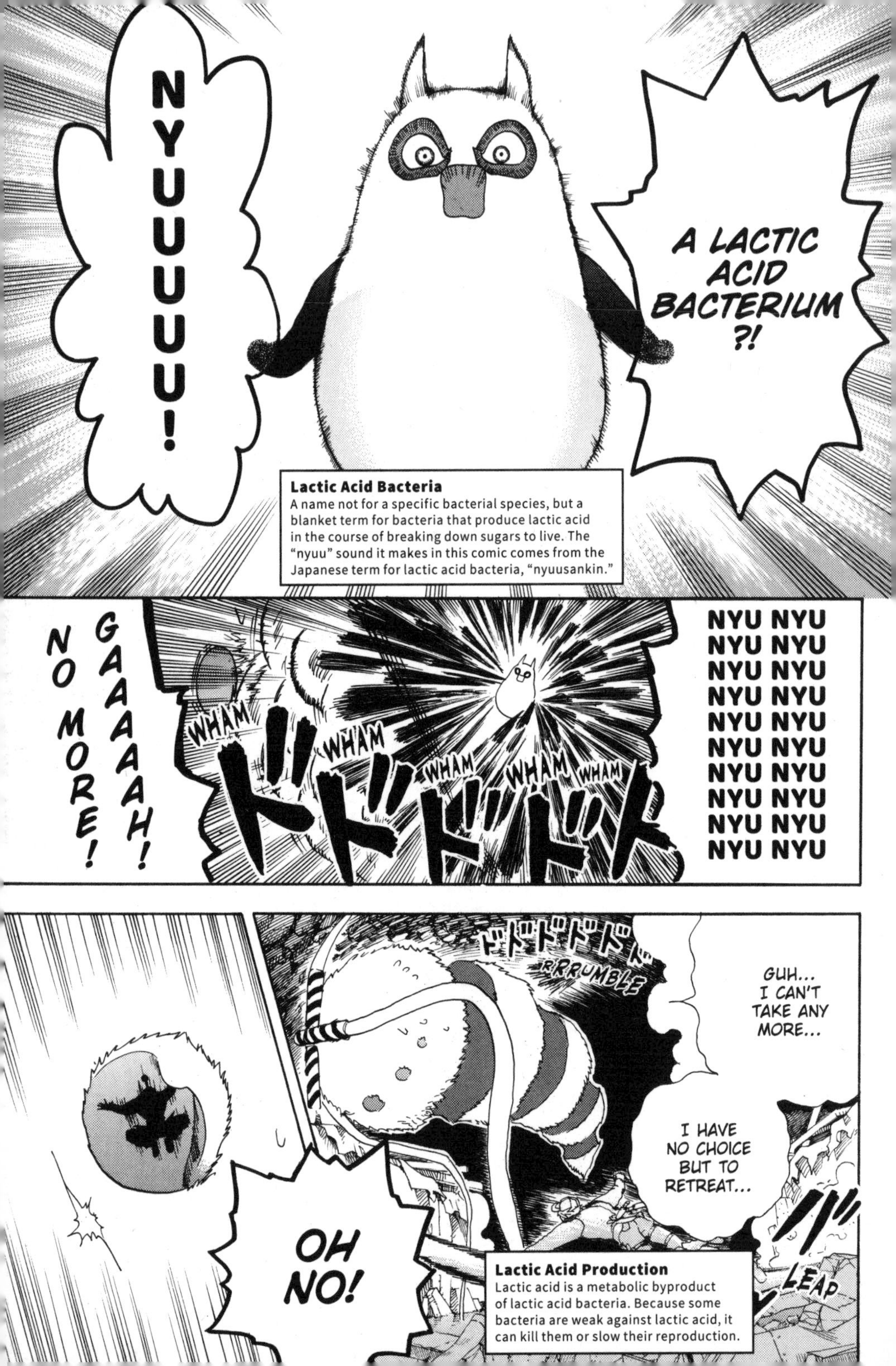
A LACTIC ACID BACTERIUM?!
NYUUUUUU!
Lactic Acid Bacteria
A name not for a specific bacterial species, but a blanket term for bacteria that produce lactic acid in the course of breaking down sugars to live. The "nyuu" sound it makes in this comic comes from the Japanese term for lactic acid bacteria, "nyuusankin."
NYU NYU NYU NYU NYU NYU NYU NYU NYU NYU NYU NYU NYU NYU NYU NYU NYU NYU NYU NYU
WHAM WHAM WHAM WHAM WHAM
GAAAAAAH!
NO MORE!
GUH... I CAN'T TAKE ANY MORE...
I HAVE NO CHOICE BUT TO RETREAT...
RRRUMBLE
LEAP
Lactic Acid Production
Lactic acid is a metabolic byproduct of lactic acid bacteria. Because some bacteria are weak against lactic acid, it can kill them or slow their reproduction.
OH NO!

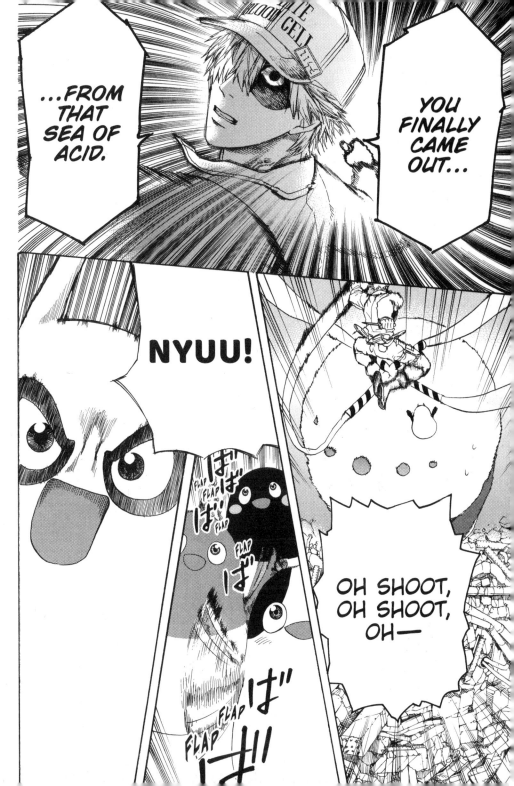

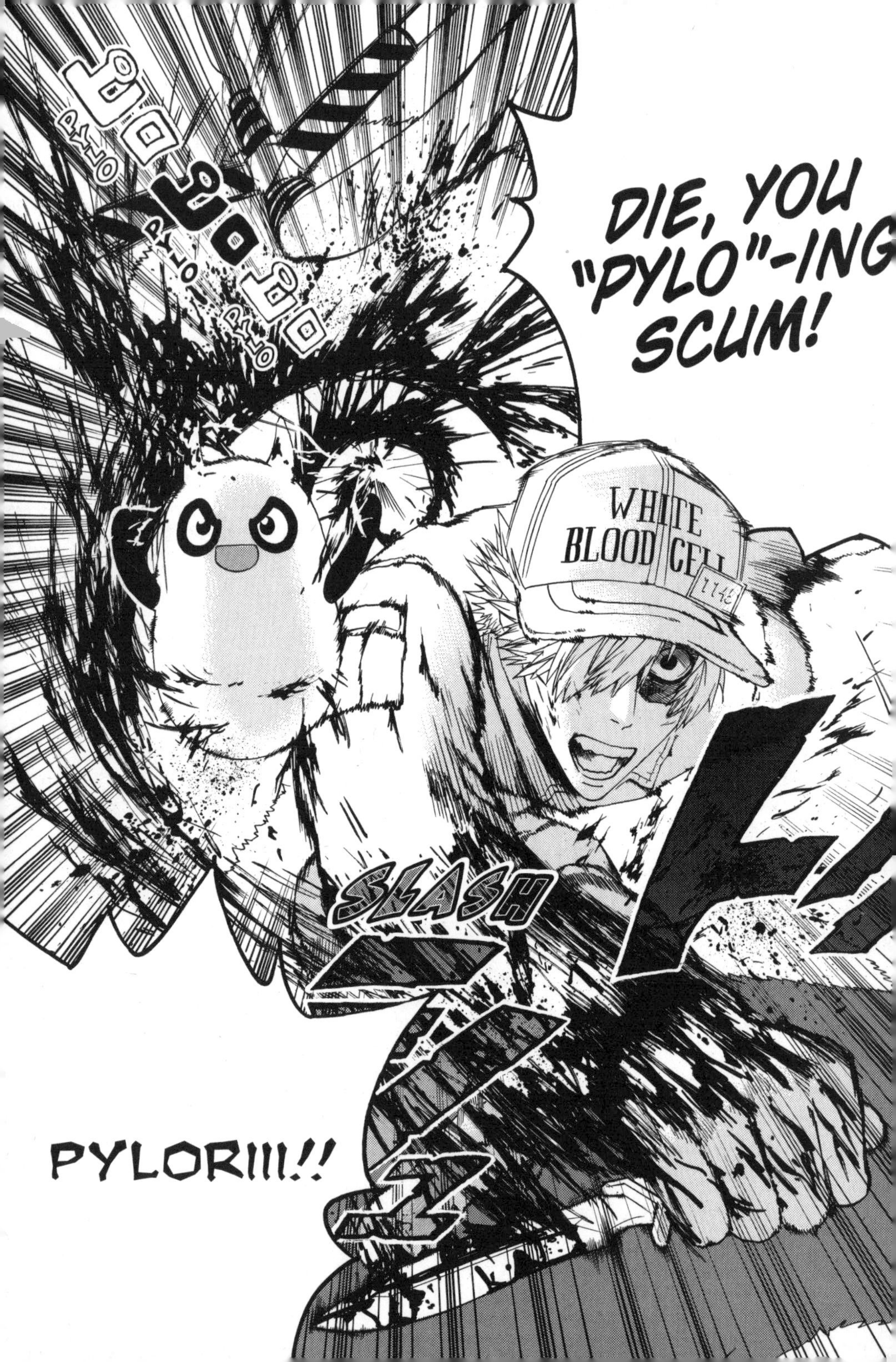
DIE, YOU "PYLO"-ING SCUM!
PYLO PYLO PYLO
WHITE BLOOD CELL
1146
SLASH
PYLORIII!!

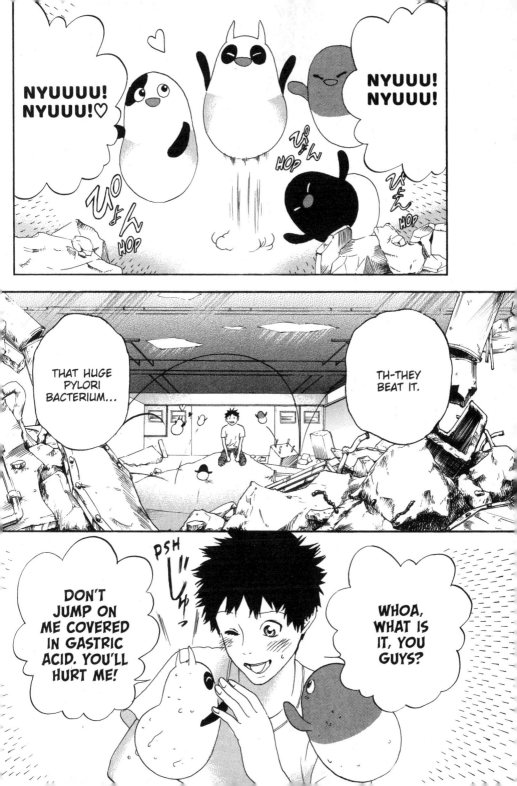

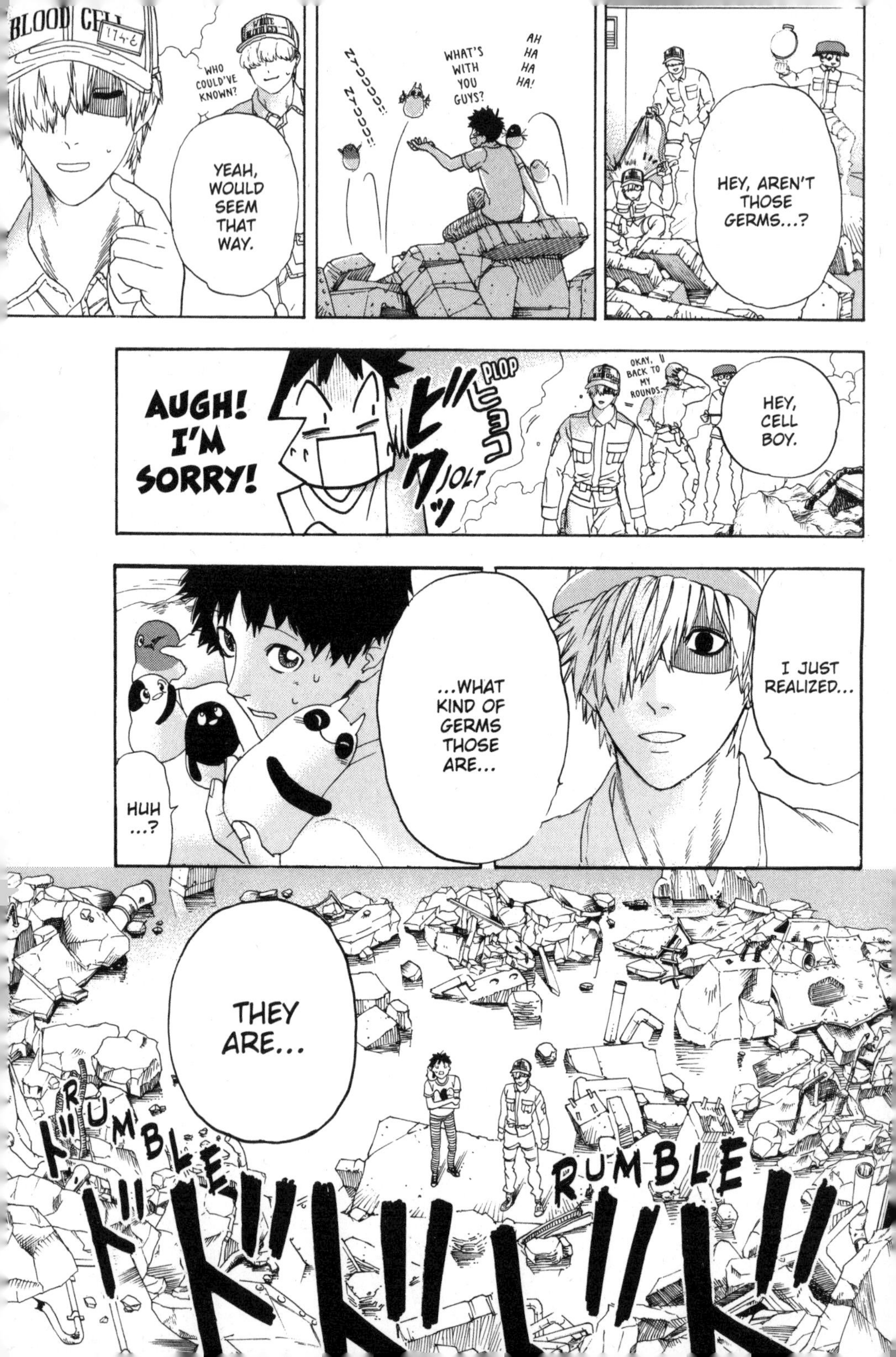
HEY, AREN'T THOSE GERMS...?
AH HA HA HA!
WHAT'S WITH YOU GUYS?
NYUUUU!!
NYUUUU!!
WHO COULD'VE KNOWN?
YEAH, WOULD SEEM THAT WAY.
HEY, CELL BOY.
OKAY, BACK TO MY ROUNDS.
PLOP
JOLT
AUGH! I'M SORRY!
I JUST REALIZED...
...WHAT KIND OF GERMS THOSE ARE...
HUH...?
THEY ARE...
RUMBLE
RUMBLE

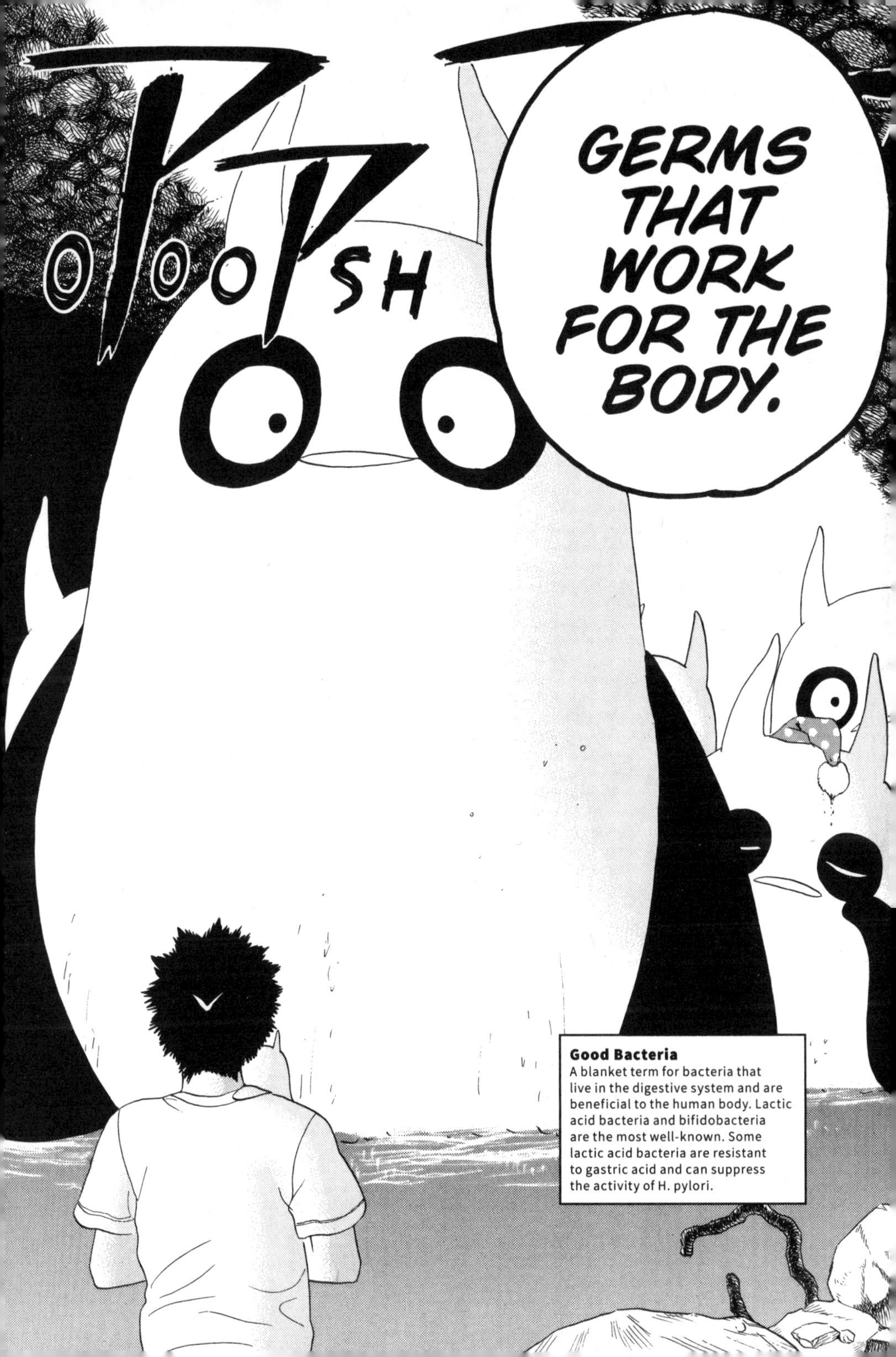
GERMS THAT WORK FOR THE BODY.
Good Bacteria
A blanket term for bacteria that live in the digestive system and are beneficial to the human body. Lactic acid bacteria and bifidobacteria are the most well-known. Some lactic acid bacteria are resistant to gastric acid and can suppress the activity of H. pylori.

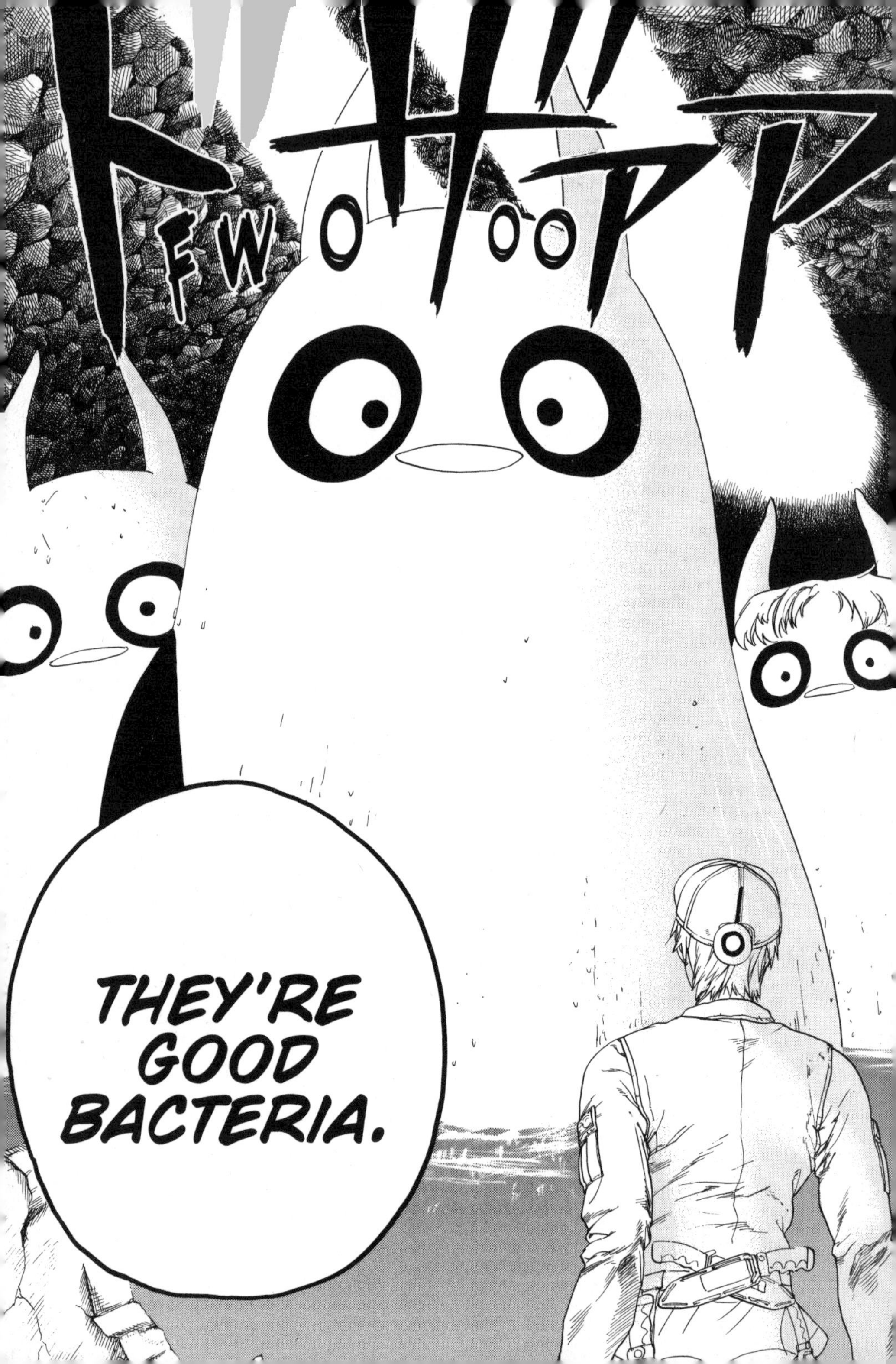

ドサザァ
FWOOOO
THEY'RE GOOD BACTERIA.

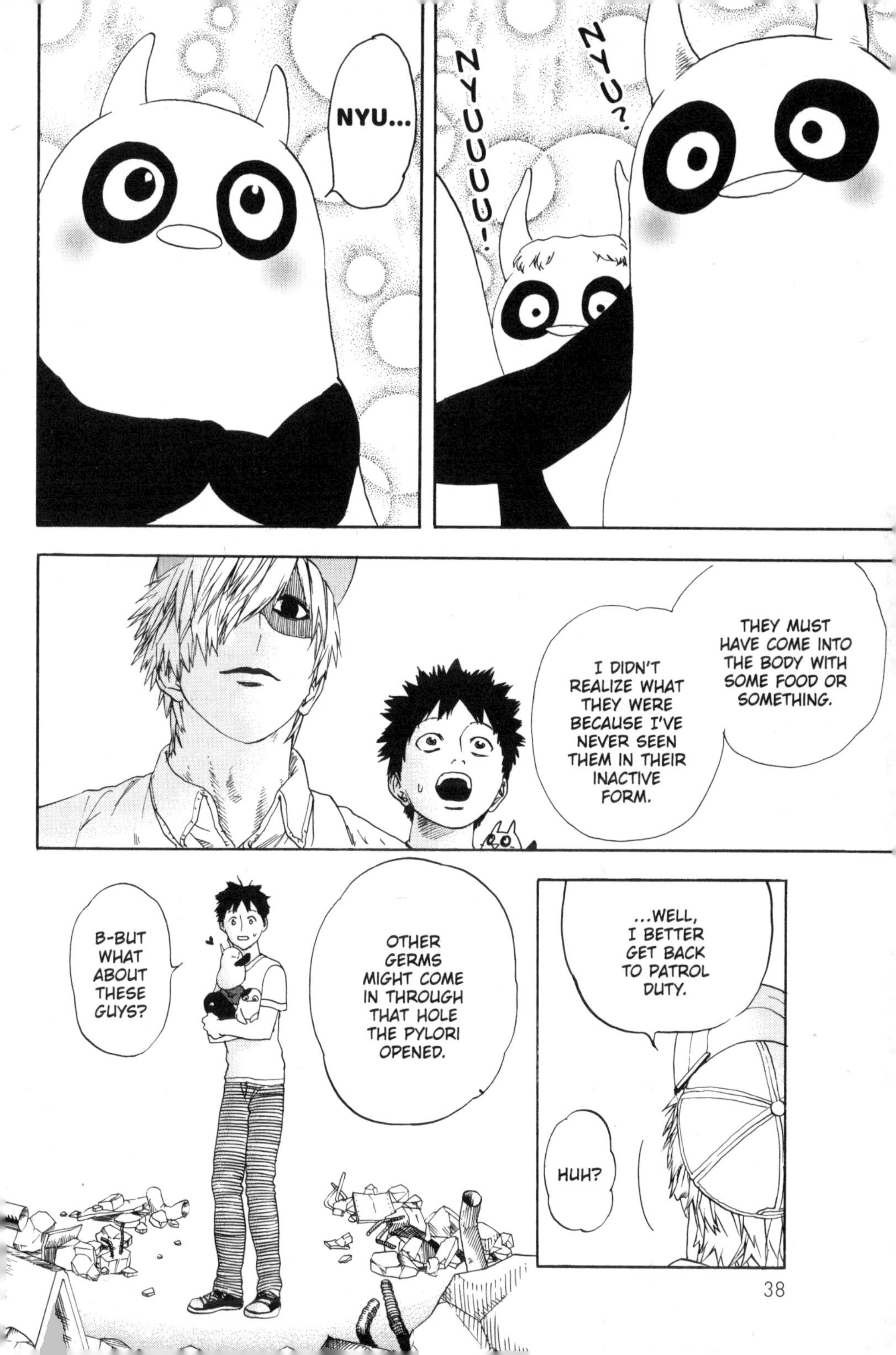
NYU?
NYUUUUU!
NYU...
THEY MUST HAVE COME INTO THE BODY WITH SOME FOOD OR SOMETHING.
I DIDN'T REALIZE WHAT THEY WERE BECAUSE I'VE NEVER SEEN THEM IN THEIR INACTIVE FORM.
...WELL, I BETTER GET BACK TO PATROL DUTY.
HUH?
OTHER GERMS MIGHT COME IN THROUGH THAT HOLE THE PYLORI OPENED.
B-BUT WHAT ABOUT THESE GUYS?

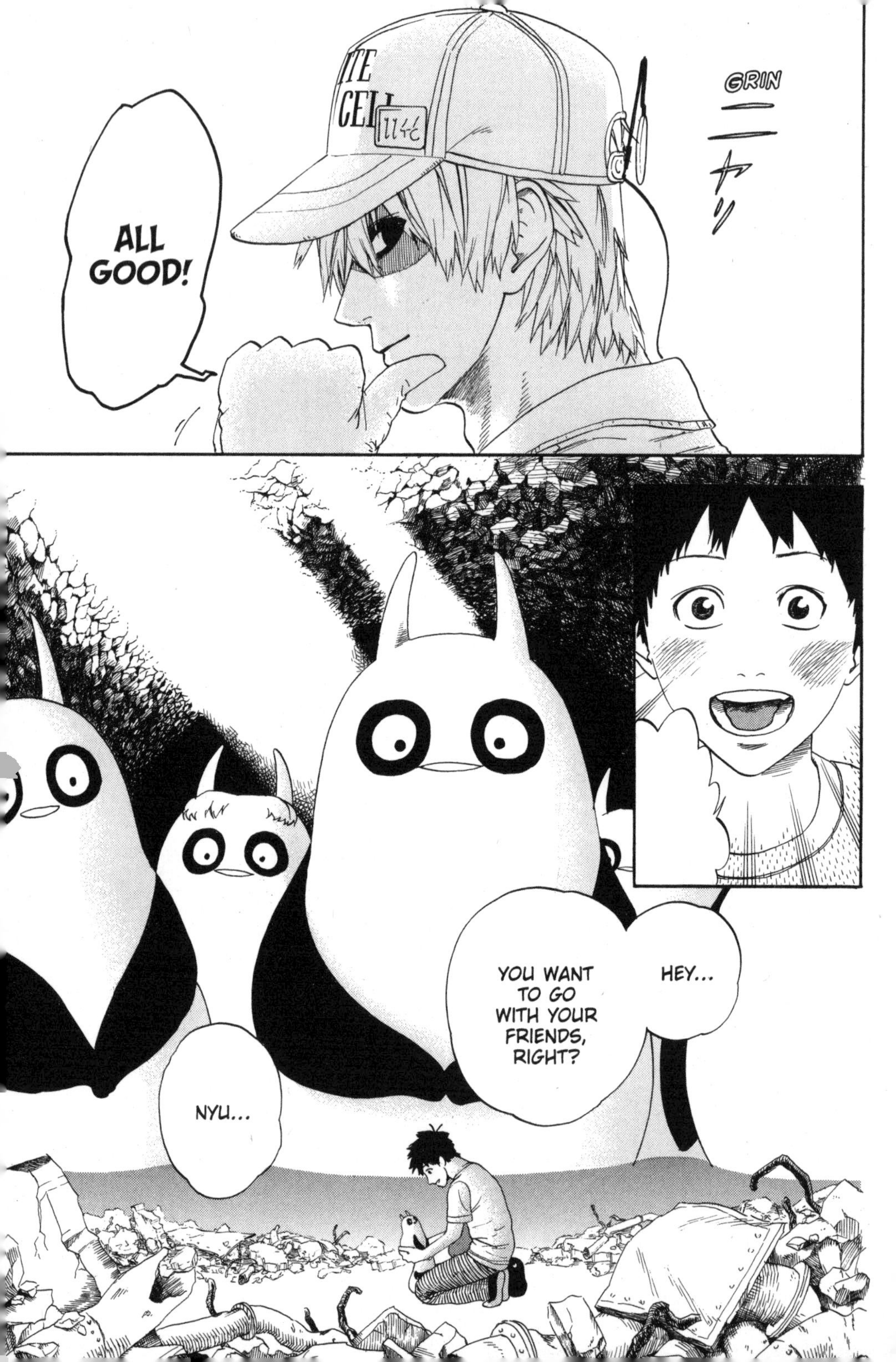
GRIN
ALL GOOD!
HEY...
YOU WANT TO GO WITH YOUR FRIENDS, RIGHT?
NYU...

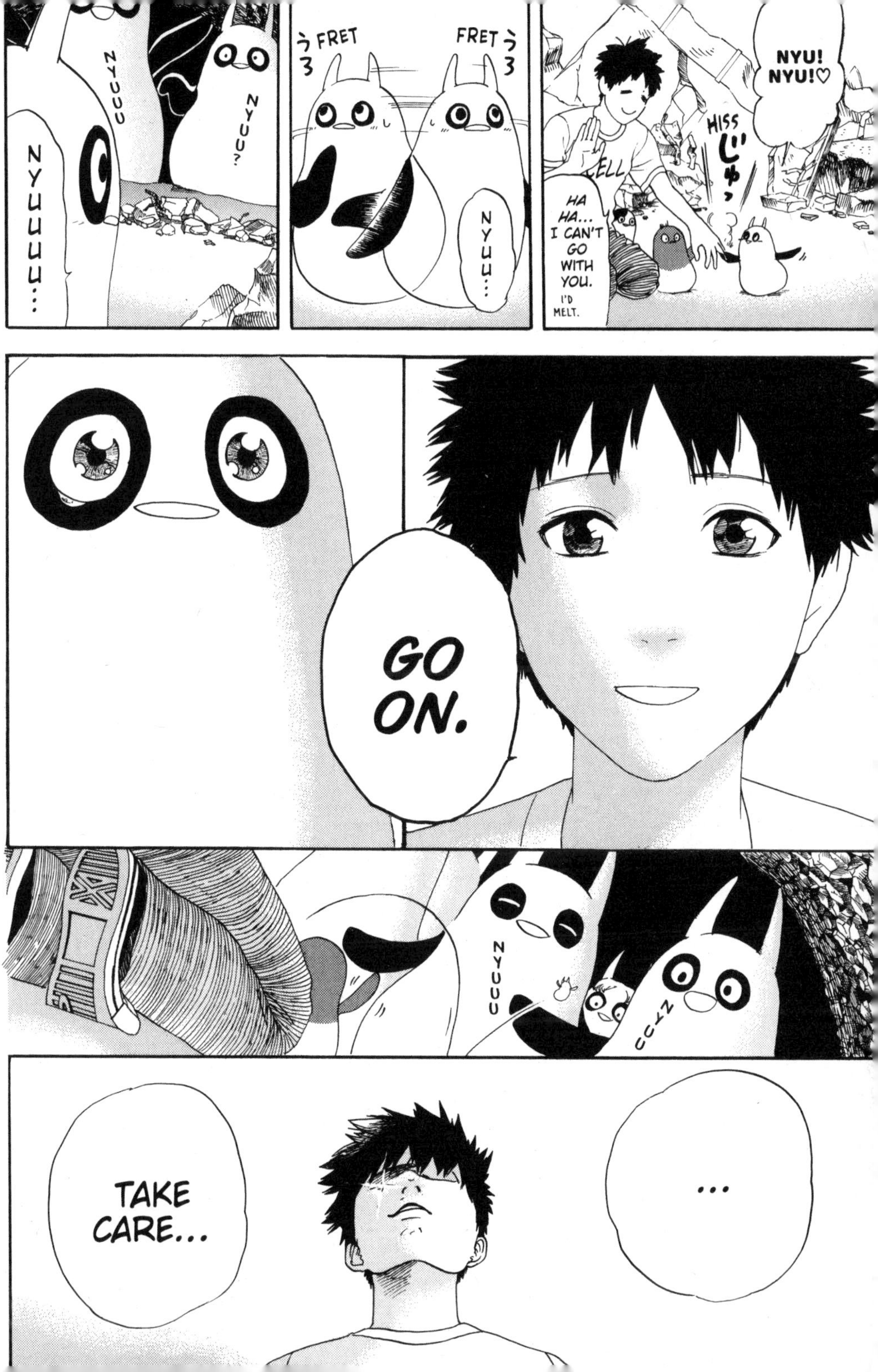
NYU! NYU!♡
HISS
じゅっ
HA HA... I CAN'T GO WITH YOU.
I'D MELT.
うろ FRET
FRET うろ
NYUU...
NYUUU
NYUU?
NYUUUUU...
GO ON.
NYUUU
...
TAKE CARE...

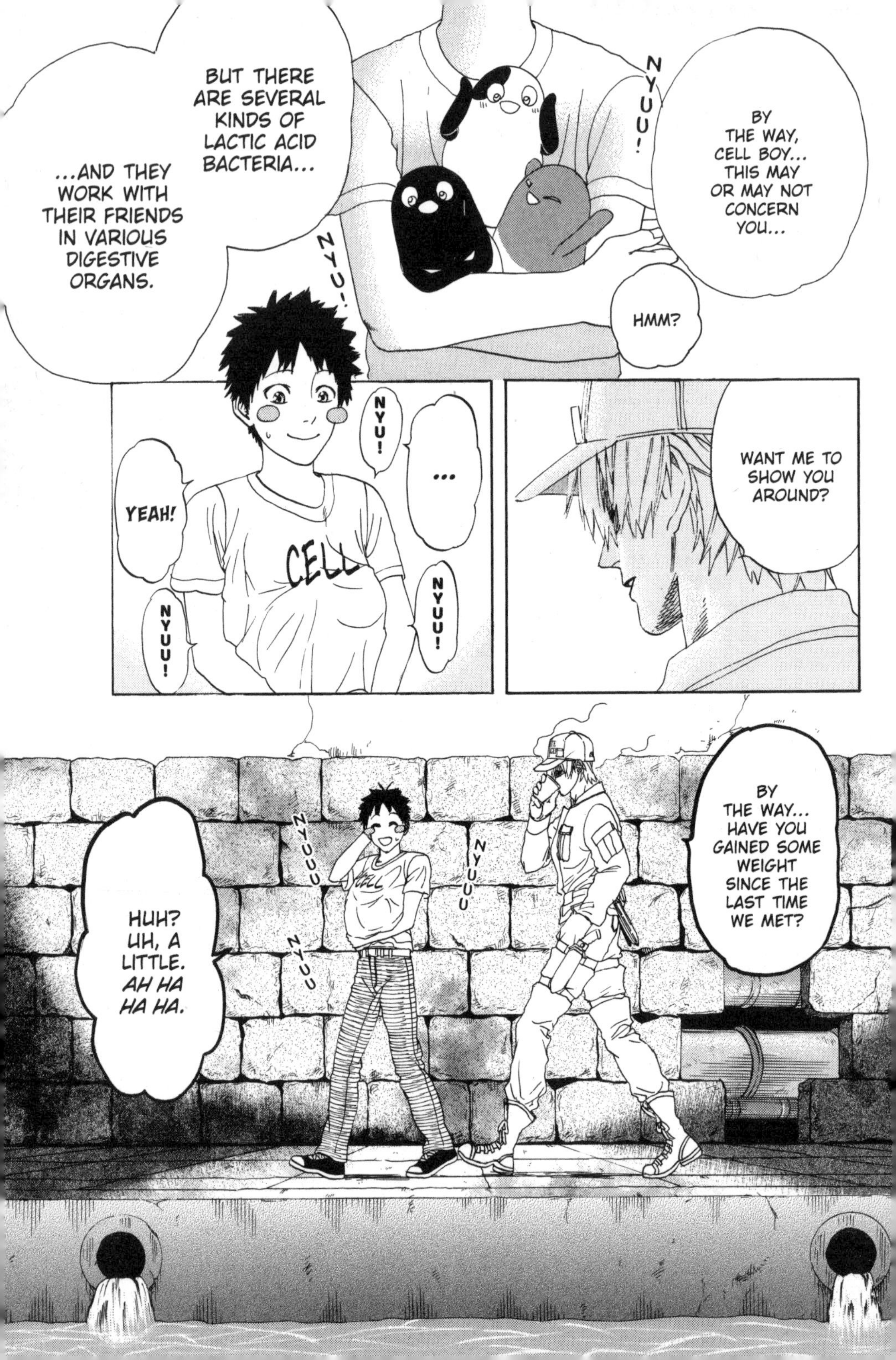
BY THE WAY, CELL BOY... THIS MAY OR MAY NOT CONCERN YOU...
NYUU!
BUT THERE ARE SEVERAL KINDS OF LACTIC ACID BACTERIA...
...AND THEY WORK WITH THEIR FRIENDS IN VARIOUS DIGESTIVE ORGANS.
NYUU!
HMM?
WANT ME TO SHOW YOU AROUND?
NYU!
...
NYUU!
YEAH!
NYUU!
BY THE WAY... HAVE YOU GAINED SOME WEIGHT SINCE THE LAST TIME WE MET?
NYUUU
NYUUU
NYUU
HUH? UH, A LITTLE. *AH HA HA HA.*

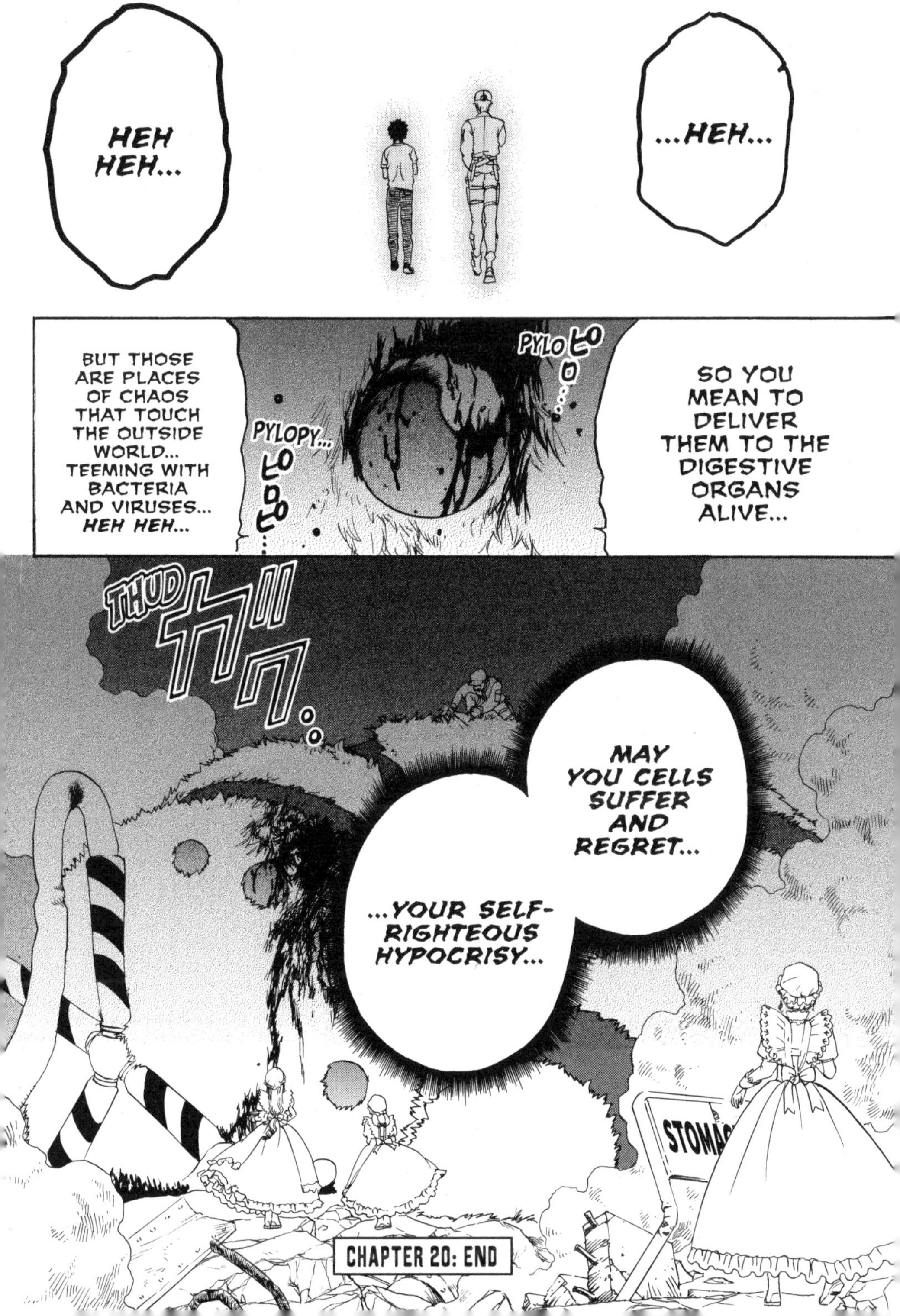

...HEH...
HEH HEH...
SO YOU MEAN TO DELIVER THEM TO THE DIGESTIVE ORGANS ALIVE...
PYLO
PYLOPY...
BUT THOSE ARE PLACES OF CHAOS THAT TOUCH THE OUTSIDE WORLD... TEEMING WITH BACTERIA AND VIRUSES... HEH HEH...
THUD
MAY YOU CELLS SUFFER AND REGRET...
...YOUR SELF-RIGHTEOUS HYPOCRISY...
CHAPTER 20: END

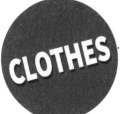
The Life and Work of White Blood Cell (Neutrophil):
What He Wears
* These are depictions created just for this comic, and differ from scientific fact.

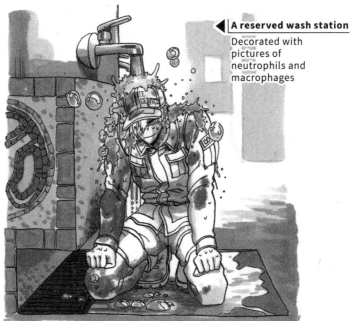

A reserved wash station
Decorated with pictures of neutrophils and macrophages

Clothes dirtied in a fight can be rinsed quickly with disinfectants and soap water. (No hot water. Cold.)

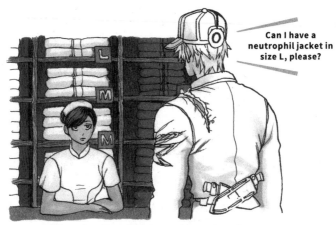

Can I have a neutrophil jacket in size L, please?

If they rip, new clothes can be retrieved at organs that work to make or store blood cells, like the red bone marrow, liver, or spleen.

Cells at Work!
はたらく細胞

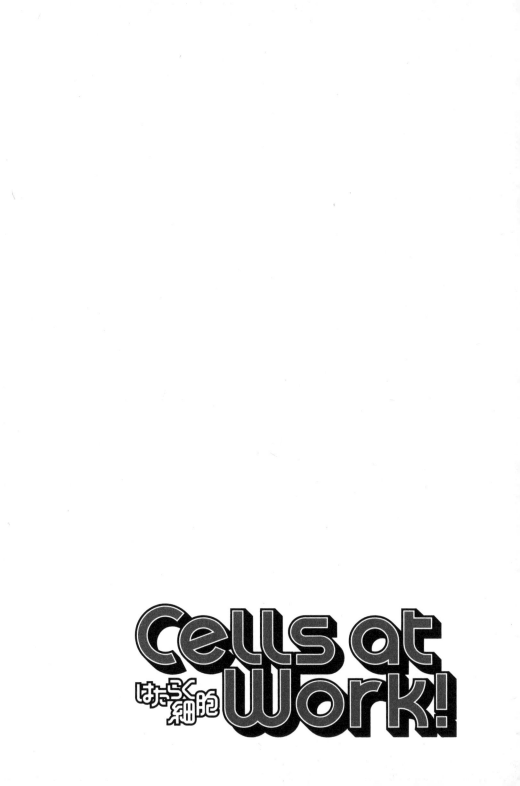

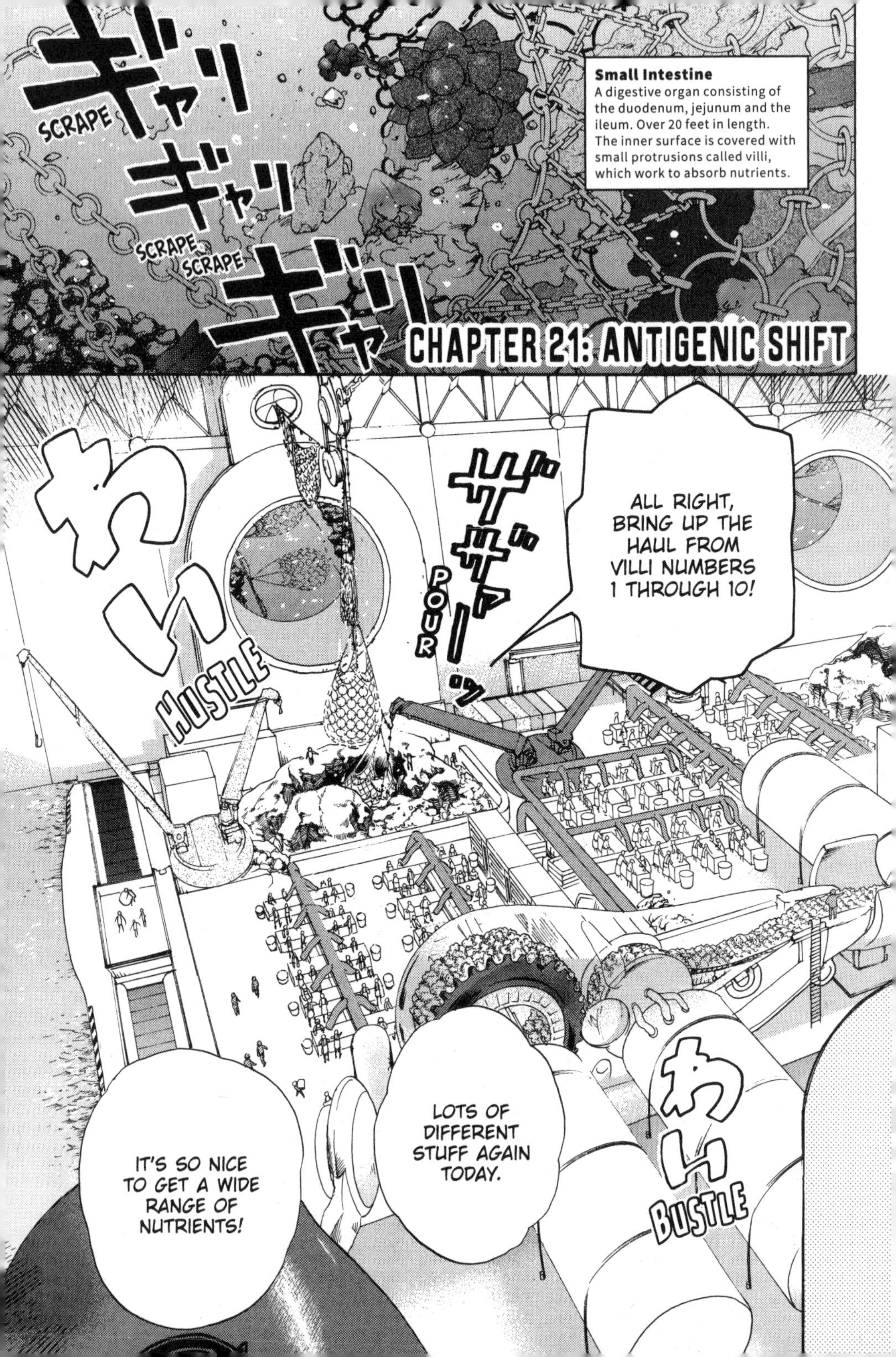

Small Intestine
A digestive organ consisting of the duodenum, jejunum and the ileum. Over 20 feet in length. The inner surface is covered with small protrusions called villi, which work to absorb nutrients.
ギャリ
SCRAPE
ギャリ
SCRAPE SCRAPE
ギャリ
CHAPTER 21: ANTIGENIC SHIFT
ALL RIGHT, BRING UP THE HAUL FROM VILLI NUMBERS 1 THROUGH 10!
ザバァーッ
POUR
わい
HUSTLE
わい
BUSTLE
LOTS OF DIFFERENT STUFF AGAIN TODAY.
IT'S SO NICE TO GET A WIDE RANGE OF NUTRIENTS!

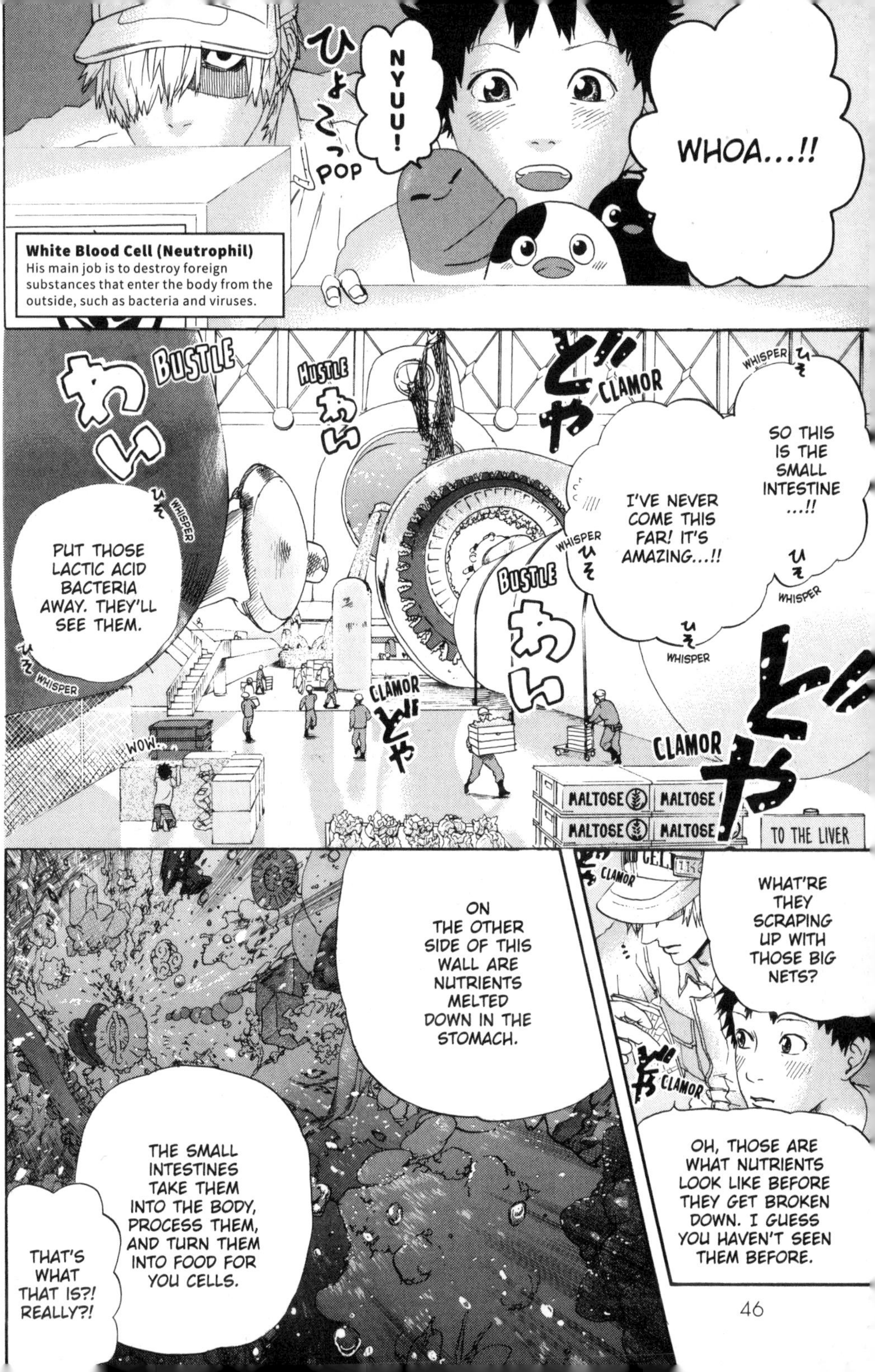
WHOA...!!
NYUU!
ひょこっ
POP
White Blood Cell (Neutrophil)
His main job is to destroy foreign substances that enter the body from the outside, such as bacteria and viruses.
WHISPER ひそ
SO THIS IS THE SMALL INTESTINE ...!!
ひそ WHISPER
どや CLAMOR
I'VE NEVER COME THIS FAR! IT'S AMAZING...!!
WHISPER ひそ
ひそ WHISPER
どや
CLAMOR
MALTOSE
MALTOSE
MALTOSE
MALTOSE
TO THE LIVER
BUSTLE
わん
HUSTLE
わん
CLAMOR
どや
WOW...
わい
BUSTLE
ひそ WHISPER
PUT THOSE LACTIC ACID BACTERIA AWAY. THEY'LL SEE THEM.
ひそ WHISPER
CLAMOR
WHAT'RE THEY SCRAPING UP WITH THOSE BIG NETS?
CLAMOR
OH, THOSE ARE WHAT NUTRIENTS LOOK LIKE BEFORE THEY GET BROKEN DOWN. I GUESS YOU HAVEN'T SEEN THEM BEFORE.
ON THE OTHER SIDE OF THIS WALL ARE NUTRIENTS MELTED DOWN IN THE STOMACH.
THE SMALL INTESTINES TAKE THEM INTO THE BODY, PROCESS THEM, AND TURN THEM INTO FOOD FOR YOU CELLS.
THAT'S WHAT THAT IS?! REALLY?!

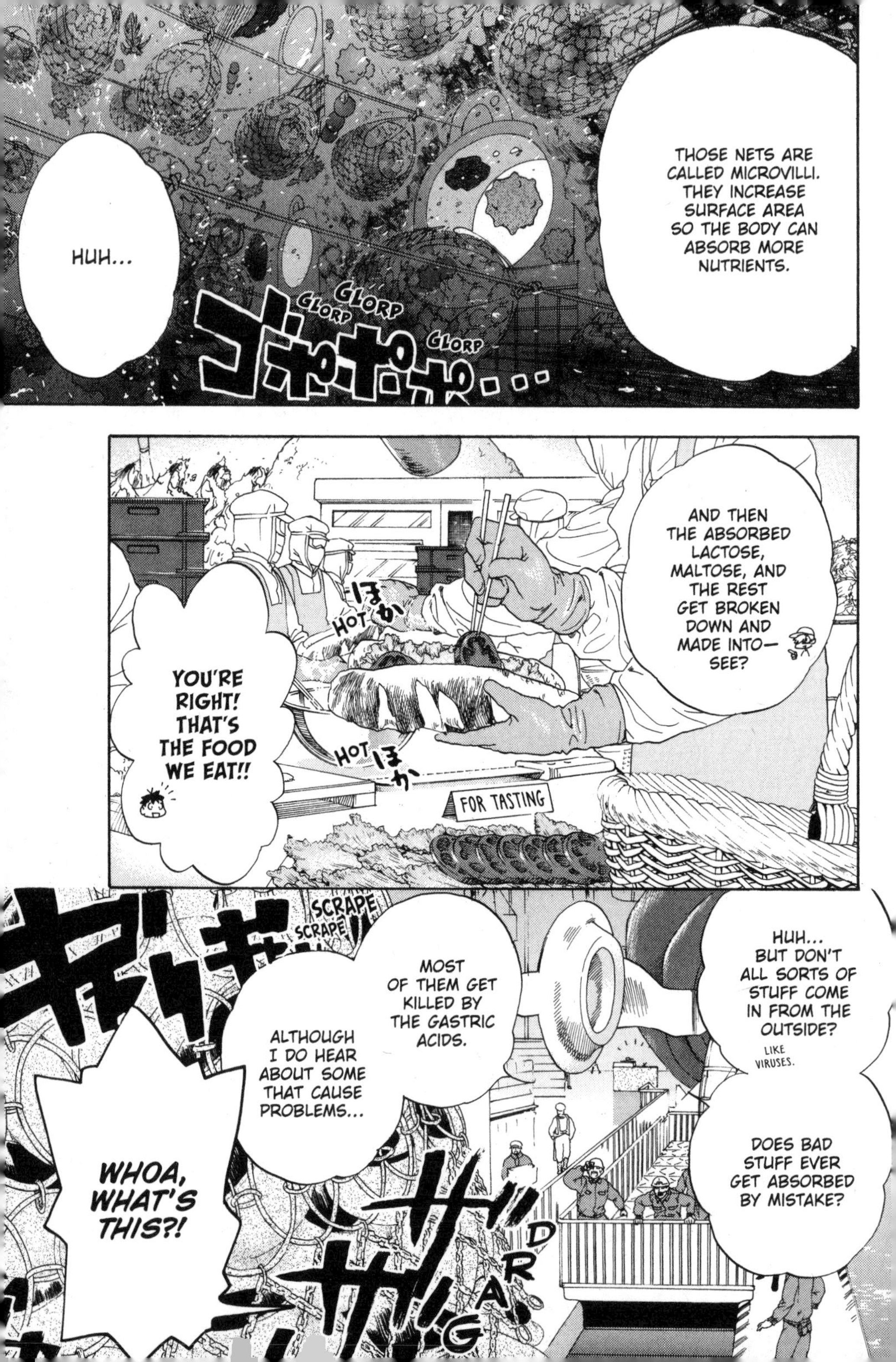
THOSE NETS ARE CALLED MICROVILLI. THEY INCREASE SURFACE AREA SO THE BODY CAN ABSORB MORE NUTRIENTS.
HUH...
ゴポポポ...
GLORP GLORP GLORP
AND THEN THE ABSORBED LACTOSE, MALTOSE, AND THE REST GET BROKEN DOWN AND MADE INTO— SEE?
ほか HOT
ほか HOT
FOR TASTING
YOU'RE RIGHT! THAT'S THE FOOD WE EAT!!
HUH... BUT DON'T ALL SORTS OF STUFF COME IN FROM THE OUTSIDE?
LIKE VIRUSES.
DOES BAD STUFF EVER GET ABSORBED BY MISTAKE?
MOST OF THEM GET KILLED BY THE GASTRIC ACIDS.
ALTHOUGH I DO HEAR ABOUT SOME THAT CAUSE PROBLEMS...
SCRAPE SCRAPE
WHOA, WHAT'S THIS?!
DRAG

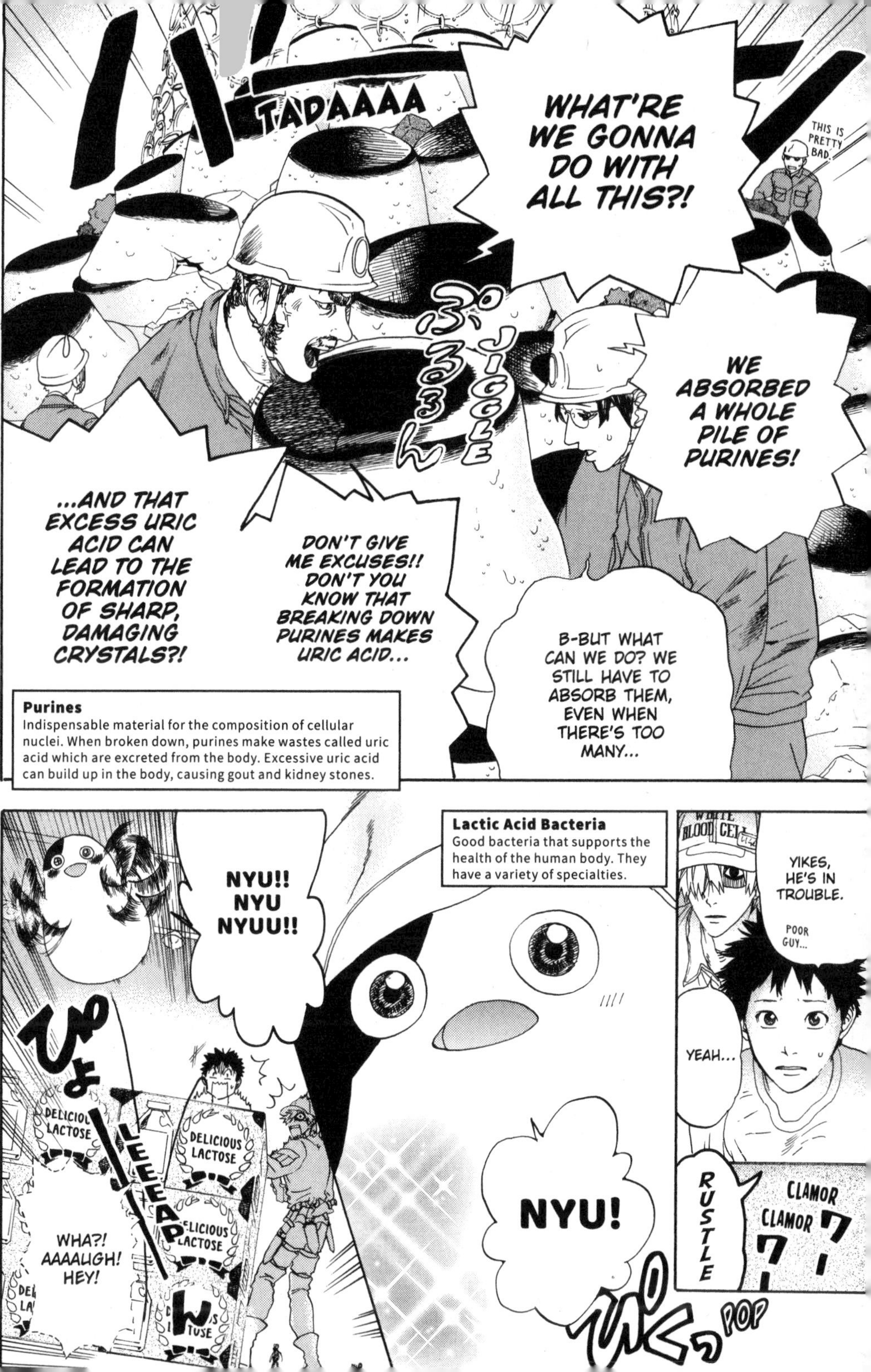
THIS IS PRETTY BAD.
WHAT'RE WE GONNA DO WITH ALL THIS?!
TADAAAA
WE ABSORBED A WHOLE PILE OF PURINES!
ぷるるん JIGGLE
B-BUT WHAT CAN WE DO? WE STILL HAVE TO ABSORB THEM, EVEN WHEN THERE'S TOO MANY...
DON'T GIVE ME EXCUSES!! DON'T YOU KNOW THAT BREAKING DOWN PURINES MAKES URIC ACID...
...AND THAT EXCESS URIC ACID CAN LEAD TO THE FORMATION OF SHARP, DAMAGING CRYSTALS?!
Purines
Indispensable material for the composition of cellular nuclei. When broken down, purines make wastes called uric acid which are excreted from the body. Excessive uric acid can build up in the body, causing gout and kidney stones.
WHITE BLOOD CELL
YIKES, HE'S IN TROUBLE.
POOR GUY...
YEAH...
RUSTLE
CLAMOR CLAMOR
Lactic Acid Bacteria
Good bacteria that supports the health of the human body. They have a variety of specialties.
NYU!! NYU NYUU!!
NYU!
POP
LEEEAP
DELICIOUS LACTOSE
DELICIOUS LACTOSE
DELICIOUS LACTOSE
WHA?! AAAAUGH! HEY!

*NOTE: THE TERM "PURINES" RESEMBLES THE JAPANESE WORD FOR "PUDDING, HENCE THEIR PUDDING-CUP APPEARANCE HERE.

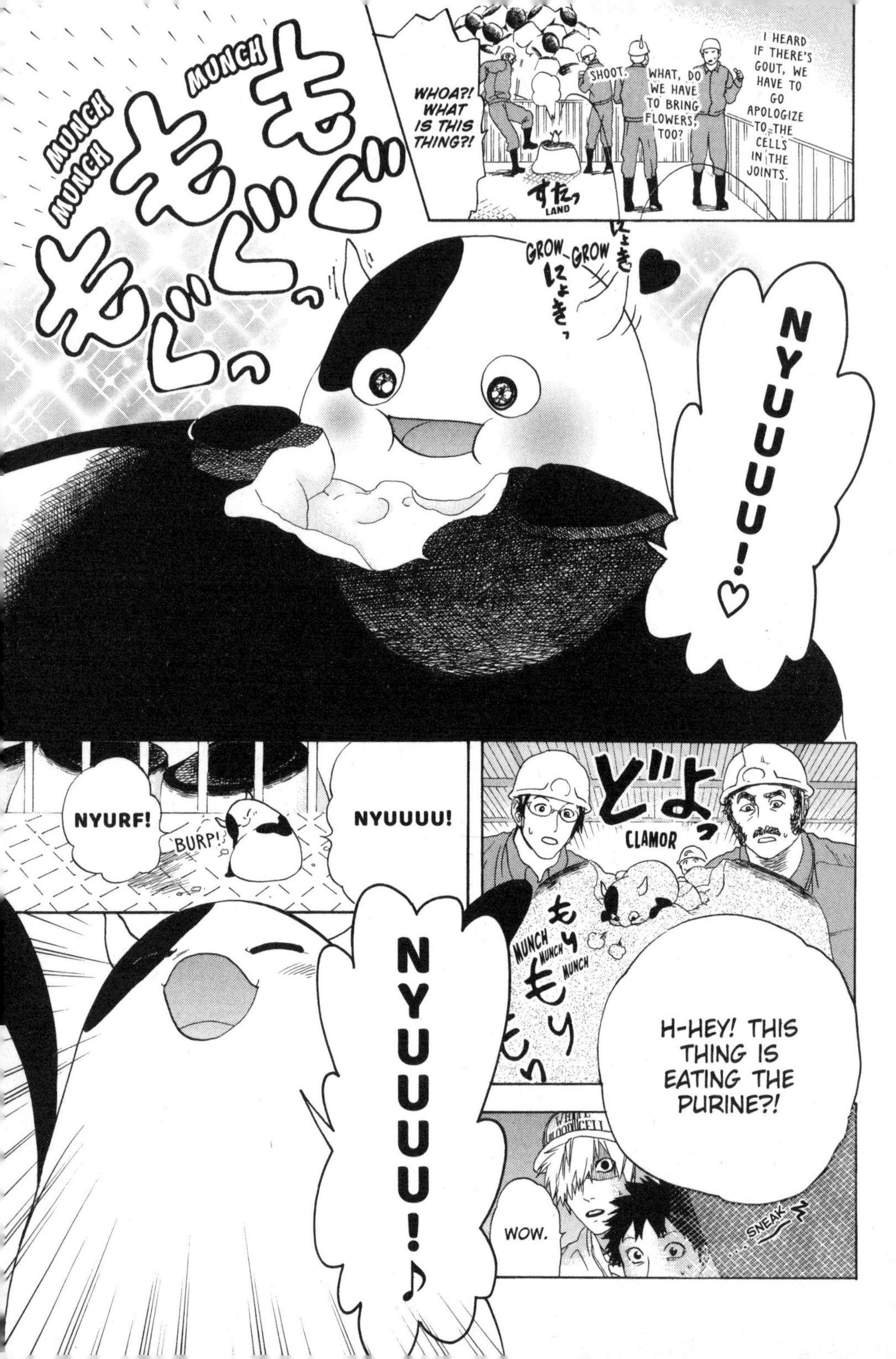
I HEARD IF THERE'S GOUT, WE HAVE TO GO APOLOGIZE TO THE CELLS IN THE JOINTS.
WHAT, DO WE HAVE TO BRING FLOWERS, TOO?
SHOOT.
WHOA?! WHAT IS THIS THING?!
すたっ
LAND
もぐもぐもぐっ
MUNCH MUNCH
MUNCH MUNCH
にょきにょきっ
GROW GROW
NYUUUUU!♡
どよっ
CLAMOR
もりもりもり
MUNCH MUNCH MUNCH
H-HEY! THIS THING IS EATING THE PURINE?!
WOW.
SNEAK
NYURF!
BURP!
NYUUUUU!
NYUUUUU!♪

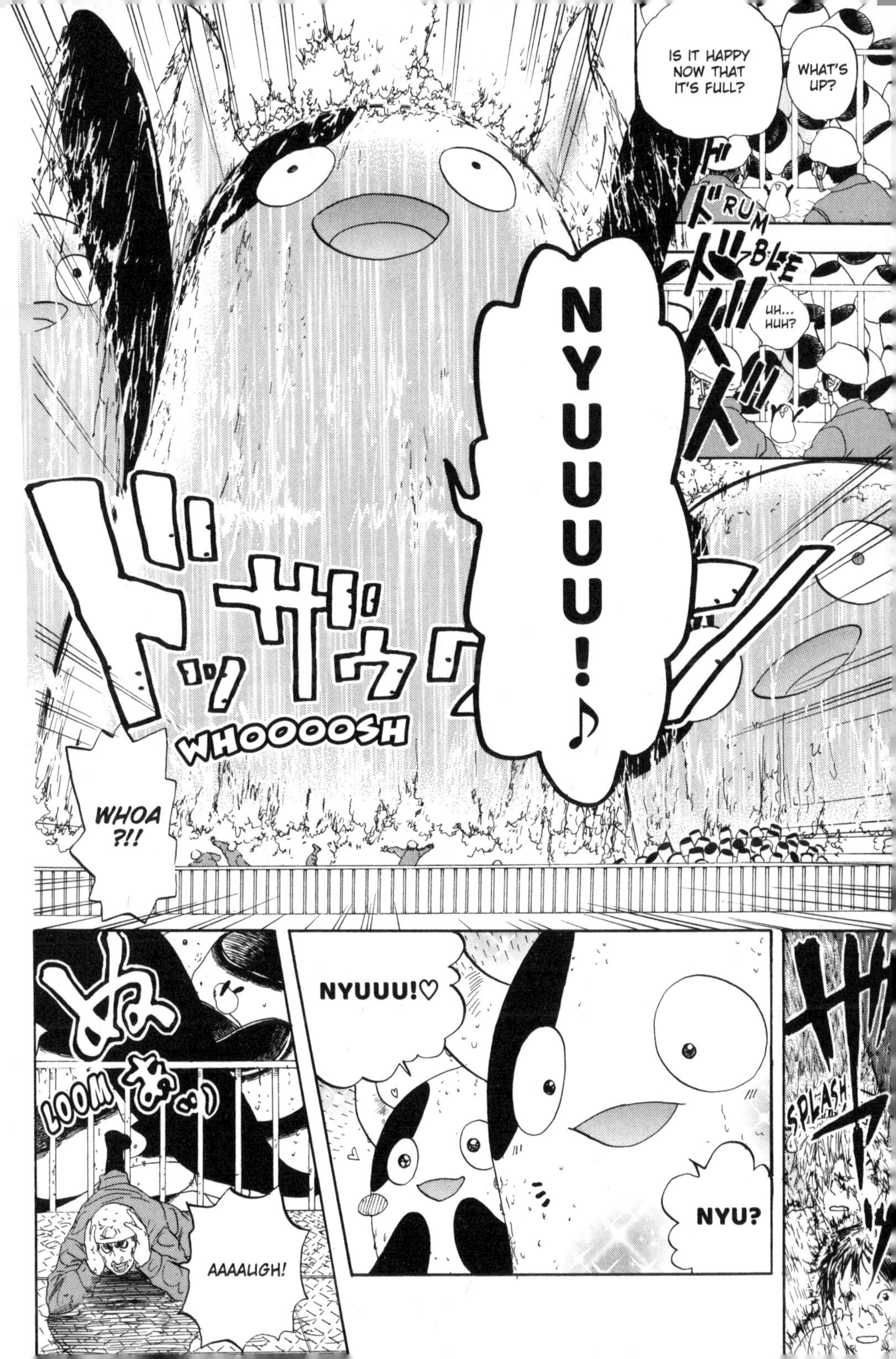
WHAT'S UP?
IS IT HAPPY NOW THAT IT'S FULL?
RUMBLE
UH... HUH?
NYUUUU!♪
WHOOOOSH
WHOA ?!!
SPLASH
NYU?
NYUUU!♡
LOOM
AAAAUGH!

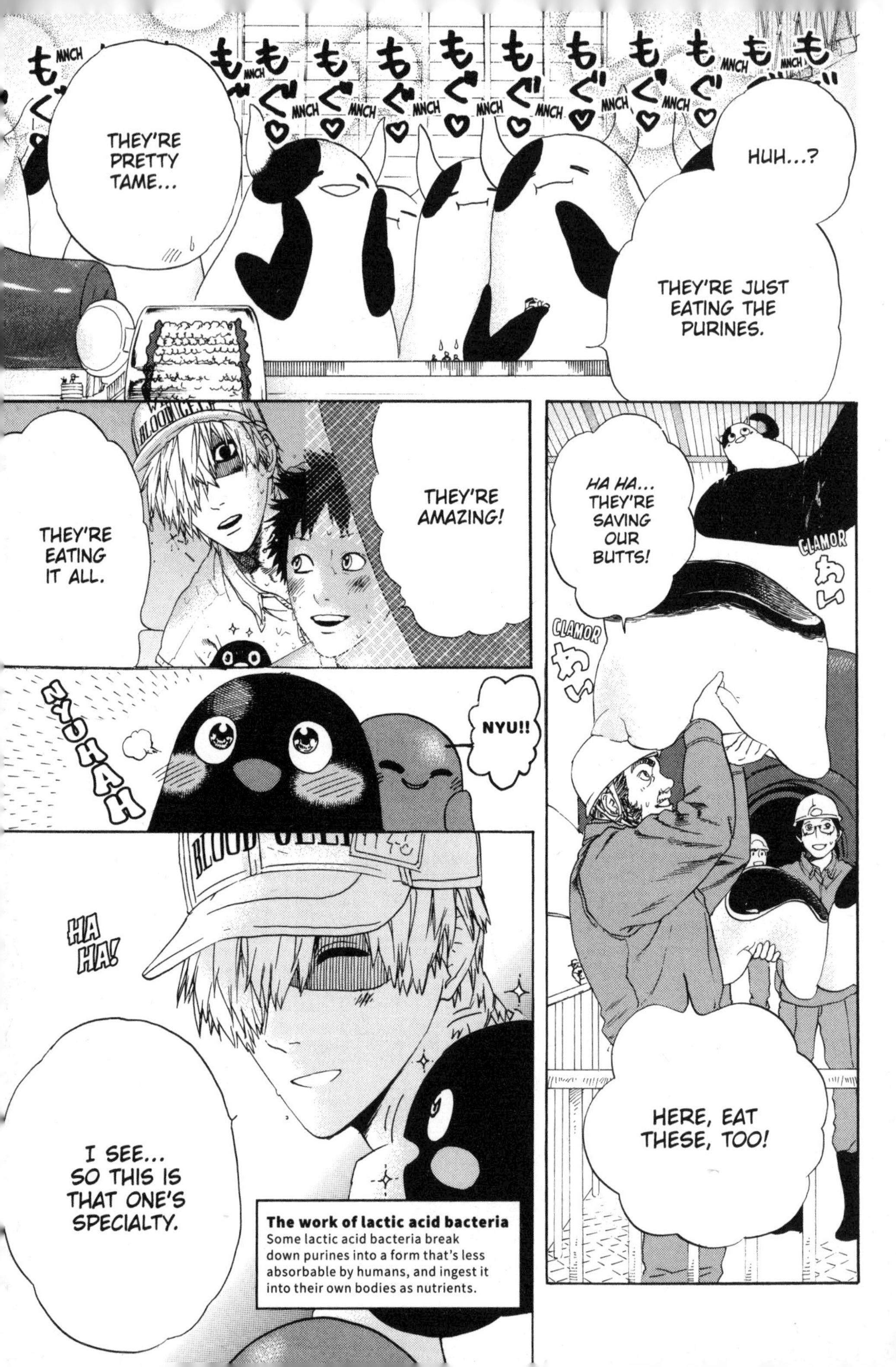
もぐ
MNCH
もぐ♡
MNCH
もぐ♡
MNCH
もぐ♡
MNCH
HUH...?
THEY'RE JUST EATING THE PURINES.
THEY'RE PRETTY TAME...
HA HA... THEY'RE SAVING OUR BUTTS!
CLAMOR
わい
CLAMOR
わい
HERE, EAT THESE, TOO!
THEY'RE AMAZING!
THEY'RE EATING IT ALL.
NYU!!
NYUHAH
HA HA!
I SEE... SO THIS IS THAT ONE'S SPECIALTY.
The work of lactic acid bacteria
Some lactic acid bacteria break down purines into a form that's less absorbable by humans, and ingest it into their own bodies as nutrients.

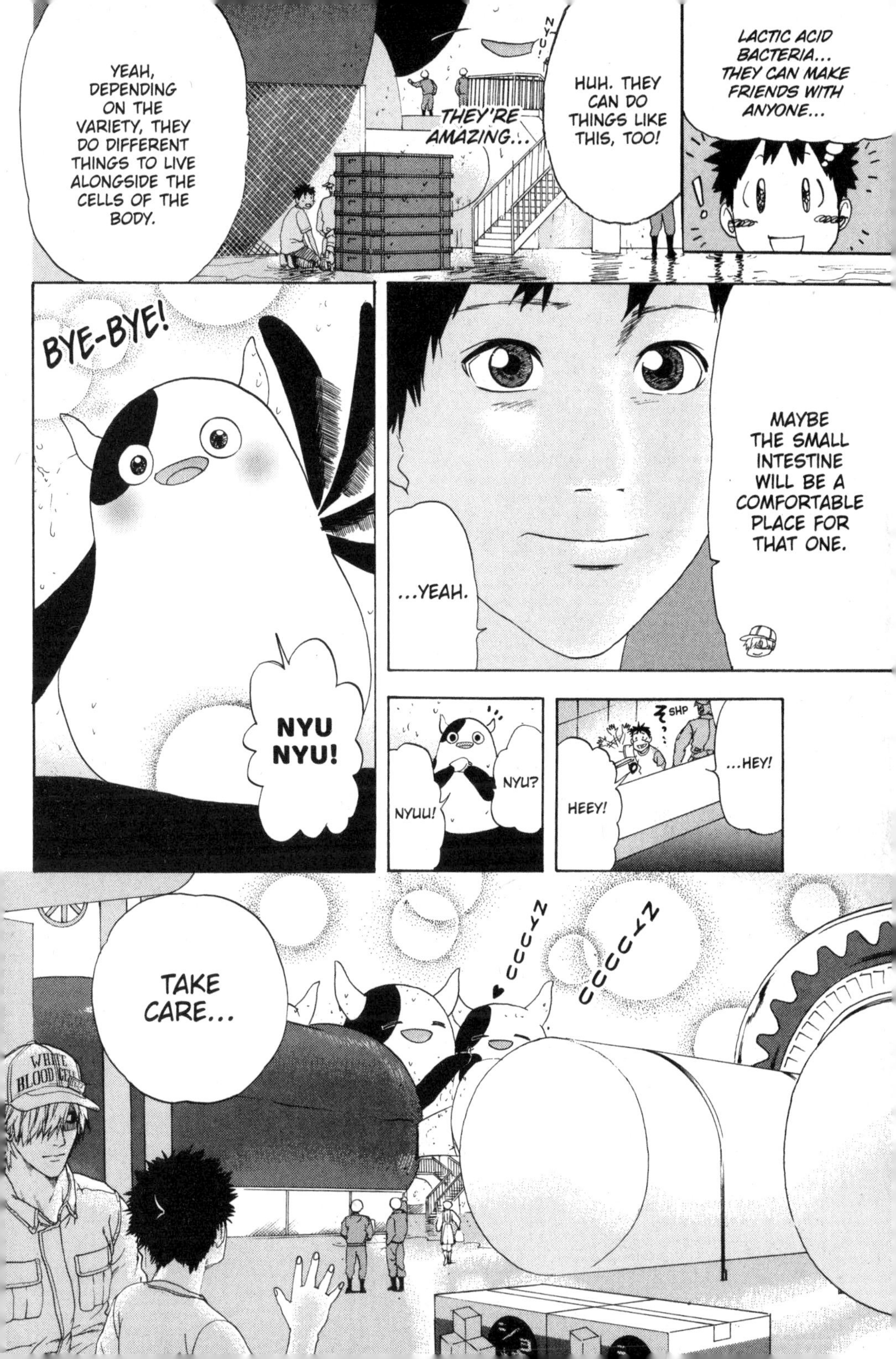
LACTIC ACID BACTERIA... THEY CAN MAKE FRIENDS WITH ANYONE...
NYU!
HUH. THEY CAN DO THINGS LIKE THIS, TOO!
THEY'RE AMAZING...
YEAH, DEPENDING ON THE VARIETY, THEY DO DIFFERENT THINGS TO LIVE ALONGSIDE THE CELLS OF THE BODY.
MAYBE THE SMALL INTESTINE WILL BE A COMFORTABLE PLACE FOR THAT ONE.
...YEAH.
...HEY!
SHP
HEEY!
NYU?
NYUU!
BYE-BYE!
NYU NYU!
TAKE CARE...

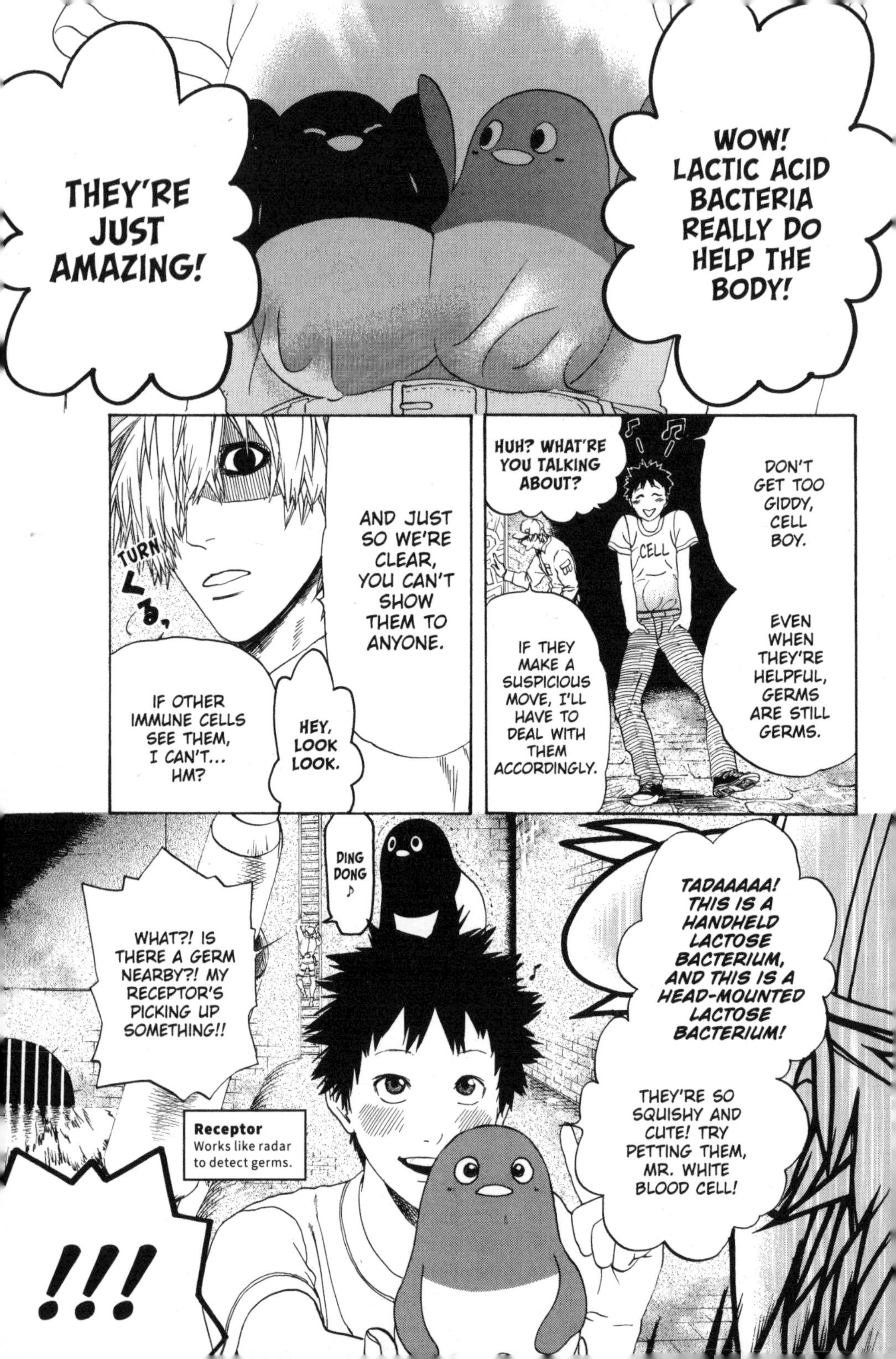
WOW! LACTIC ACID BACTERIA REALLY DO HELP THE BODY!
THEY'RE JUST AMAZING!
DON'T GET TOO GIDDY, CELL BOY.
HUH? WHAT'RE YOU TALKING ABOUT?
CELL
EVEN WHEN THEY'RE HELPFUL, GERMS ARE STILL GERMS.
IF THEY MAKE A SUSPICIOUS MOVE, I'LL HAVE TO DEAL WITH THEM ACCORDINGLY.
AND JUST SO WE'RE CLEAR, YOU CAN'T SHOW THEM TO ANYONE.
TURN くる
HEY, LOOK LOOK.
IF OTHER IMMUNE CELLS SEE THEM, I CAN'T... HM?
TADAAAAA! THIS IS A HANDHELD LACTOSE BACTERIUM, AND THIS IS A HEAD-MOUNTED LACTOSE BACTERIUM!
DING DONG ♪
WHAT?! IS THERE A GERM NEARBY?! MY RECEPTOR'S PICKING UP SOMETHING!!
THEY'RE SO SQUISHY AND CUTE! TRY PETTING THEM, MR. WHITE BLOOD CELL!
Receptor
Works like radar to detect germs.
!!!

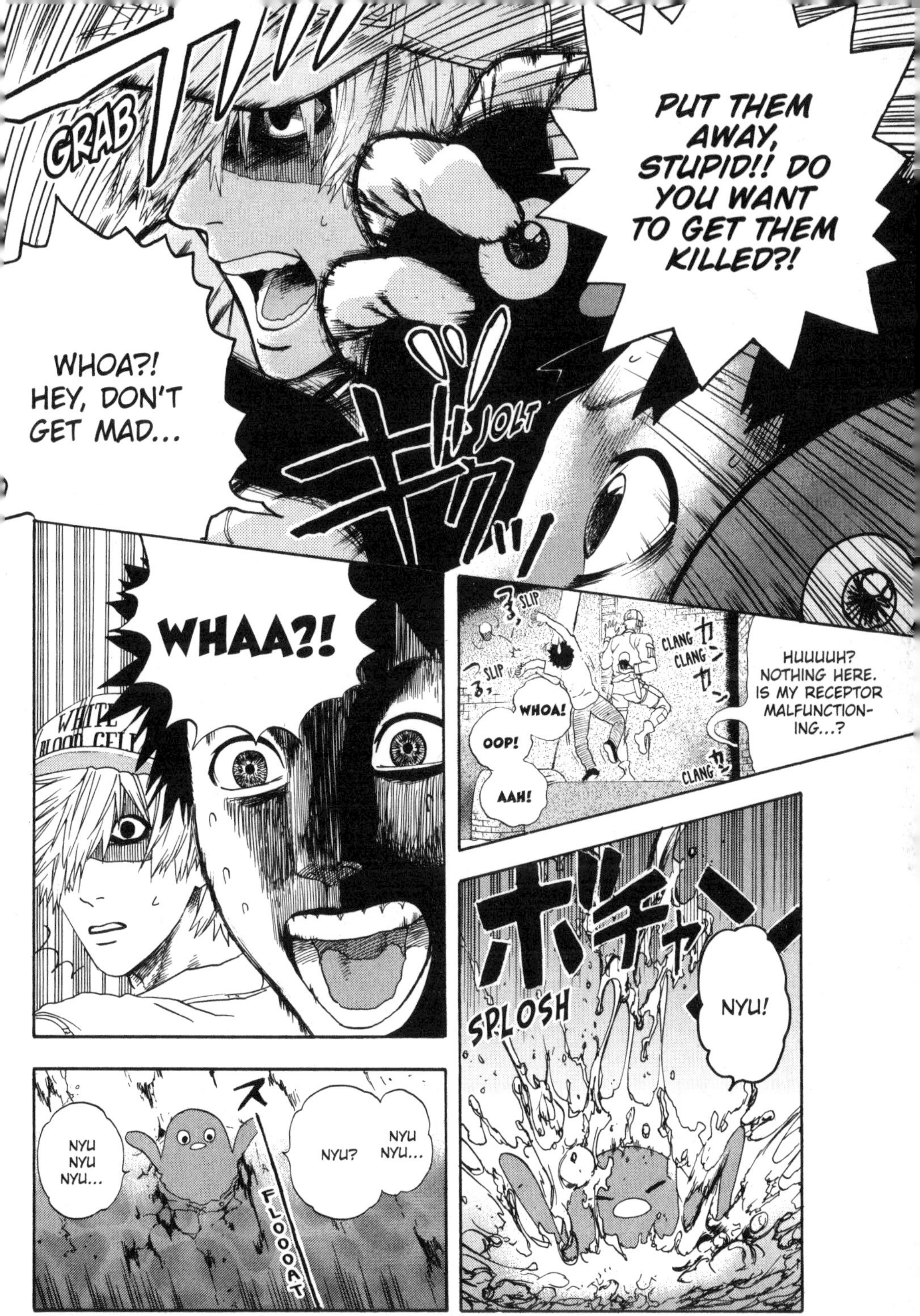

PUT THEM AWAY, STUPID!! DO YOU WANT TO GET THEM KILLED?!
GRAB
JOLT
WHOA?! HEY, DON'T GET MAD...
HUUUUH? NOTHING HERE. IS MY RECEPTOR MALFUNCTION-ING...?
CLANG CLANG
CLANG
SLIP
SLIP
WHOA!
OOP!
AAH!
WHAA?!
WHITE BLOOD CELL
NYU!
SPLOSH
NYU NYU...
NYU?
FLOOOAT
NYU NYU NYU...

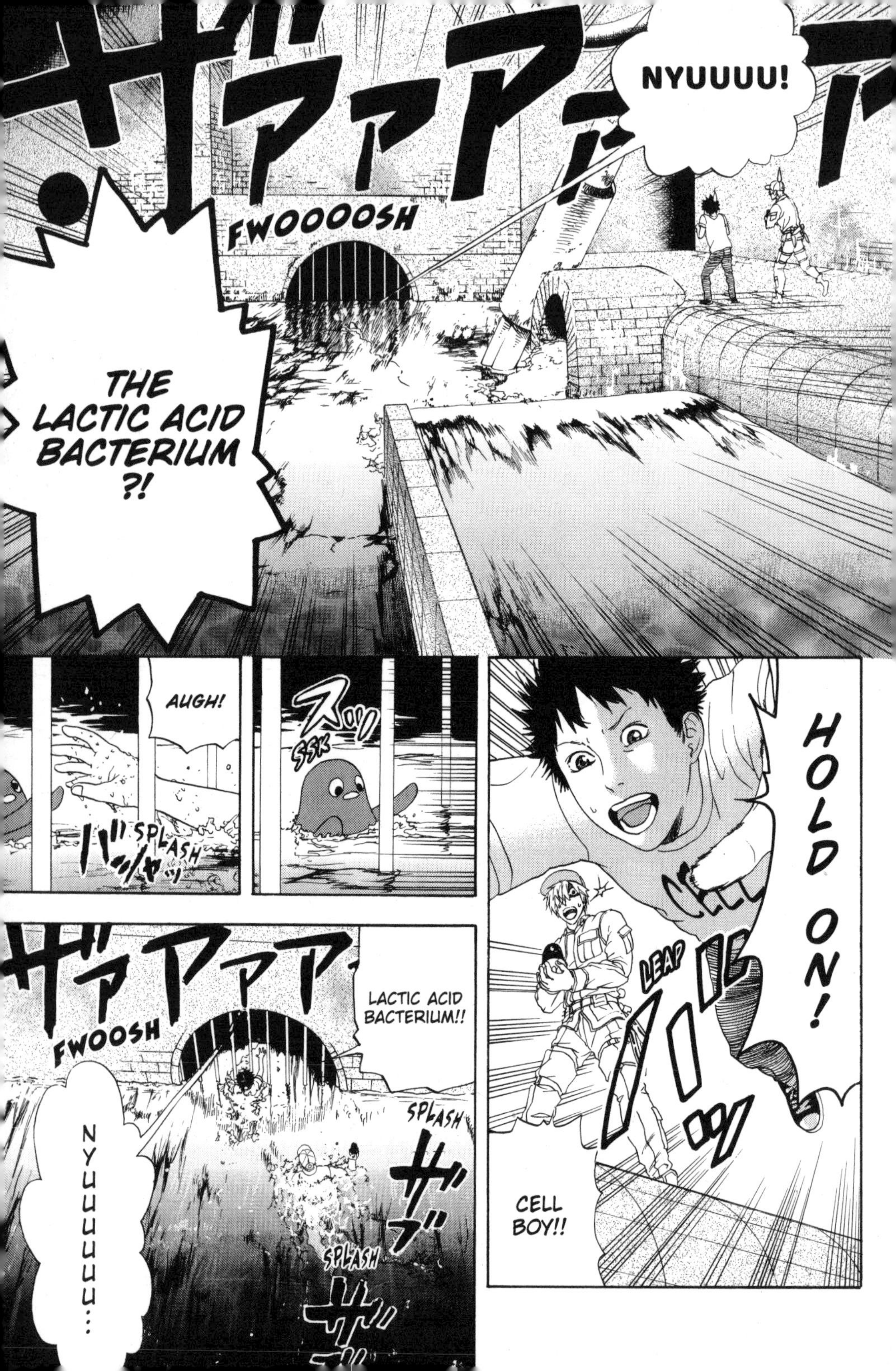

NYUUUUU!
FWOOOOSH
THE LACTIC ACID BACTERIUM ?!
HOLD ON!
LEAP
CELL BOY!!
SSK
AUGH!
SPLASH
LACTIC ACID BACTERIUM!!
FWOOSH
SPLASH
NYUUUUUUU...
SPLASH

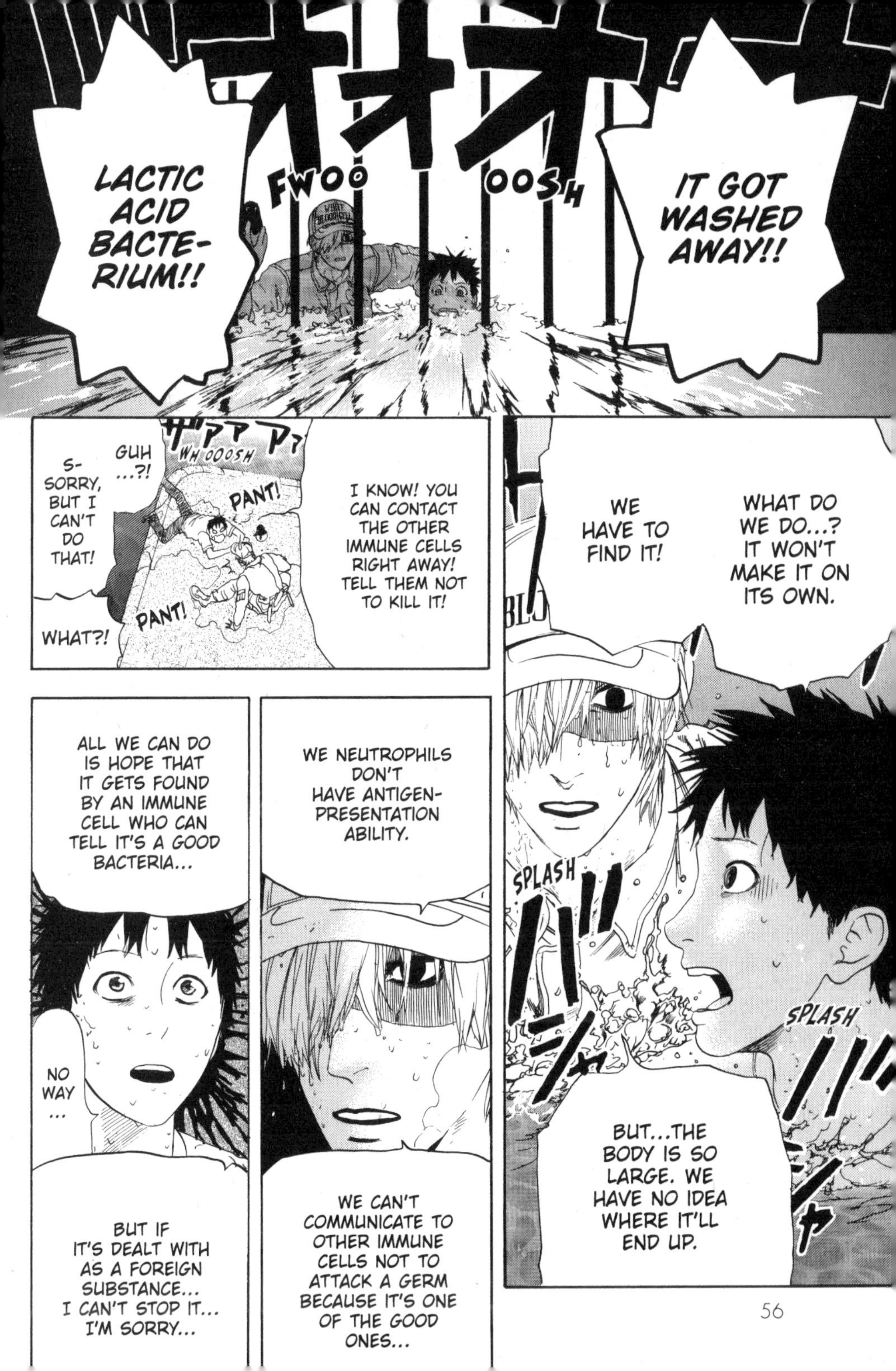
IT GOT WASHED AWAY!!
FWOOOOSH
LACTIC ACID BACTERIUM!!
WHAT DO WE DO...? IT WON'T MAKE IT ON ITS OWN.
WE HAVE TO FIND IT!
SPLASH
SPLASH
BUT...THE BODY IS SO LARGE. WE HAVE NO IDEA WHERE IT'LL END UP.
I KNOW! YOU CAN CONTACT THE OTHER IMMUNE CELLS RIGHT AWAY! TELL THEM NOT TO KILL IT!
WHOOOSH
GUH ...?!
S-SORRY, BUT I CAN'T DO THAT!
PANT!
PANT!
WHAT?!
WE NEUTROPHILS DON'T HAVE ANTIGEN-PRESENTATION ABILITY.
WE CAN'T COMMUNICATE TO OTHER IMMUNE CELLS NOT TO ATTACK A GERM BECAUSE IT'S ONE OF THE GOOD ONES...
ALL WE CAN DO IS HOPE THAT IT GETS FOUND BY AN IMMUNE CELL WHO CAN TELL IT'S A GOOD BACTERIA...
NO WAY ...
BUT IF IT'S DEALT WITH AS A FOREIGN SUBSTANCE... I CAN'T STOP IT... I'M SORRY...

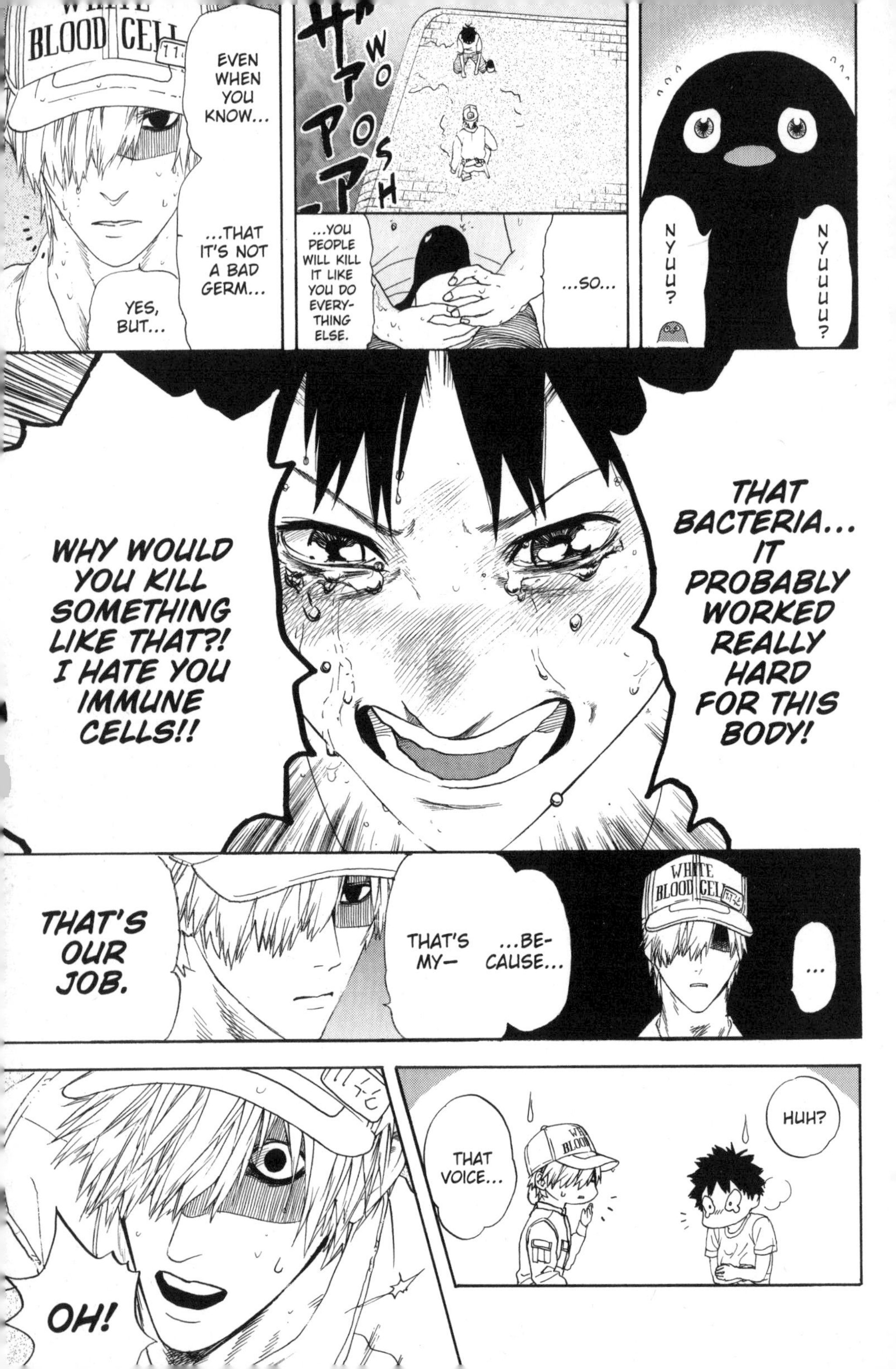
NYUUUUU?
NYUUU?
WOOSH
...SO...
...YOU PEOPLE WILL KILL IT LIKE YOU DO EVERYTHING ELSE.
EVEN WHEN YOU KNOW...
...THAT IT'S NOT A BAD GERM...
YES, BUT...
THAT BACTERIA... IT PROBABLY WORKED REALLY HARD FOR THIS BODY!
WHY WOULD YOU KILL SOMETHING LIKE THAT?! I HATE YOU IMMUNE CELLS!!
...
...BE-CAUSE...
THAT'S MY—
THAT'S OUR JOB.
HUH?
THAT VOICE...
OH!

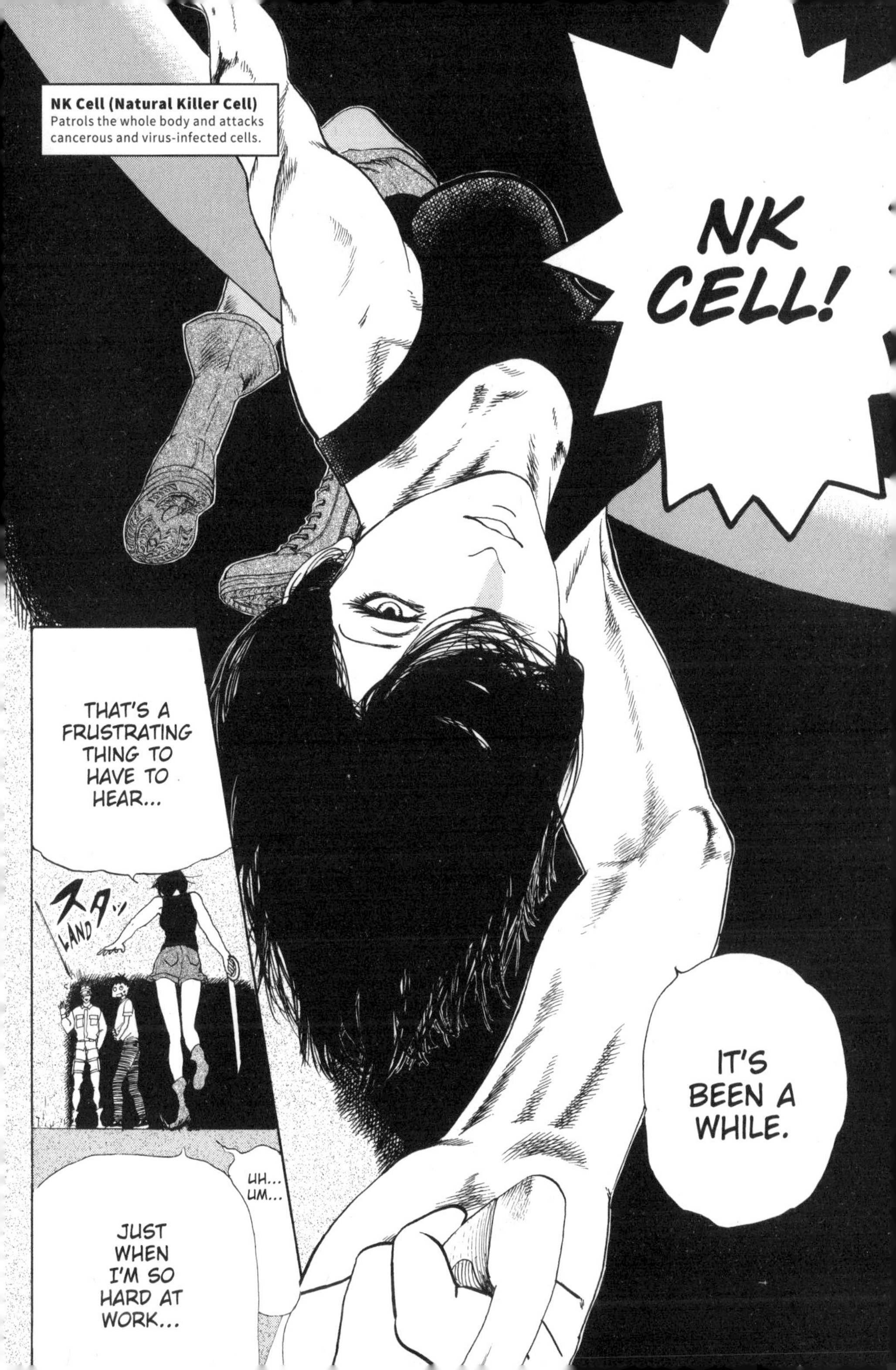
NK CELL!
NK Cell (Natural Killer Cell)
Patrols the whole body and attacks cancerous and virus-infected cells.
IT'S BEEN A WHILE.
THAT'S A FRUSTRATING THING TO HAVE TO HEAR...
スタッ LAND
UH... UM...
JUST WHEN I'M SO HARD AT WORK...

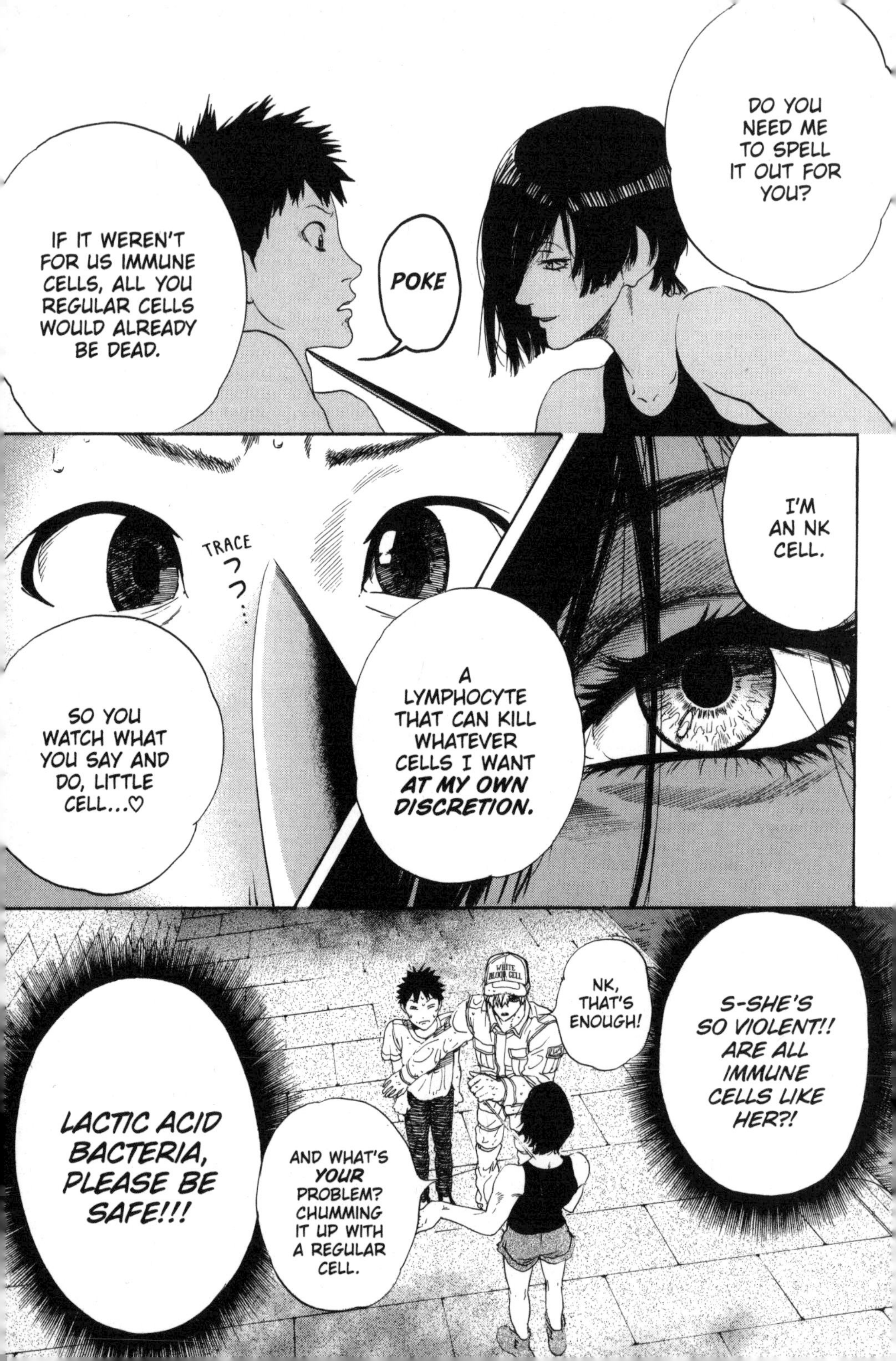
DO YOU NEED ME TO SPELL IT OUT FOR YOU?
POKE
IF IT WEREN'T FOR US IMMUNE CELLS, ALL YOU REGULAR CELLS WOULD ALREADY BE DEAD.
I'M AN NK CELL.
A LYMPHOCYTE THAT CAN KILL WHATEVER CELLS I WANT AT MY OWN DISCRETION.
TRACE
SO YOU WATCH WHAT YOU SAY AND DO, LITTLE CELL...♡
S-SHE'S SO VIOLENT!! ARE ALL IMMUNE CELLS LIKE HER?!
NK, THAT'S ENOUGH!
WHITE BLOOD CELL
AND WHAT'S YOUR PROBLEM? CHUMMING IT UP WITH A REGULAR CELL.
LACTIC ACID BACTERIA, PLEASE BE SAFE!!!

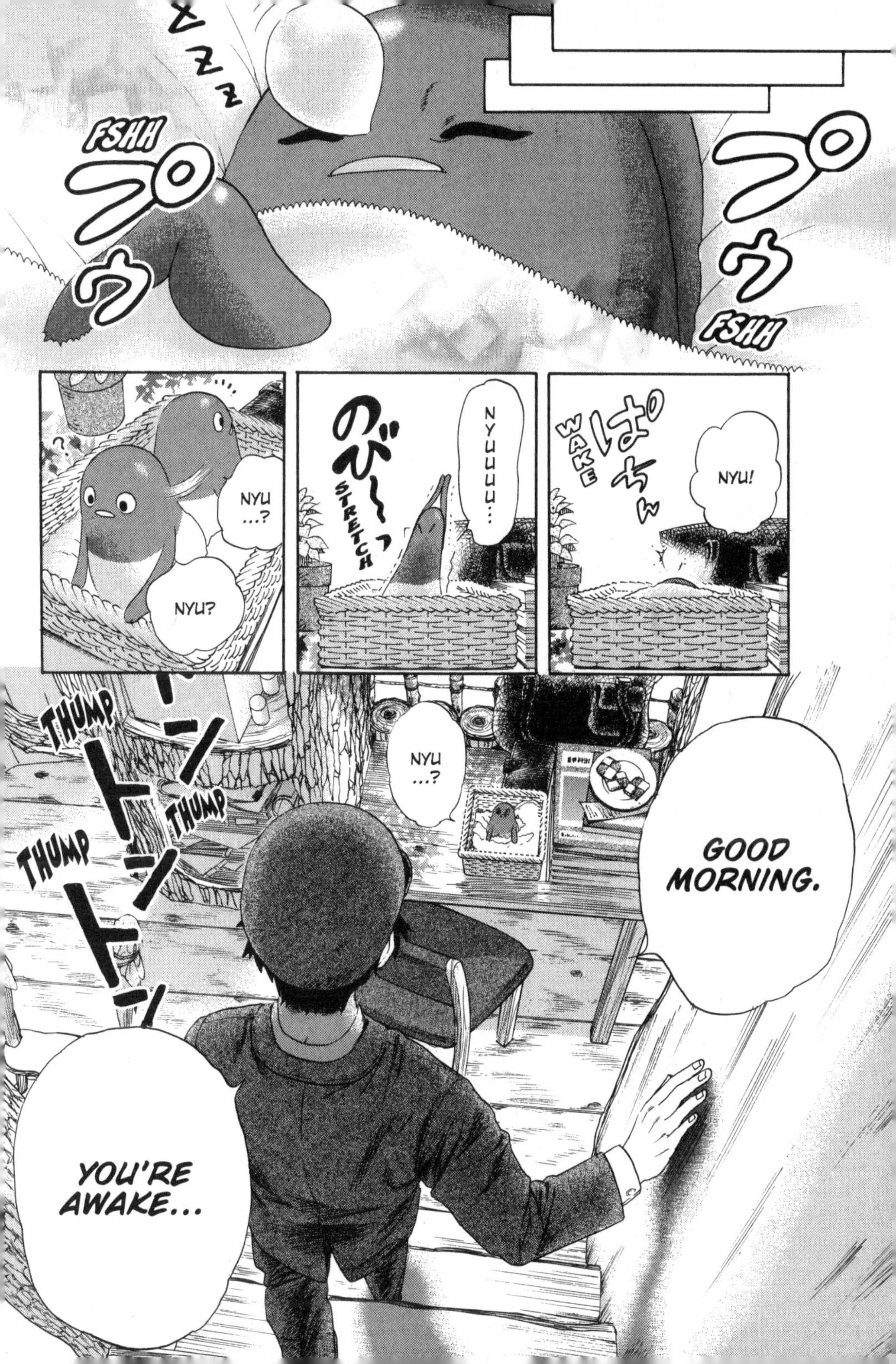

プウ
FSHH
ZZZ
FSHH
プウ
ぱちん
WAKE
NYU!
のび〜っ
STRETCH
NYUUUUU...
NYU ...?
NYU?
GOOD MORNING.
NYU ...?
トーン
THUMP
トーン
THUMP
トーン
THUMP
YOU'RE AWAKE...

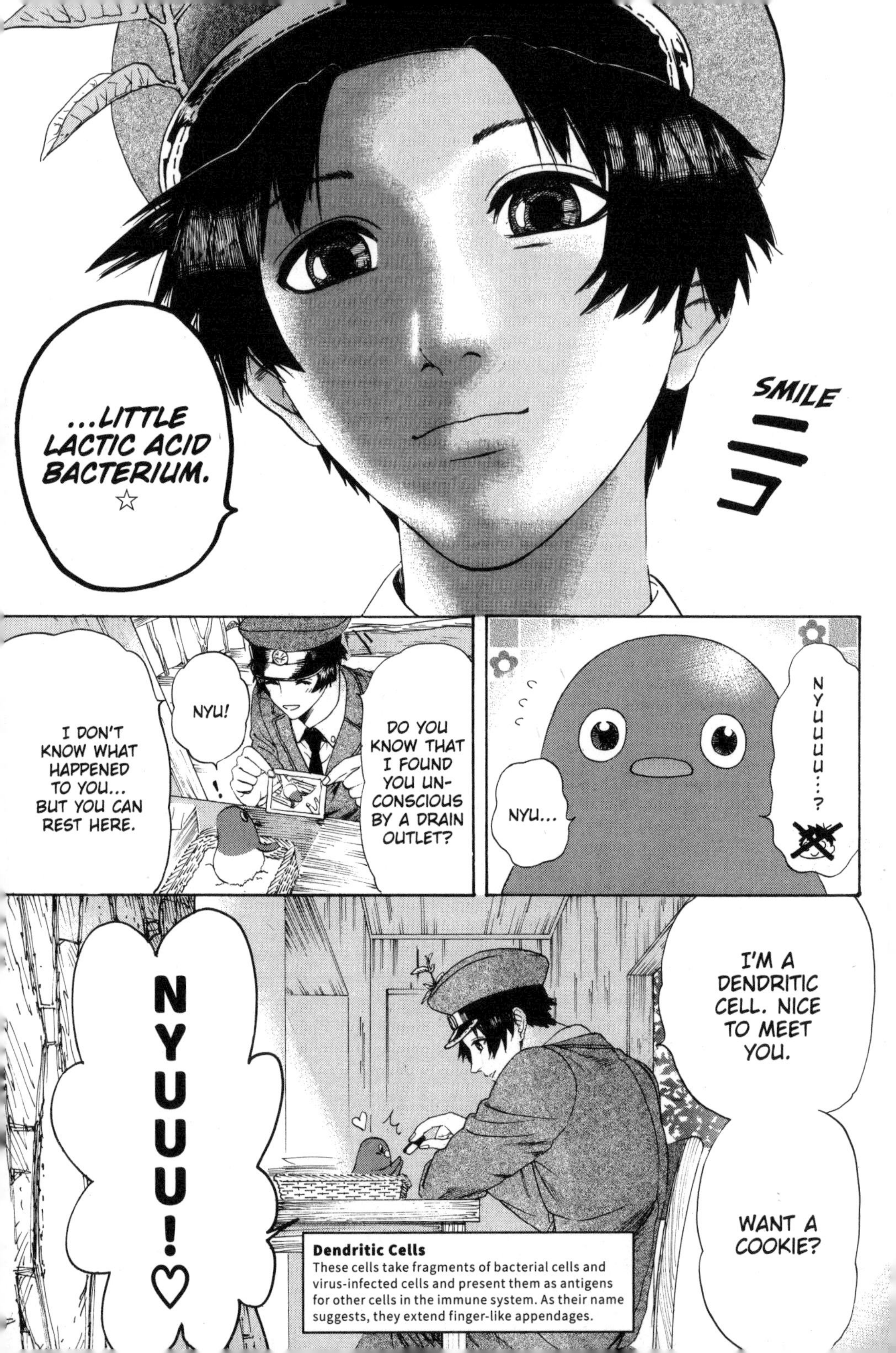
...LITTLE LACTIC ACID BACTERIUM. ☆
SMILE
NYUUUU...?
NYU...
DO YOU KNOW THAT I FOUND YOU UN-CONSCIOUS BY A DRAIN OUTLET?
NYU!
!
I DON'T KNOW WHAT HAPPENED TO YOU... BUT YOU CAN REST HERE.
I'M A DENDRITIC CELL. NICE TO MEET YOU.
WANT A COOKIE?
NYUUU!♡
Dendritic Cells
These cells take fragments of bacterial cells and virus-infected cells and present them as antigens for other cells in the immune system. As their name suggests, they extend finger-like appendages.

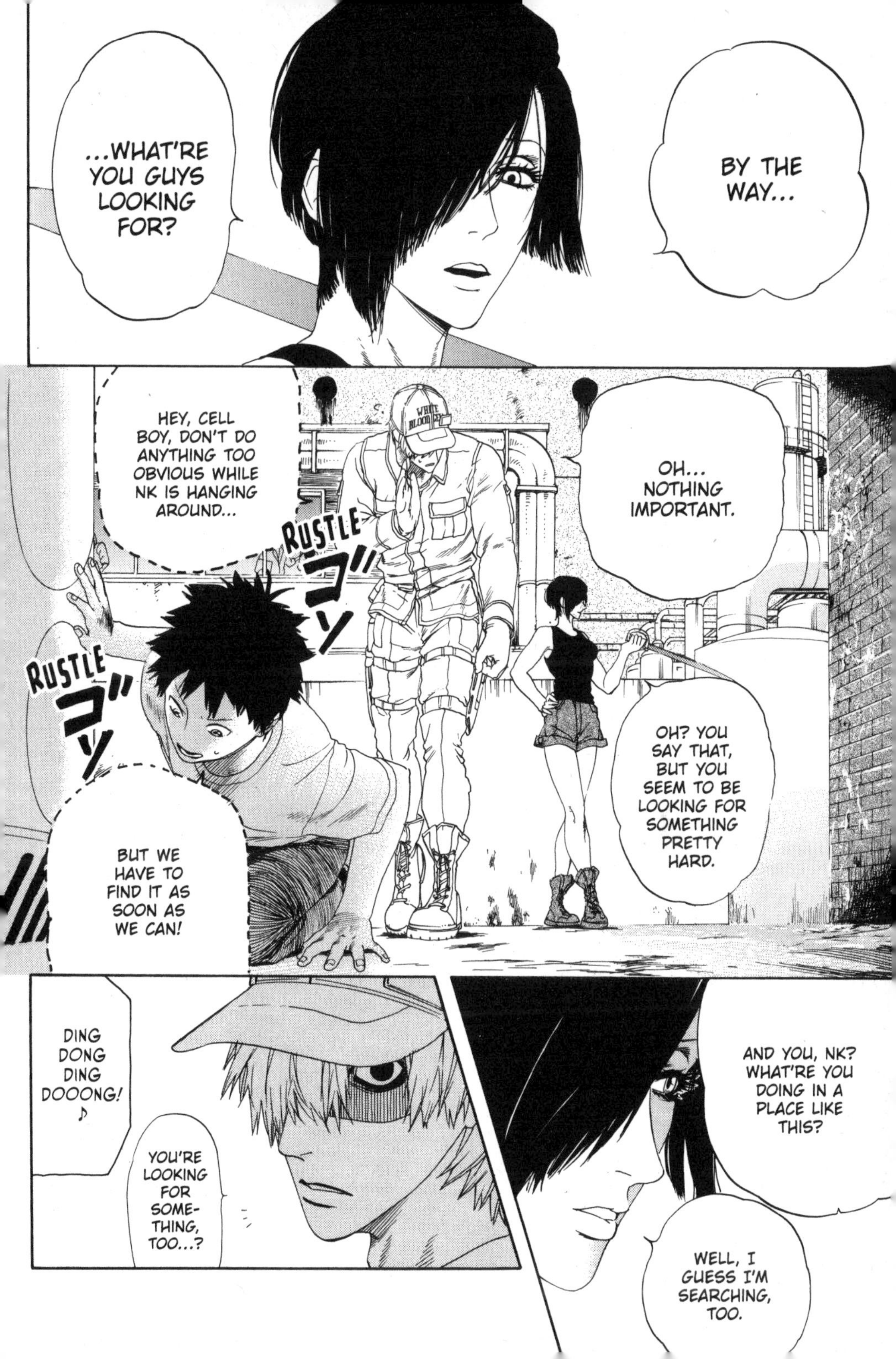
BY THE WAY...
...WHAT'RE YOU GUYS LOOKING FOR?
OH... NOTHING IMPORTANT.
OH? YOU SAY THAT, BUT YOU SEEM TO BE LOOKING FOR SOMETHING PRETTY HARD.
RUSTLE ゴソ
HEY, CELL BOY, DON'T DO ANYTHING TOO OBVIOUS WHILE NK IS HANGING AROUND...
RUSTLE ゴソ
BUT WE HAVE TO FIND IT AS SOON AS WE CAN!
AND YOU, NK? WHAT'RE YOU DOING IN A PLACE LIKE THIS?
WELL, I GUESS I'M SEARCHING, TOO.
DING DONG DING DOOONG! ♪
YOU'RE LOOKING FOR SOME-THING, TOO...?

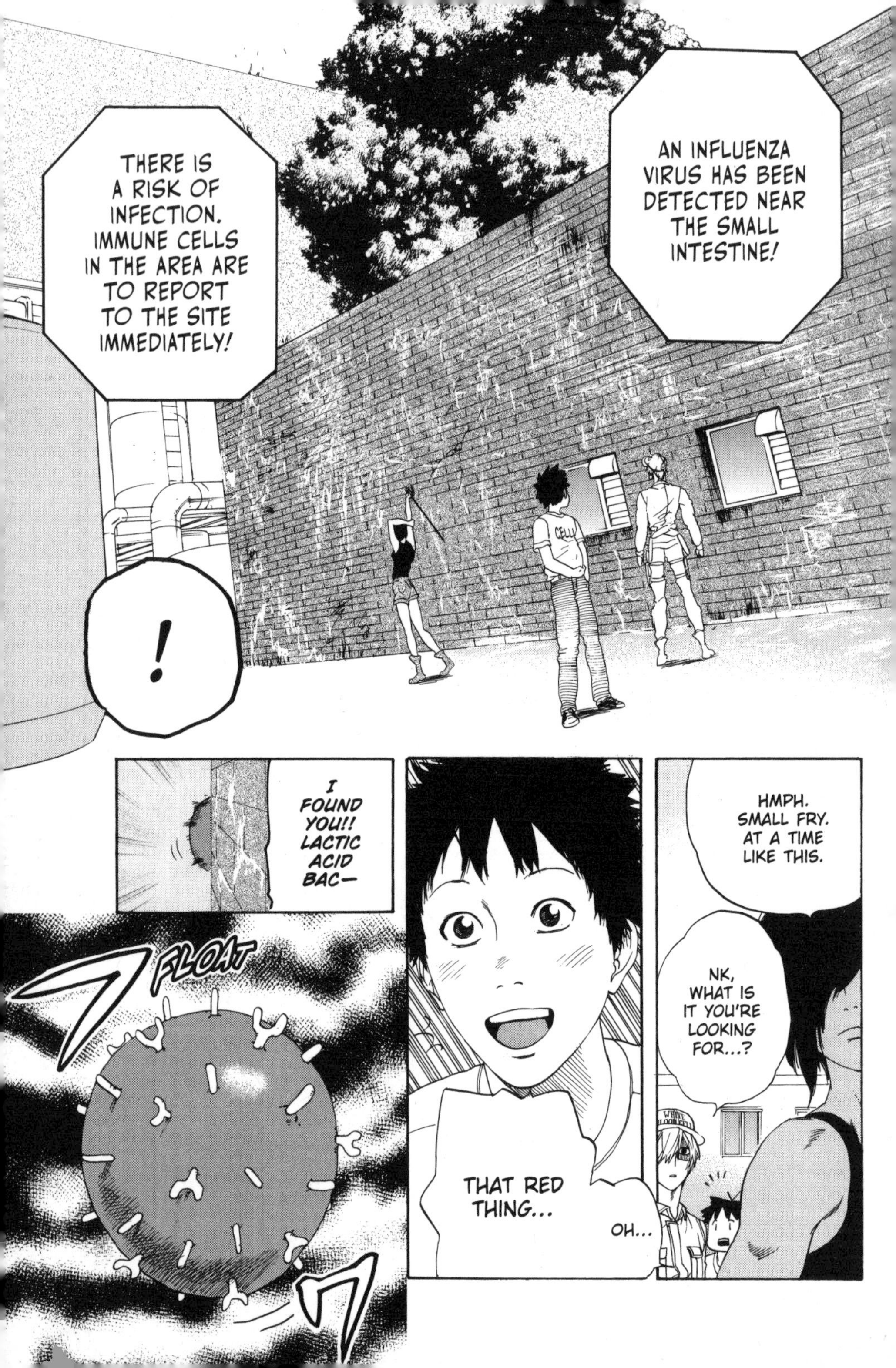
AN INFLUENZA VIRUS HAS BEEN DETECTED NEAR THE SMALL INTESTINE!
THERE IS A RISK OF INFECTION. IMMUNE CELLS IN THE AREA ARE TO REPORT TO THE SITE IMMEDIATELY!
!
HMPH. SMALL FRY. AT A TIME LIKE THIS.
NK, WHAT IS IT YOU'RE LOOKING FOR...?
THAT RED THING...
OH...
I FOUND YOU!! LACTIC ACID BAC—
FLOAT

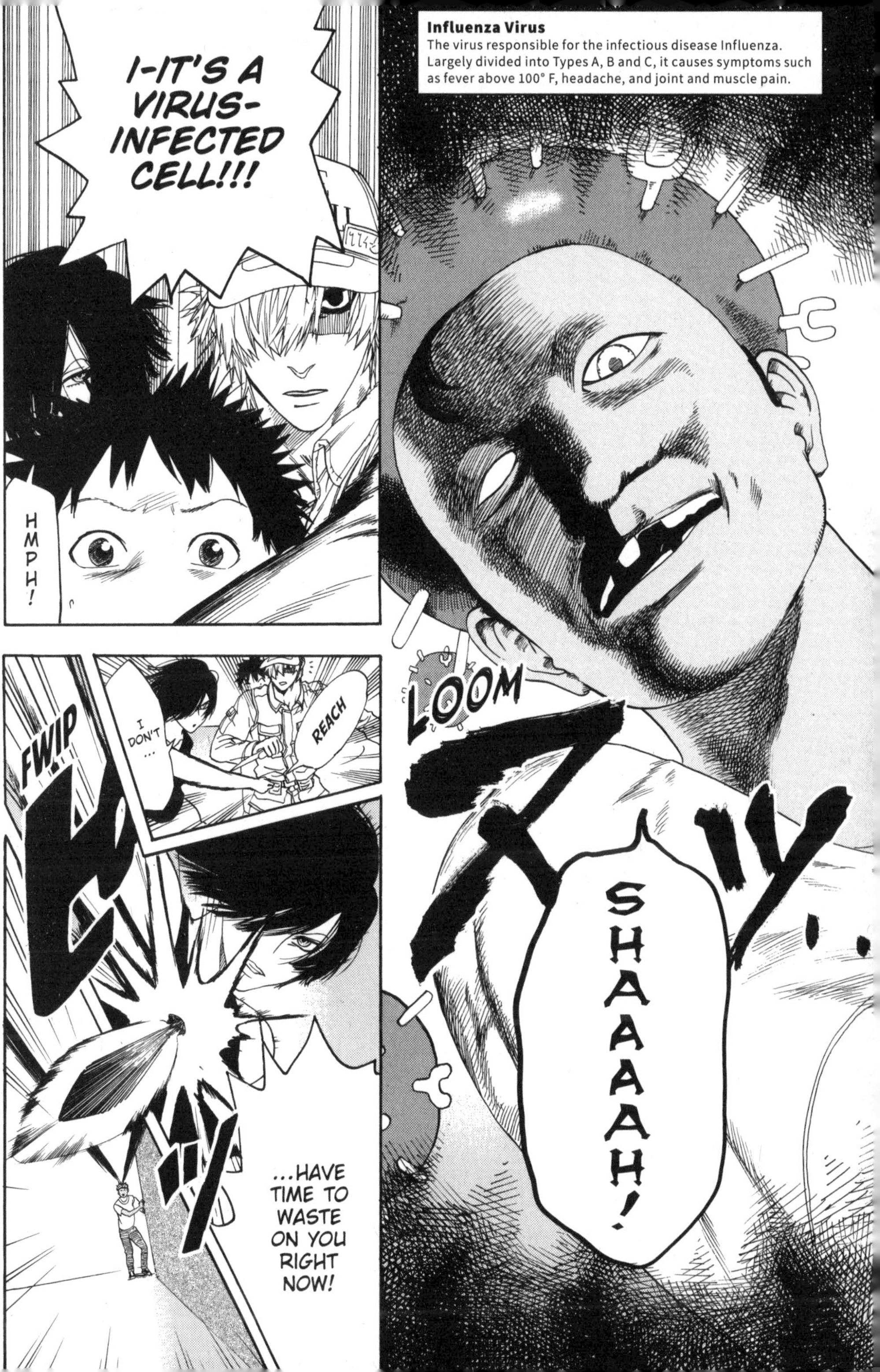
Influenza Virus
The virus responsible for the infectious disease Influenza. Largely divided into Types A, B and C, it causes symptoms such as fever above 100° F, headache, and joint and muscle pain.
LOOM
SHAAAAH!
I-IT'S A VIRUS-INFECTED CELL!!!
HMPH!
REACH
I DON'T...
FWIP
...HAVE TIME TO WASTE ON YOU RIGHT NOW!

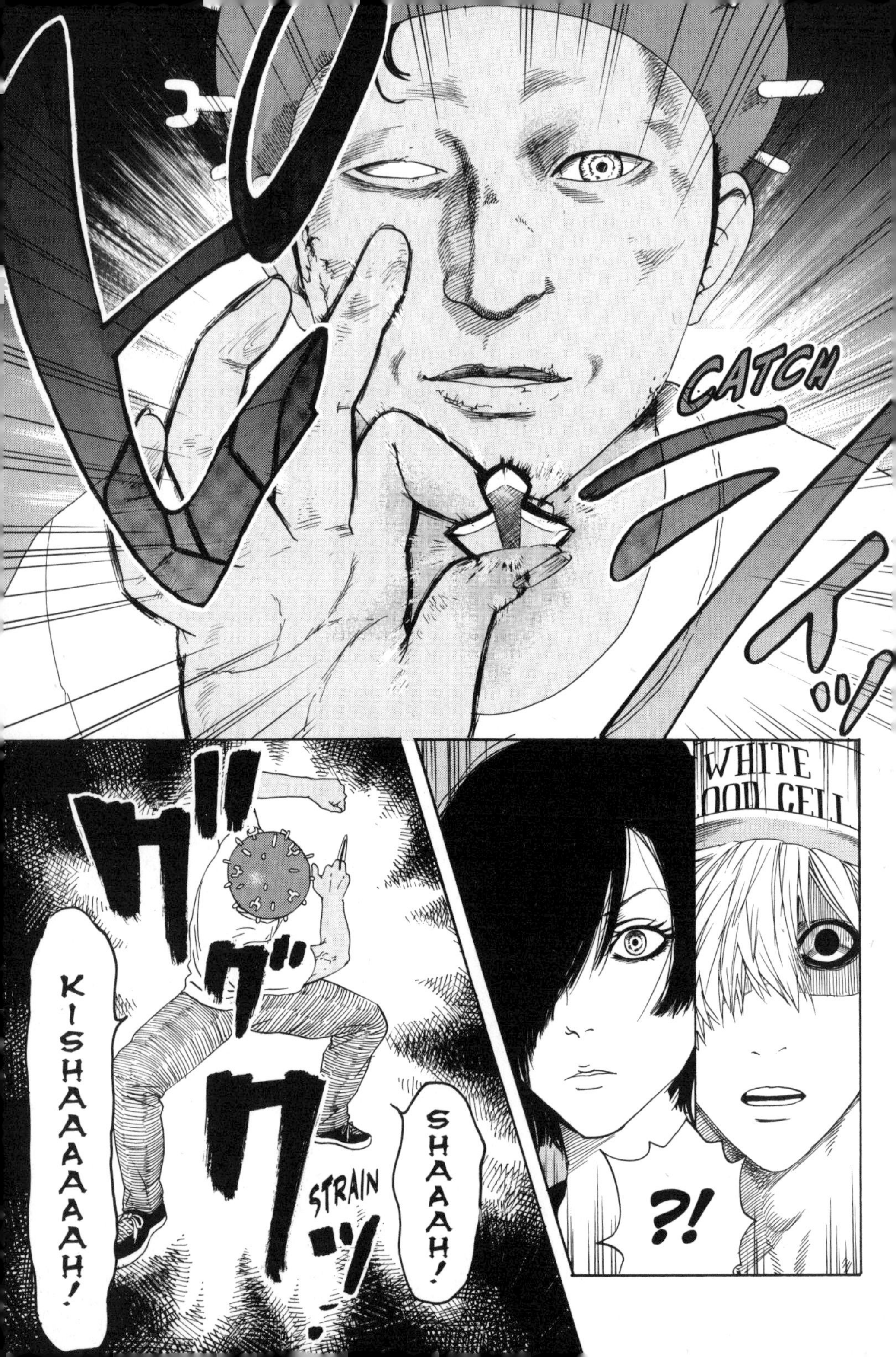
CATCH
WHITE
OOD CELL
?!
KISHAAAAAAAH!
SHAAAH!
STRAIN

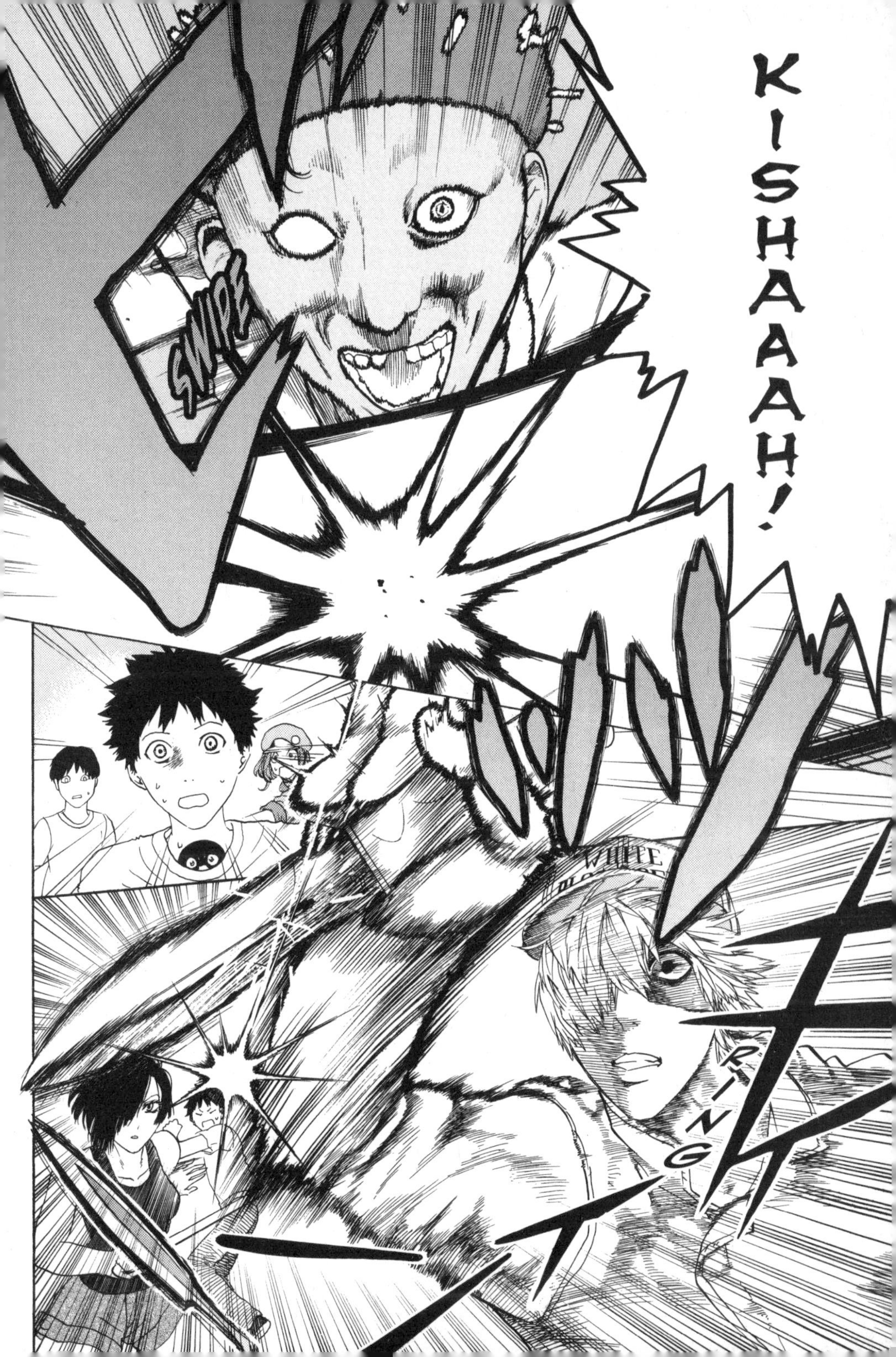
KISHAAAH!
SWIPE
RING

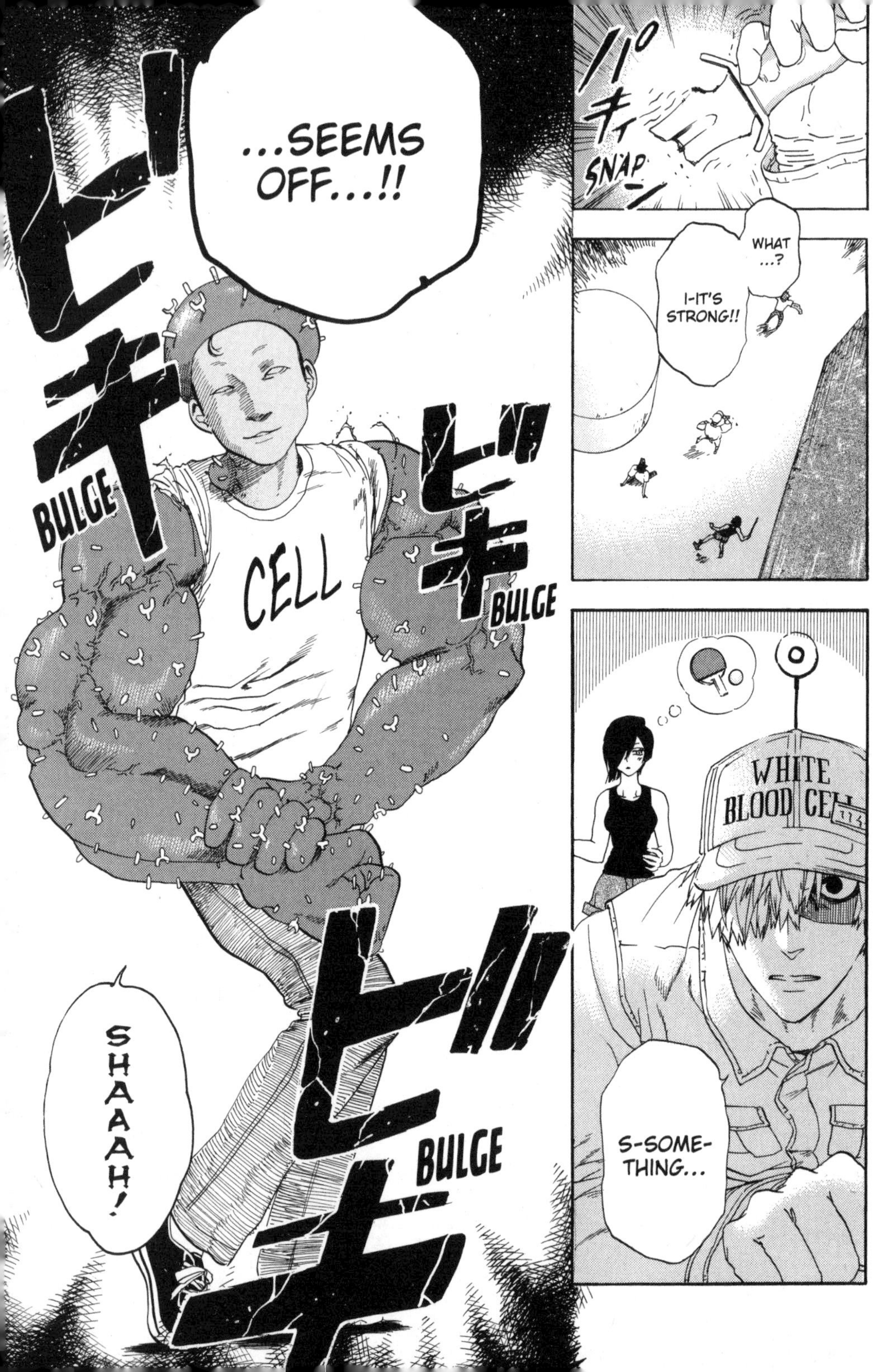
SNAP
WHAT ...?
I-IT'S STRONG!!
S-SOME-THING...
...SEEMS OFF...!!
BULGE
BULGE
CELL
SHAAAH!
BULGE
WHITE BLOOD CELL

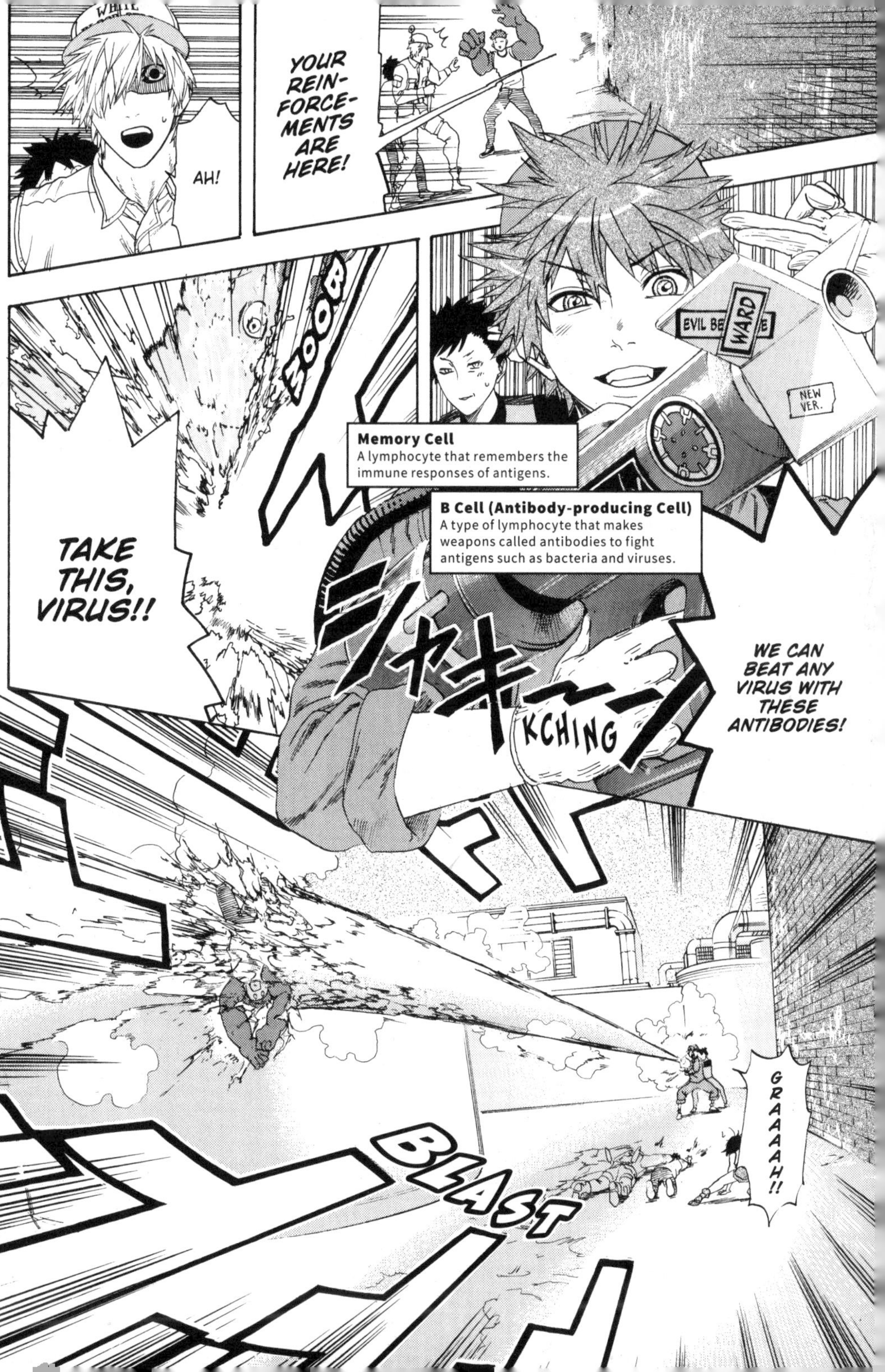

YOUR REIN-FORCE-MENTS ARE HERE!
AH!
EVIL BE WARD E
NEW VER.
Memory Cell
A lymphocyte that remembers the immune responses of antigens.
B Cell (Antibody-producing Cell)
A type of lymphocyte that makes weapons called antibodies to fight antigens such as bacteria and viruses.
シャキーン
KCHING
WE CAN BEAT ANY VIRUS WITH THESE ANTIBODIES!
ZOOB
TAKE THIS, VIRUS!!
GRAAAAH!!
BLAST

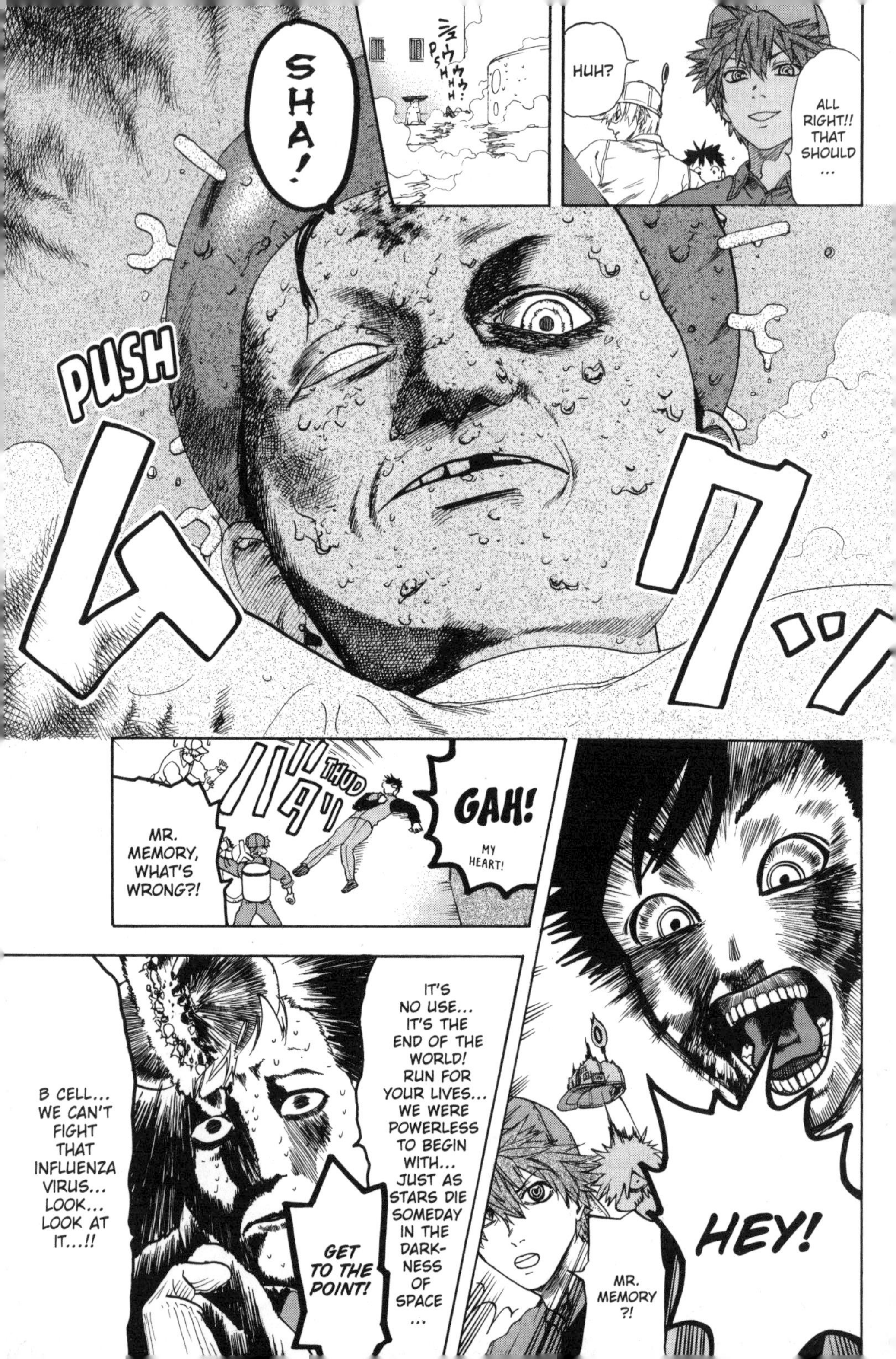
ALL RIGHT!! THAT SHOULD ...
HUH?
シュウウウ
PSHHHH
SHA!
PUSH
ムクッ
HEY!
MR. MEMORY?!
GAH!
MY HEART!
THUD
バタッ
MR. MEMORY, WHAT'S WRONG?!
IT'S NO USE... IT'S THE END OF THE WORLD! RUN FOR YOUR LIVES... WE WERE POWERLESS TO BEGIN WITH... JUST AS STARS DIE SOMEDAY IN THE DARKNESS OF SPACE ...
B CELL... WE CAN'T FIGHT THAT INFLUENZA VIRUS... LOOK... LOOK AT IT...!!
GET TO THE POINT!

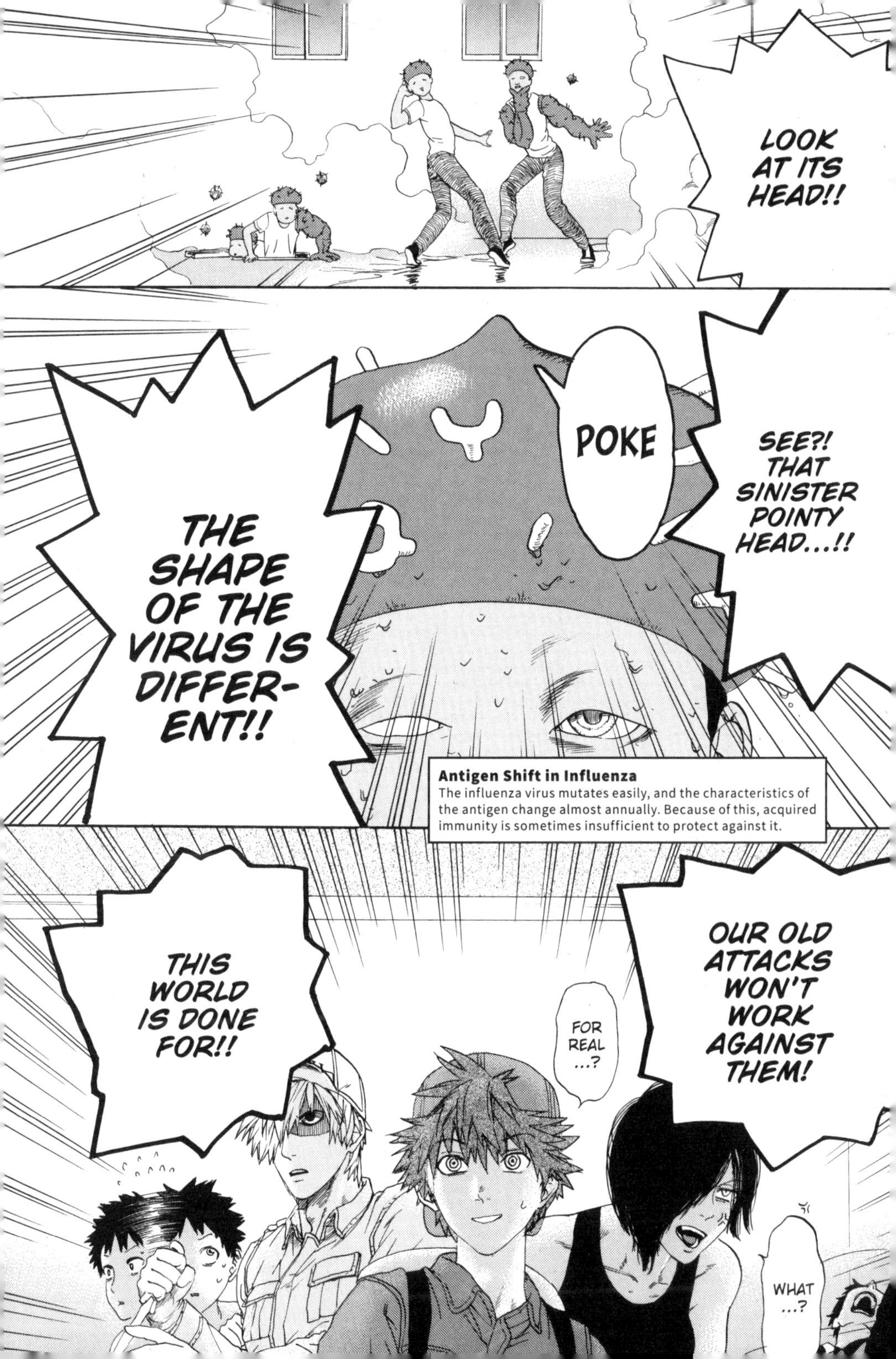
LOOK AT ITS HEAD!!
SEE?! THAT SINISTER POINTY HEAD...!!
POKE
THE SHAPE OF THE VIRUS IS DIFFER-ENT!!
Antigen Shift in Influenza
The influenza virus mutates easily, and the characteristics of the antigen change almost annually. Because of this, acquired immunity is sometimes insufficient to protect against it.
OUR OLD ATTACKS WON'T WORK AGAINST THEM!
FOR REAL ...?
THIS WORLD IS DONE FOR!!
WHAT ...?

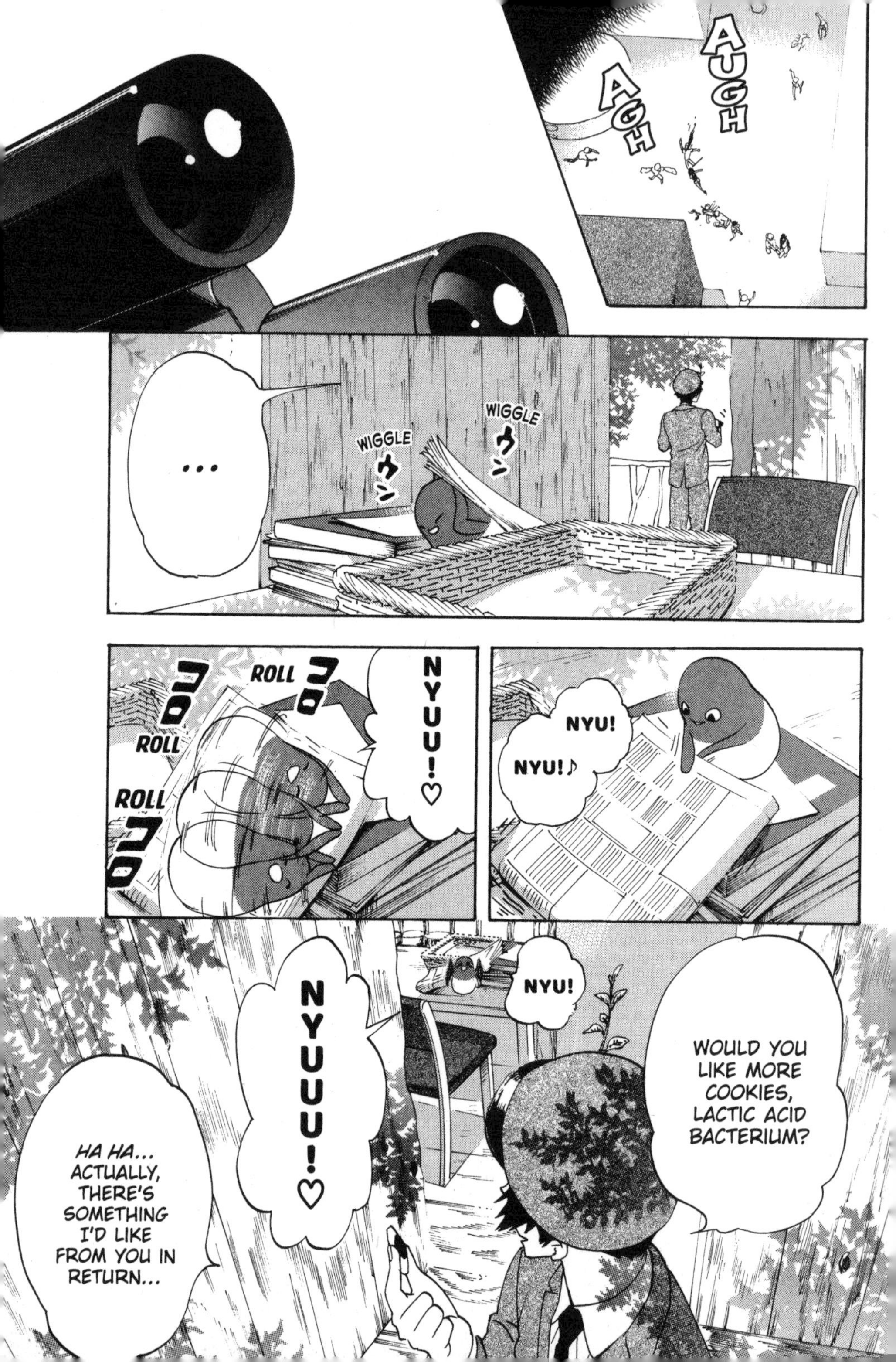
AUGH
AGH
WIGGLE ウン
WIGGLE ウン
...
NYU!
NYU!♪
NYUU!♡
ROLL コロ
ROLL
ROLL コロ
WOULD YOU LIKE MORE COOKIES, LACTIC ACID BACTERIUM?
NYU!
NYUUU!♡
HA HA... ACTUALLY, THERE'S SOMETHING I'D LIKE FROM YOU IN RETURN...

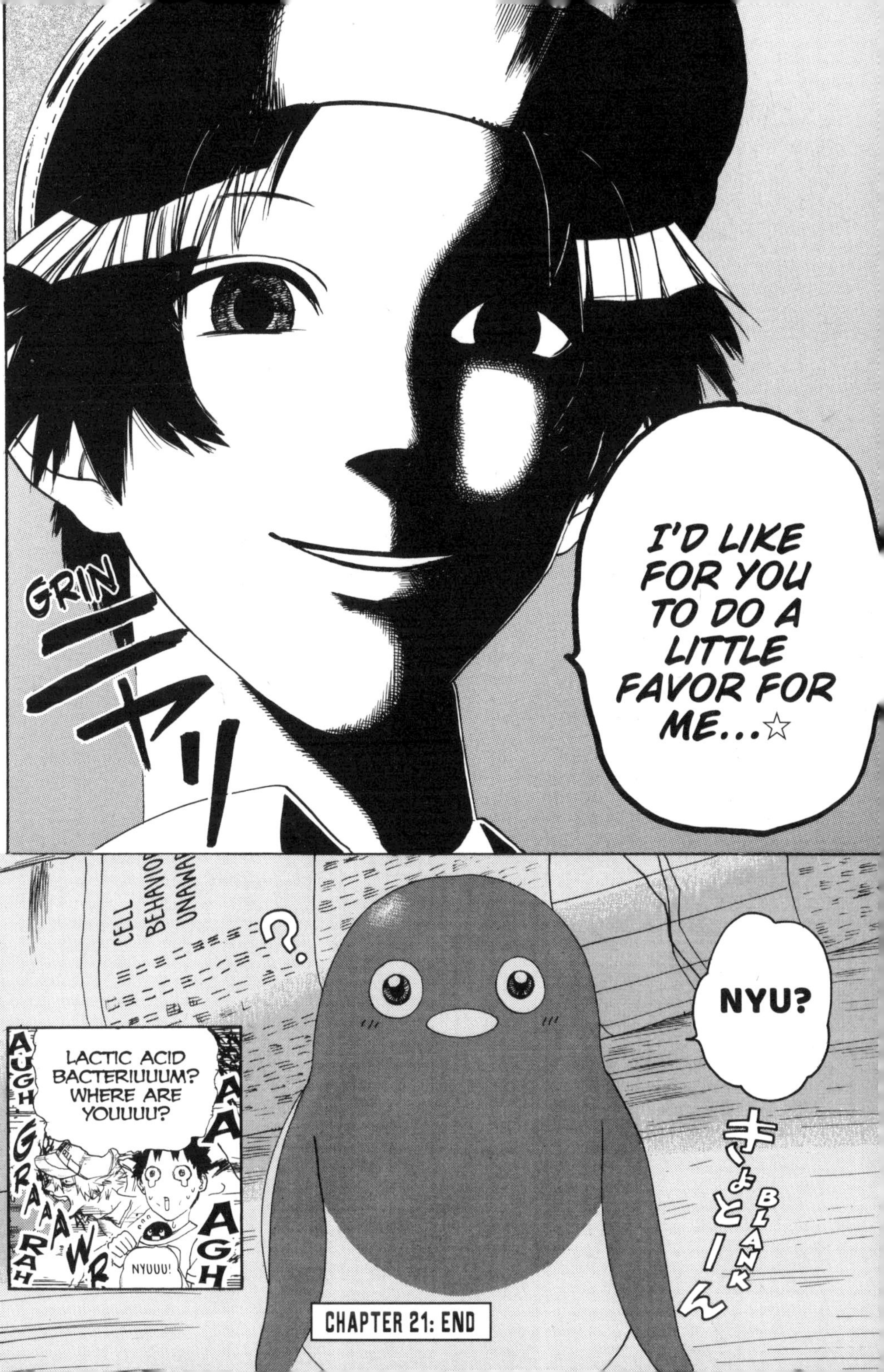
I'D LIKE FOR YOU TO DO A LITTLE FAVOR FOR ME...☆
GRIN
NYU?
BLANK
CELL
LACTIC ACID BACTERIUUUM? WHERE ARE YOUUUU?
AUGH
NYUUU!
CHAPTER 21: END

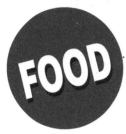
FOOD

The Life and Work of White Blood Cell (Neutrophil):
What He Eats

*These are depictions created just for this comic, and differ from scientific fact.

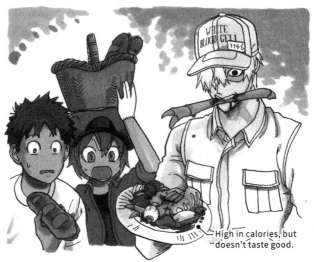

High in calories, but doesn't taste good.

He eats bacteria and viruses for nutrients.

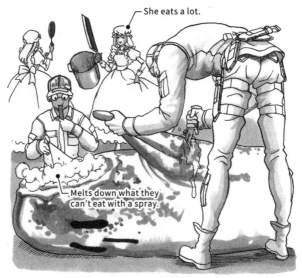

She eats a lot.

Melts down what they can't eat with a spray.

When there's more than he can eat, he gets help from the macrophages.

Cells at Work!

はたらく細胞

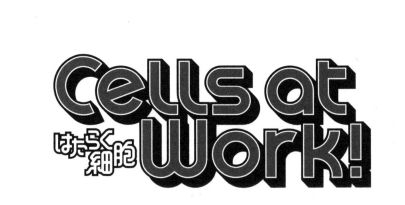

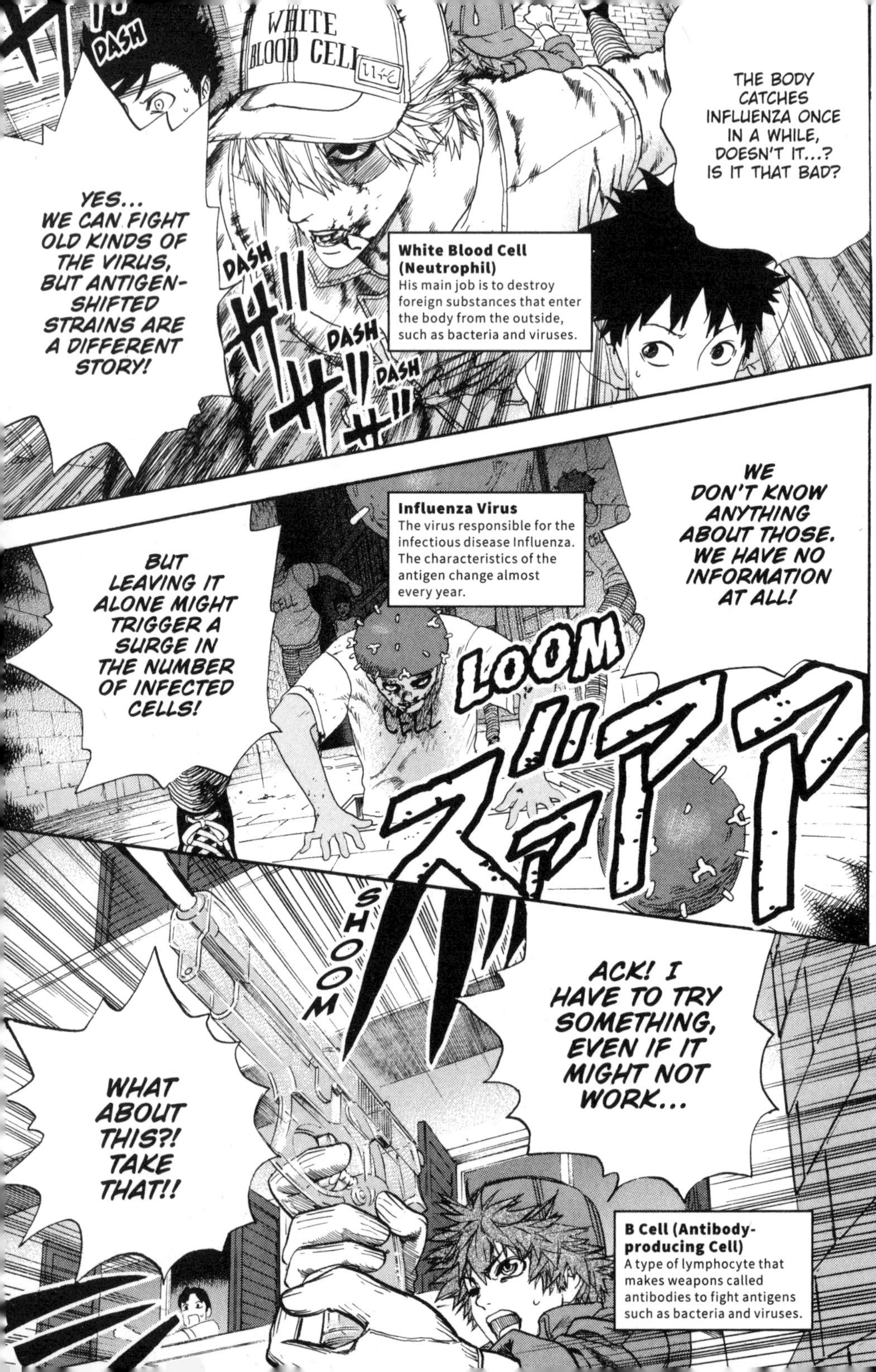

WHITE BLOOD CELL
THE BODY CATCHES INFLUENZA ONCE IN A WHILE, DOESN'T IT...? IS IT THAT BAD?
DASH
White Blood Cell (Neutrophil)
His main job is to destroy foreign substances that enter the body from the outside, such as bacteria and viruses.
DASH
DASH
DASH
YES... WE CAN FIGHT OLD KINDS OF THE VIRUS, BUT ANTIGEN-SHIFTED STRAINS ARE A DIFFERENT STORY!
WE DON'T KNOW ANYTHING ABOUT THOSE. WE HAVE NO INFORMATION AT ALL!
LOOM
Influenza Virus
The virus responsible for the infectious disease Influenza. The characteristics of the antigen change almost every year.
BUT LEAVING IT ALONE MIGHT TRIGGER A SURGE IN THE NUMBER OF INFECTED CELLS!
ACK! I HAVE TO TRY SOMETHING, EVEN IF IT MIGHT NOT WORK...
SHOOOM
B Cell (Antibody-producing Cell)
A type of lymphocyte that makes weapons called antibodies to fight antigens such as bacteria and viruses.
WHAT ABOUT THIS?! TAKE THAT!!

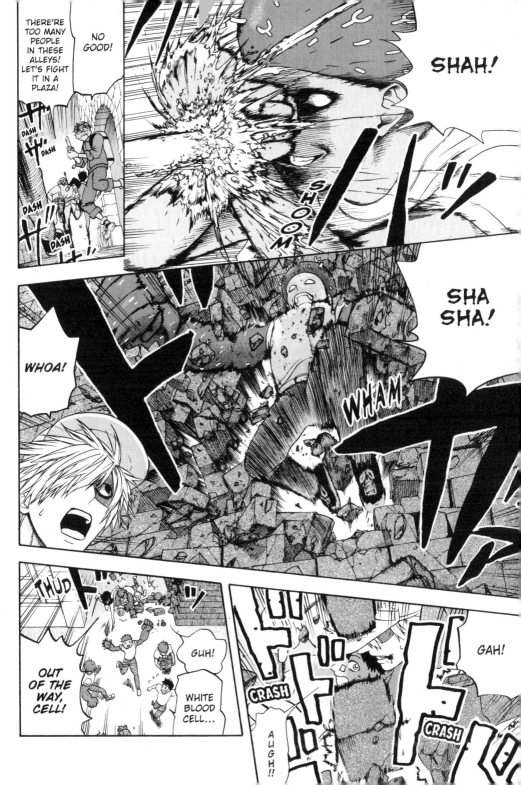

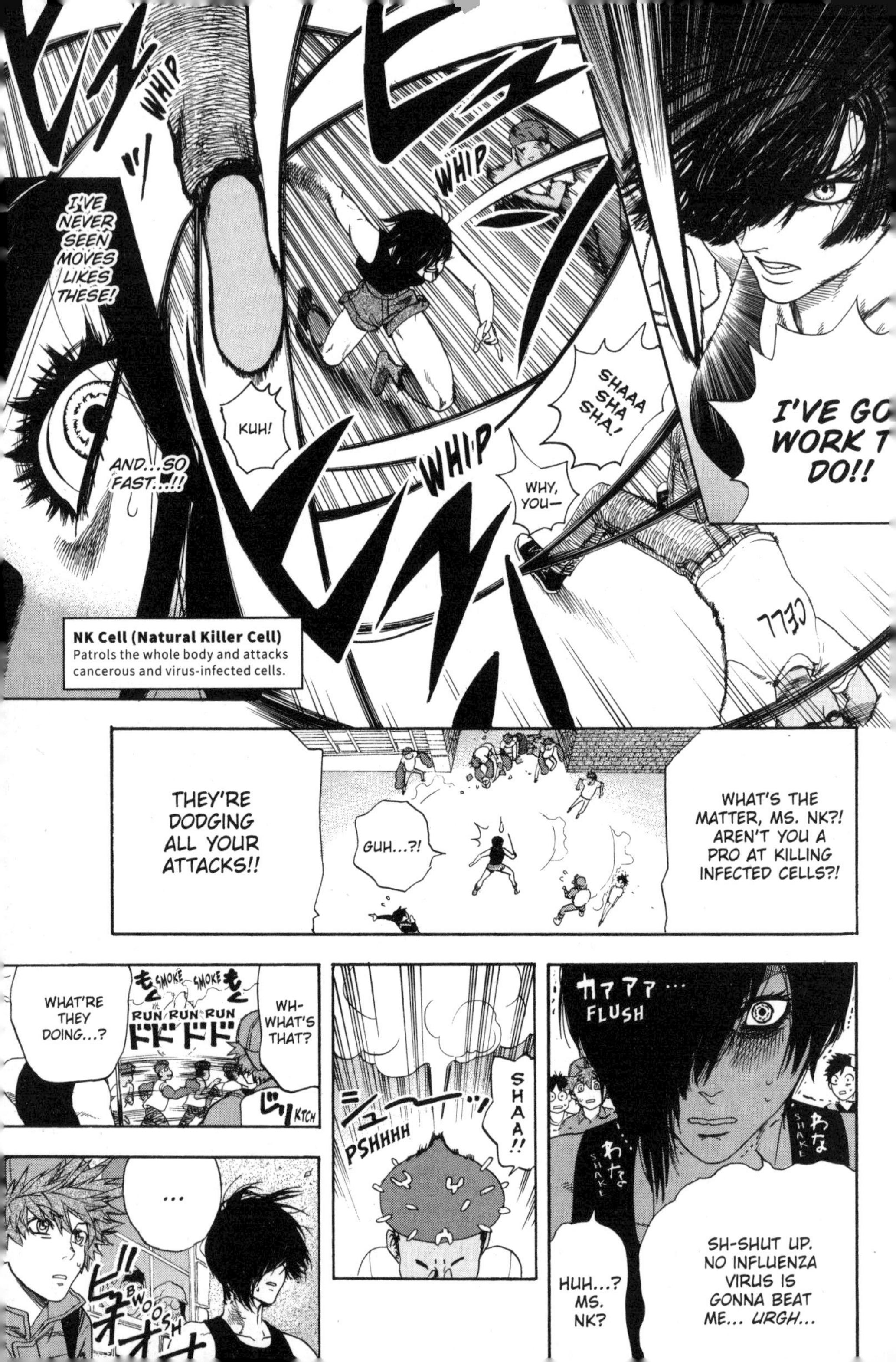
I'VE GO
WORK T
DO!!
SHAAA SHA SHA!
WHY, YOU—
WHIP
WHIP
WHIP
KUH!
I'VE NEVER SEEN MOVES LIKES THESE!
AND...SO FAST...!!
NK Cell (Natural Killer Cell)
Patrols the whole body and attacks cancerous and virus-infected cells.
CELL
WHAT'S THE MATTER, MS. NK?! AREN'T YOU A PRO AT KILLING INFECTED CELLS?!
GUH...?!
THEY'RE DODGING ALL YOUR ATTACKS!!
カァァァ...
FLUSH
SHAKE
SHAKE
SH-SHUT UP. NO INFLUENZA VIRUS IS GONNA BEAT ME... URGH...
HUH...? MS. NK?
SHAA!!
PSHHHH
WH- WHAT'S THAT?
SMOKE
SMOKE
WHAT'RE THEY DOING...?
RUN RUN RUN
KTCH
...
BWOOSH

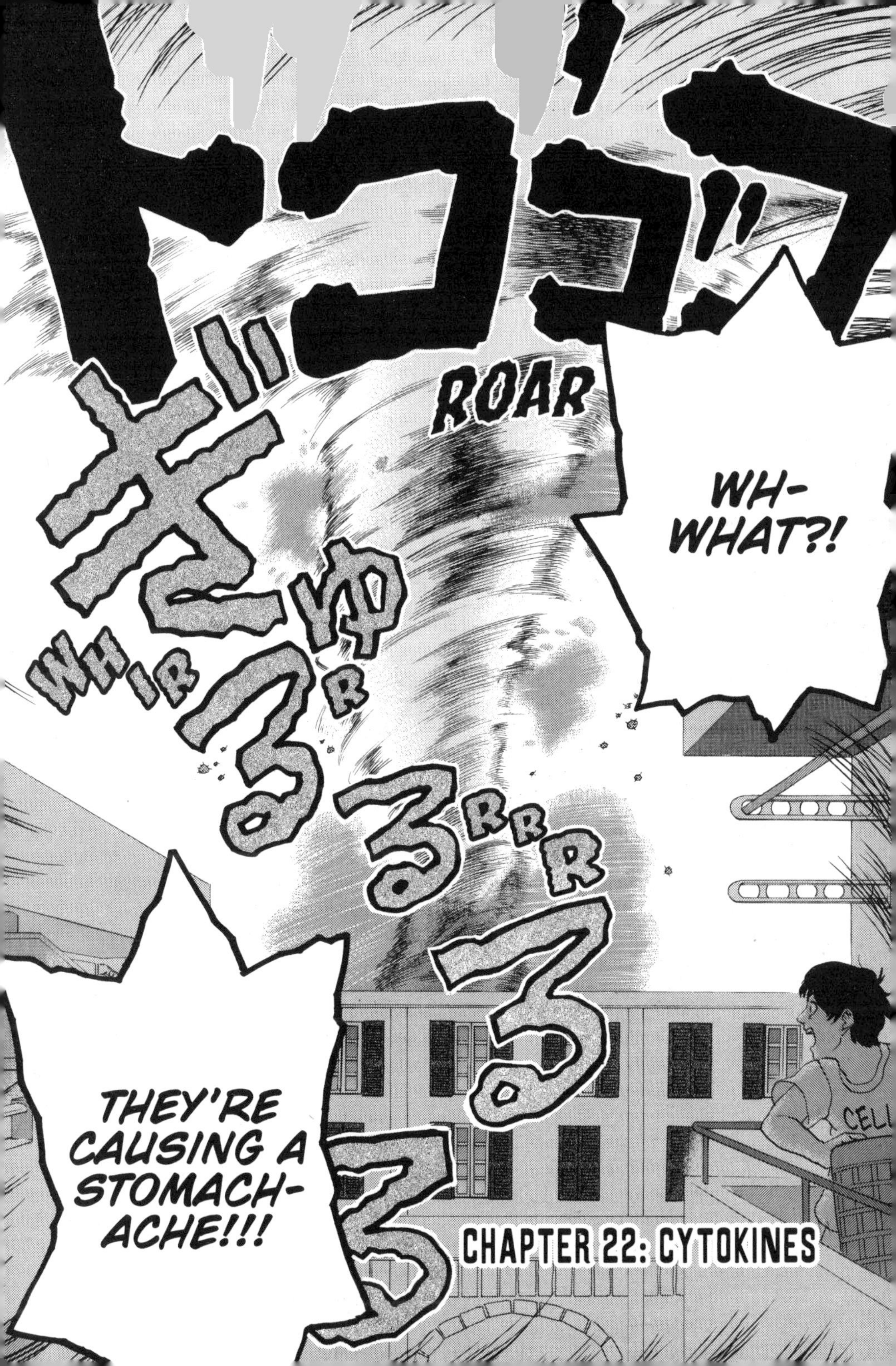

WH-
WHAT?!
ROAR
WHIRRRRR
THEY'RE CAUSING A STOMACH-ACHE!!!
CHAPTER 22: CYTOKINES

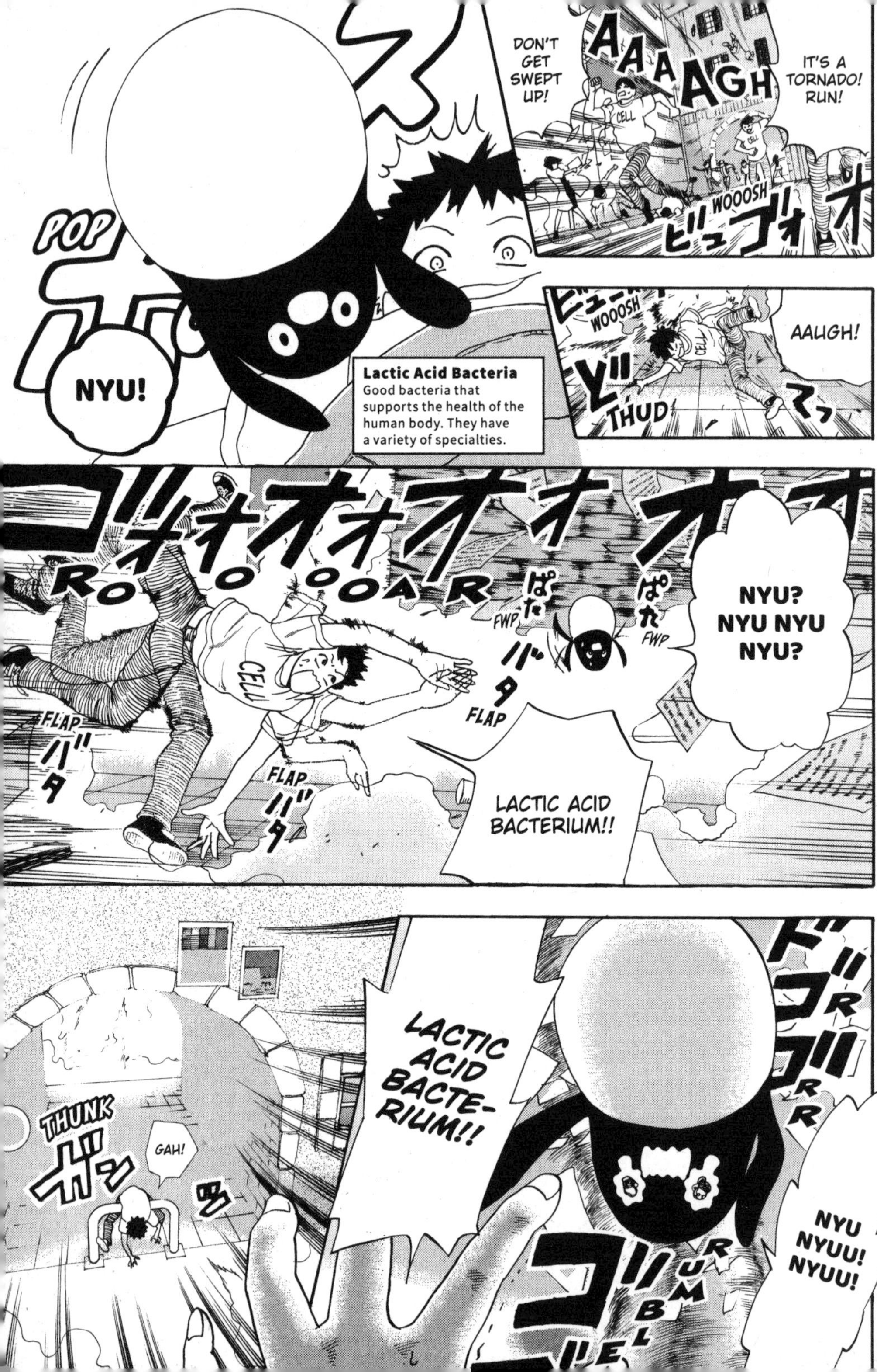

IT'S A TORNADO! RUN!
AAAAGH
DON'T GET SWEPT UP!
WOOOSH
AAUGH!
WOOOSH
THUD
POP
NYU!
Lactic Acid Bacteria
Good bacteria that supports the health of the human body. They have a variety of specialties.
ROOOOAR
NYU? NYU NYU NYU?
FWP
FWP
FLAP
LACTIC ACID BACTERIUM!!
FLAP
FLAP
GRRR
NYU NYUU! NYUU!
RUMBLE
LACTIC ACID BACTERIUM!!
THUNK
GAH!

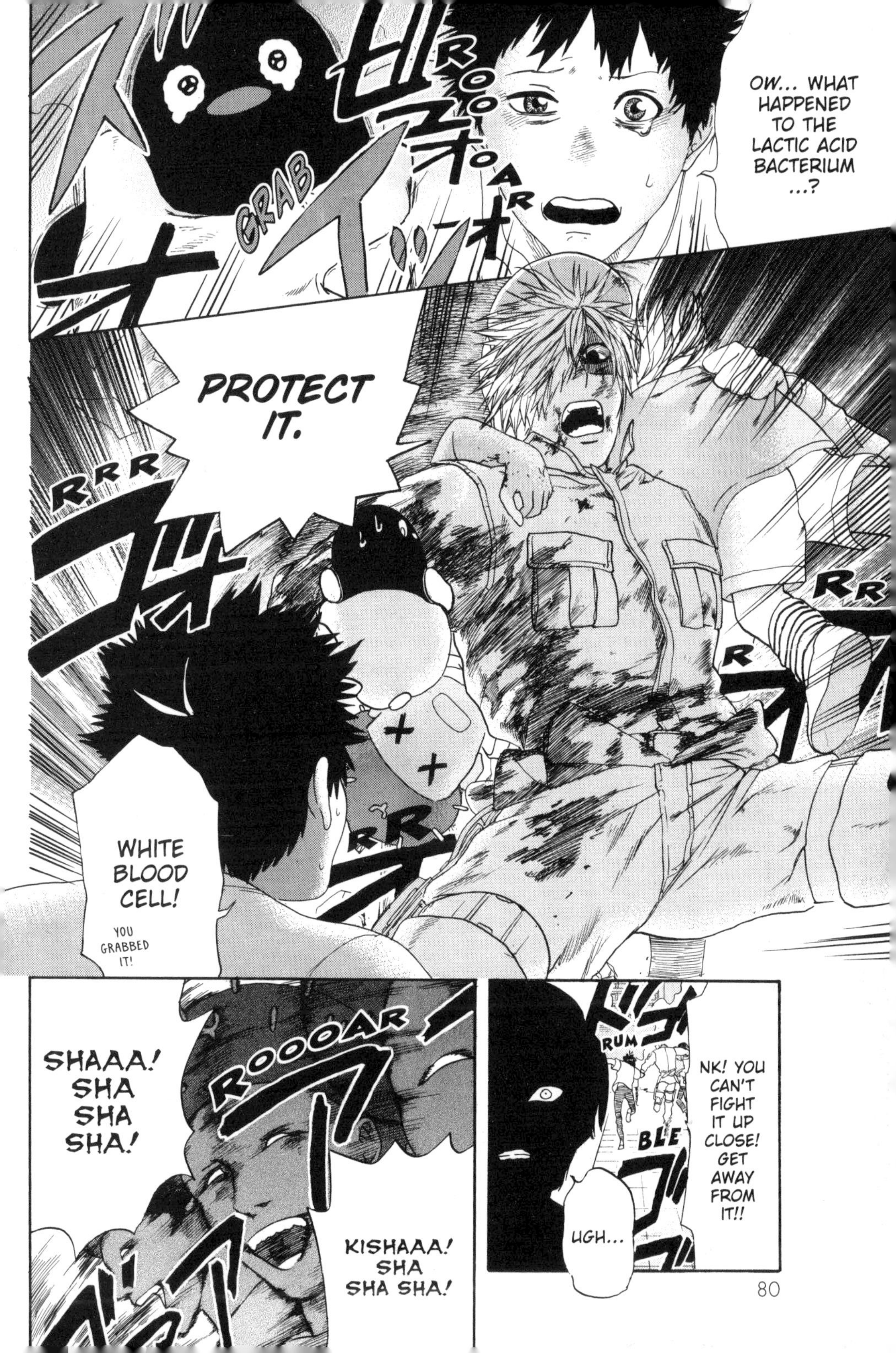
OW... WHAT HAPPENED TO THE LACTIC ACID BACTERIUM ...?
ROOOAR
GRAB
PROTECT IT.
RR
R
RRR
WHITE BLOOD CELL!
YOU GRABBED IT!
RR
RUM
NK! YOU CAN'T FIGHT IT UP CLOSE! GET AWAY FROM IT!!
BLE
UGH...
ROOOAR
SHAAA! SHA SHA SHA!
KISHAAA! SHA SHA SHA!

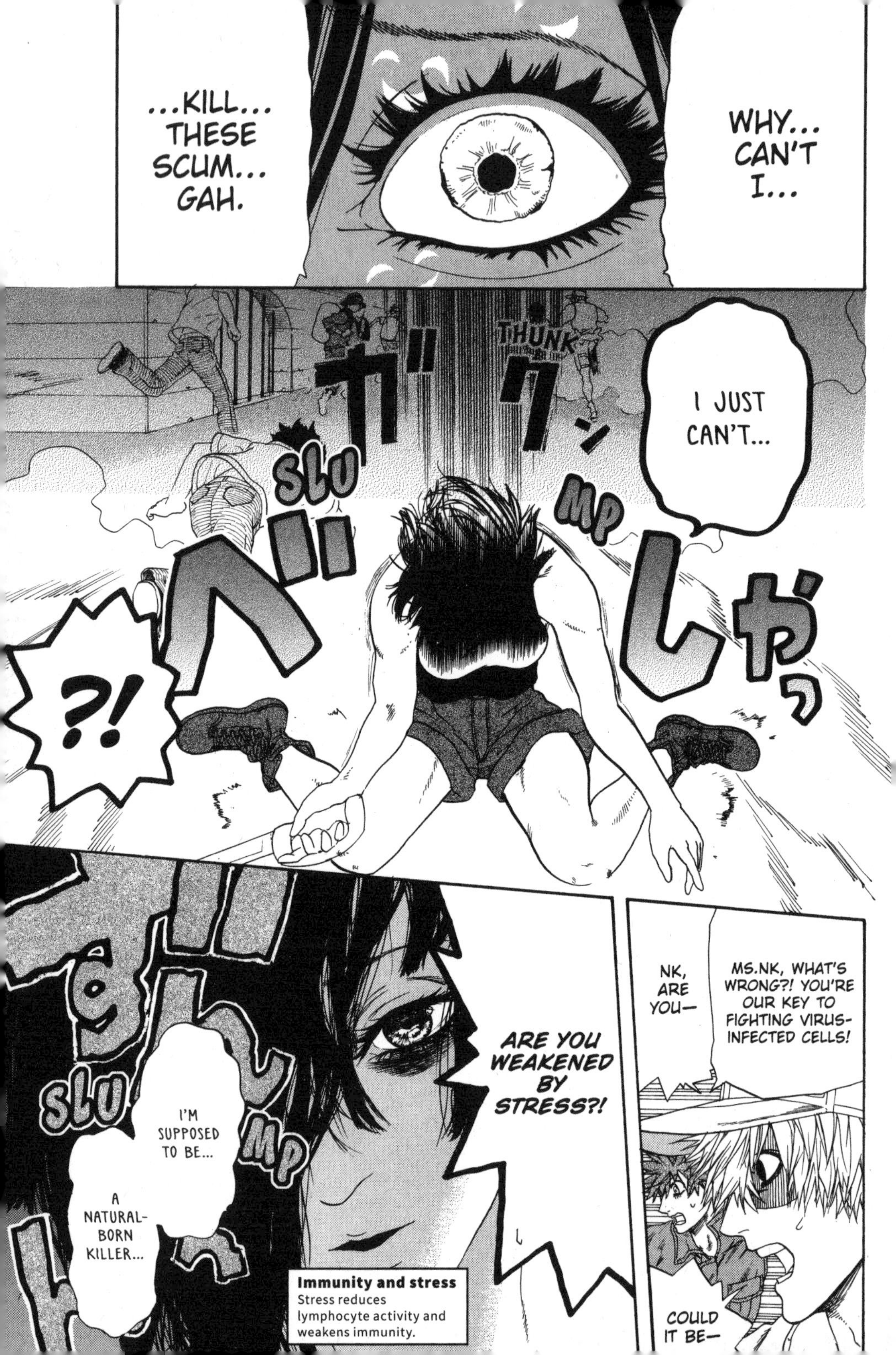
WHY... CAN'T I...
...KILL... THESE SCUM... GAH.
I JUST CAN'T...
THUNK
ガクッ
SLUMP
べしゃっ
?!
MS.NK, WHAT'S WRONG?! YOU'RE OUR KEY TO FIGHTING VIRUS-INFECTED CELLS!
NK, ARE YOU—
COULD IT BE—
ARE YOU WEAKENED BY STRESS?!
I'M SUPPOSED TO BE...
A NATURAL-BORN KILLER...
SLUMP
Immunity and stress
Stress reduces lymphocyte activity and weakens immunity.

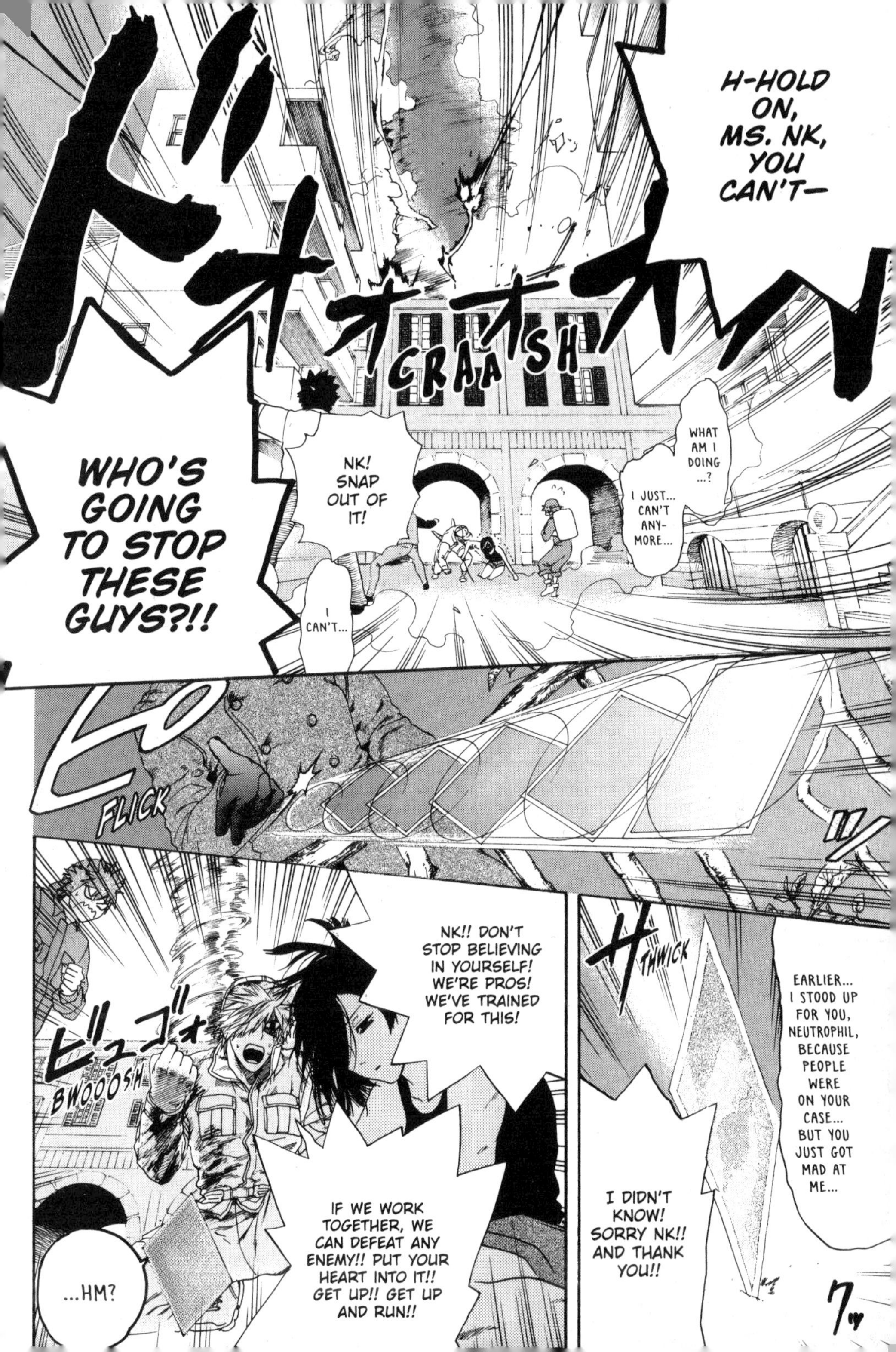

H-HOLD ON, MS. NK, YOU CAN'T—
CRAAASH
WHAT AM I DOING ...?
I JUST... CAN'T ANYMORE...
NK! SNAP OUT OF IT!
I CAN'T...
WHO'S GOING TO STOP THESE GUYS?!!
FLICK
THWICK
EARLIER... I STOOD UP FOR YOU, NEUTROPHIL, BECAUSE PEOPLE WERE ON YOUR CASE... BUT YOU JUST GOT MAD AT ME...
I DIDN'T KNOW! SORRY NK!! AND THANK YOU!!
NK!! DON'T STOP BELIEVING IN YOURSELF! WE'RE PROS! WE'VE TRAINED FOR THIS!
BWOOOSH
IF WE WORK TOGETHER, WE CAN DEFEAT ANY ENEMY!! PUT YOUR HEART INTO IT!! GET UP!! GET UP AND RUN!!
...HM?

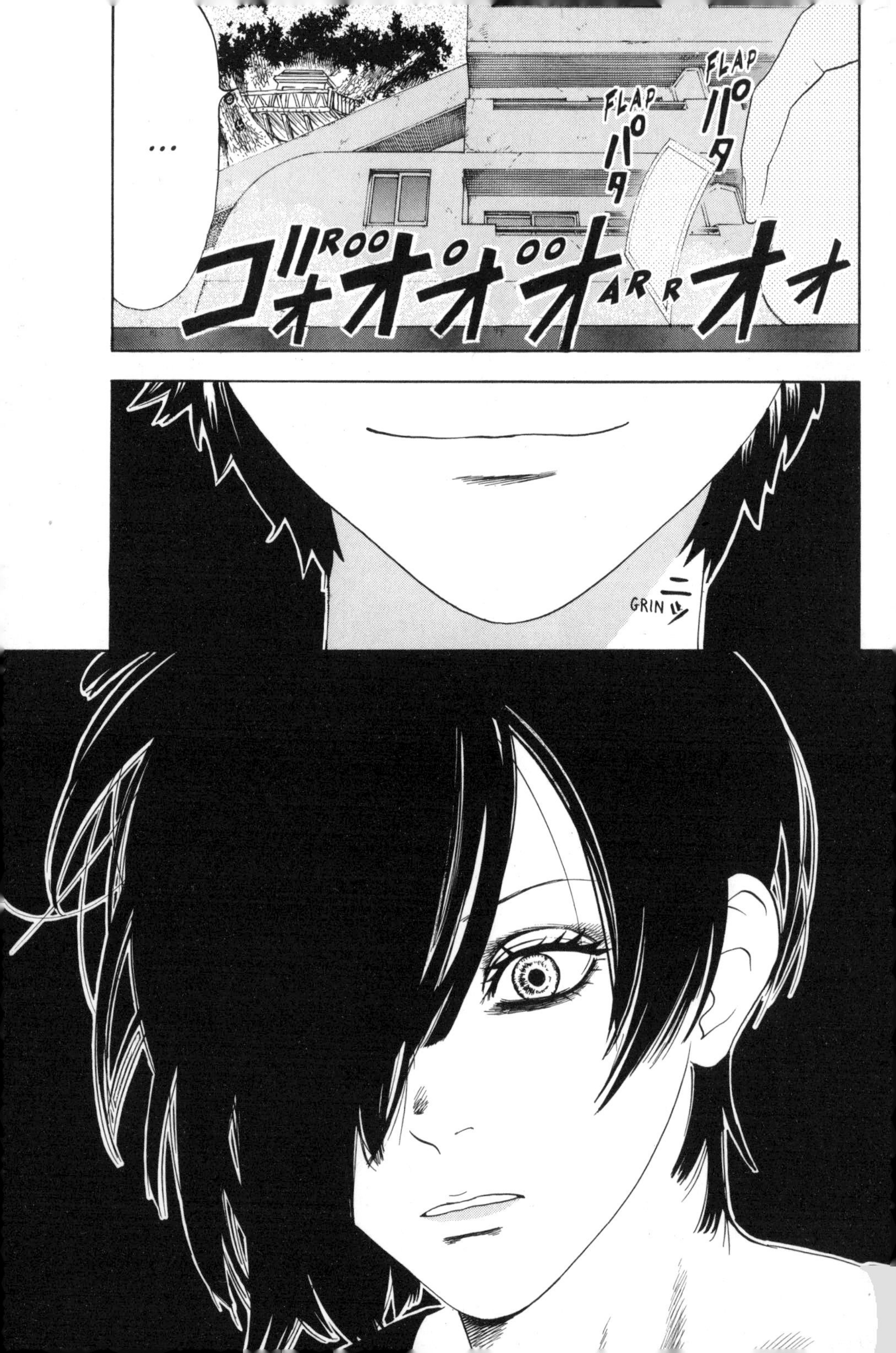
FLAP パタ
FLAP パタ
ROOOOOARR ゴォオオオオオオ
...
GRIN ニッ

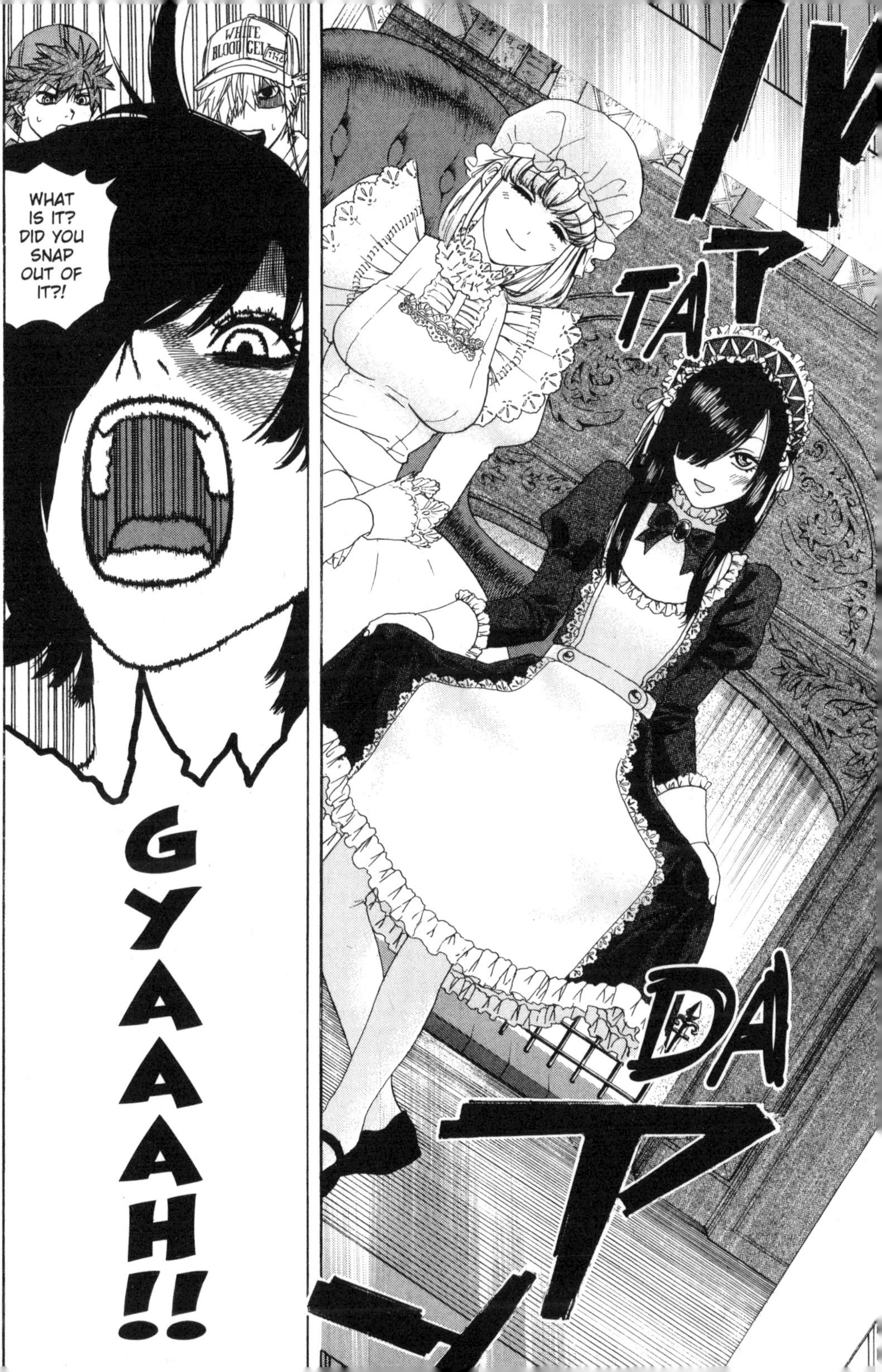
TA
DA
WHAT IS IT? DID YOU SNAP OUT OF IT?!
GYAAAH!!

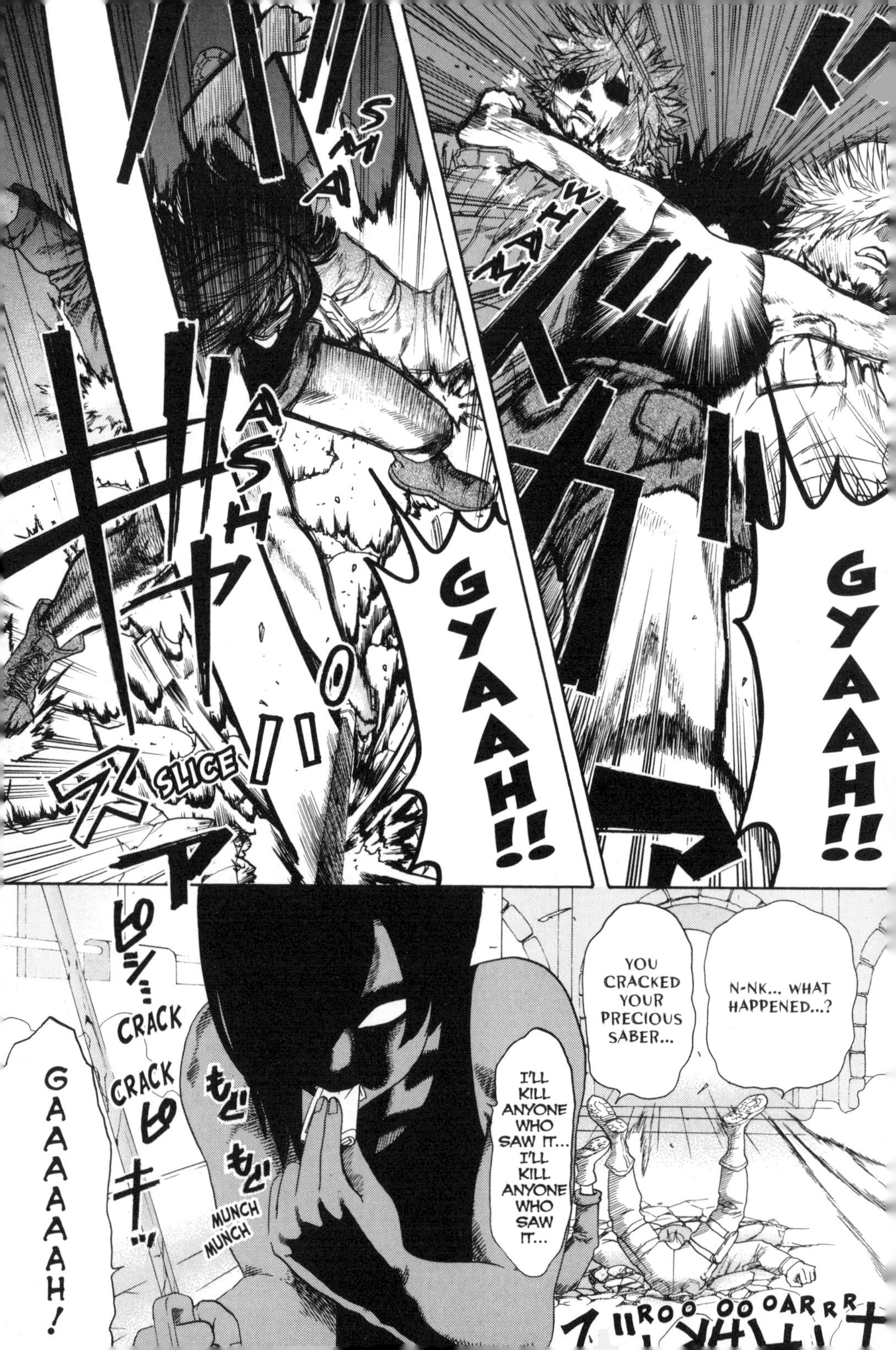

WHAM
GYAAH!!
SMA
ASH
SLICE
GYAAH!!
N-NK... WHAT HAPPENED...?
YOU CRACKED YOUR PRECIOUS SABER...
I'LL KILL ANYONE WHO SAW IT... I'LL KILL ANYONE WHO SAW IT...
もぐ もぐ
MUNCH MUNCH
CRACK
CRACK
GAAAAAAAH!
ROO OO OARRR

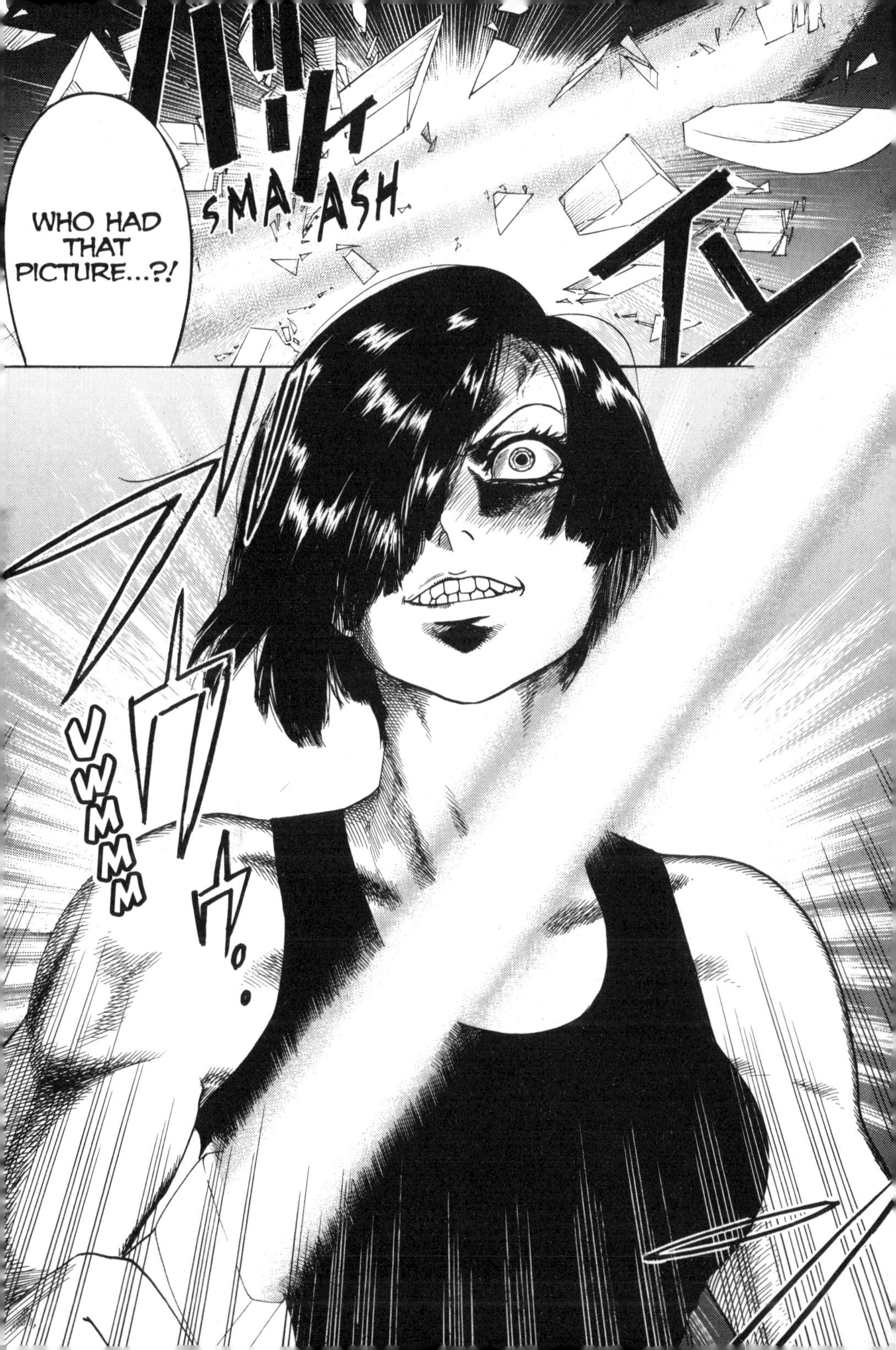
SMASH
WHO HAD THAT PICTURE...?!
VWMMM

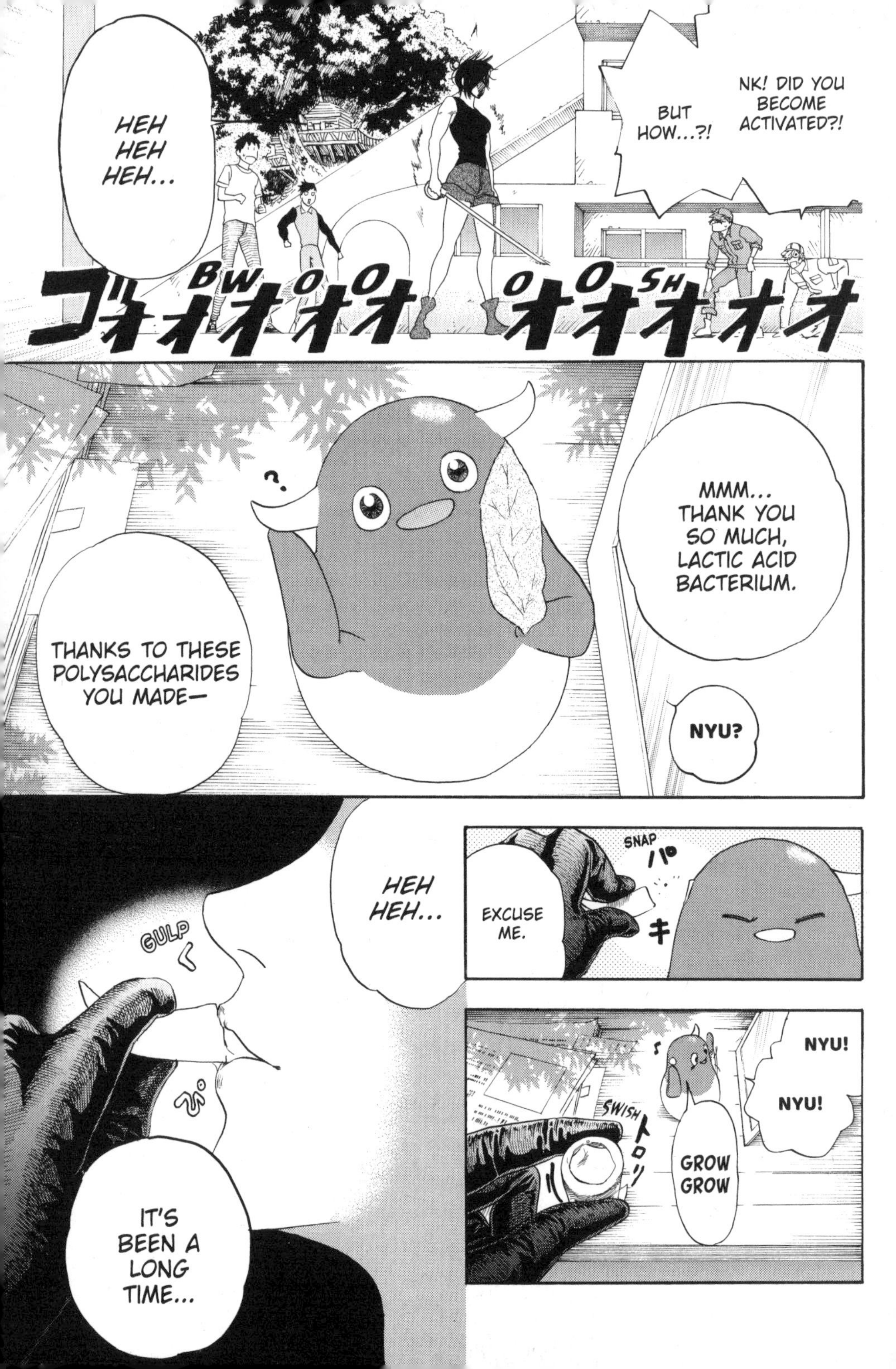
NK! DID YOU BECOME ACTIVATED?!
BUT HOW...?!
HEH HEH HEH...
BWOOOOSH
MMM... THANK YOU SO MUCH, LACTIC ACID BACTERIUM.
THANKS TO THESE POLYSACCHARIDES YOU MADE—
NYU?
SNAP
EXCUSE ME.
NYU!
NYU!
SWISH
GROW GROW
HEH HEH...
GULP
IT'S BEEN A LONG TIME...

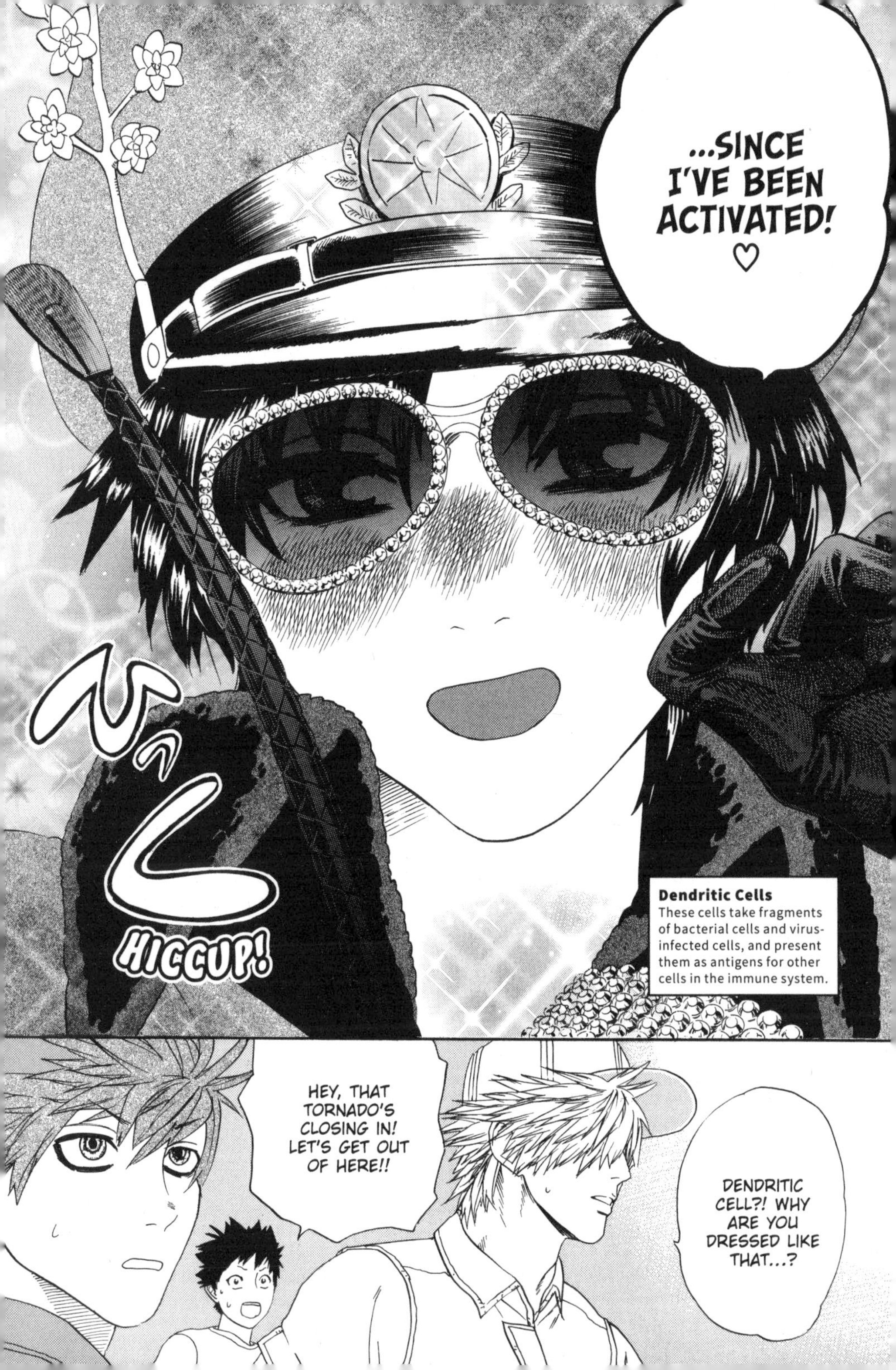
...SINCE I'VE BEEN ACTIVATED! ♡
HICCUP!
Dendritic Cells
These cells take fragments of bacterial cells and virus-infected cells, and present them as antigens for other cells in the immune system.
DENDRITIC CELL?! WHY ARE YOU DRESSED LIKE THAT...?
HEY, THAT TORNADO'S CLOSING IN! LET'S GET OUT OF HERE!!

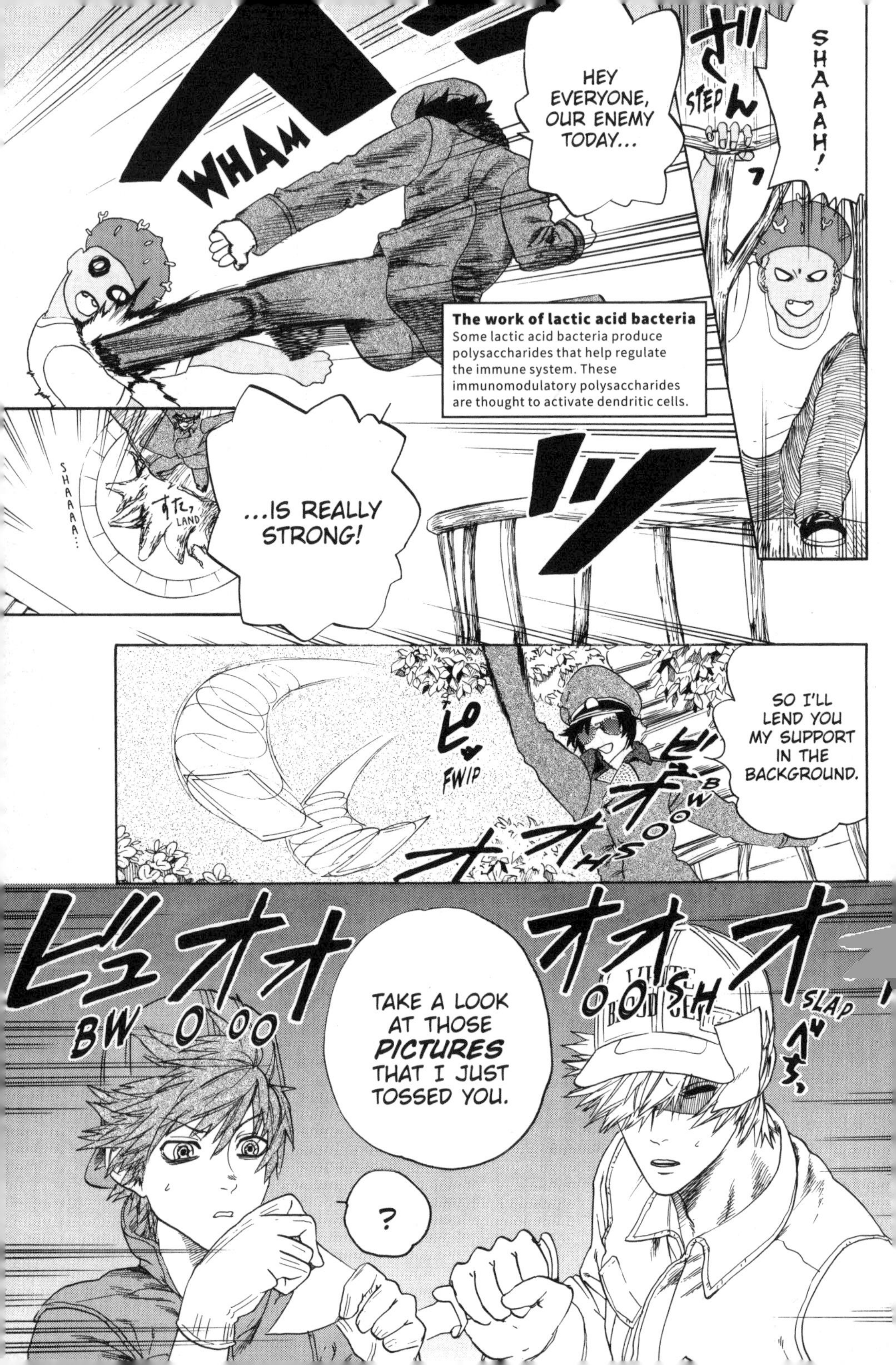

SHAAAAH!
STEP
WHAM
HEY EVERYONE, OUR ENEMY TODAY...
The work of lactic acid bacteria
Some lactic acid bacteria produce polysaccharides that help regulate the immune system. These immunomodulatory polysaccharides are thought to activate dendritic cells.
...IS REALLY STRONG!
LAND
SHAAAAA...
SO I'LL LEND YOU MY SUPPORT IN THE BACKGROUND.
BWOOSH
FWIP
SLAP
TAKE A LOOK AT THOSE PICTURES THAT I JUST TOSSED YOU.
BWOOOOOSH
?

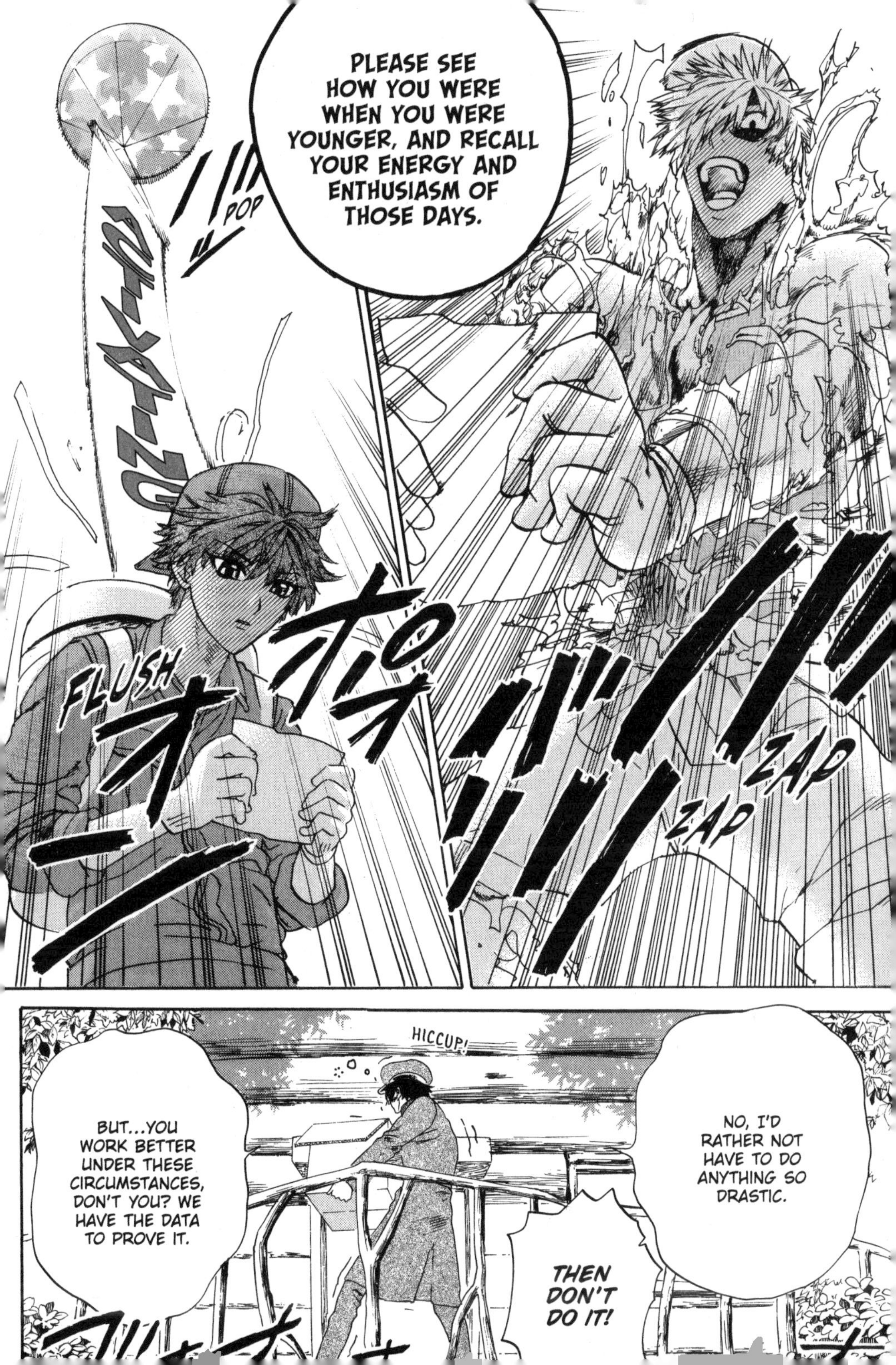
PLEASE SEE HOW YOU WERE WHEN YOU WERE YOUNGER, AND RECALL YOUR ENERGY AND ENTHUSIASM OF THOSE DAYS.
ZAP
ZAP
POP
SPLATTING
FLUSH
NO, I'D RATHER NOT HAVE TO DO ANYTHING SO DRASTIC.
HICCUP!
THEN DON'T DO IT!
BUT...YOU WORK BETTER UNDER THESE CIRCUMSTANCES, DON'T YOU? WE HAVE THE DATA TO PROVE IT.

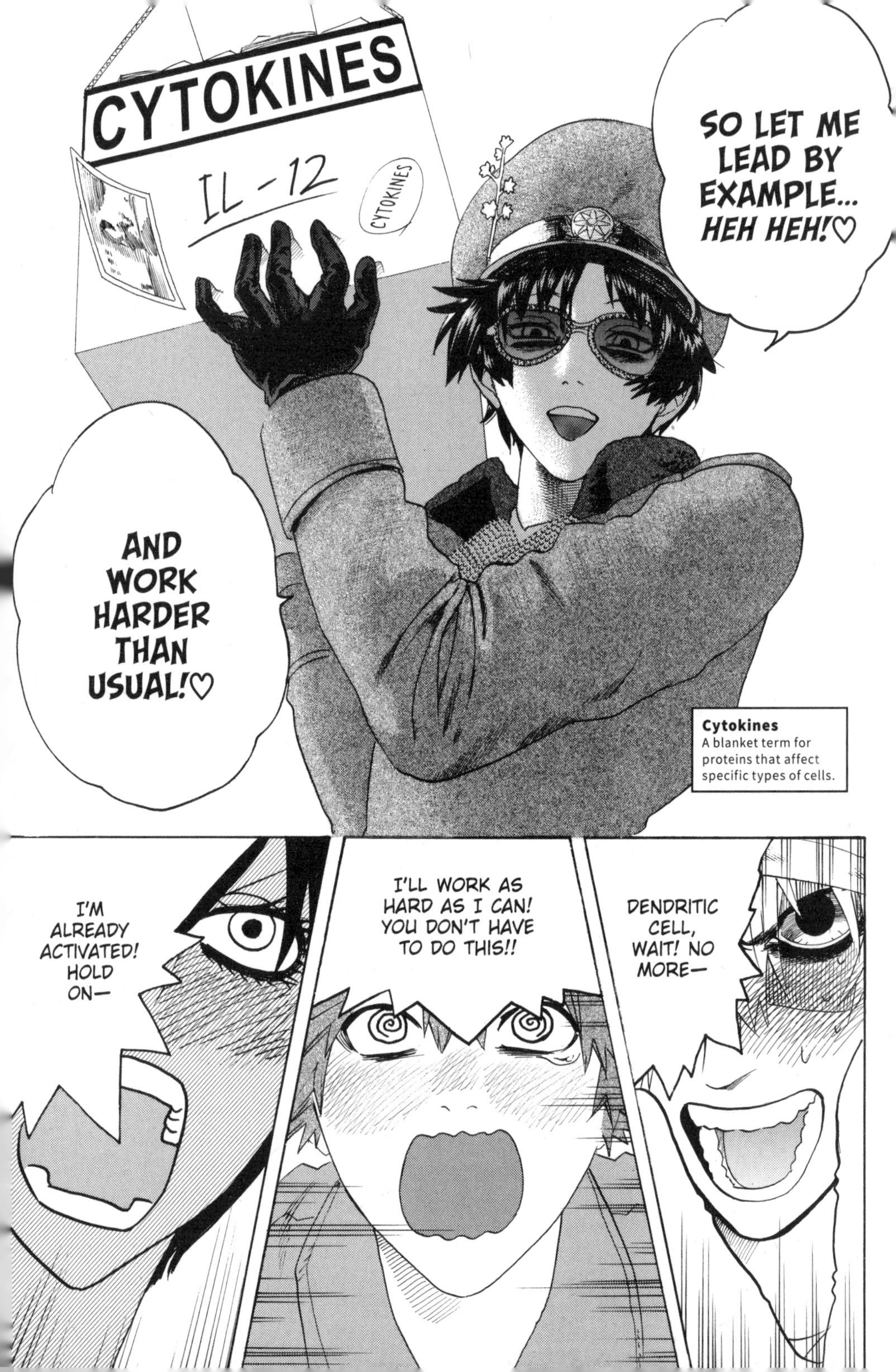
SO LET ME LEAD BY EXAMPLE... HEH HEH!♡
CYTOKINES
IL-12
CYTOKINES
AND WORK HARDER THAN USUAL!♡
Cytokines
A blanket term for proteins that affect specific types of cells.
DENDRITIC CELL, WAIT! NO MORE—
I'LL WORK AS HARD AS I CAN! YOU DON'T HAVE TO DO THIS!!
I'M ALREADY ACTIVATED! HOLD ON—

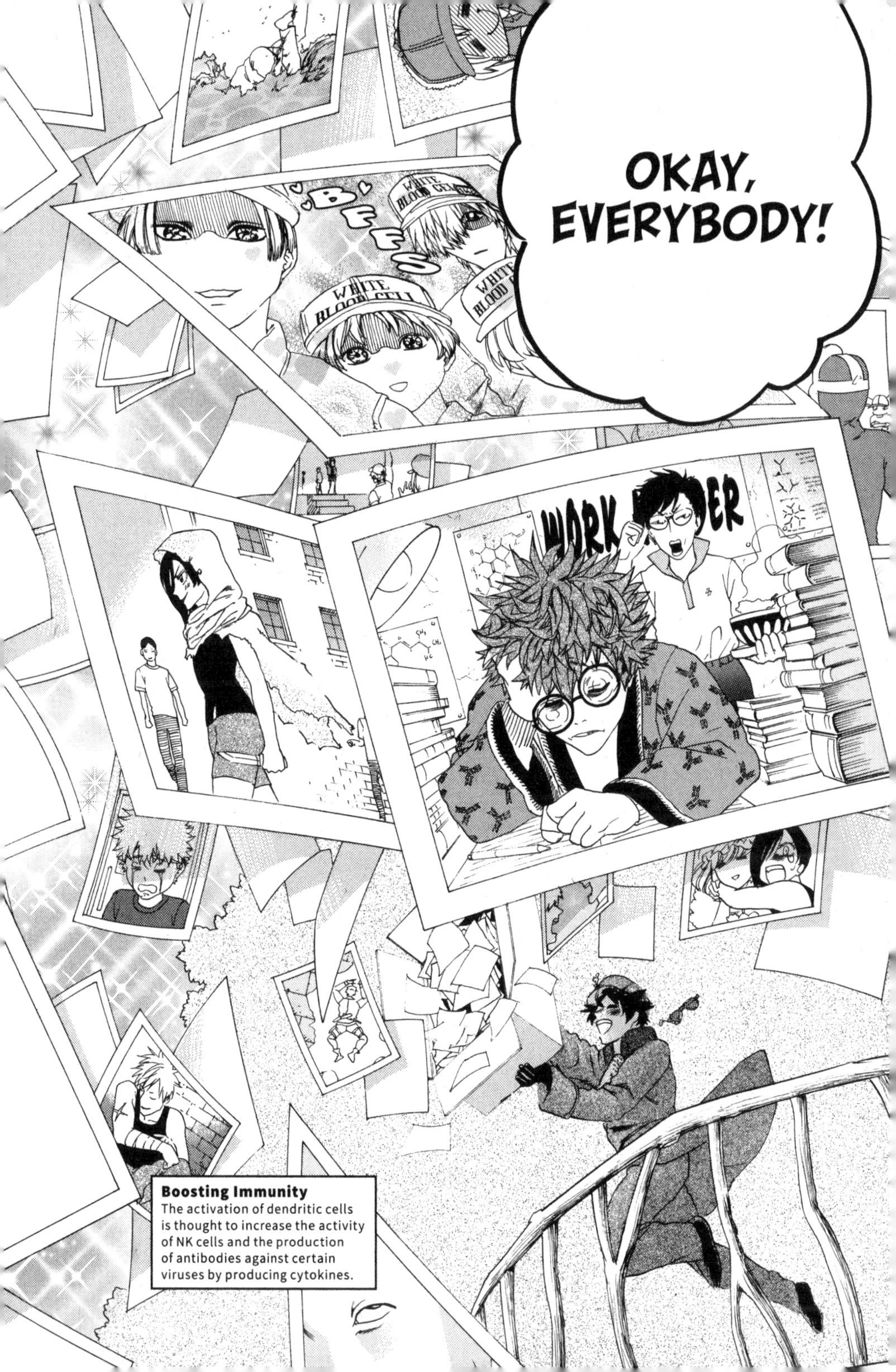
OKAY, EVERYBODY!
BFFS
WHITE BLOOD CELL
Boosting Immunity
The activation of dendritic cells is thought to increase the activity of NK cells and the production of antibodies against certain viruses by producing cytokines.

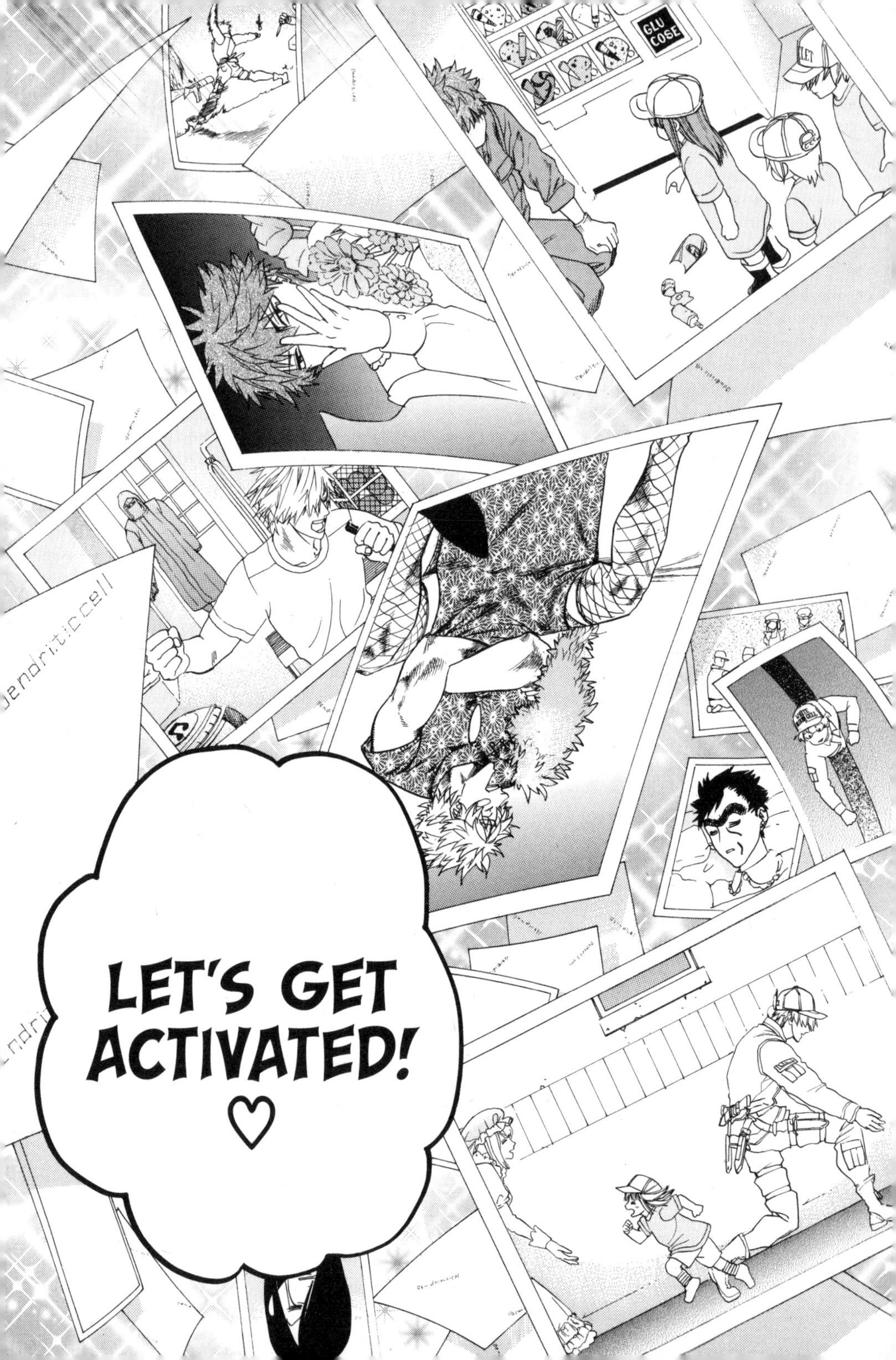
GLU COSE
dendritic cell
LET'S GET ACTIVATED! ♡

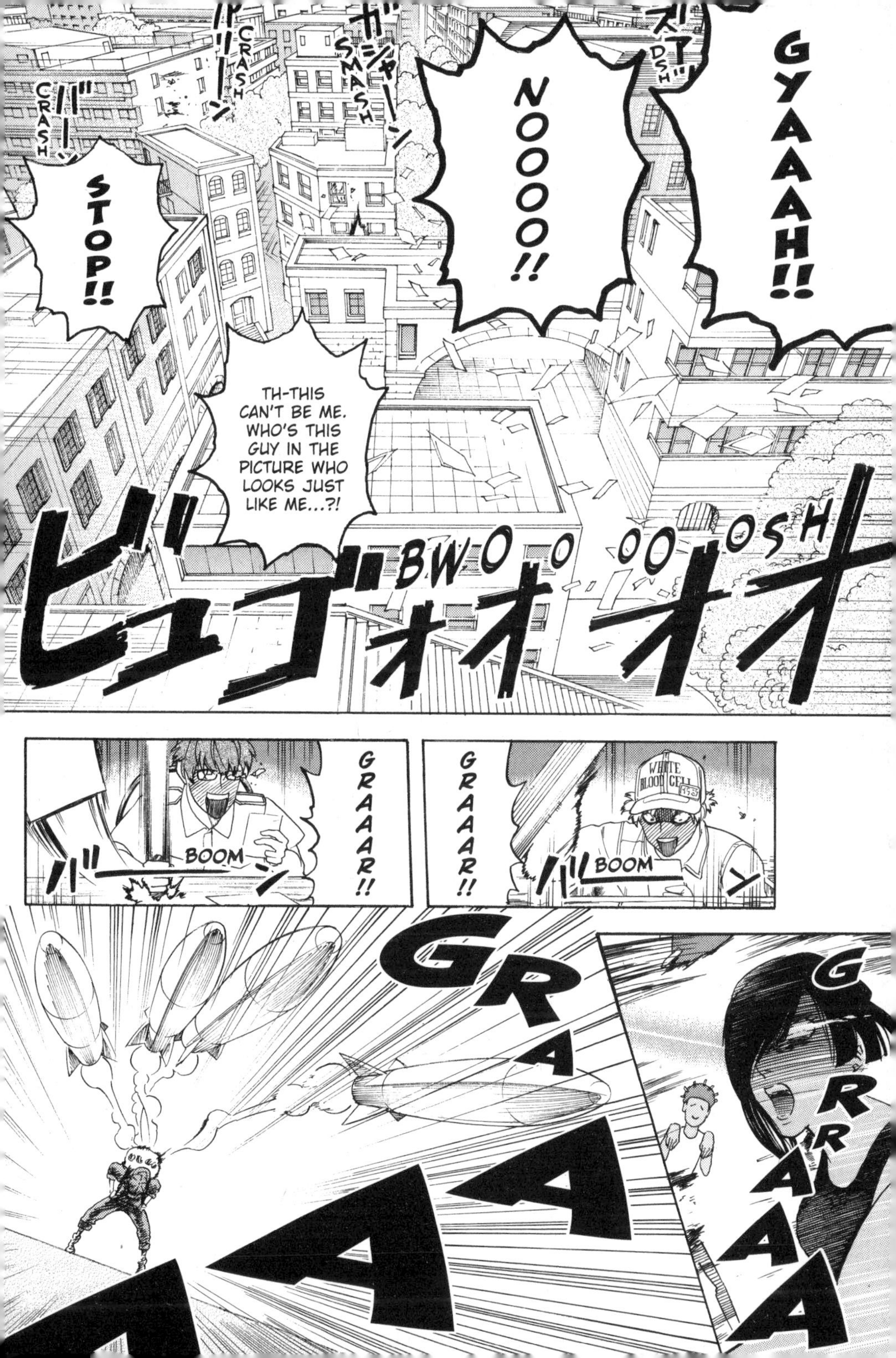
GYAAAAH!!
DSH
NOOOOO!!
SMASH
CRASH
CRASH
STOP!!
TH-THIS CAN'T BE ME. WHO'S THIS GUY IN THE PICTURE WHO LOOKS JUST LIKE ME...?!
BWOOOOOSH
GRAAAAR!!
BOOM
GRAAAAR!!
BOOM
GRRAAAAA
GRAAAAA

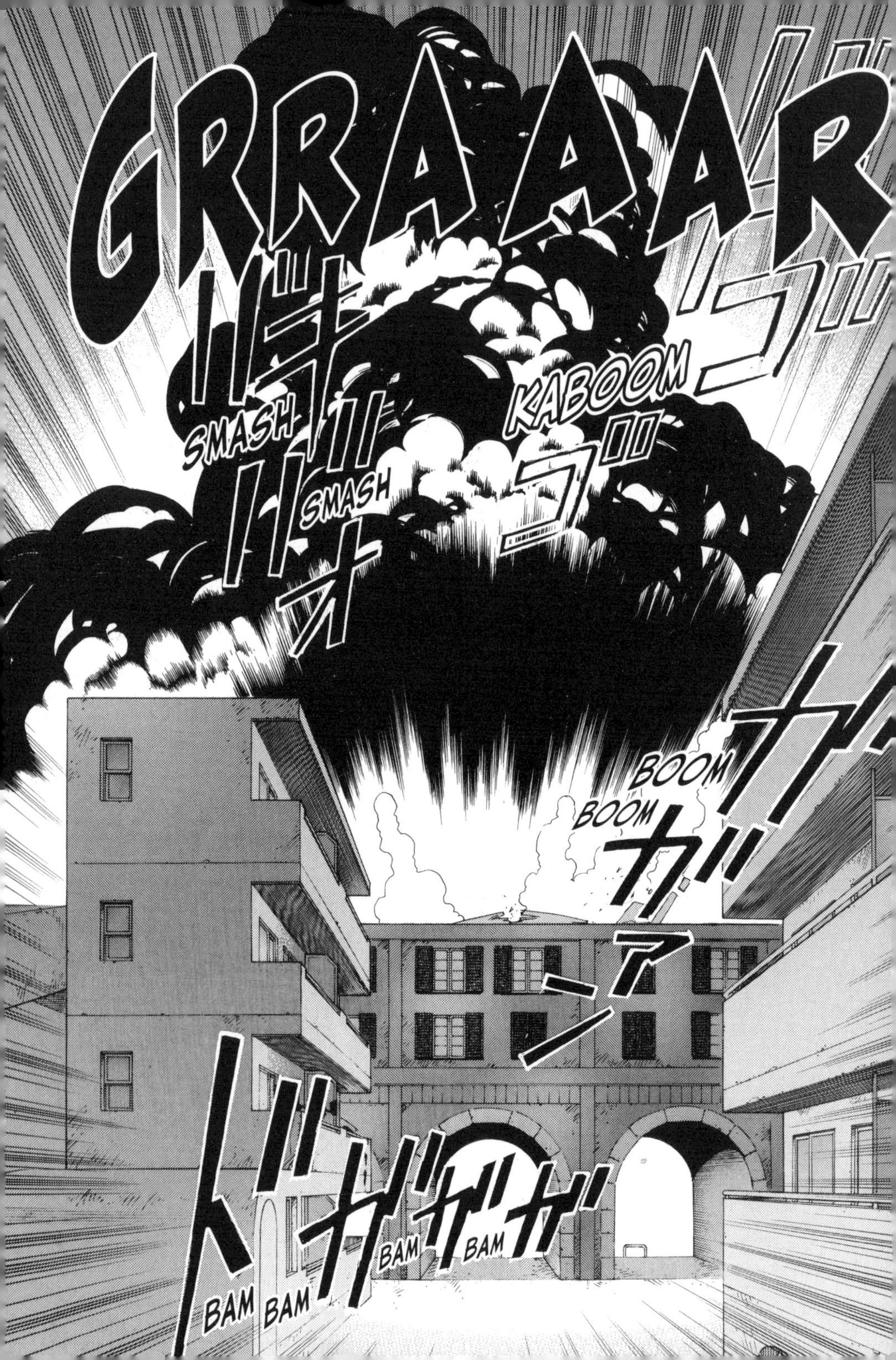
GRRAAAR
KABOOM
SMASH
SMASH
BOOM
BOOM
BAM
BAM
BAM
BAM

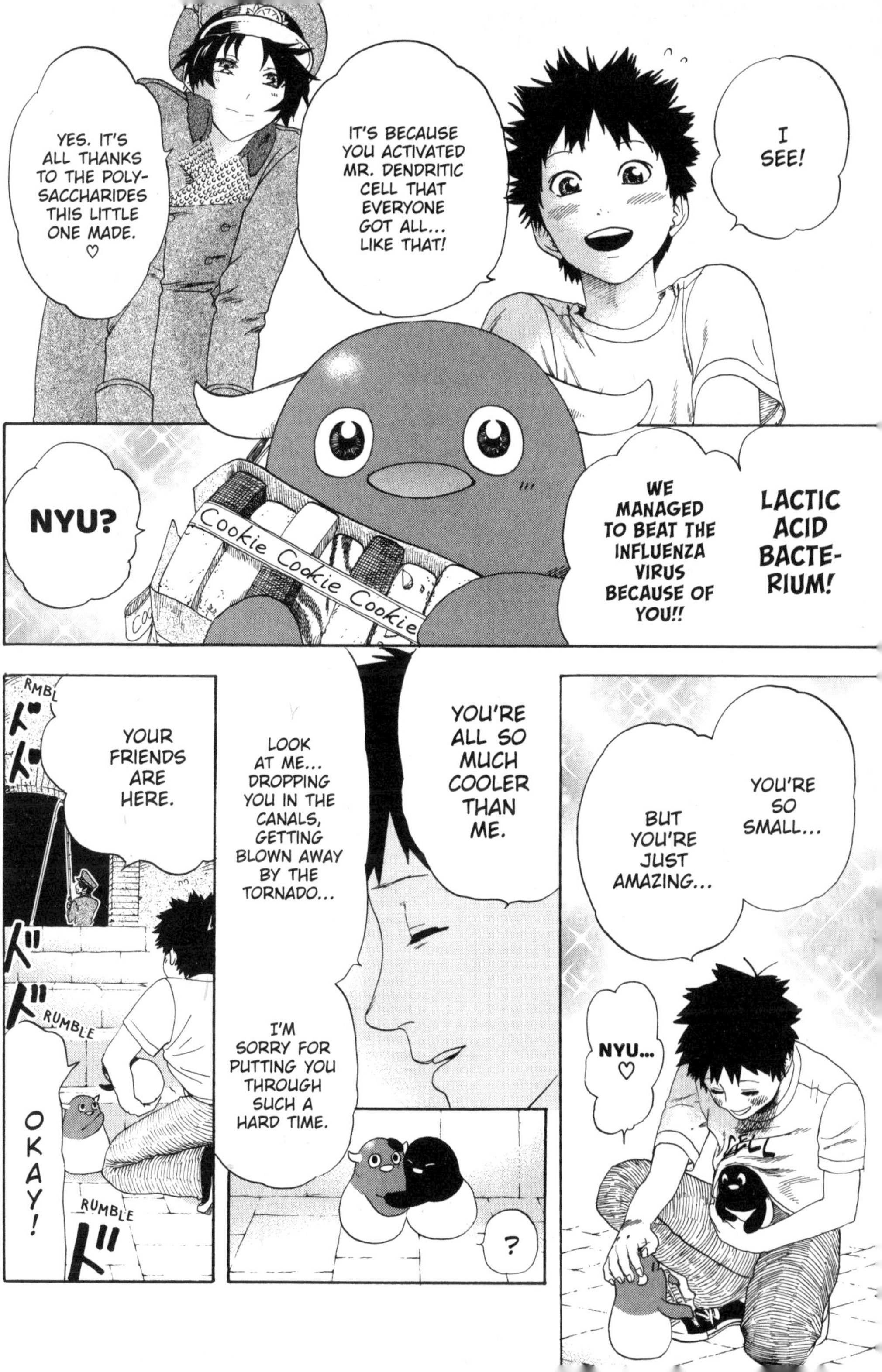
I SEE!
IT'S BECAUSE YOU ACTIVATED MR. DENDRITIC CELL THAT EVERYONE GOT ALL... LIKE THAT!
YES. IT'S ALL THANKS TO THE POLY-SACCHARIDES THIS LITTLE ONE MADE. ♡
LACTIC ACID BACTE-RIUM!
WE MANAGED TO BEAT THE INFLUENZA VIRUS BECAUSE OF YOU!!
NYU?
YOU'RE SO SMALL...
BUT YOU'RE JUST AMAZING...
NYU... ♡
YOU'RE ALL SO MUCH COOLER THAN ME.
LOOK AT ME... DROPPING YOU IN THE CANALS, GETTING BLOWN AWAY BY THE TORNADO...
I'M SORRY FOR PUTTING YOU THROUGH SUCH A HARD TIME.
?
RMBL
YOUR FRIENDS ARE HERE.
RUMBLE
OKAY!
RUMBLE

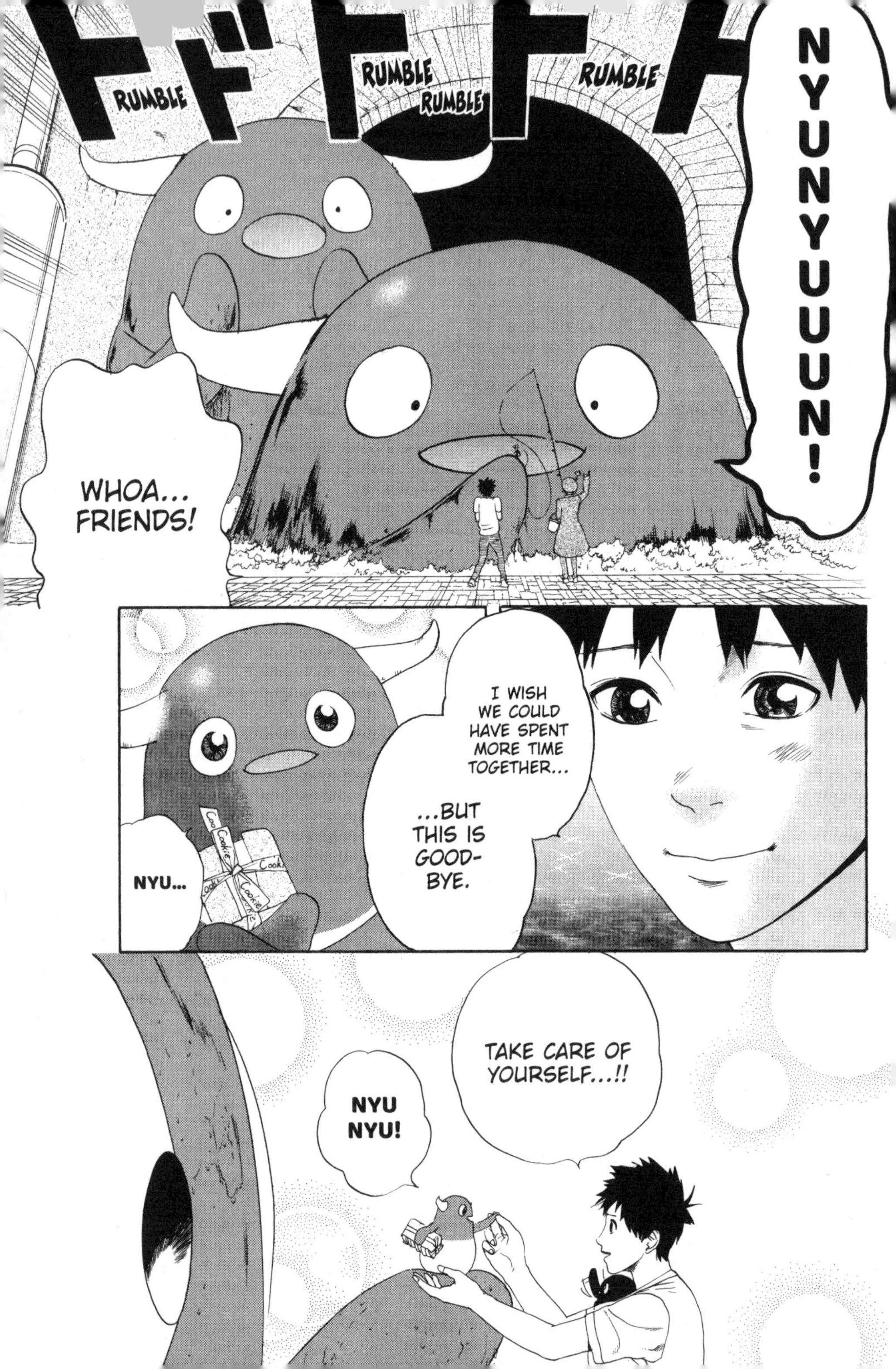
NYUNYUUUUN!
RUMBLE
RUMBLE
RUMBLE
RUMBLE
WHOA... FRIENDS!
I WISH WE COULD HAVE SPENT MORE TIME TOGETHER...
...BUT THIS IS GOOD-BYE.
NYU...
TAKE CARE OF YOURSELF...!!
NYU NYU!

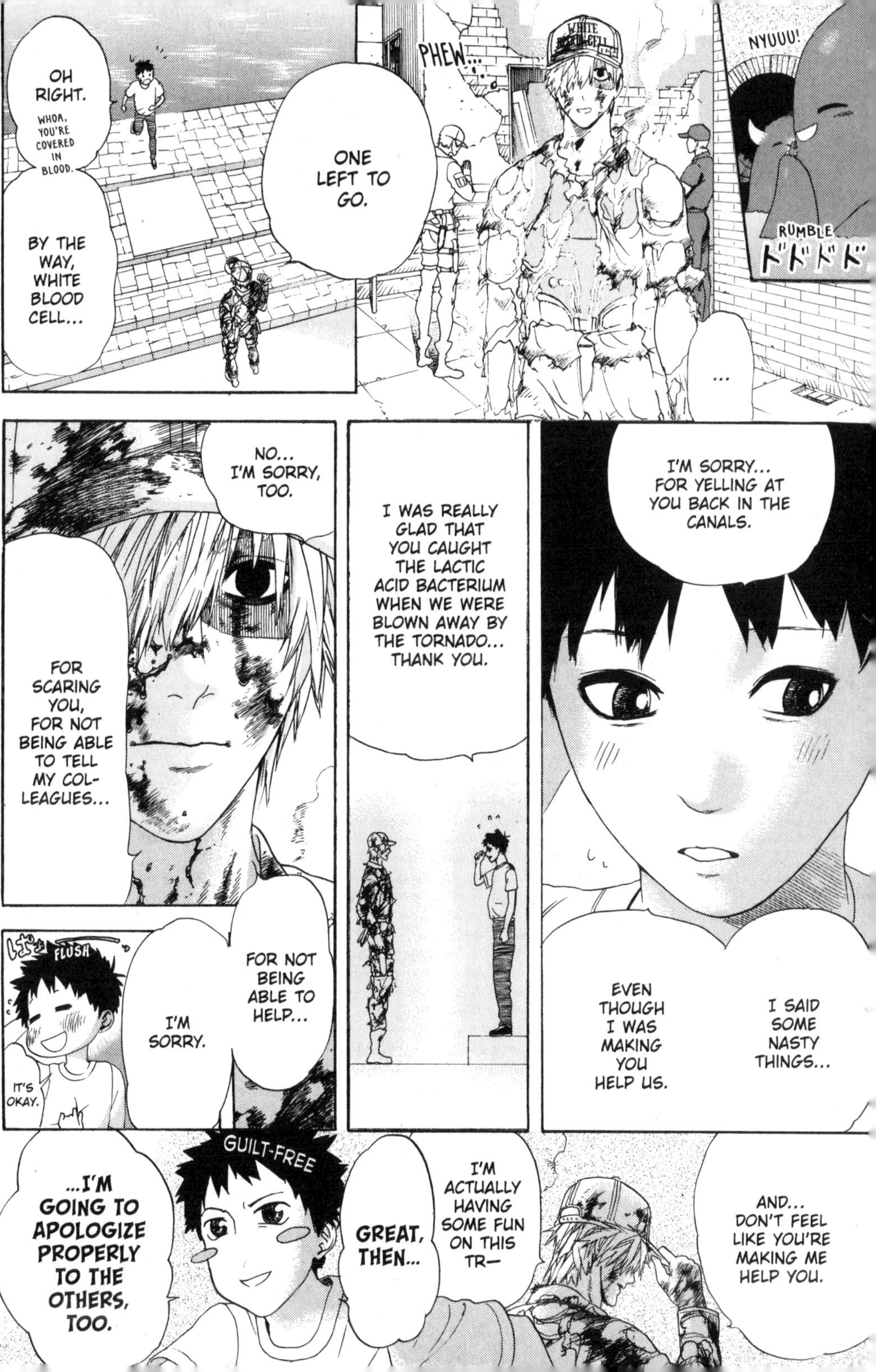
NYUUU!
RUMBLE
ドドドド
PHEW...
ONE LEFT TO GO.
...
OH RIGHT.
WHOA, YOU'RE COVERED IN BLOOD.
BY THE WAY, WHITE BLOOD CELL...
I'M SORRY... FOR YELLING AT YOU BACK IN THE CANALS.
I SAID SOME NASTY THINGS...
EVEN THOUGH I WAS MAKING YOU HELP US.
I WAS REALLY GLAD THAT YOU CAUGHT THE LACTIC ACID BACTERIUM WHEN WE WERE BLOWN AWAY BY THE TORNADO... THANK YOU.
NO... I'M SORRY, TOO.
FOR SCARING YOU, FOR NOT BEING ABLE TO TELL MY COL-LEAGUES...
FOR NOT BEING ABLE TO HELP...
I'M SORRY.
FLUSH
IT'S OKAY.
AND... DON'T FEEL LIKE YOU'RE MAKING ME HELP YOU.
I'M ACTUALLY HAVING SOME FUN ON THIS TR—
GREAT, THEN...
GUILT-FREE
...I'M GOING TO APOLOGIZE PROPERLY TO THE OTHERS, TOO.

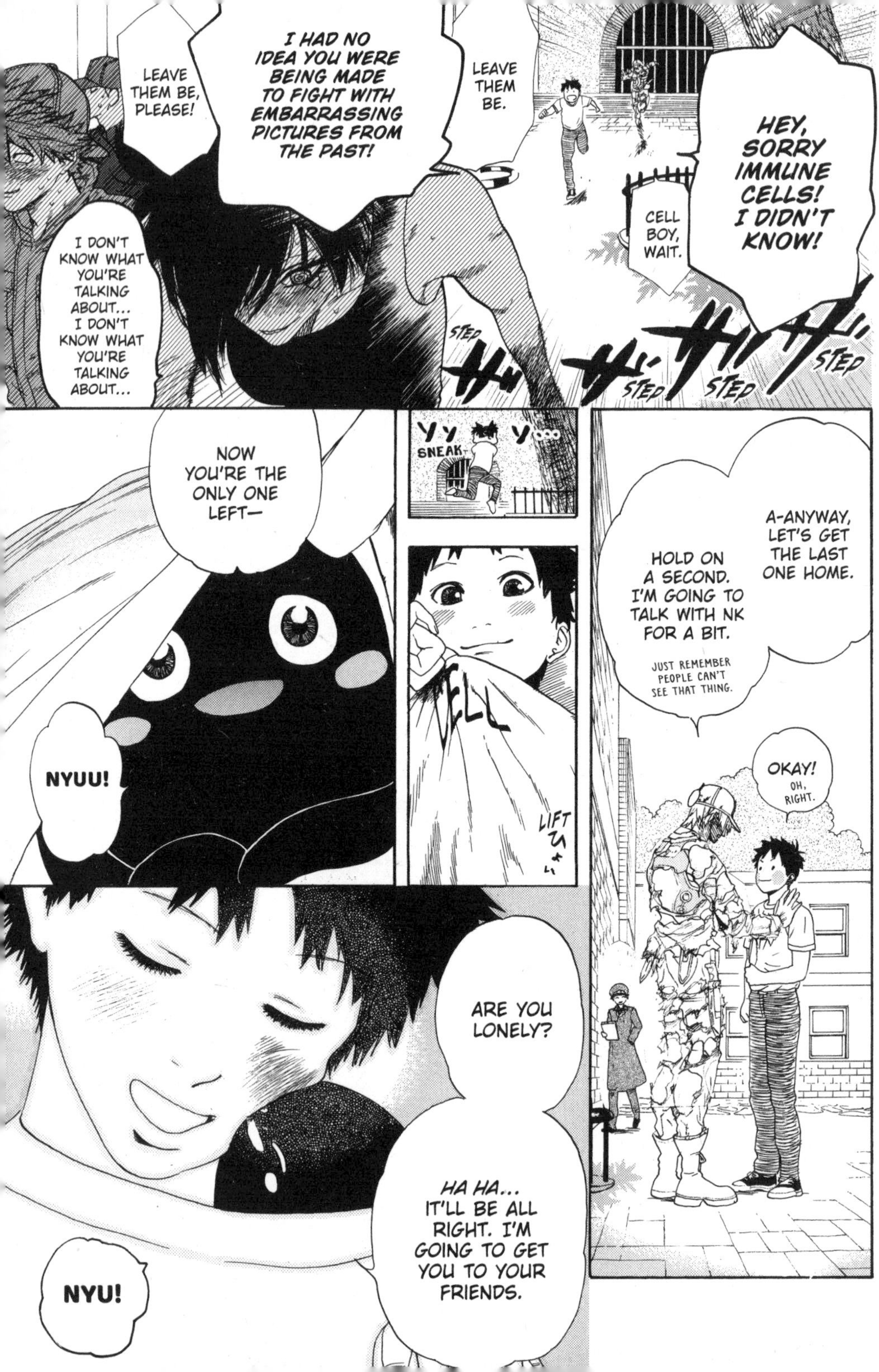
HEY, SORRY IMMUNE CELLS! I DIDN'T KNOW!
CELL BOY, WAIT.
LEAVE THEM BE.
I HAD NO IDEA YOU WERE BEING MADE TO FIGHT WITH EMBARRASSING PICTURES FROM THE PAST!
LEAVE THEM BE, PLEASE!
I DON'T KNOW WHAT YOU'RE TALKING ABOUT... I DON'T KNOW WHAT YOU'RE TALKING ABOUT...
STEP STEP STEP STEP STEP
A-ANYWAY, LET'S GET THE LAST ONE HOME.
HOLD ON A SECOND. I'M GOING TO TALK WITH NK FOR A BIT.
JUST REMEMBER PEOPLE CAN'T SEE THAT THING.
OKAY!
OH, RIGHT.
SNEAK
LIFT
NOW YOU'RE THE ONLY ONE LEFT—
NYUU!
ARE YOU LONELY?
HA HA... IT'LL BE ALL RIGHT. I'M GOING TO GET YOU TO YOUR FRIENDS.
NYU!

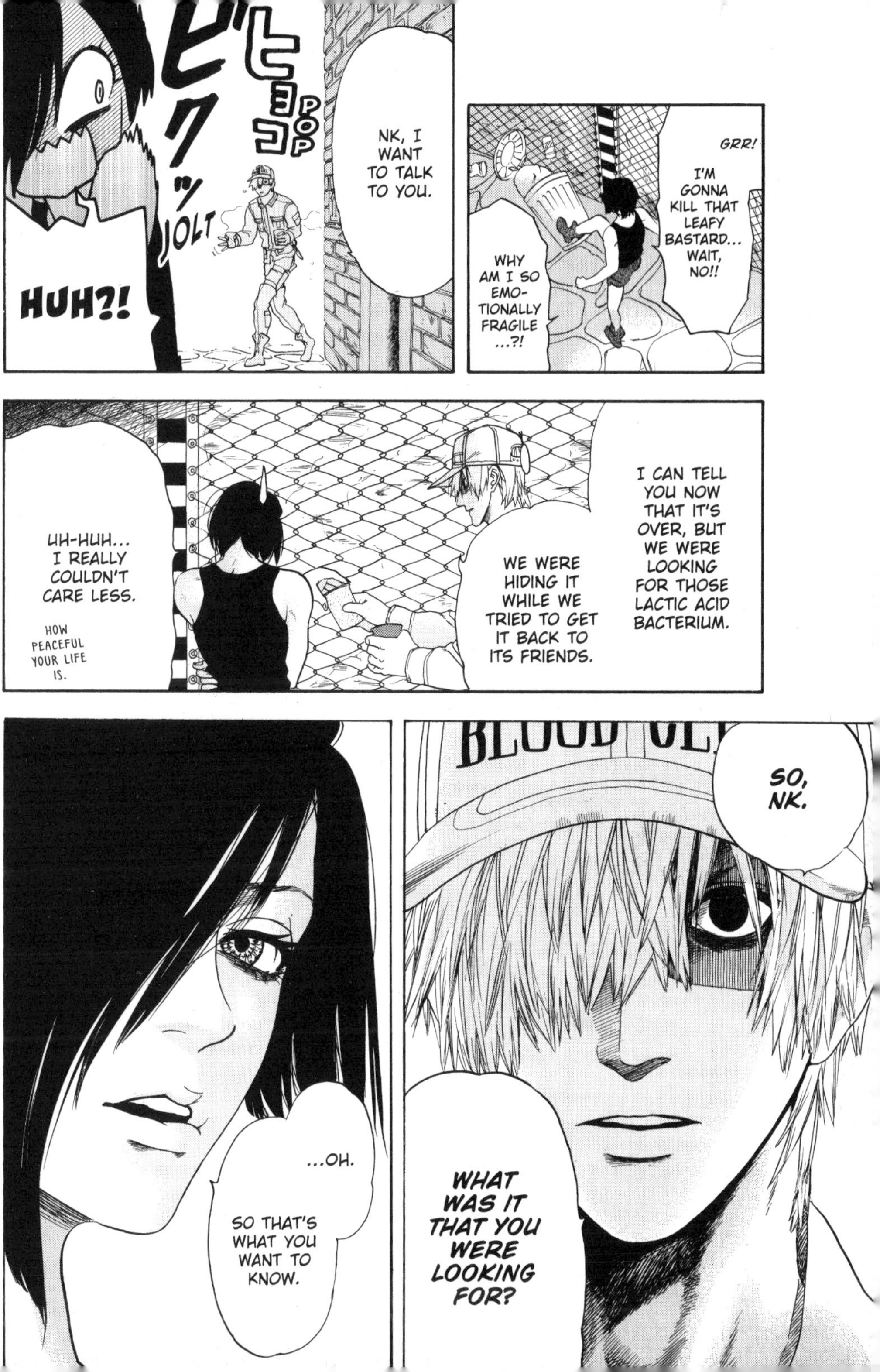

GRR!
I'M GONNA KILL THAT LEAFY BASTARD... WAIT, NO!!
WHY AM I SO EMOTIONALLY FRAGILE ...?!
NK, I WANT TO TALK TO YOU.
ピョコ
POP
ビクッ
JOLT
HUH?!
I CAN TELL YOU NOW THAT IT'S OVER, BUT WE WERE LOOKING FOR THOSE LACTIC ACID BACTERIUM.
WE WERE HIDING IT WHILE WE TRIED TO GET IT BACK TO ITS FRIENDS.
UH-HUH... I REALLY COULDN'T CARE LESS.
HOW PEACEFUL YOUR LIFE IS.
SO, NK.
WHAT WAS IT THAT YOU WERE LOOKING FOR?
...OH.
SO THAT'S WHAT YOU WANT TO KNOW.

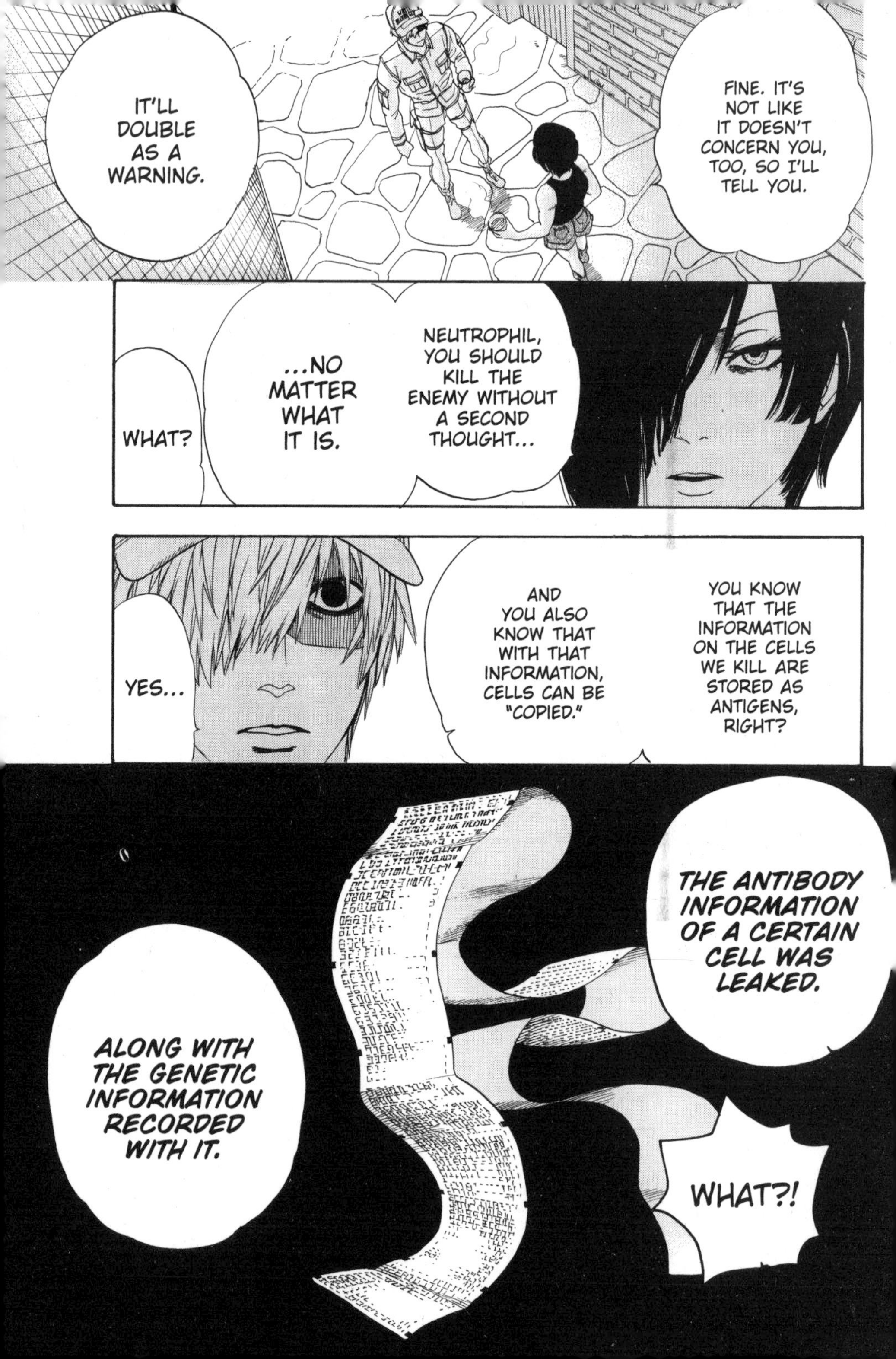
FINE. IT'S NOT LIKE IT DOESN'T CONCERN YOU, TOO, SO I'LL TELL YOU.
IT'LL DOUBLE AS A WARNING.
NEUTROPHIL, YOU SHOULD KILL THE ENEMY WITHOUT A SECOND THOUGHT...
...NO MATTER WHAT IT IS.
WHAT?
YOU KNOW THAT THE INFORMATION ON THE CELLS WE KILL ARE STORED AS ANTIGENS, RIGHT?
AND YOU ALSO KNOW THAT WITH THAT INFORMATION, CELLS CAN BE "COPIED."
YES...
THE ANTIBODY INFORMATION OF A CERTAIN CELL WAS LEAKED.
ALONG WITH THE GENETIC INFORMATION RECORDED WITH IT.
WHAT?!

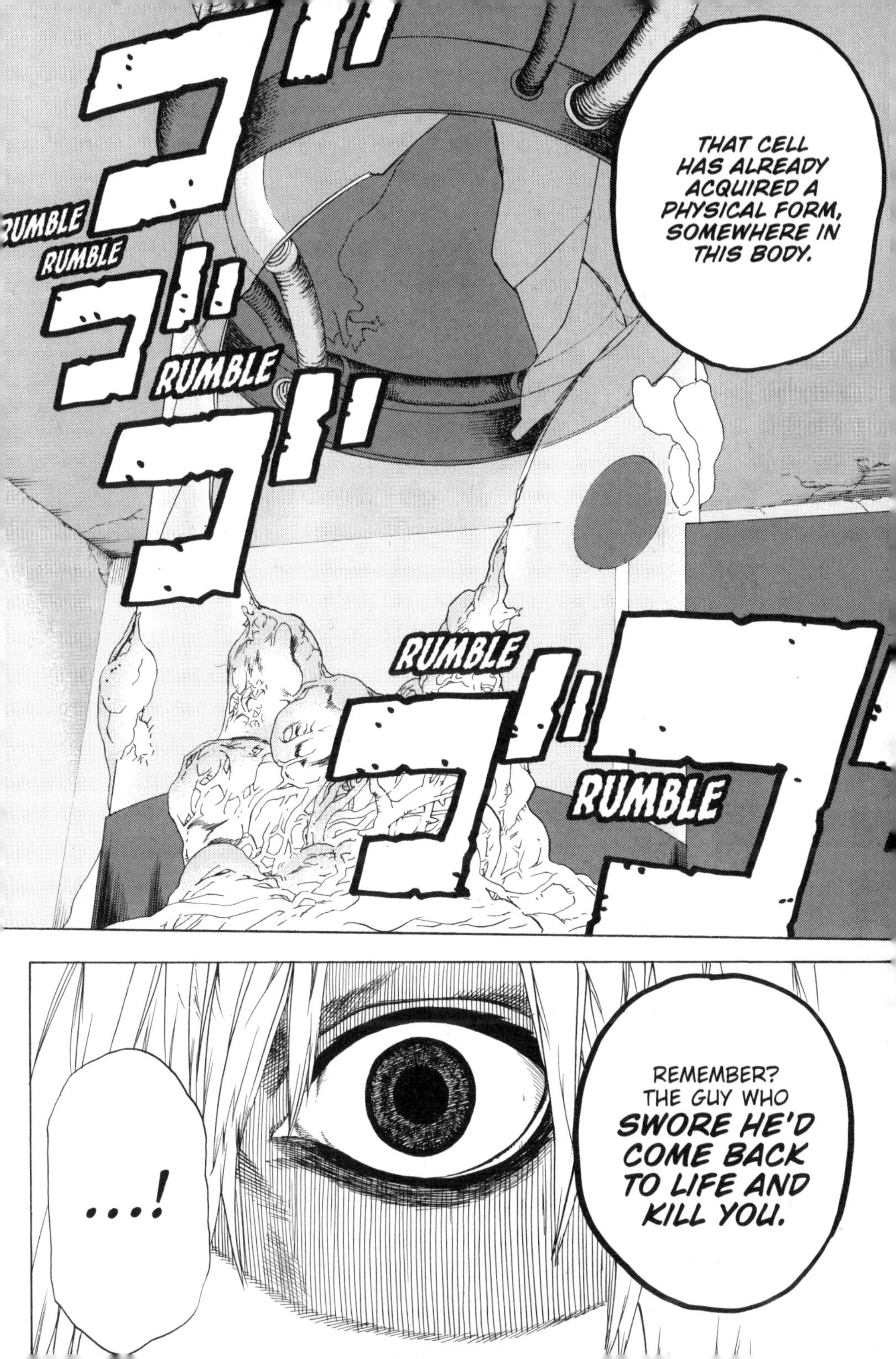
THAT CELL HAS ALREADY ACQUIRED A PHYSICAL FORM, SOMEWHERE IN THIS BODY.
RUMBLE
RUMBLE
RUMBLE
RUMBLE
RUMBLE
REMEMBER? THE GUY WHO SWORE HE'D COME BACK TO LIFE AND KILL YOU.
...!

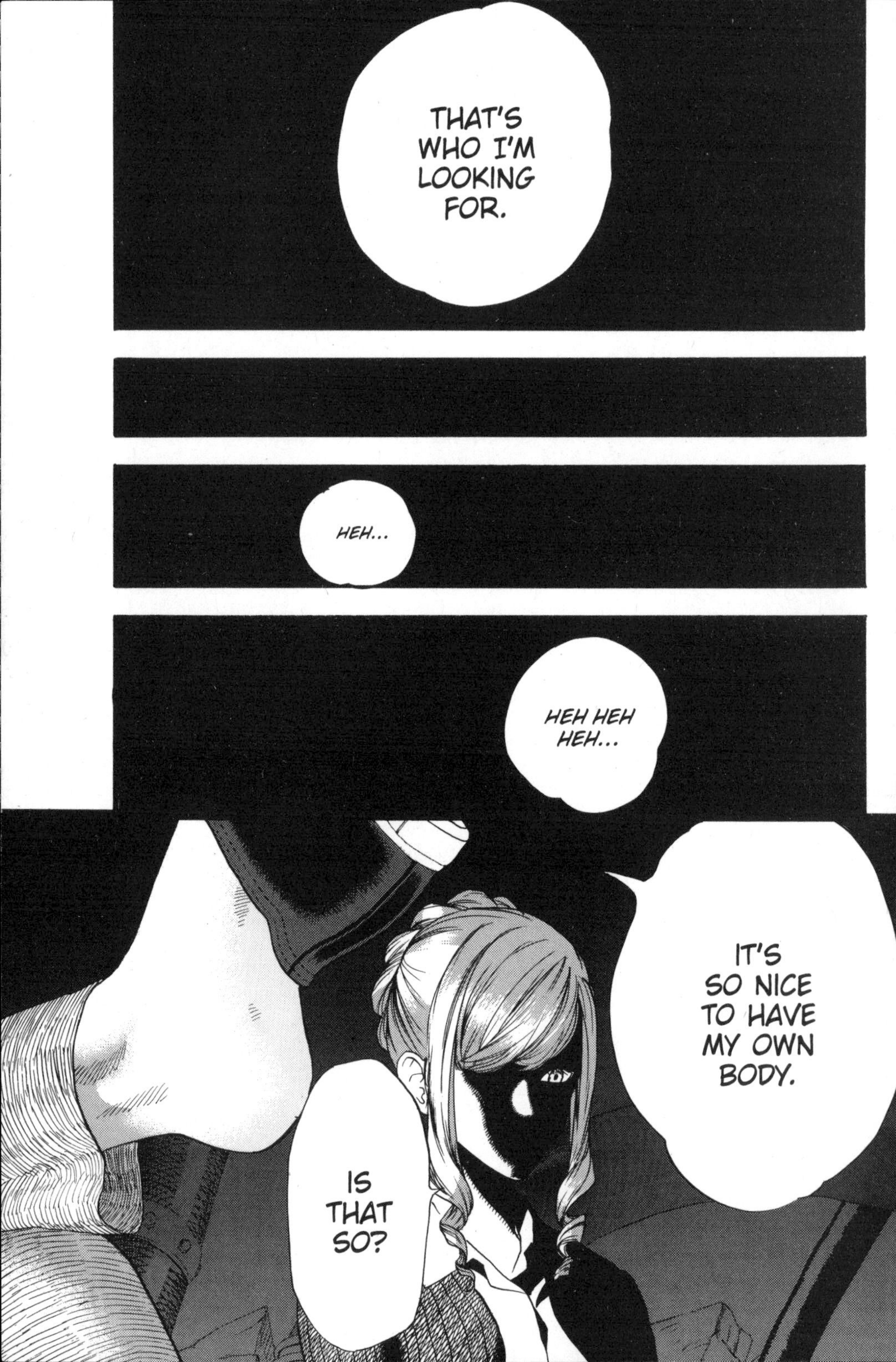
THAT'S WHO I'M LOOKING FOR.
HEH...
HEH HEH HEH...
IT'S SO NICE TO HAVE MY OWN BODY.
IS THAT SO?

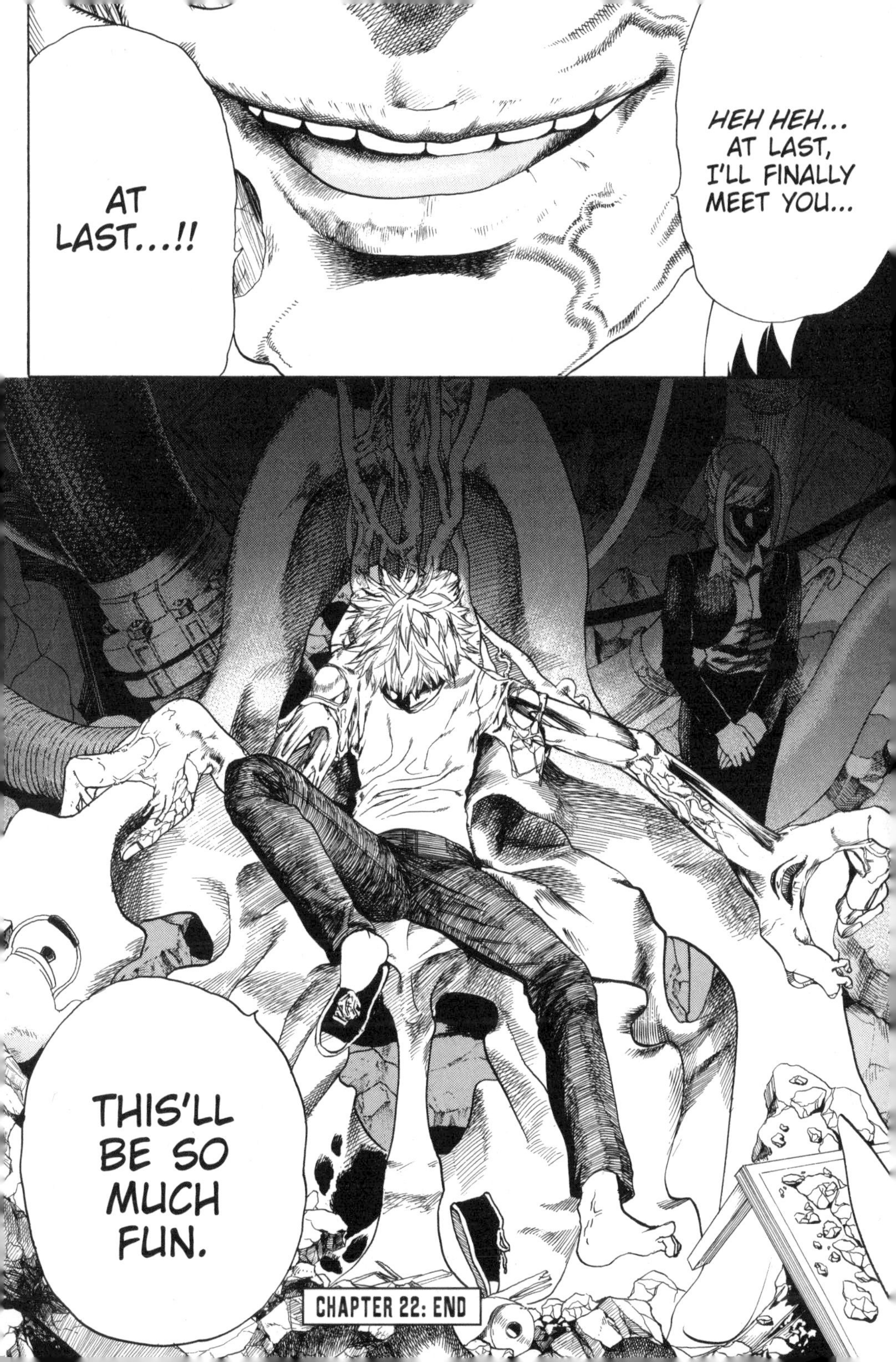
HEH HEH... AT LAST, I'LL FINALLY MEET YOU...
AT LAST...!!
THIS'LL BE SO MUCH FUN.
CHAPTER 22: END

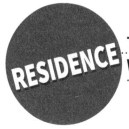
RESIDENCE

The Life and Work of White Blood Cell (Neutrophil):
Where He Lives
* These are depictions created just for this comic, and differ from scientific fact.

Even though neutrophils patrol the body at all hours, there are places where they can rest. They live in the circulating and marginating pools in the blood vessels.

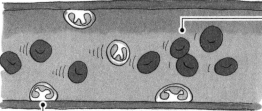

Circulating pools flow in the middle of the blood vessel.

Marginating pools stick to the vessel walls or flow slowly.

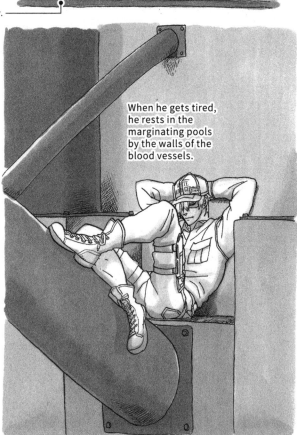

When he gets tired, he rests in the marginating pools by the walls of the blood vessels.

はたらく細胞

Cells at Work!

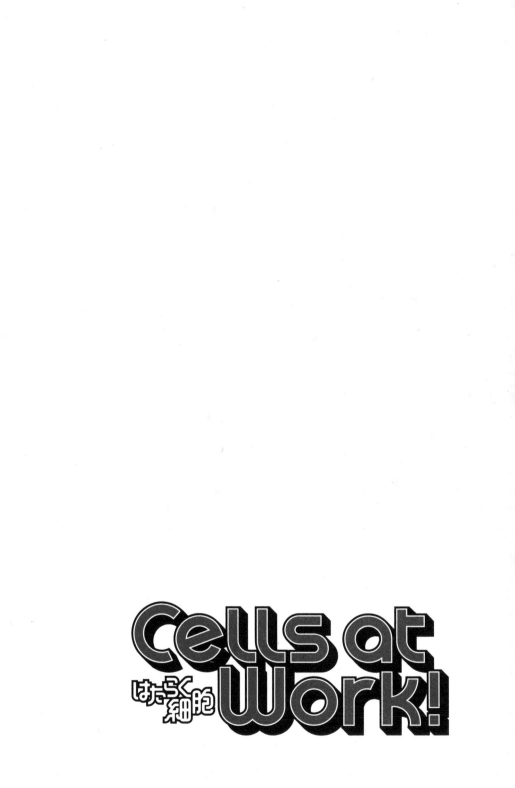

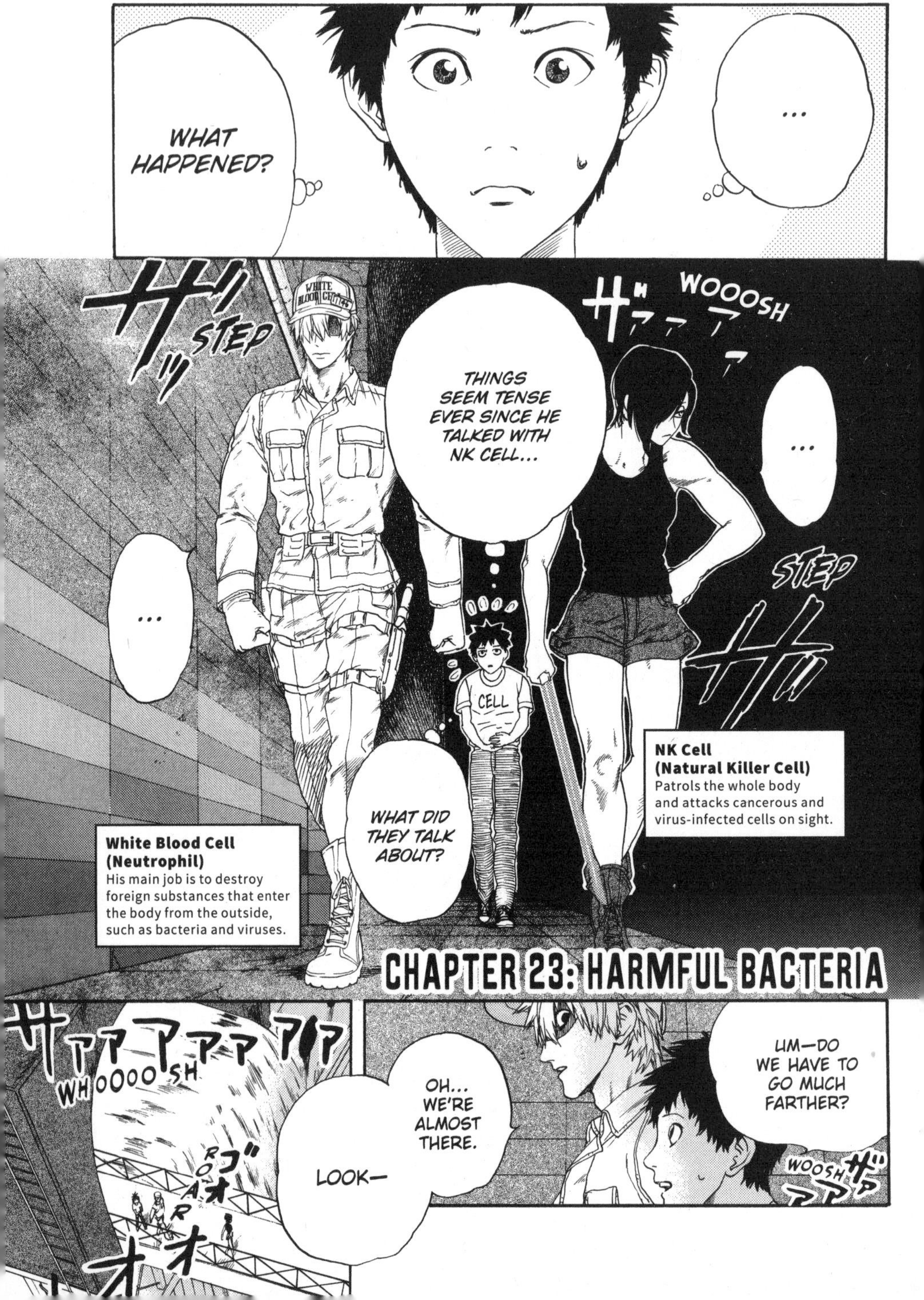
...
WHAT HAPPENED?
WOOOSH
...
THINGS SEEM TENSE EVER SINCE HE TALKED WITH NK CELL...
STEP
NK Cell (Natural Killer Cell)
Patrols the whole body and attacks cancerous and virus-infected cells on sight.
STEP
...
WHAT DID THEY TALK ABOUT?
White Blood Cell (Neutrophil)
His main job is to destroy foreign substances that enter the body from the outside, such as bacteria and viruses.
CHAPTER 23: HARMFUL BACTERIA
UM—DO WE HAVE TO GO MUCH FARTHER?
WOOSH
OH... WE'RE ALMOST THERE.
LOOK—
WHOOOOSH
ROAR

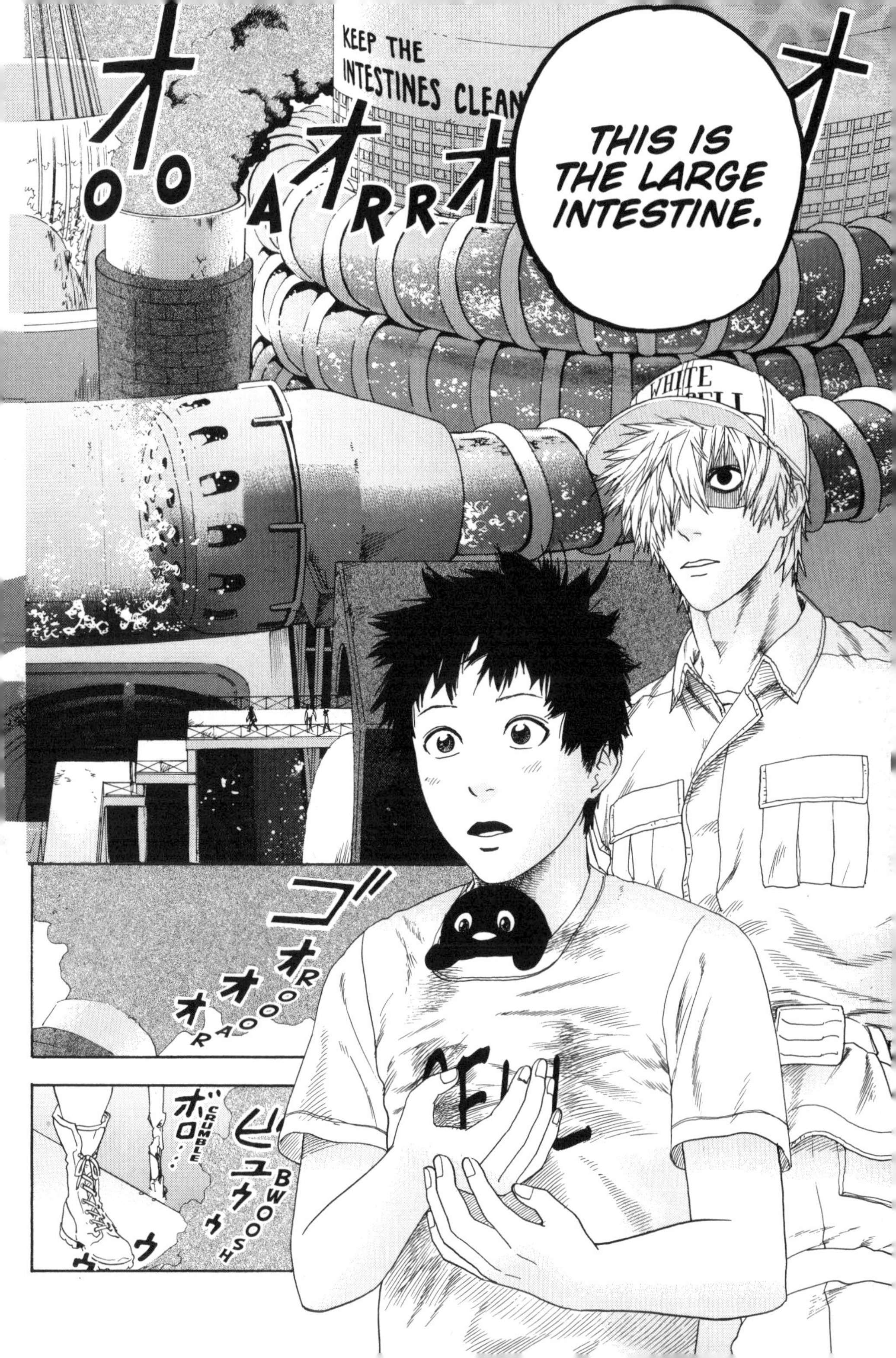
KEEP THE INTESTINES CLEAN
OOARR
THIS IS THE LARGE INTESTINE.
ROOOAR
CRUMBLE
BWOOSH

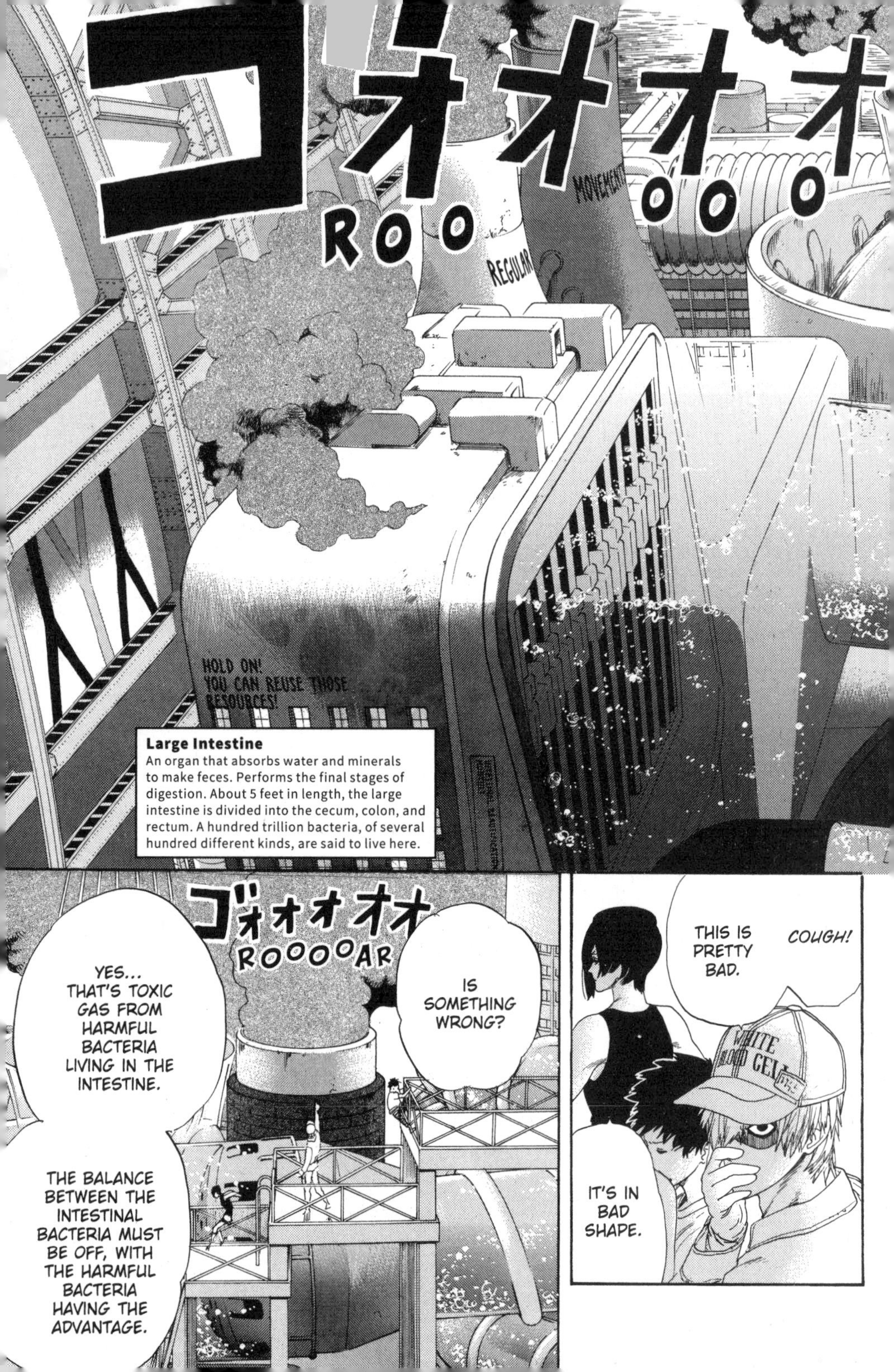

コオオオオ
ROOOOO
MOVEMENT
REGULAR
HOLD ON! YOU CAN REUSE THOSE RESOURCES!
Large Intestine
An organ that absorbs water and minerals to make feces. Performs the final stages of digestion. About 5 feet in length, the large intestine is divided into the cecum, colon, and rectum. A hundred trillion bacteria, of several hundred different kinds, are said to live here.
COUGH!
THIS IS PRETTY BAD.
IT'S IN BAD SHAPE.
ゴォオオオオ
ROOOOAR
IS SOMETHING WRONG?
YES... THAT'S TOXIC GAS FROM HARMFUL BACTERIA LIVING IN THE INTESTINE.
THE BALANCE BETWEEN THE INTESTINAL BACTERIA MUST BE OFF, WITH THE HARMFUL BACTERIA HAVING THE ADVANTAGE.

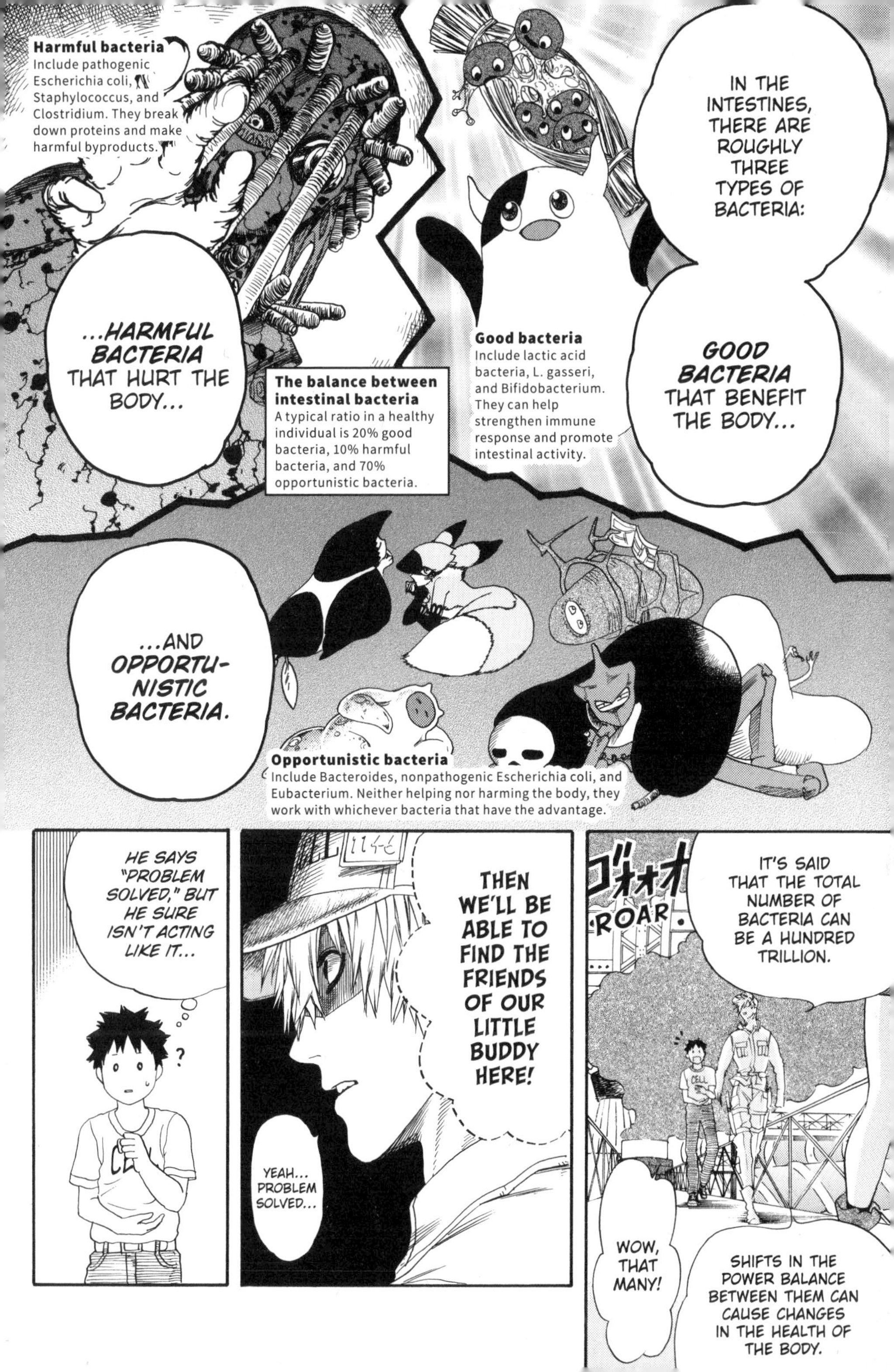
IN THE INTESTINES, THERE ARE ROUGHLY THREE TYPES OF BACTERIA:
GOOD BACTERIA THAT BENEFIT THE BODY...
Good bacteria
Include lactic acid bacteria, L. gasseri, and Bifidobacterium. They can help strengthen immune response and promote intestinal activity.
...HARMFUL BACTERIA THAT HURT THE BODY...
Harmful bacteria
Include pathogenic Escherichia coli, Staphylococcus, and Clostridium. They break down proteins and make harmful byproducts.
The balance between intestinal bacteria
A typical ratio in a healthy individual is 20% good bacteria, 10% harmful bacteria, and 70% opportunistic bacteria.
...AND OPPORTUNISTIC BACTERIA.
Opportunistic bacteria
Include Bacteroides, nonpathogenic Escherichia coli, and Eubacterium. Neither helping nor harming the body, they work with whichever bacteria that have the advantage.
ゴォオオ
ROAR
IT'S SAID THAT THE TOTAL NUMBER OF BACTERIA CAN BE A HUNDRED TRILLION.
SHIFTS IN THE POWER BALANCE BETWEEN THEM CAN CAUSE CHANGES IN THE HEALTH OF THE BODY.
WOW, THAT MANY!
THEN WE'LL BE ABLE TO FIND THE FRIENDS OF OUR LITTLE BUDDY HERE!
YEAH... PROBLEM SOLVED...
HE SAYS "PROBLEM SOLVED," BUT HE SURE ISN'T ACTING LIKE IT...
?

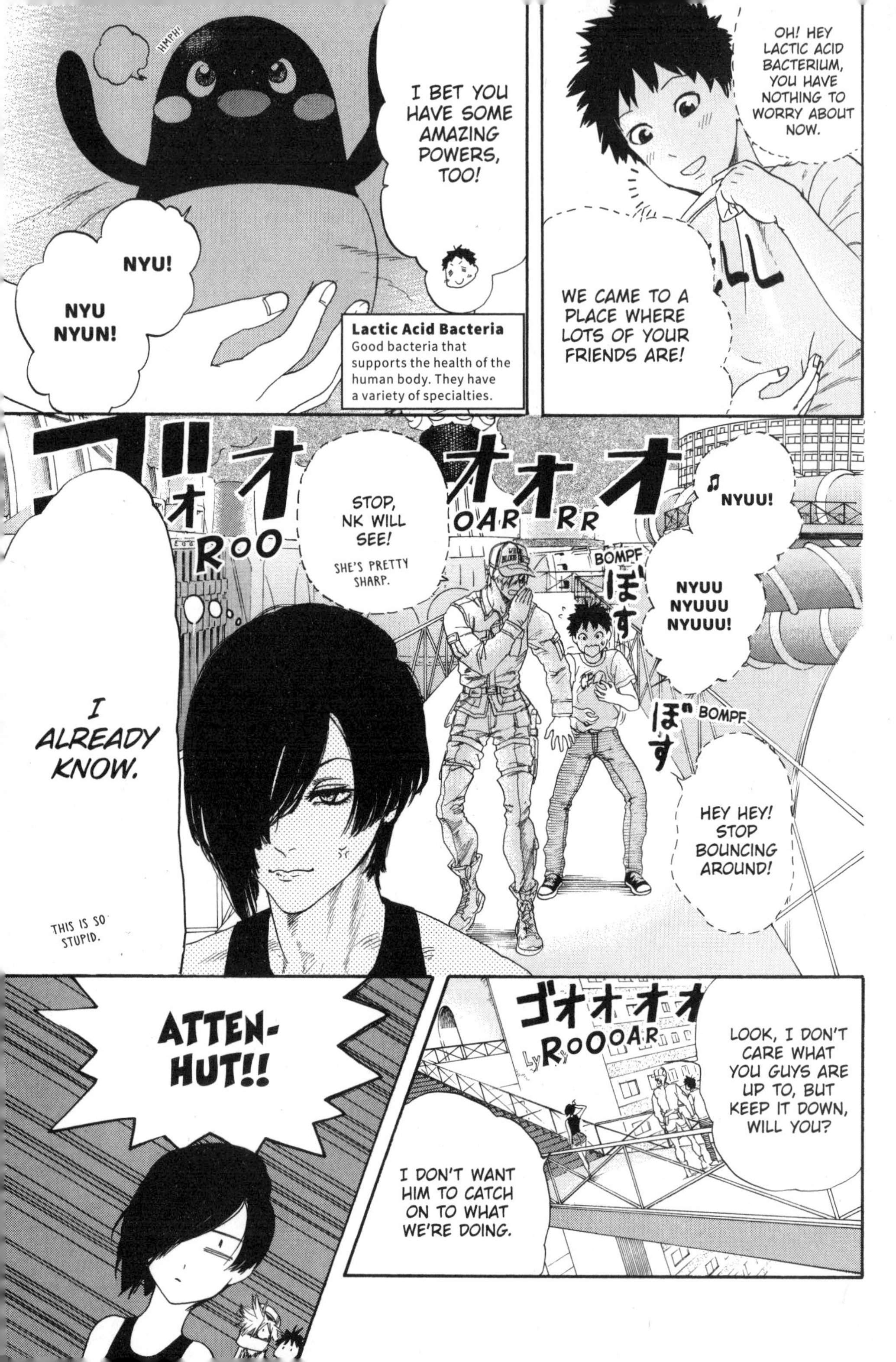
OH! HEY LACTIC ACID BACTERIUM, YOU HAVE NOTHING TO WORRY ABOUT NOW.
WE CAME TO A PLACE WHERE LOTS OF YOUR FRIENDS ARE!
I BET YOU HAVE SOME AMAZING POWERS, TOO!
HMPH!
NYU!
NYU NYUN!
Lactic Acid Bacteria
Good bacteria that supports the health of the human body. They have a variety of specialties.
ゴオオオオ
ROOOARRR
♪ NYUU!
NYUU NYUUU NYUUU!
ぼす
BOMPF
ぼす
BOMPF
HEY HEY! STOP BOUNCING AROUND!
STOP, NK WILL SEE!
SHE'S PRETTY SHARP.
I ALREADY KNOW.
THIS IS SO STUPID.
ゴオオオオ
ROOOAR
LOOK, I DON'T CARE WHAT YOU GUYS ARE UP TO, BUT KEEP IT DOWN, WILL YOU?
I DON'T WANT HIM TO CATCH ON TO WHAT WE'RE DOING.
ATTEN-HUT!!

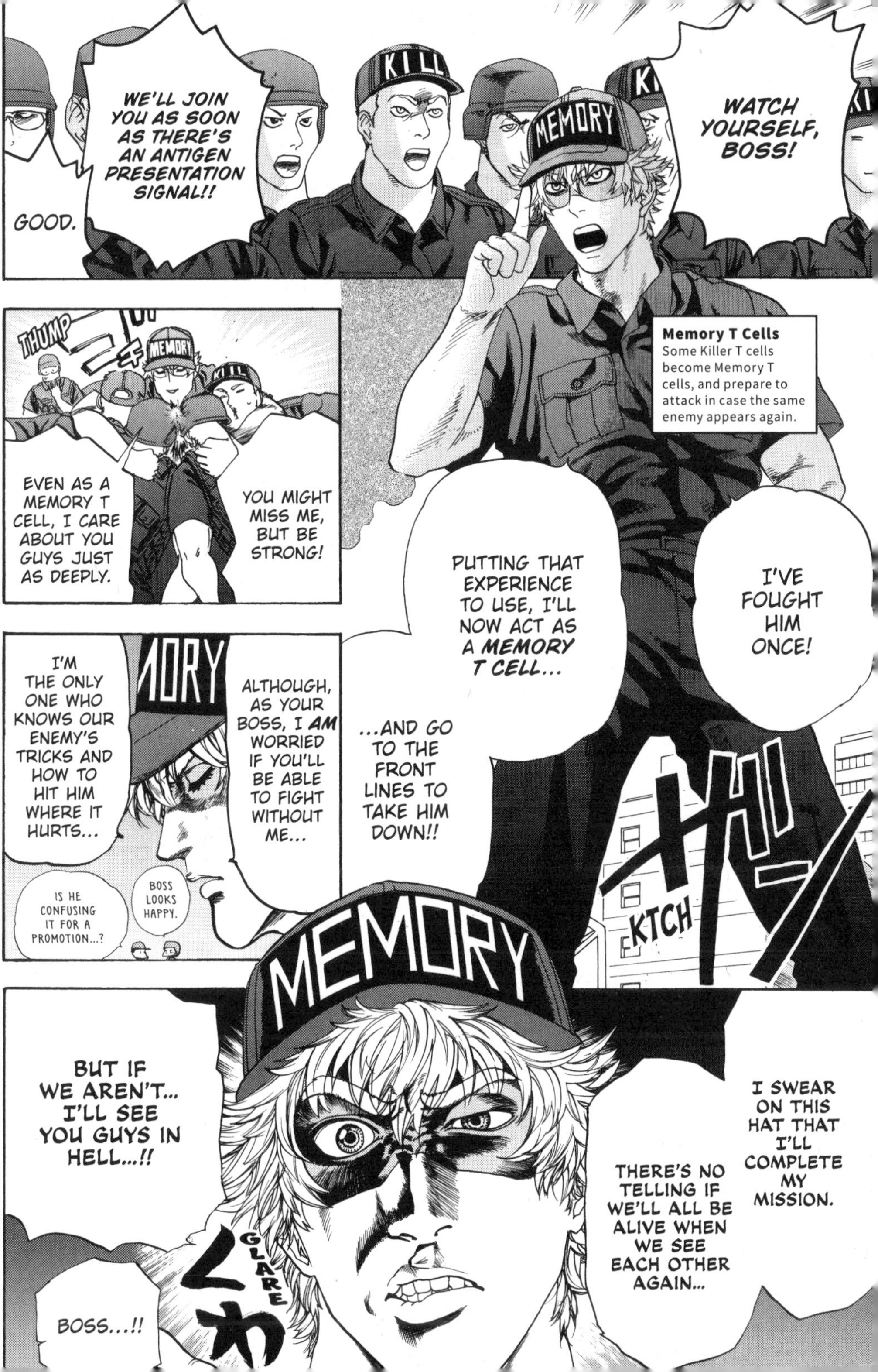
WATCH YOURSELF, BOSS!
WE'LL JOIN YOU AS SOON AS THERE'S AN ANTIGEN PRESENTATION SIGNAL!!
GOOD.
Memory T Cells
Some Killer T cells become Memory T cells, and prepare to attack in case the same enemy appears again.
I'VE FOUGHT HIM ONCE!
PUTTING THAT EXPERIENCE TO USE, I'LL NOW ACT AS A *MEMORY T CELL*...
...AND GO TO THE FRONT LINES TO TAKE HIM DOWN!!
KTCH
THUMP
YOU MIGHT MISS ME, BUT BE STRONG!
EVEN AS A MEMORY T CELL, I CARE ABOUT YOU GUYS JUST AS DEEPLY.
ALTHOUGH, AS YOUR BOSS, I *AM* WORRIED IF YOU'LL BE ABLE TO FIGHT WITHOUT ME...
I'M THE ONLY ONE WHO KNOWS OUR ENEMY'S TRICKS AND HOW TO HIT HIM WHERE IT HURTS...
BOSS LOOKS HAPPY.
IS HE CONFUSING IT FOR A PROMOTION...?
I SWEAR ON THIS HAT THAT I'LL COMPLETE MY MISSION.
THERE'S NO TELLING IF WE'LL ALL BE ALIVE WHEN WE SEE EACH OTHER AGAIN...
BUT IF WE AREN'T... I'LL SEE YOU GUYS IN HELL...!!
GLARE
BOSS...!!

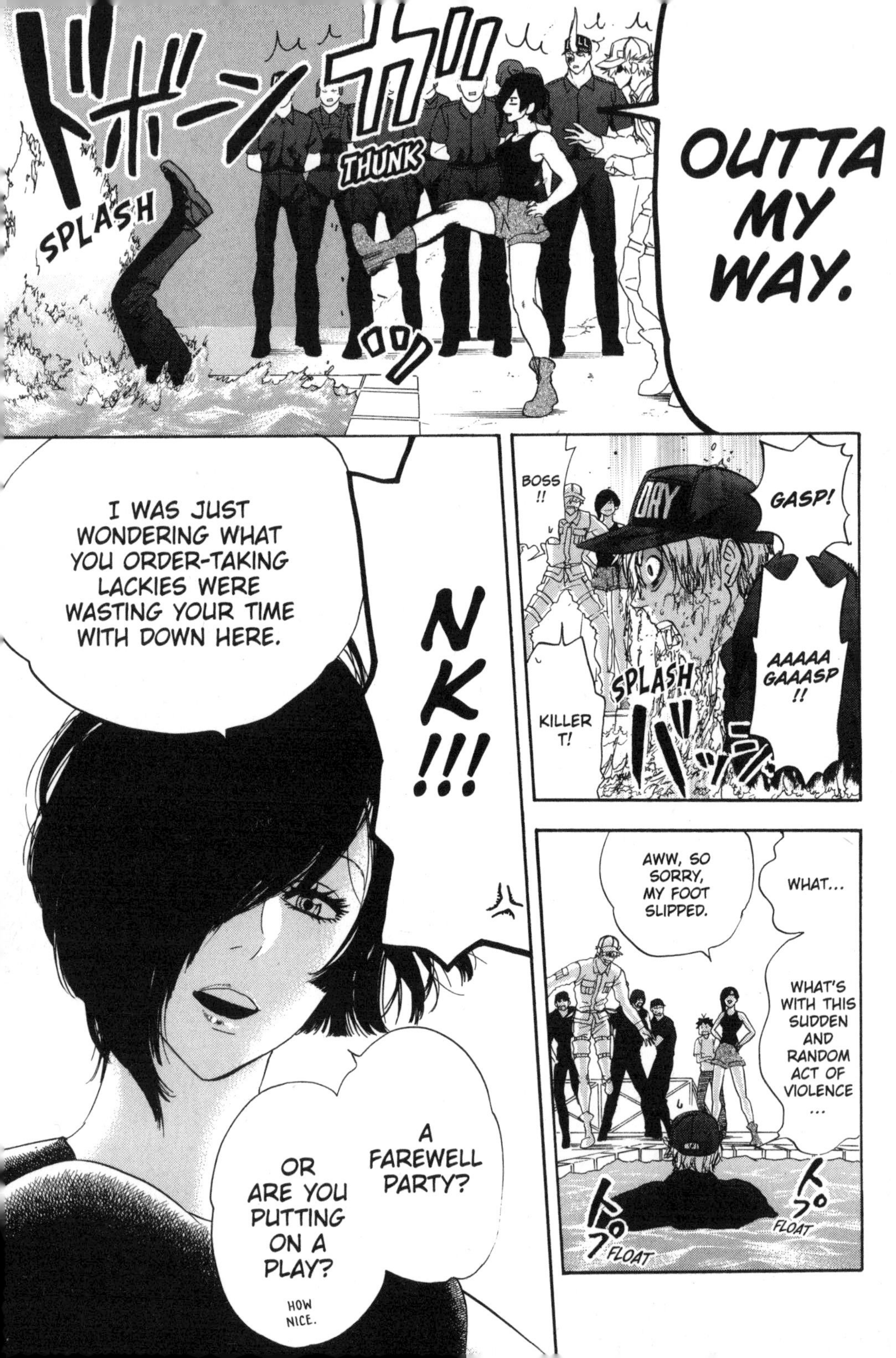
OUTTA MY WAY.
ガッ
THUNK
ドボーン
SPLASH
GASP!
AAAAA GAAASP !!
BOSS !!
KILLER T!
SPLASH
WHAT...
AWW, SO SORRY, MY FOOT SLIPPED.
WHAT'S WITH THIS SUDDEN AND RANDOM ACT OF VIOLENCE ...
FLOAT
FLOAT
NK!!!
I WAS JUST WONDERING WHAT YOU ORDER-TAKING LACKIES WERE WASTING YOUR TIME WITH DOWN HERE.
A FAREWELL PARTY?
OR ARE YOU PUTTING ON A PLAY?
HOW NICE.

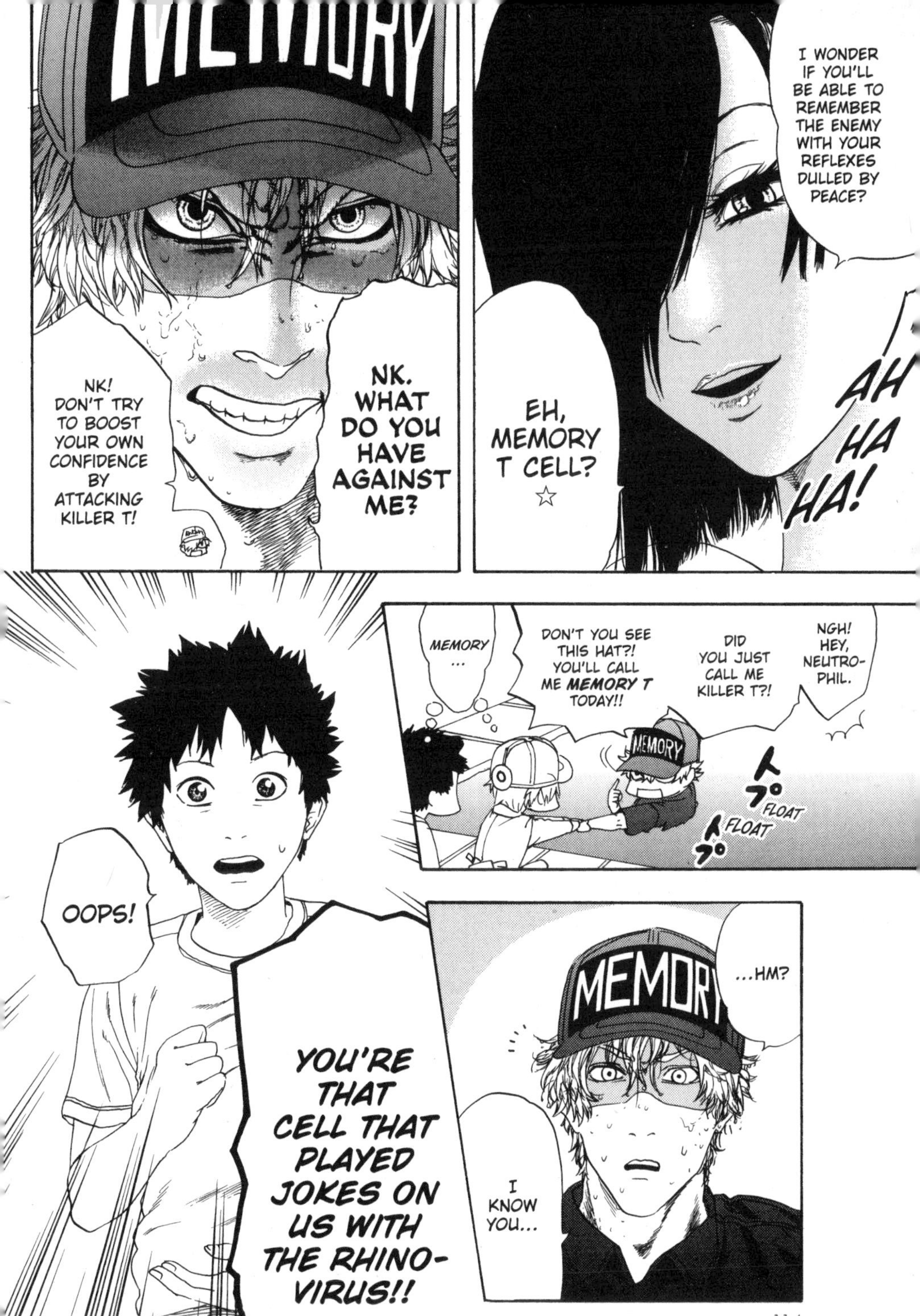
I WONDER IF YOU'LL BE ABLE TO REMEMBER THE ENEMY WITH YOUR REFLEXES DULLED BY PEACE?
EH, MEMORY T CELL? ☆
AH HA HA!
NK. WHAT DO YOU HAVE AGAINST ME?
NK! DON'T TRY TO BOOST YOUR OWN CONFIDENCE BY ATTACKING KILLER T!
NGH! HEY, NEUTROPHIL.
DID YOU JUST CALL ME KILLER T?!
DON'T YOU SEE THIS HAT?! YOU'LL CALL ME MEMORY T TODAY!!
MEMORY ...
MEMORY
FLOAT
FLOAT
...HM?
MEMORY
I KNOW YOU...
OOPS!
YOU'RE THAT CELL THAT PLAYED JOKES ON US WITH THE RHINO-VIRUS!!

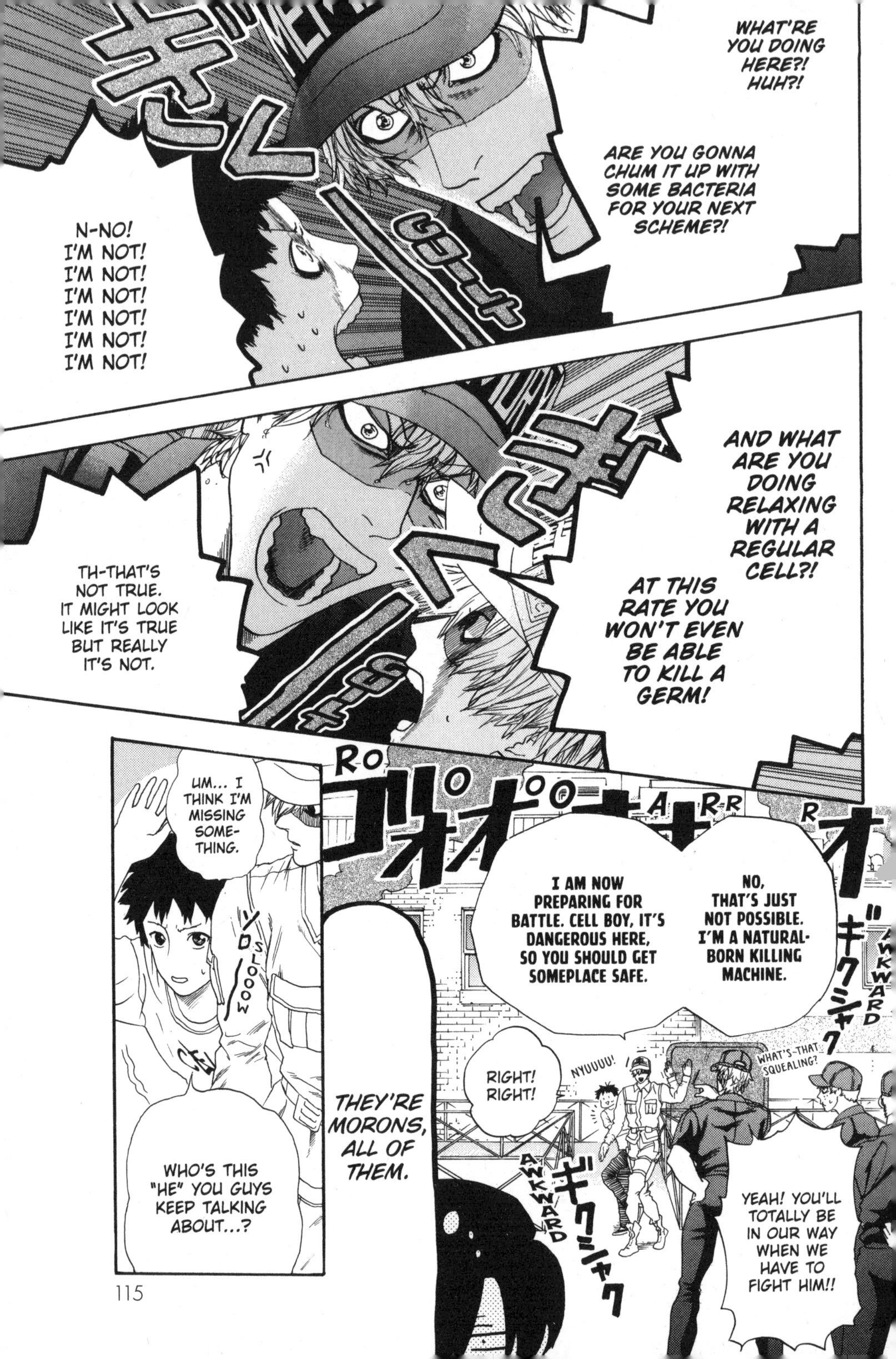
WHAT'RE YOU DOING HERE?! HUH?!
ARE YOU GONNA CHUM IT UP WITH SOME BACTERIA FOR YOUR NEXT SCHEME?!
N-NO! I'M NOT! I'M NOT! I'M NOT! I'M NOT! I'M NOT! I'M NOT!
AND WHAT ARE YOU DOING RELAXING WITH A REGULAR CELL?!
AT THIS RATE YOU WON'T EVEN BE ABLE TO KILL A GERM!
TH-THAT'S NOT TRUE. IT MIGHT LOOK LIKE IT'S TRUE BUT REALLY IT'S NOT.
RO-O-O-A-R-R-R
NO, THAT'S JUST NOT POSSIBLE. I'M A NATURAL-BORN KILLING MACHINE.
I AM NOW PREPARING FOR BATTLE. CELL BOY, IT'S DANGEROUS HERE, SO YOU SHOULD GET SOMEPLACE SAFE.
AWKWARD
WHAT'S THAT SQUEALING?
NYUUUU!
RIGHT! RIGHT!
YEAH! YOU'LL TOTALLY BE IN OUR WAY WHEN WE HAVE TO FIGHT HIM!!
AWKWARD
THEY'RE MORONS, ALL OF THEM.
UM... I THINK I'M MISSING SOME-THING.
SLOOOOW
WHO'S THIS "HE" YOU GUYS KEEP TALKING ABOUT...?

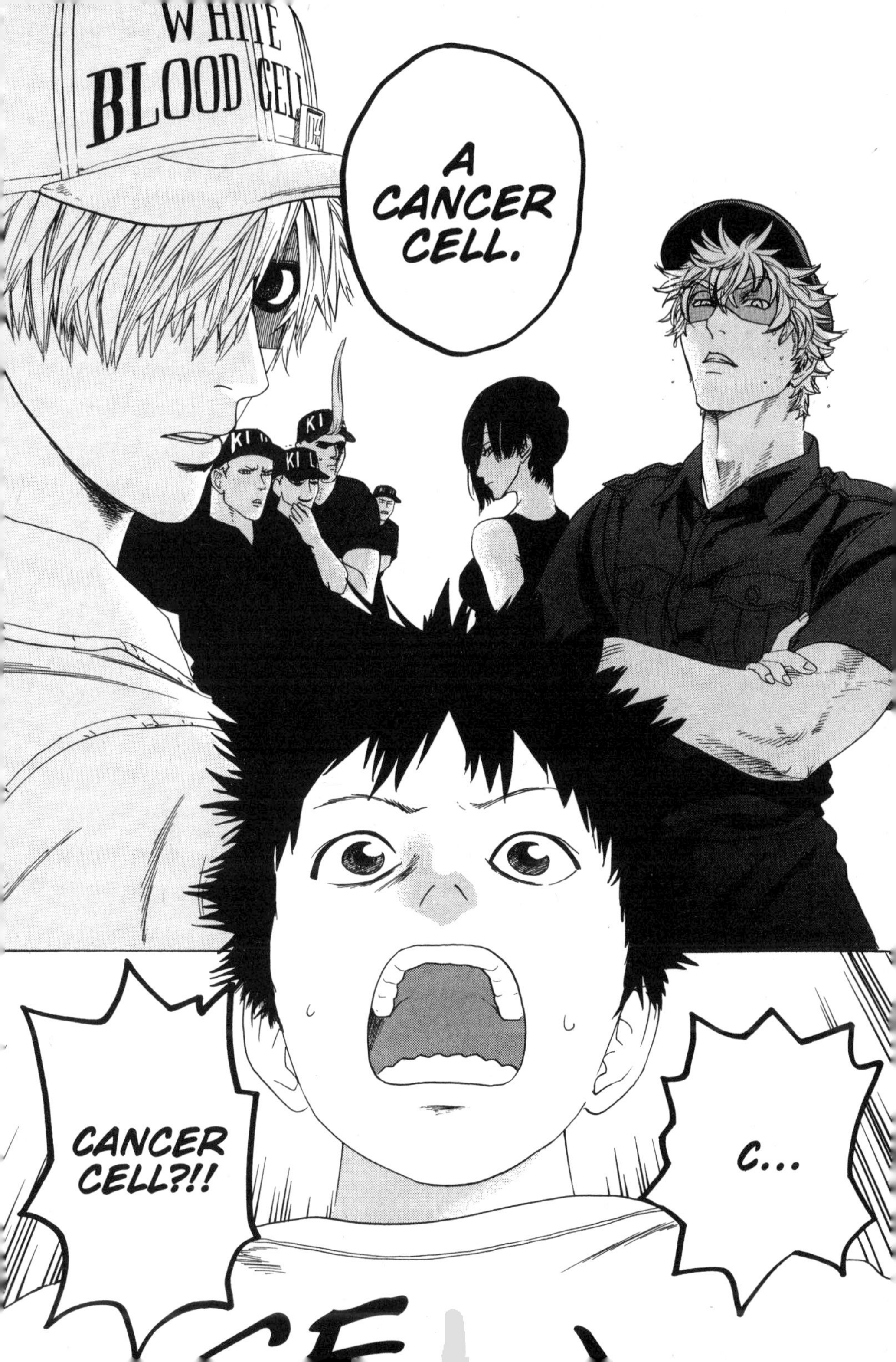
A CANCER CELL.
WHITE BLOOD CELL
C...
CANCER CELL?!!

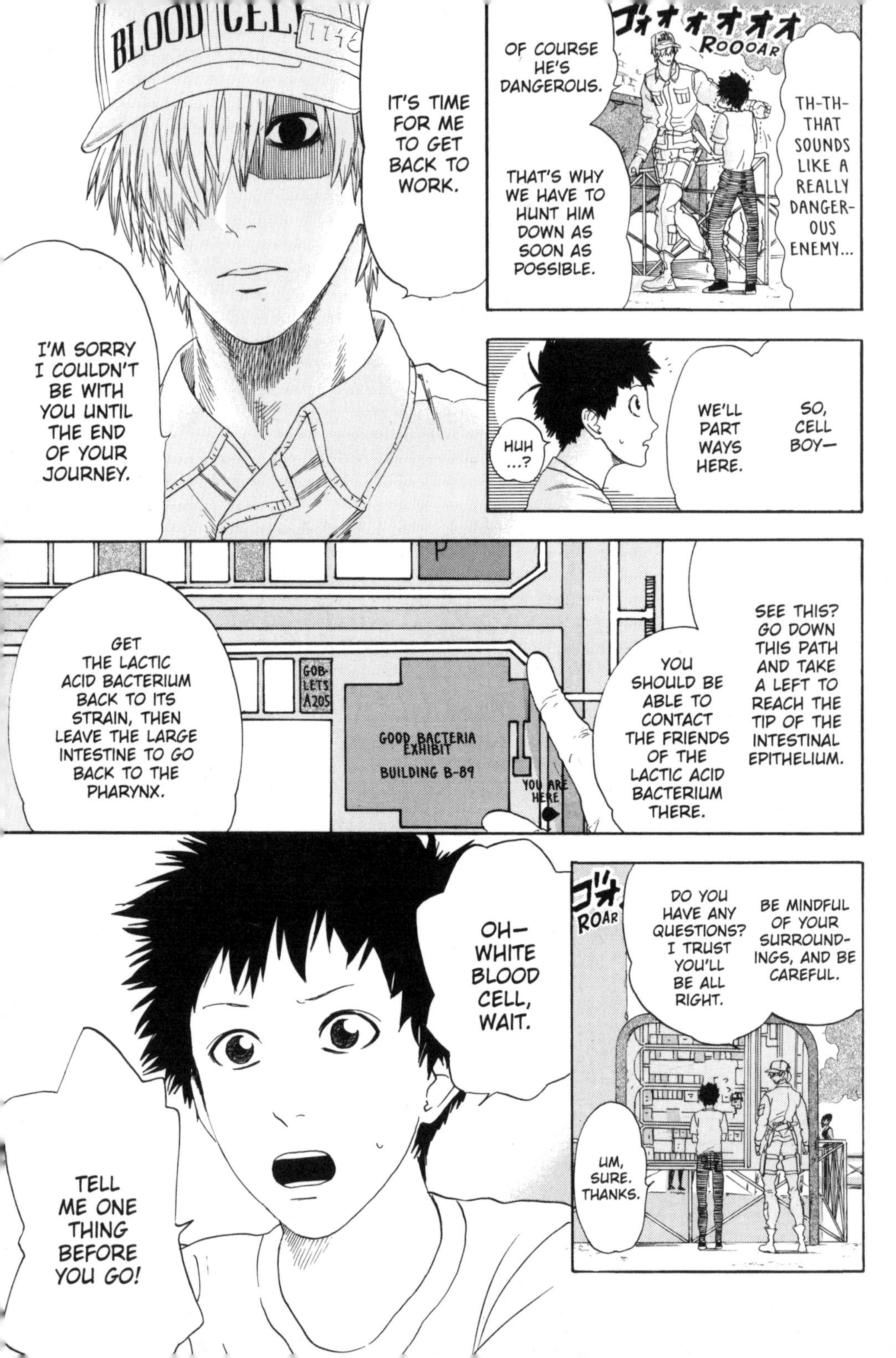
ゴォォオオオ ROOOAR
TH-TH-THAT SOUNDS LIKE A REALLY DANGER-OUS ENEMY...
OF COURSE HE'S DANGEROUS.
THAT'S WHY WE HAVE TO HUNT HIM DOWN AS SOON AS POSSIBLE.
SO, CELL BOY—
WE'LL PART WAYS HERE.
HUH ...?
IT'S TIME FOR ME TO GET BACK TO WORK.
I'M SORRY I COULDN'T BE WITH YOU UNTIL THE END OF YOUR JOURNEY.
SEE THIS? GO DOWN THIS PATH AND TAKE A LEFT TO REACH THE TIP OF THE INTESTINAL EPITHELIUM.
YOU SHOULD BE ABLE TO CONTACT THE FRIENDS OF THE LACTIC ACID BACTERIUM THERE.
YOU ARE HERE
GOOD BACTERIA EXHIBIT
BUILDING B-89
GOB-LETS A205
GET THE LACTIC ACID BACTERIUM BACK TO ITS STRAIN, THEN LEAVE THE LARGE INTESTINE TO GO BACK TO THE PHARYNX.
BE MINDFUL OF YOUR SURROUND-INGS, AND BE CAREFUL.
DO YOU HAVE ANY QUESTIONS? I TRUST YOU'LL BE ALL RIGHT.
ゴォ ROAR
UM, SURE. THANKS.
OH— WHITE BLOOD CELL, WAIT.
TELL ME ONE THING BEFORE YOU GO!

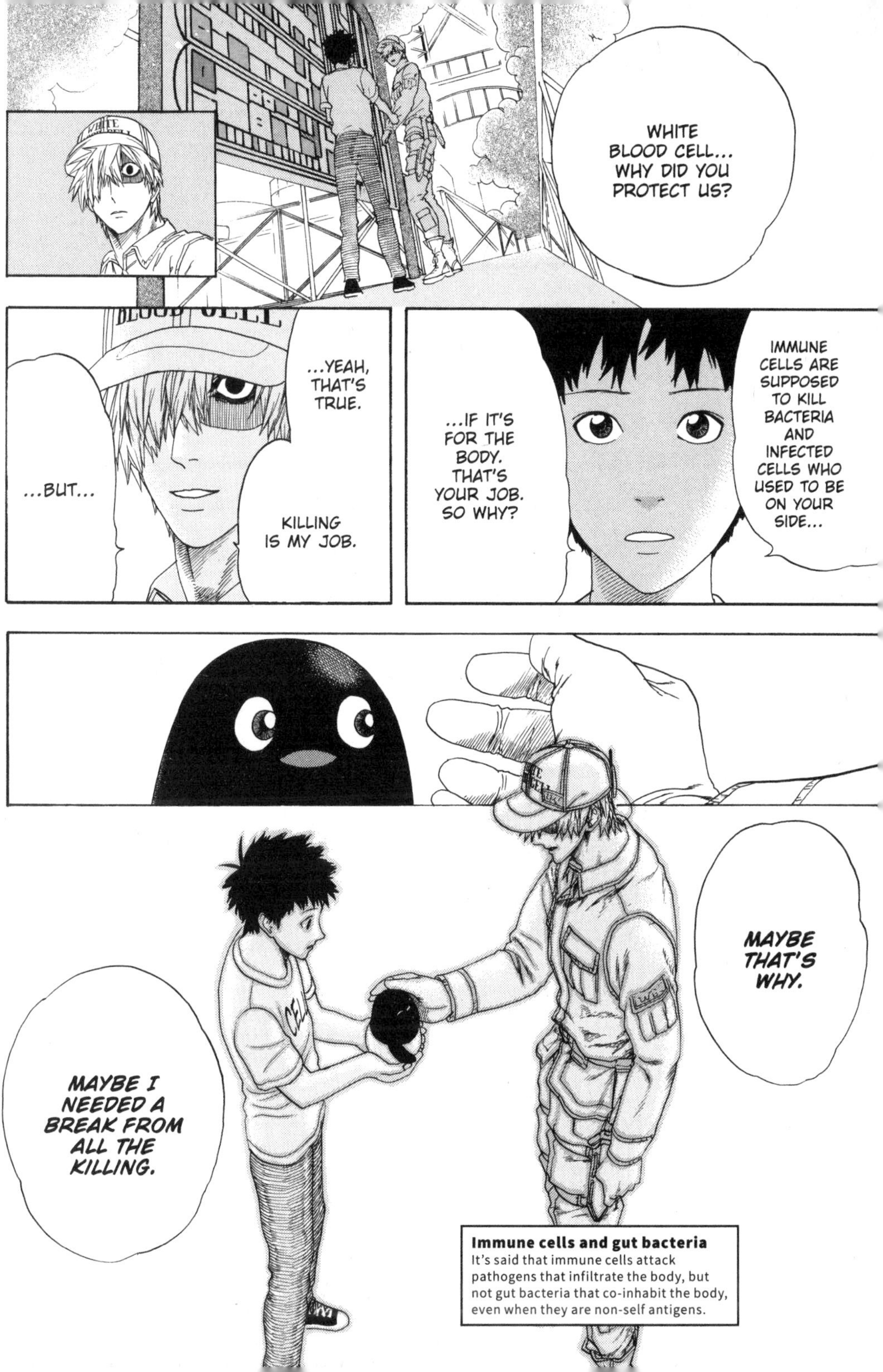
WHITE BLOOD CELL... WHY DID YOU PROTECT US?
IMMUNE CELLS ARE SUPPOSED TO KILL BACTERIA AND INFECTED CELLS WHO USED TO BE ON YOUR SIDE...
...IF IT'S FOR THE BODY. THAT'S YOUR JOB. SO WHY?
...YEAH, THAT'S TRUE.
KILLING IS MY JOB.
...BUT...
MAYBE THAT'S WHY.
MAYBE I NEEDED A BREAK FROM ALL THE KILLING.

Immune cells and gut bacteria
It's said that immune cells attack pathogens that infiltrate the body, but not gut bacteria that co-inhabit the body, even when they are non-self antigens.

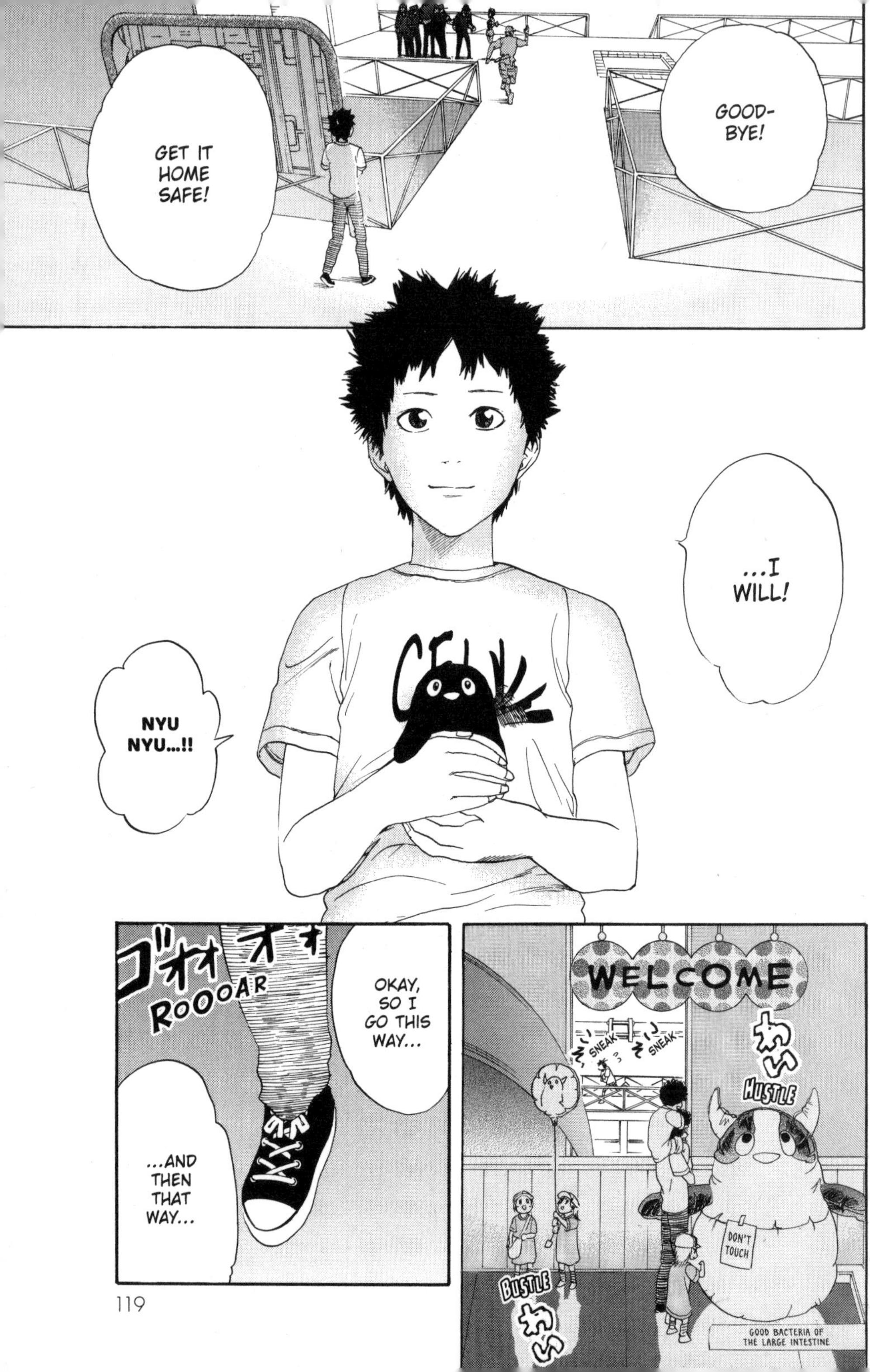
GOOD-BYE!
GET IT HOME SAFE!
...I WILL!
NYU NYU...!!
WELCOME
SNEAK
SNEAK
HUSTLE
DON'T TOUCH
BUSTLE
GOOD BACTERIA OF THE LARGE INTESTINE
ROOOAR
OKAY, SO I GO THIS WAY...
...AND THEN THAT WAY...

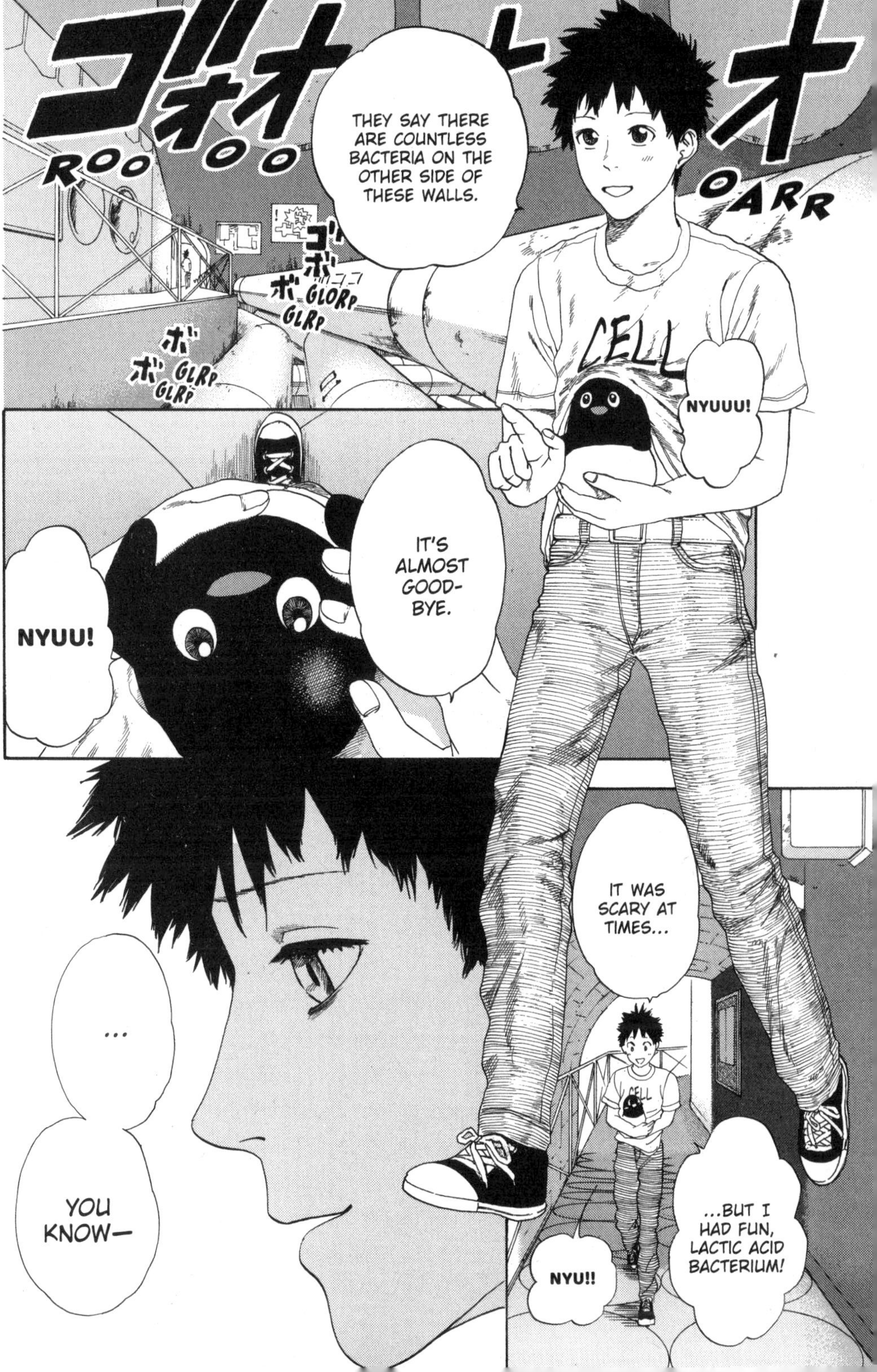
ゴォオ オ
ROOOOOARR
THEY SAY THERE ARE COUNTLESS BACTERIA ON THE OTHER SIDE OF THESE WALLS.
ゴボ GLORP
ボ GLRP
ボ GLRP
ボ GLRP
NYUUU!
IT'S ALMOST GOOD-BYE.
NYUU!
IT WAS SCARY AT TIMES...
...BUT I HAD FUN, LACTIC ACID BACTERIUM!
NYU!!
...
YOU KNOW—

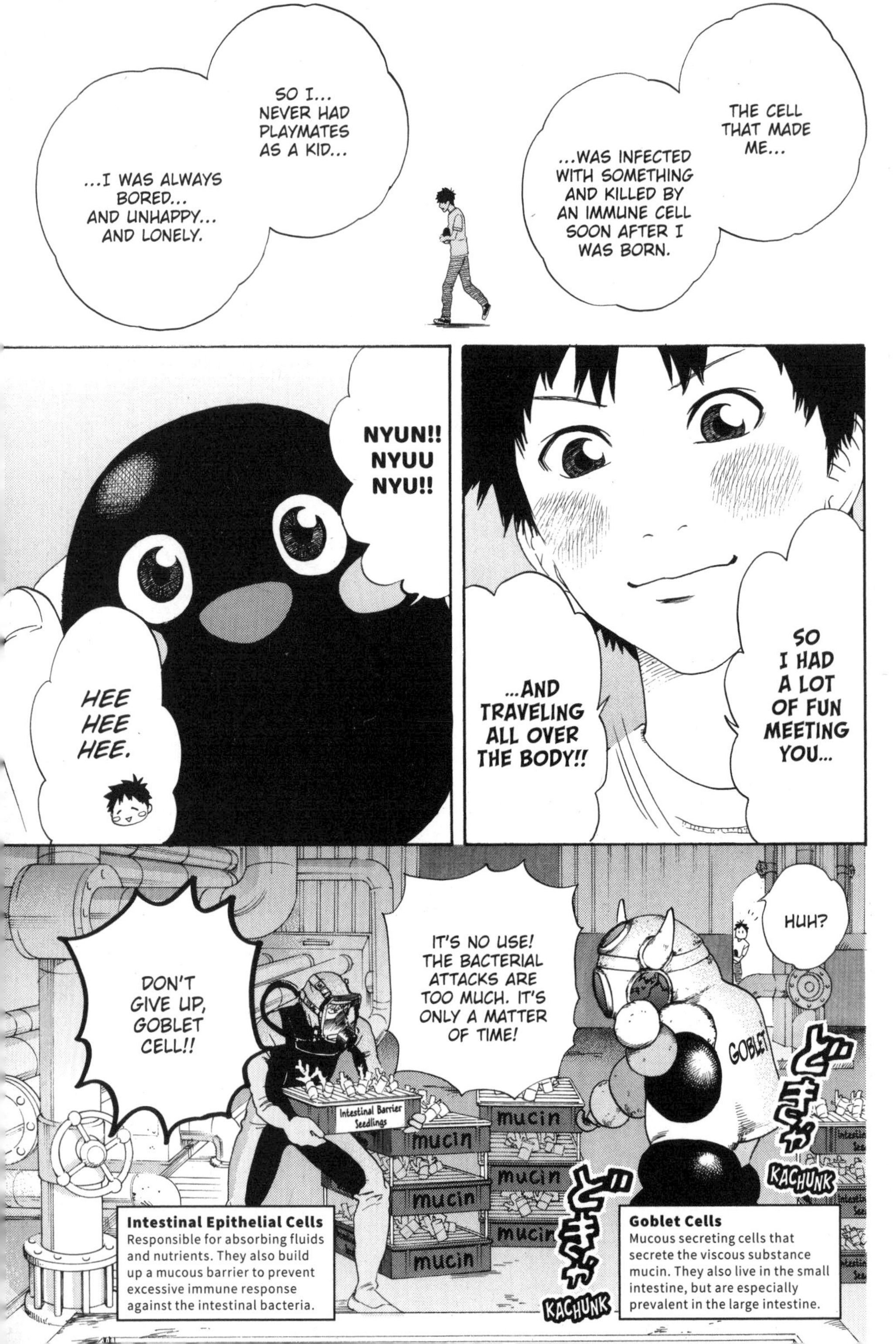
THE CELL THAT MADE ME...
...WAS INFECTED WITH SOMETHING AND KILLED BY AN IMMUNE CELL SOON AFTER I WAS BORN.
SO I... NEVER HAD PLAYMATES AS A KID...
...I WAS ALWAYS BORED... AND UNHAPPY... AND LONELY.
SO I HAD A LOT OF FUN MEETING YOU...
...AND TRAVELING ALL OVER THE BODY!!
NYUN!! NYUU NYU!!
HEE HEE HEE.
HUH?
GOBLET
KACHUNK
KACHUNK
Goblet Cells
Mucous secreting cells that secrete the viscous substance mucin. They also live in the small intestine, but are especially prevalent in the large intestine.
IT'S NO USE! THE BACTERIAL ATTACKS ARE TOO MUCH. IT'S ONLY A MATTER OF TIME!
mucin
Intestinal Barrier Seedlings
DON'T GIVE UP, GOBLET CELL!!
Intestinal Epithelial Cells
Responsible for absorbing fluids and nutrients. They also build up a mucous barrier to prevent excessive immune response against the intestinal bacteria.

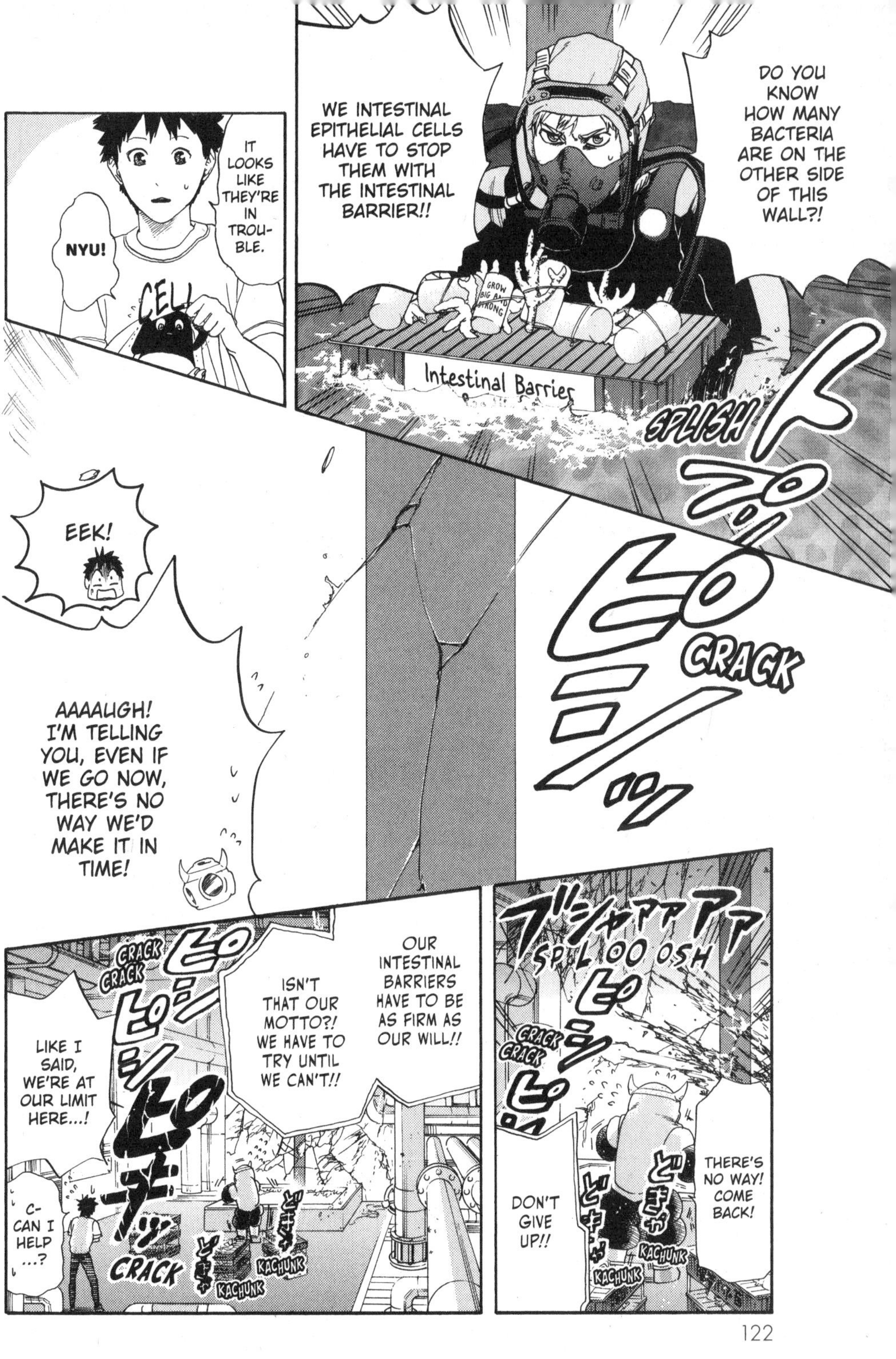
DO YOU KNOW HOW MANY BACTERIA ARE ON THE OTHER SIDE OF THIS WALL?!
WE INTESTINAL EPITHELIAL CELLS HAVE TO STOP THEM WITH THE INTESTINAL BARRIER!!
GROW BIG AND STRONG
Intestinal Barrier
SPLISH
IT LOOKS LIKE THEY'RE IN TROUBLE.
NYU!
CELL
CRACK
EEK!
AAAAUGH! I'M TELLING YOU, EVEN IF WE GO NOW, THERE'S NO WAY WE'D MAKE IT IN TIME!
SPLOOOSH
CRACK CRACK
THERE'S NO WAY! COME BACK!
DON'T GIVE UP!!
KACHUNK
KACHUNK
OUR INTESTINAL BARRIERS HAVE TO BE AS FIRM AS OUR WILL!!
ISN'T THAT OUR MOTTO?! WE HAVE TO TRY UNTIL WE CAN'T!!
CRACK CRACK
LIKE I SAID, WE'RE AT OUR LIMIT HERE...!
C-CAN I HELP ...?
CRACK
KACHUNK
KACHUNK

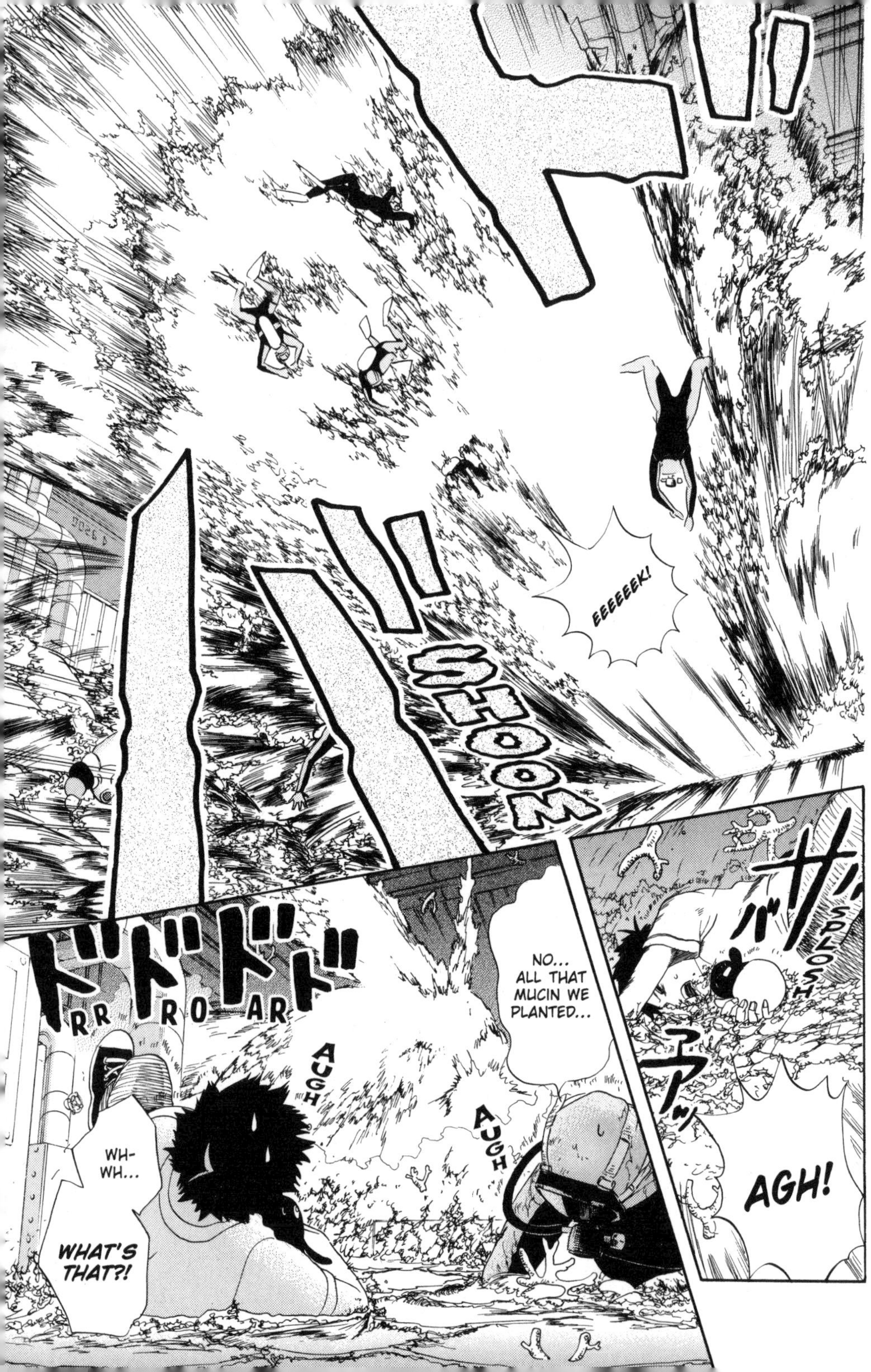
EEEEEEK!
SHOOM
SPLOSH
AGH!
NO... ALL THAT MUCIN WE PLANTED...
RRROAR
AUGH
AUGH
WH-WH...
WHAT'S THAT?!

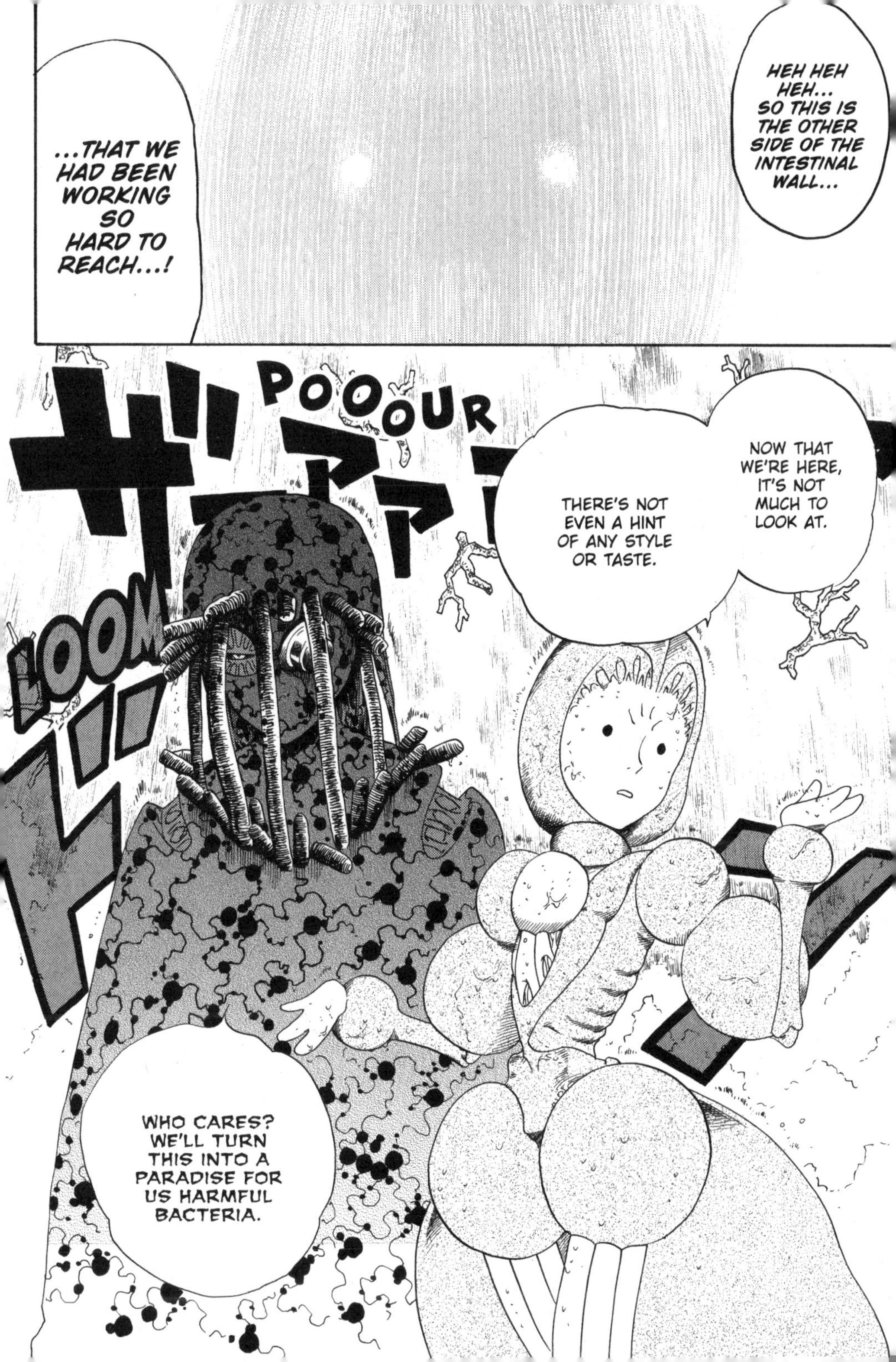
HEH HEH HEH... SO THIS IS THE OTHER SIDE OF THE INTESTINAL WALL...
...THAT WE HAD BEEN WORKING SO HARD TO REACH...!
POOOUR
LOOM
NOW THAT WE'RE HERE, IT'S NOT MUCH TO LOOK AT.
THERE'S NOT EVEN A HINT OF ANY STYLE OR TASTE.
WHO CARES? WE'LL TURN THIS INTO A PARADISE FOR US HARMFUL BACTERIA.

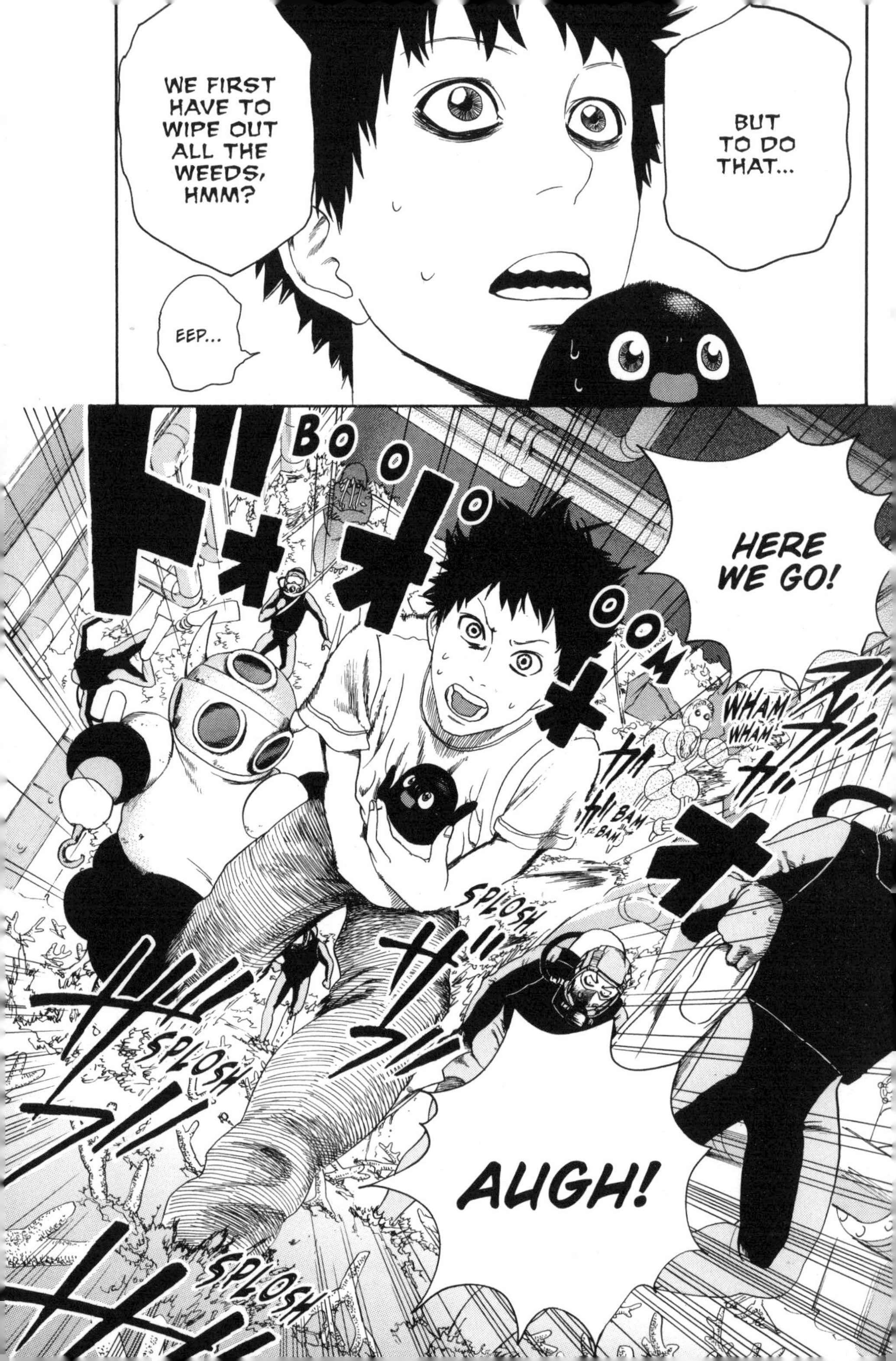
WE FIRST HAVE TO WIPE OUT ALL THE WEEDS, HMM?
BUT TO DO THAT...
EEP...
BOOOOOOM
HERE WE GO!
WHAM WHAM
BAM BAM
SPLOSH
SPLOSH
AUGH!
SPLOSH

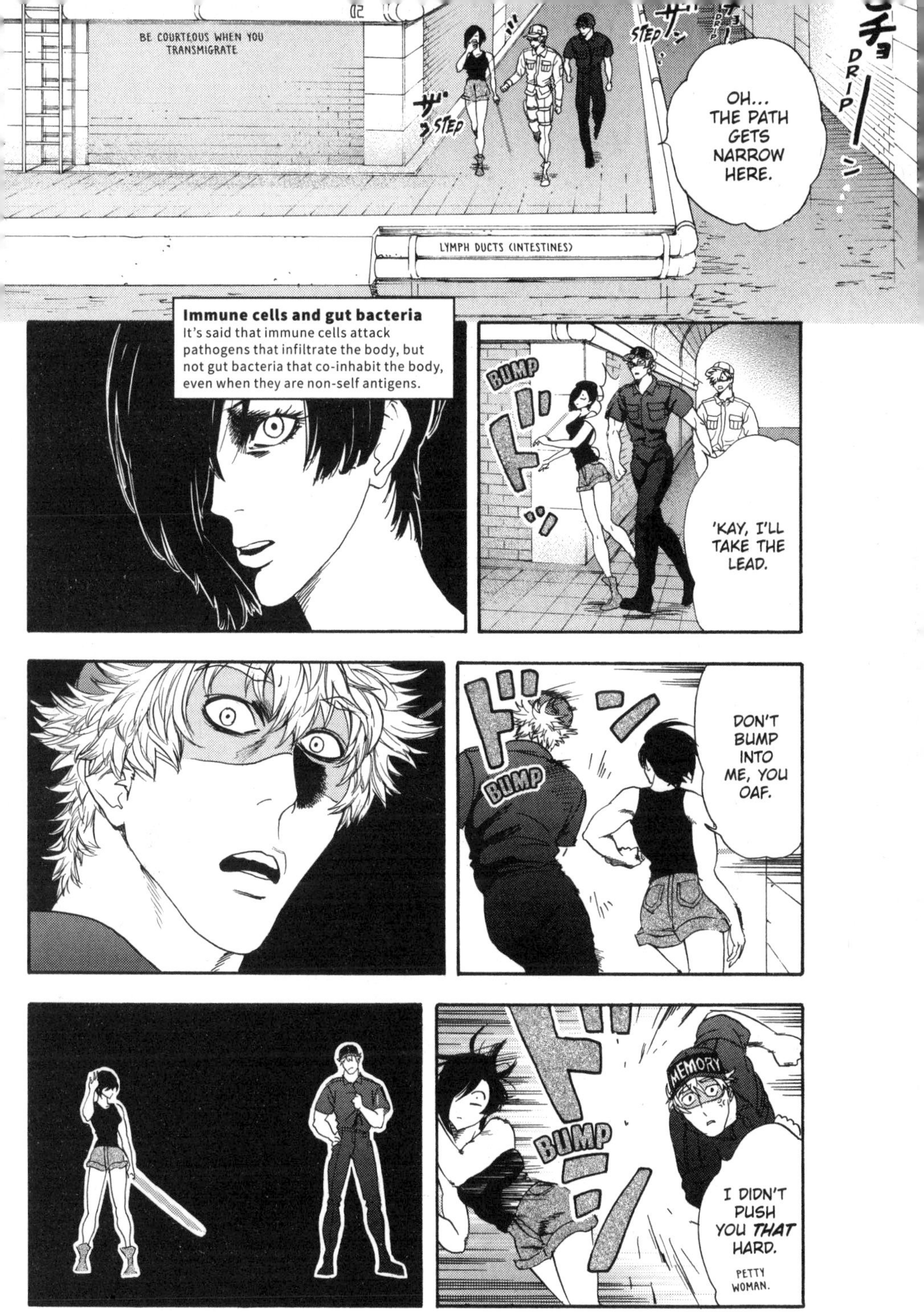
DRIP
OH... THE PATH GETS NARROW HERE.
DRIP
STEP
STEP
BE COURTEOUS WHEN YOU TRANSMIGRATE
LYMPH DUCTS (INTESTINES)
BUMP
'KAY, I'LL TAKE THE LEAD.
Immune cells and gut bacteria
It's said that immune cells attack pathogens that infiltrate the body, but not gut bacteria that co-inhabit the body, even when they are non-self antigens.
BUMP
DON'T BUMP INTO ME, YOU OAF.
MEMORY
BUMP
I DIDN'T PUSH YOU *THAT* HARD.
PETTY WOMAN.

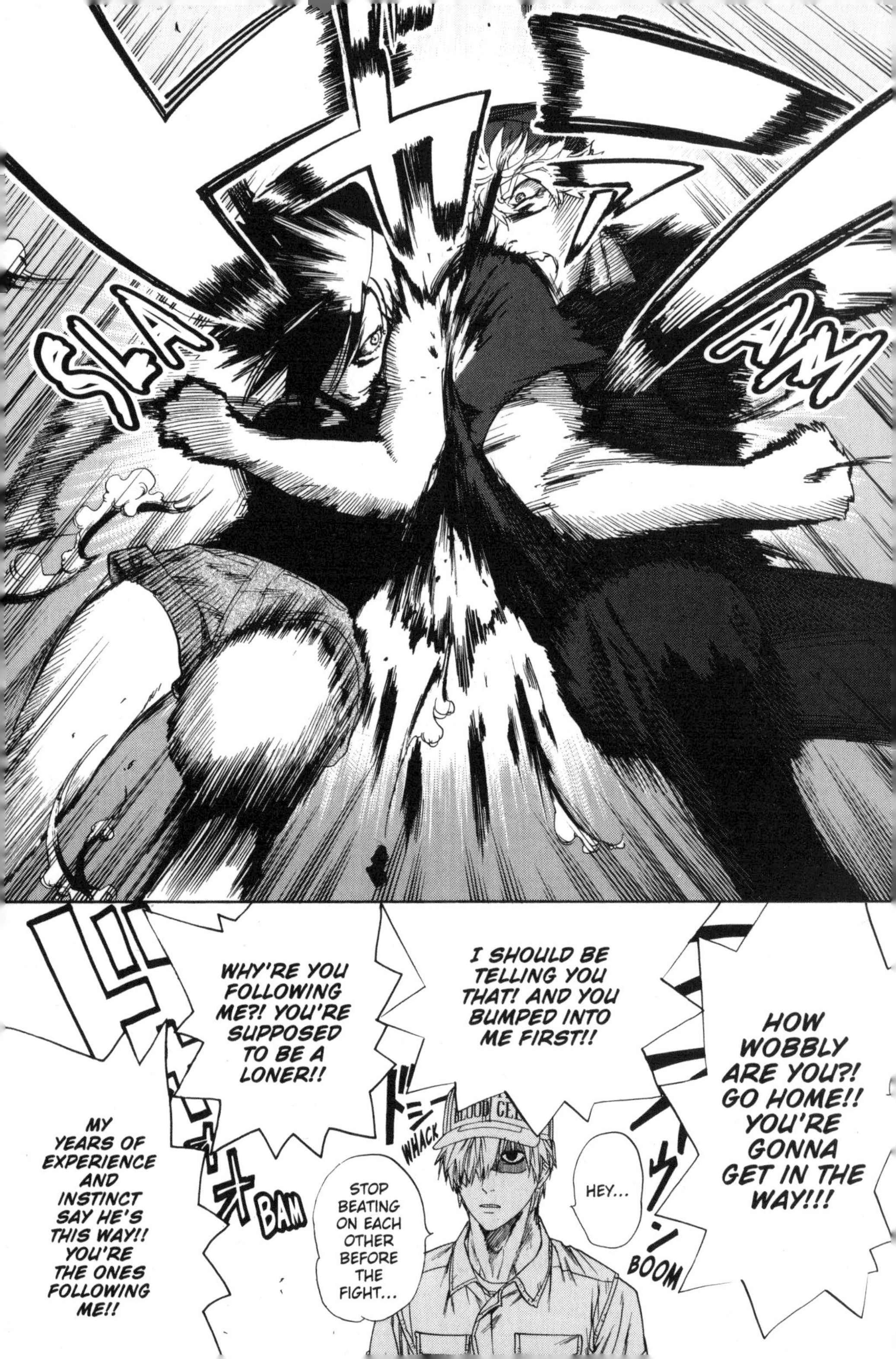
SLA
AM
HOW WOBBLY ARE YOU?! GO HOME!! YOU'RE GONNA GET IN THE WAY!!!
BOOM
I SHOULD BE TELLING YOU THAT! AND YOU BUMPED INTO ME FIRST!!
HEY...
WHACK
WHY'RE YOU FOLLOWING ME?! YOU'RE SUPPOSED TO BE A LONER!!
STOP BEATING ON EACH OTHER BEFORE THE FIGHT...
BAM
MY YEARS OF EXPERIENCE AND INSTINCT SAY HE'S THIS WAY!! YOU'RE THE ONES FOLLOWING ME!!

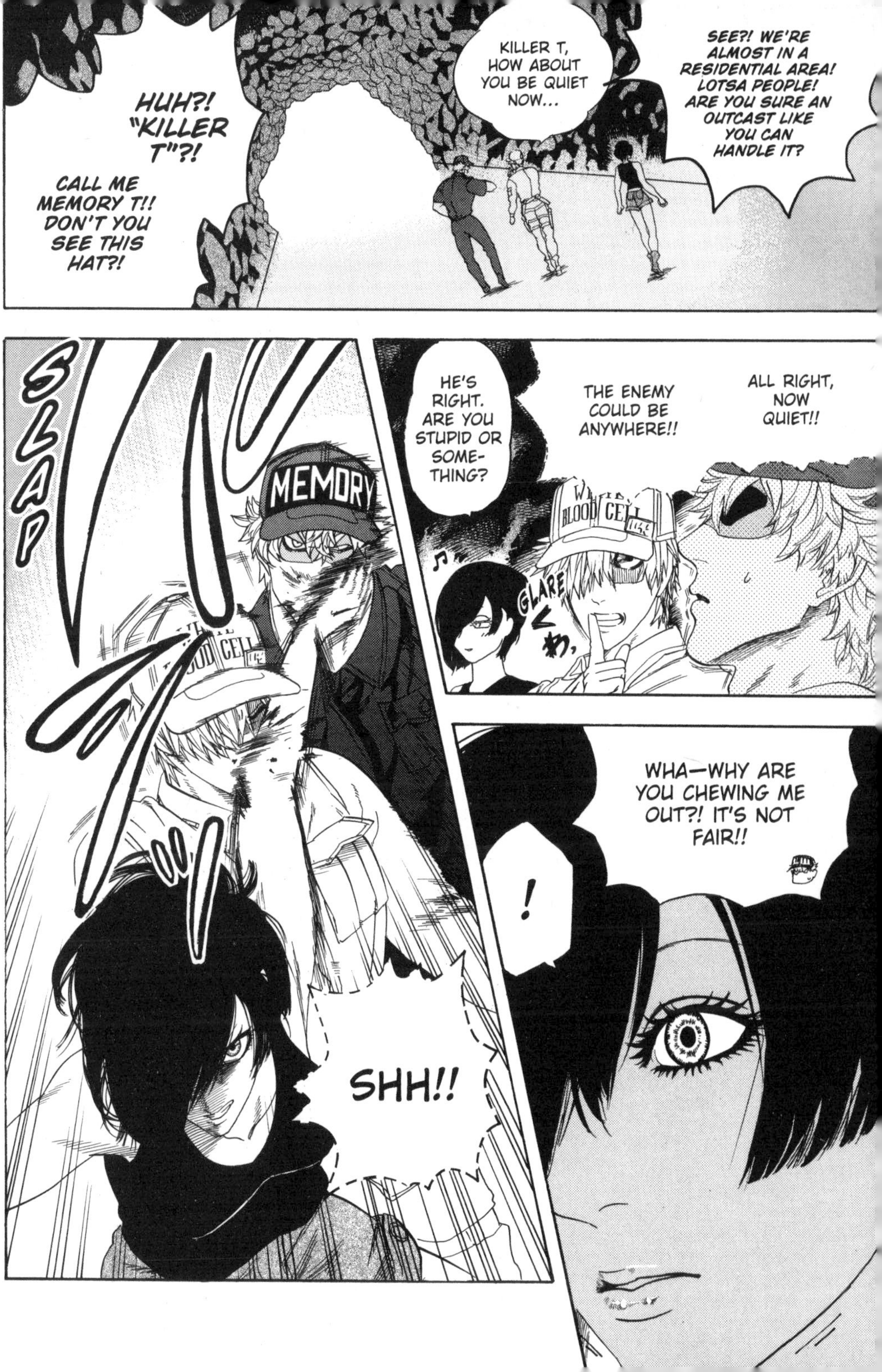
SEE?! WE'RE ALMOST IN A RESIDENTIAL AREA! LOTSA PEOPLE! ARE YOU SURE AN OUTCAST LIKE YOU CAN HANDLE IT?
KILLER T, HOW ABOUT YOU BE QUIET NOW...
HUH?! "KILLER T"?!
CALL ME MEMORY T!! DON'T YOU SEE THIS HAT?!
ALL RIGHT, NOW QUIET!!
THE ENEMY COULD BE ANYWHERE!!
HE'S RIGHT. ARE YOU STUPID OR SOME-THING?
GLARE
WHA—WHY ARE YOU CHEWING ME OUT?! IT'S NOT FAIR!!
!
SLAP
MEMORY
SHH!!

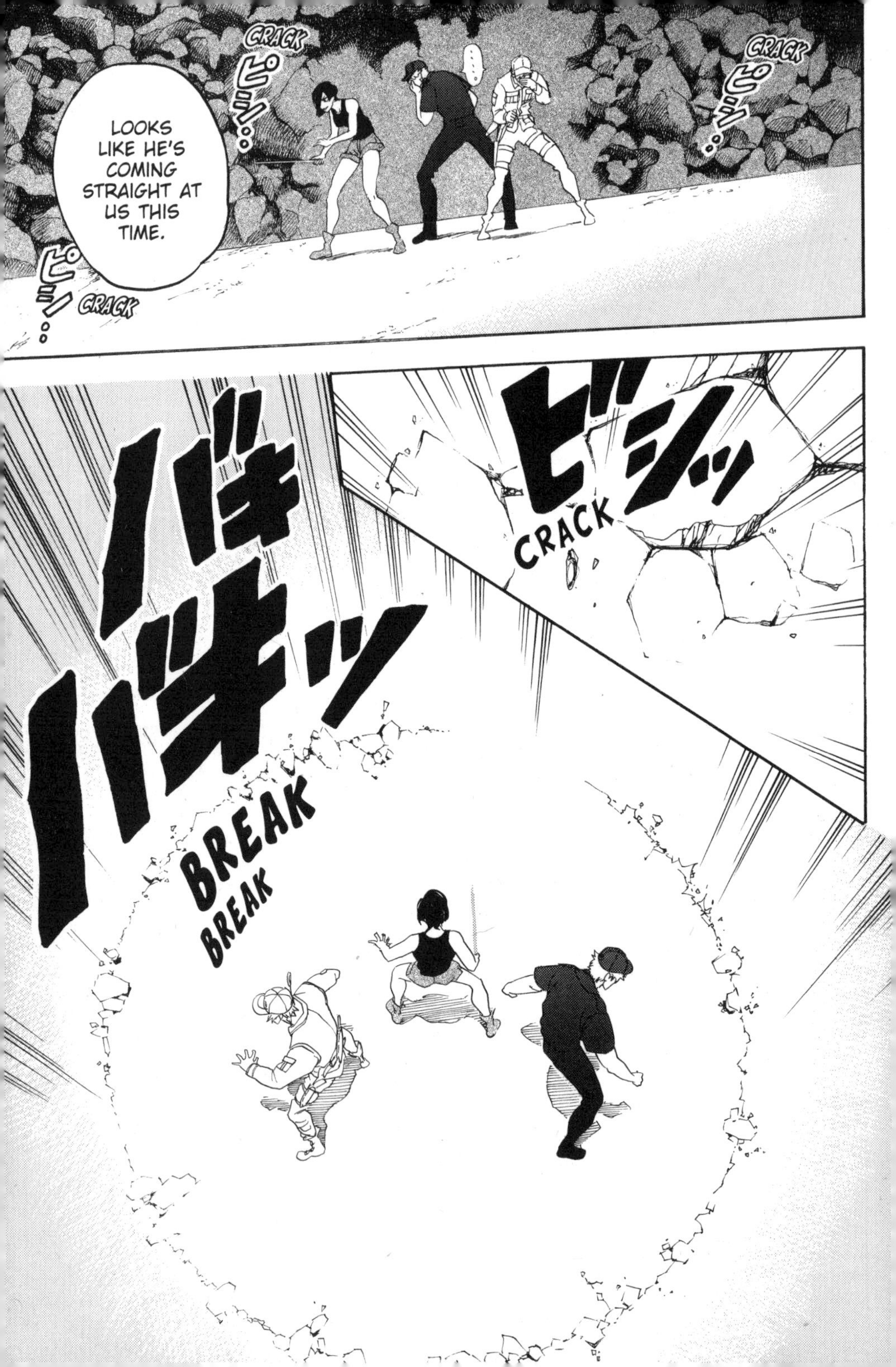
CRACK
ピシ…
…
LOOKS LIKE HE'S COMING STRAIGHT AT US THIS TIME.
CRACK
ピシ…
CRACK
ピシ…
ビシッ
CRACK
バキバキッ
BREAK
BREAK

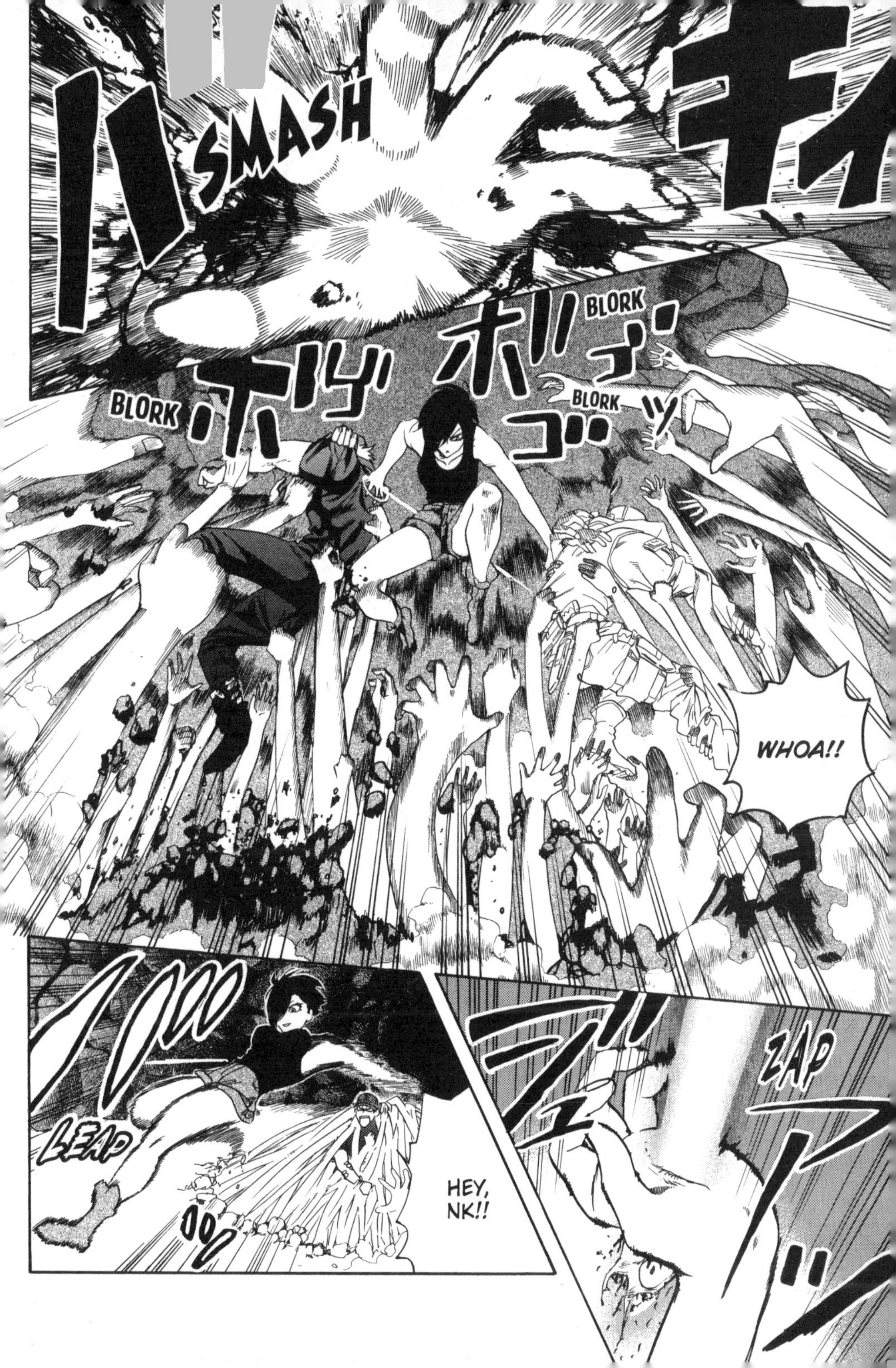
SMASH
BLORK
BLORK
BLORK
WHOA!!
ZAP
LEAP
HEY, NK!!

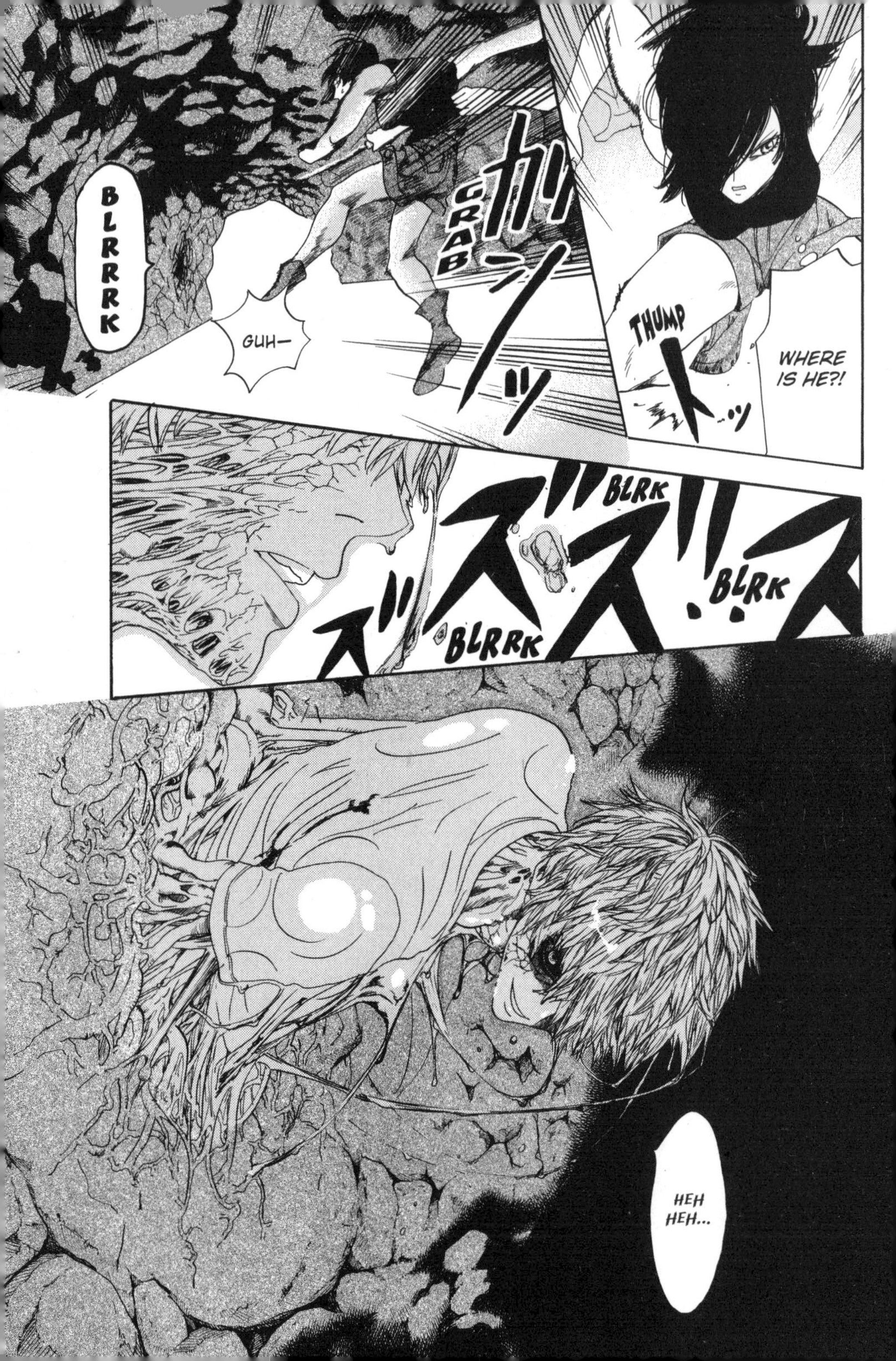
WHERE IS HE?!
THUMP
GRAB
GUH—
BLRRRK
BLRK
BLRK
BLRRRK
HEH HEH...

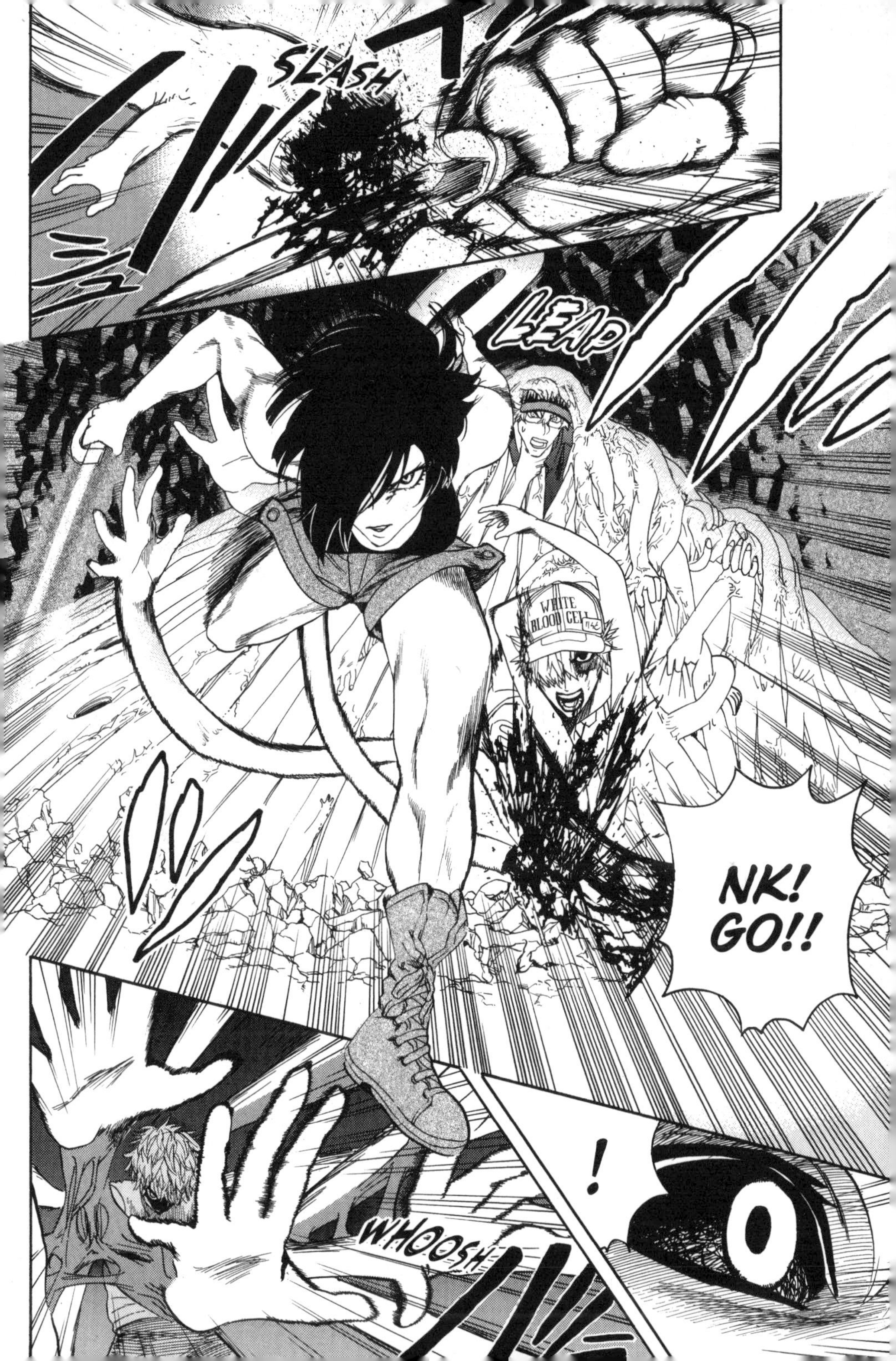
SLASH
LEAP
WHITE BLOOD CELL
NK! GO!!
!
WHOOSH

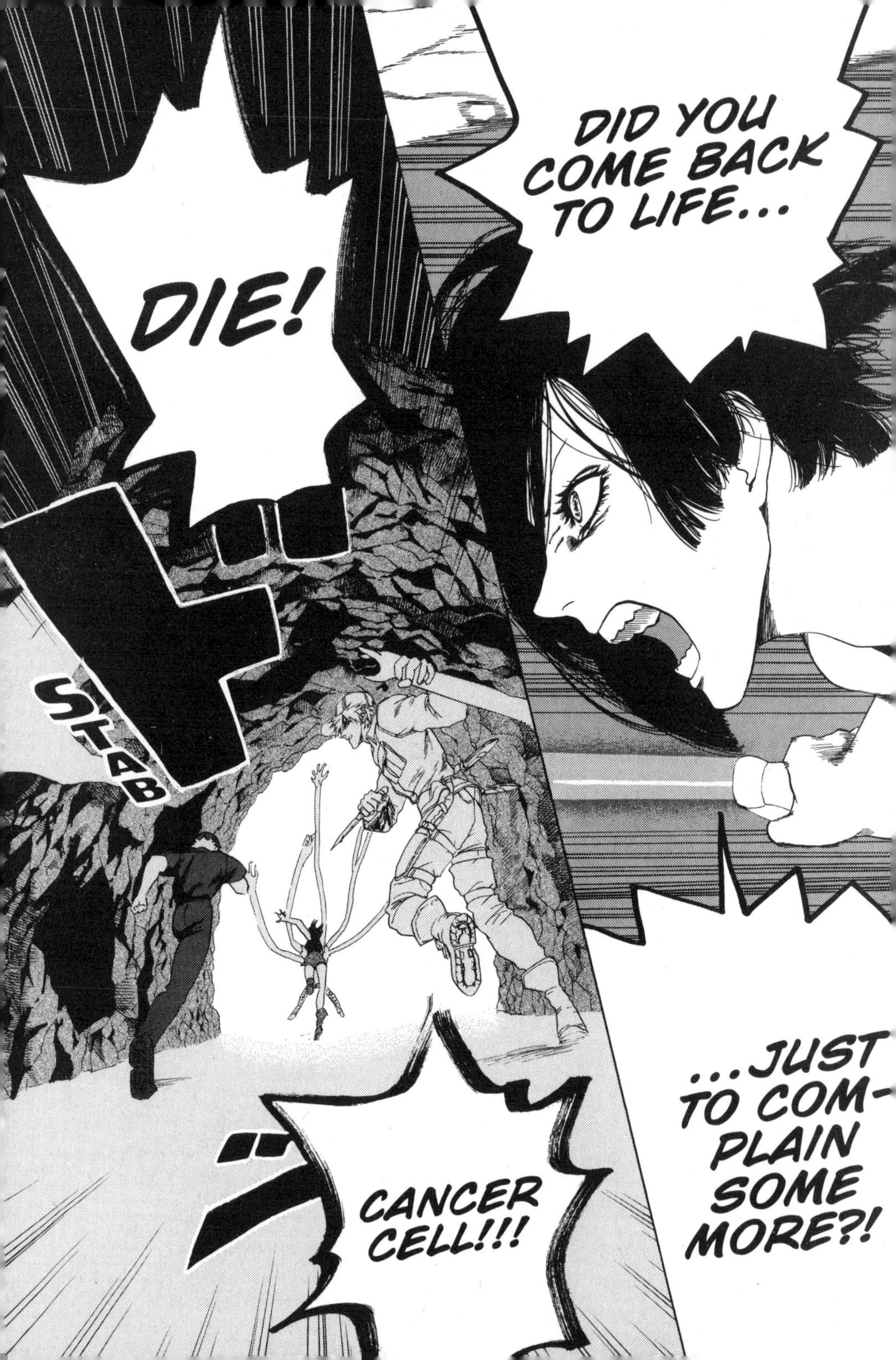
DID YOU COME BACK TO LIFE...
...JUST TO COM-PLAIN SOME MORE?!
DIE!
STAB
CANCER CELL!!!

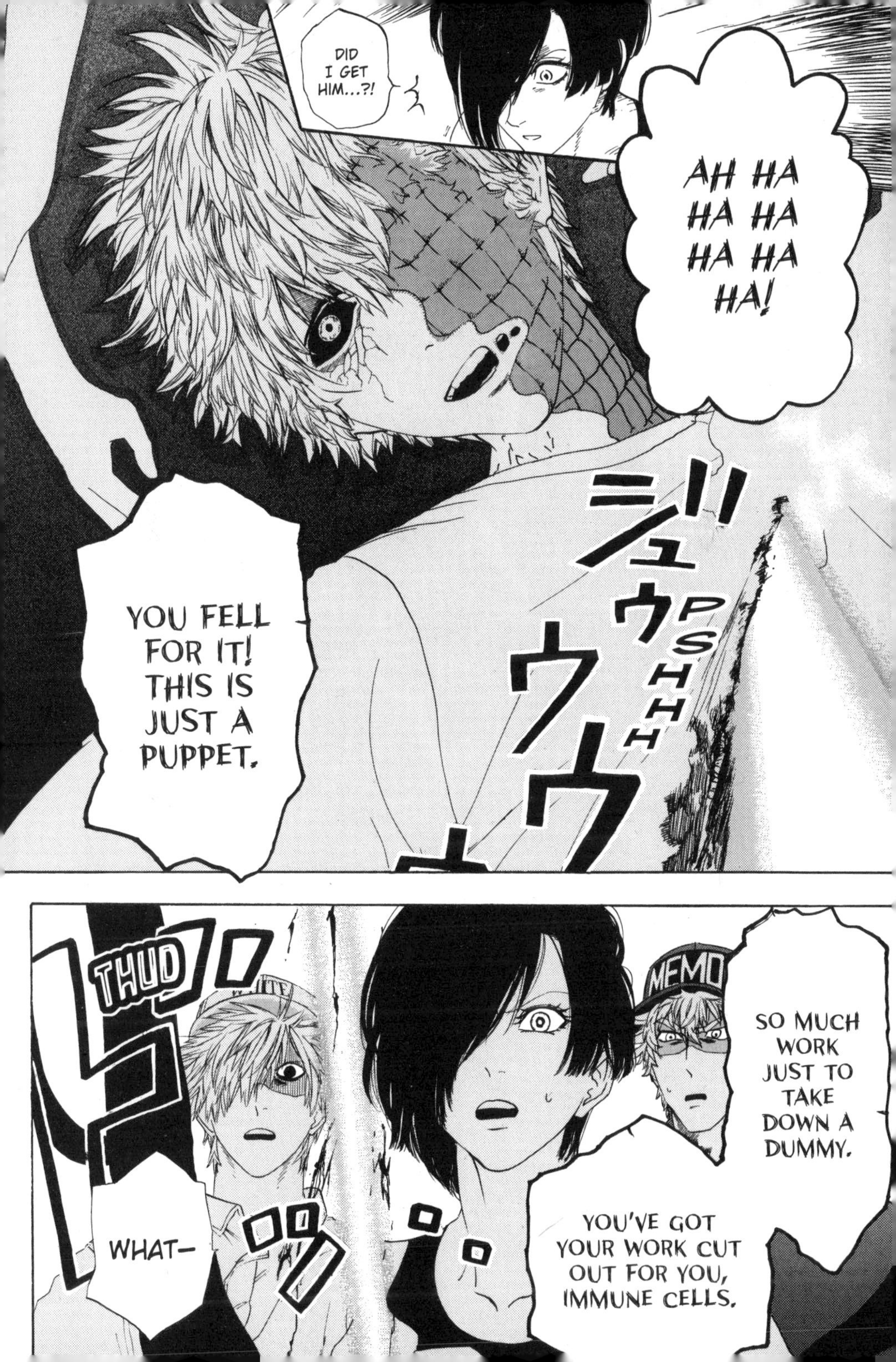
DID I GET HIM...?!
AH HA HA HA HA HA HA!
ジュウウウ
PSHHHH
YOU FELL FOR IT! THIS IS JUST A PUPPET.
SO MUCH WORK JUST TO TAKE DOWN A DUMMY.
YOU'VE GOT YOUR WORK CUT OUT FOR YOU, IMMUNE CELLS.
THUD
WHAT-

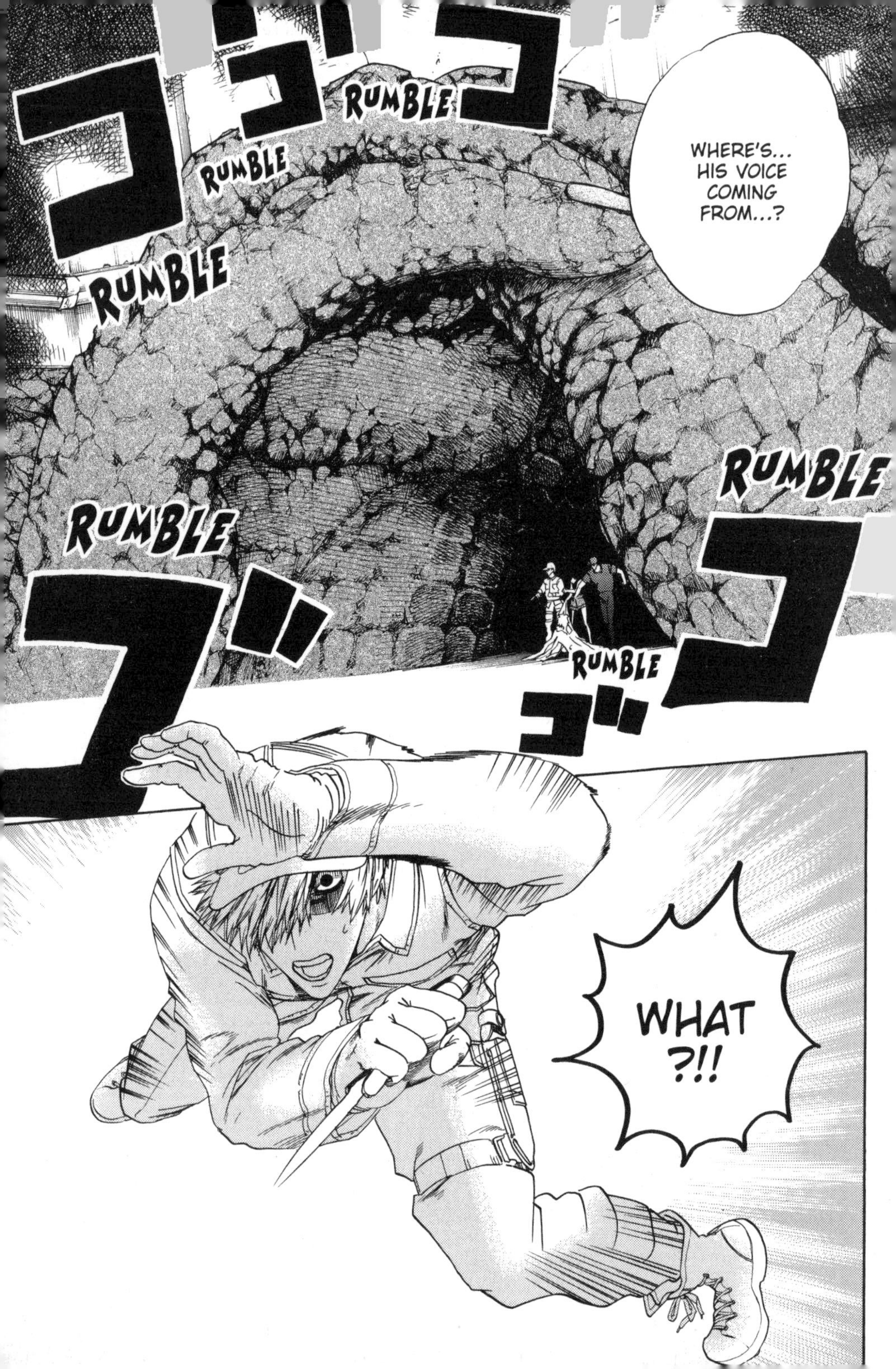
WHERE'S...
HIS VOICE
COMING
FROM...?
RUMBLE
RUMBLE
RUMBLE
RUMBLE
RUMBLE
RUMBLE
WHAT
?!!

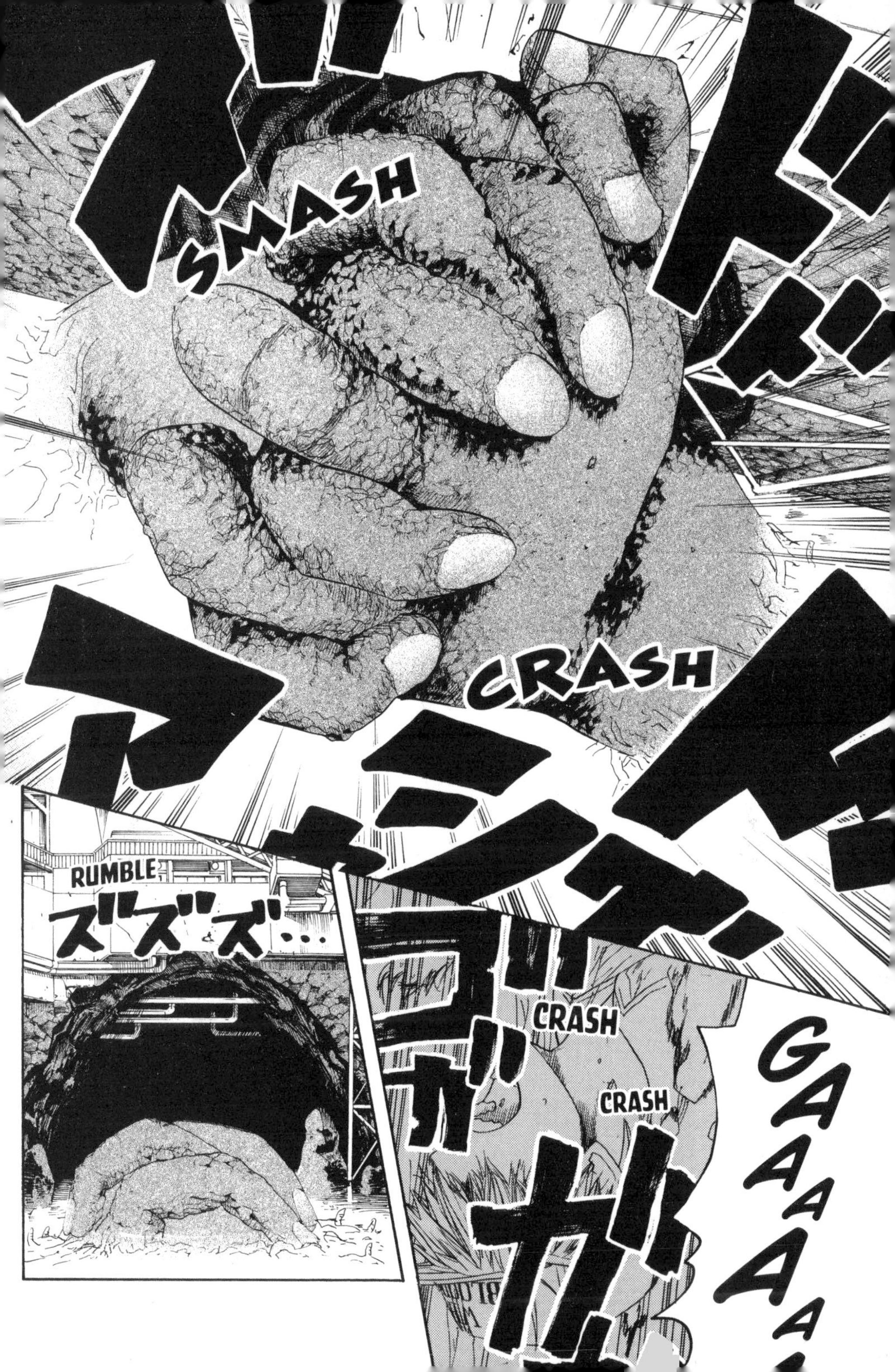
SMASH
CRASH
CRASH
CRASH
GAAAAA
RUMBLE
ズズズ...

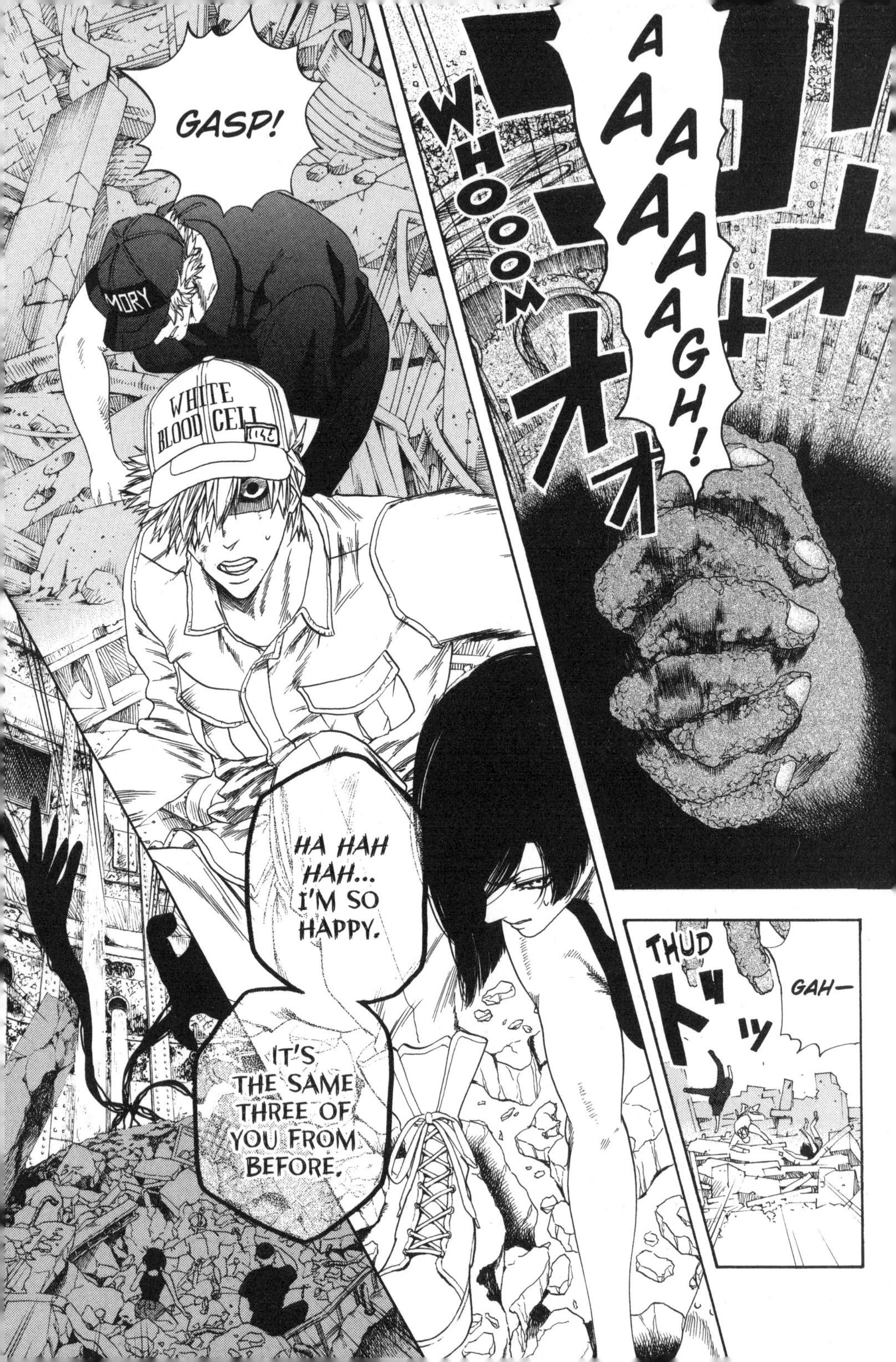
WHOOOM
AAAAAAGH!
THUD
ドッ
GAH—
GASP!
WHITE BLOOD CELL
HA HAH HAH... I'M SO HAPPY.
IT'S THE SAME THREE OF YOU FROM BEFORE.

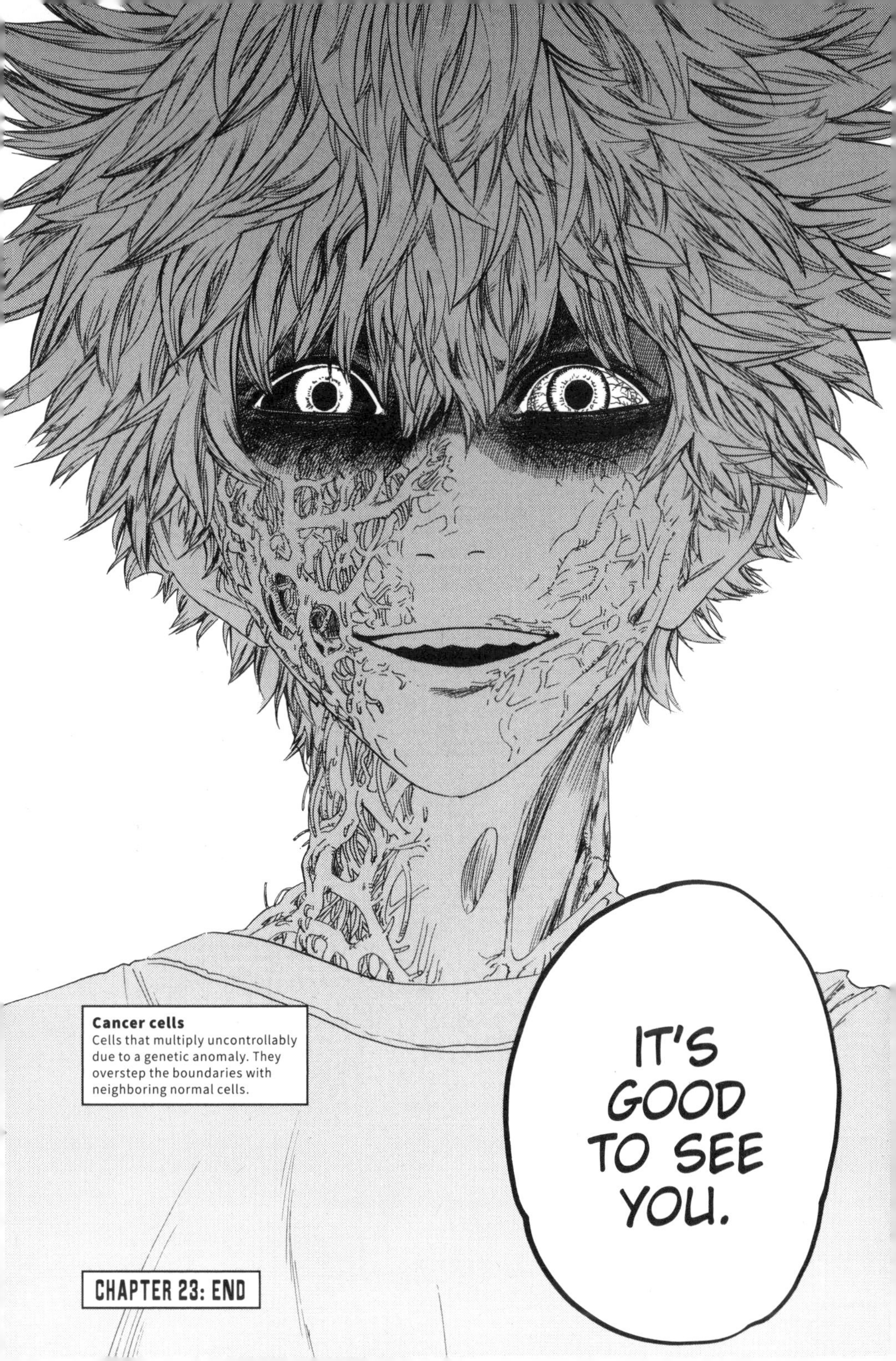
IT'S GOOD TO SEE YOU.
Cancer cells
Cells that multiply uncontrollably due to a genetic anomaly. They overstep the boundaries with neighboring normal cells.
CHAPTER 23: END

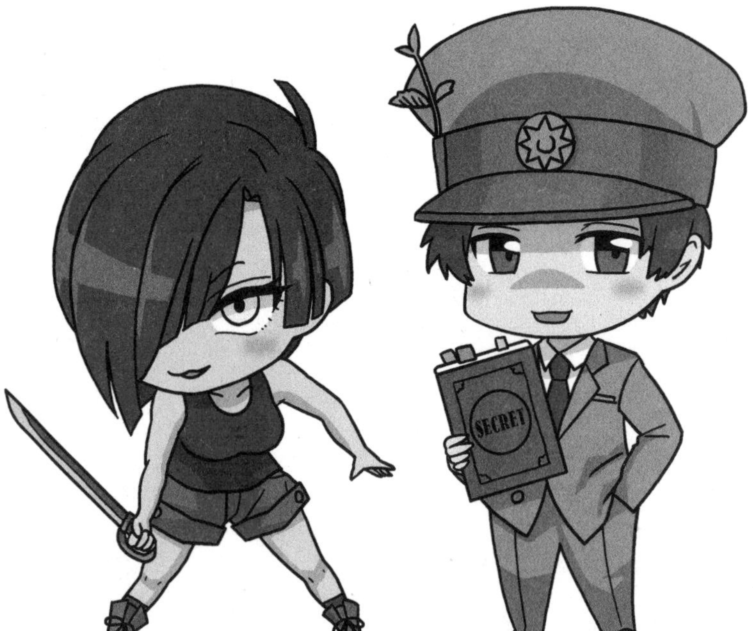
SECRET

はたらく細胞

Cells at Work!

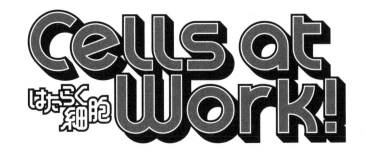

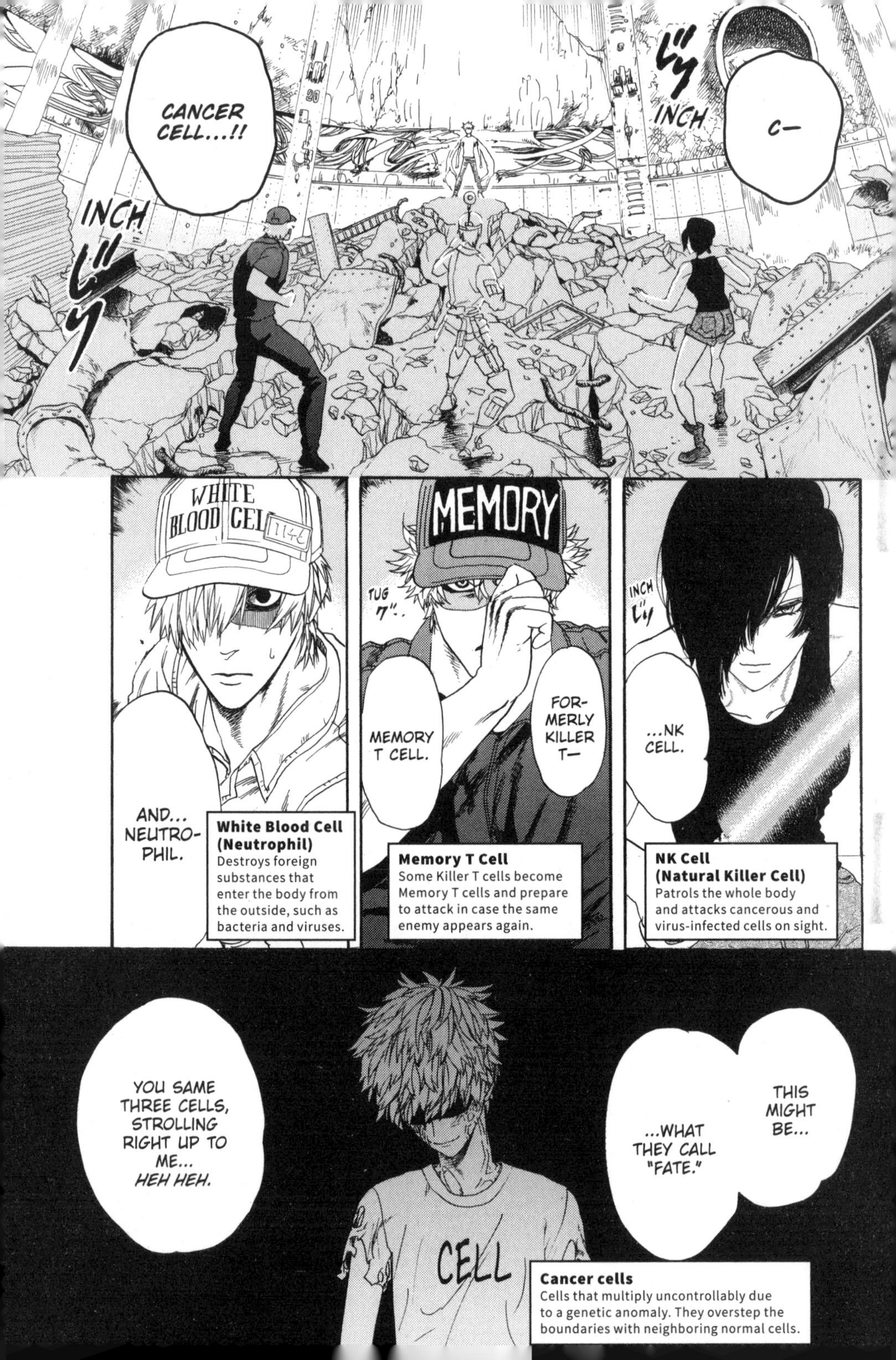
INCH
C—
CANCER CELL...!!
INCH
INCH
...NK CELL.
NK Cell (Natural Killer Cell)
Patrols the whole body and attacks cancerous and virus-infected cells on sight.
MEMORY
TUG
FOR-MERLY KILLER T—
MEMORY T CELL.
Memory T Cell
Some Killer T cells become Memory T cells and prepare to attack in case the same enemy appears again.
WHITE BLOOD CELL
1146
AND... NEUTRO-PHIL.
White Blood Cell (Neutrophil)
Destroys foreign substances that enter the body from the outside, such as bacteria and viruses.
THIS MIGHT BE...
...WHAT THEY CALL "FATE."
YOU SAME THREE CELLS, STROLLING RIGHT UP TO ME... HEH HEH.
CELL
Cancer cells
Cells that multiply uncontrollably due to a genetic anomaly. They overstep the boundaries with neighboring normal cells.

CHAPTER 24: CANCER CELL II (PART I)

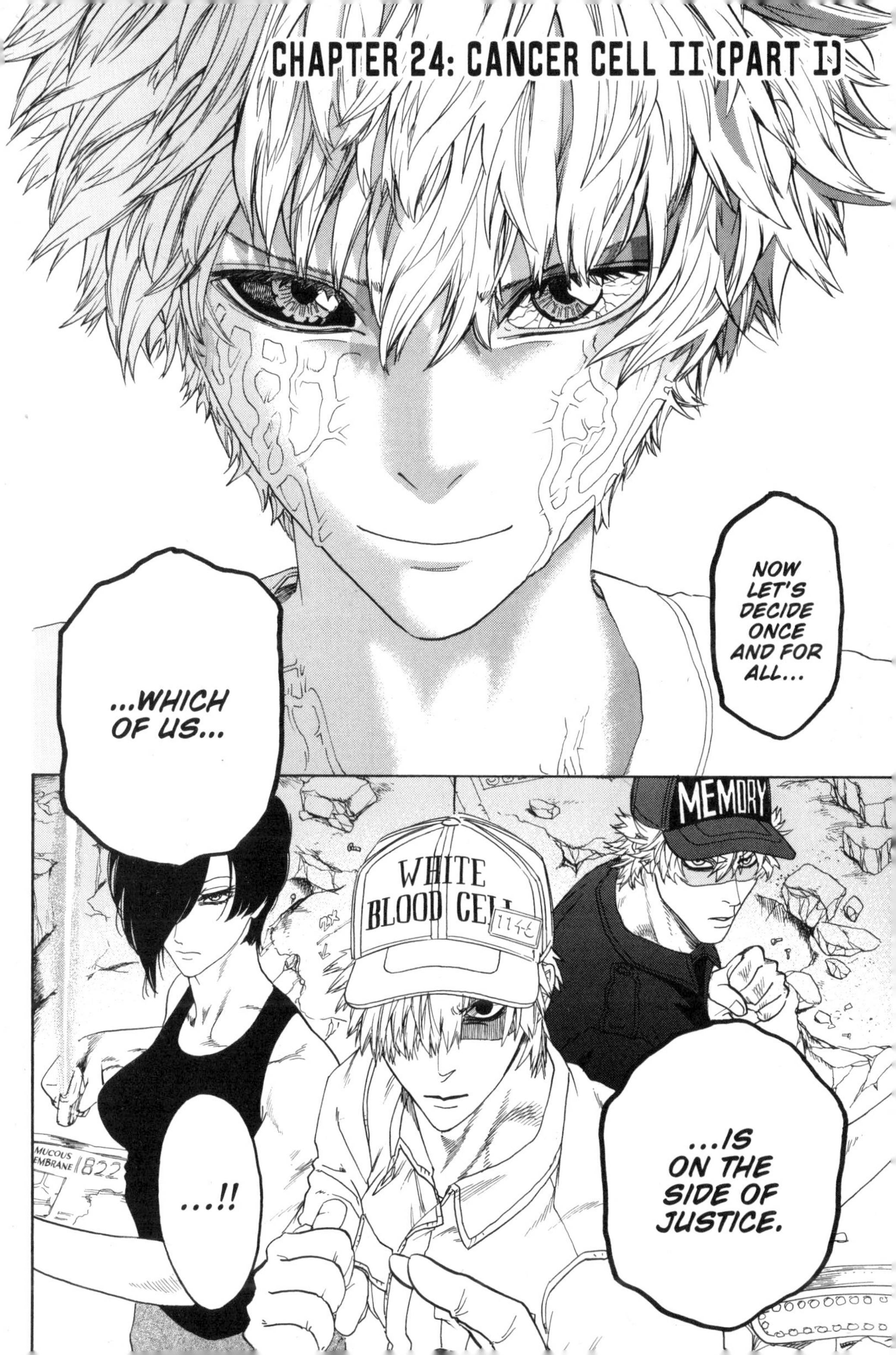
NOW LET'S DECIDE ONCE AND FOR ALL...
...WHICH OF US...
MEMORY
WHITE BLOOD CELL
1146
...IS ON THE SIDE OF JUSTICE.
...!!

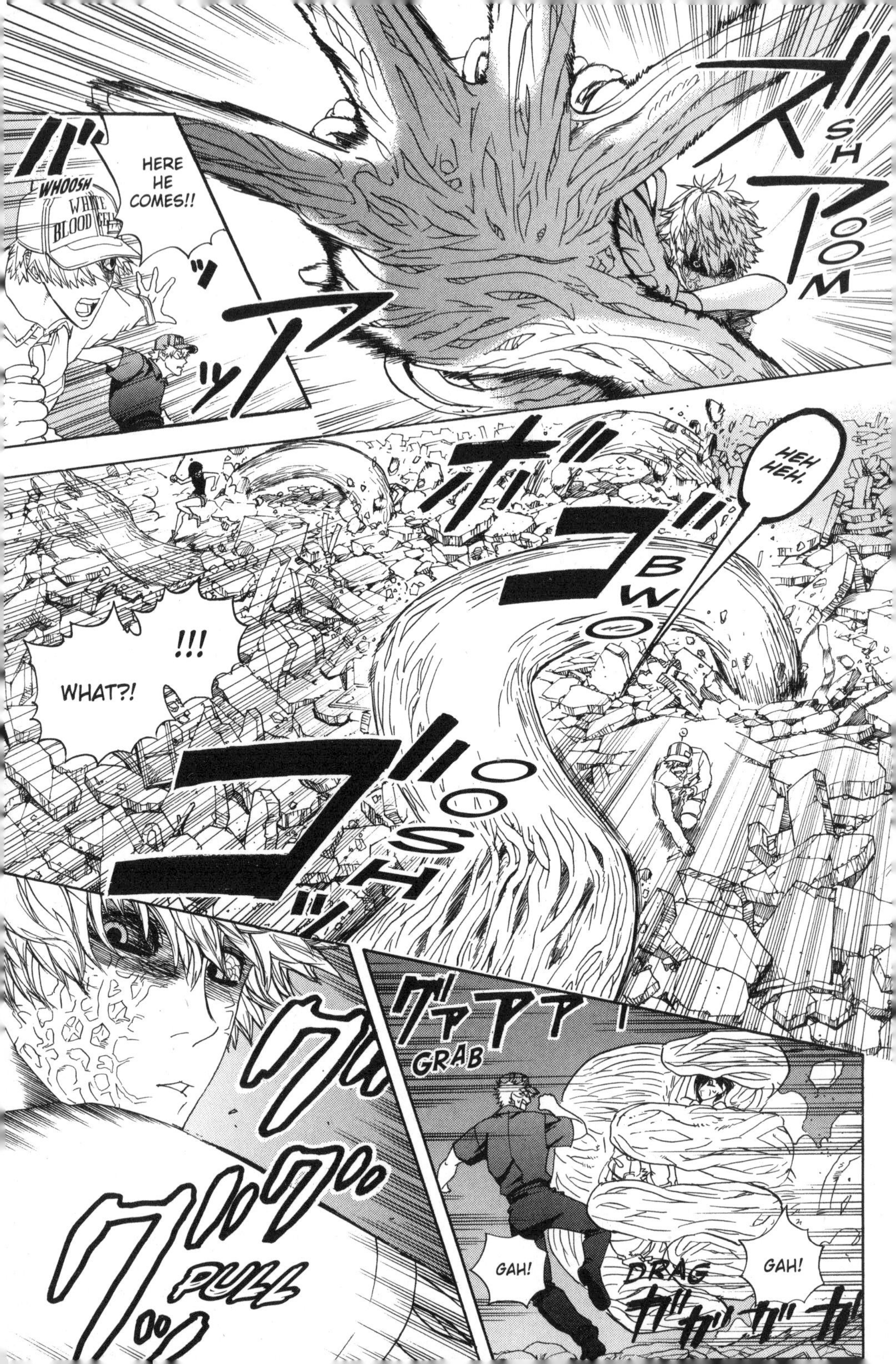SHOOOM
WHOOSH
HERE HE COMES!!
HEH HEH.
BWOO
!!!
WHAT?!
OOSH
GRAB
GAH!
DRAG
GAH!
PULL

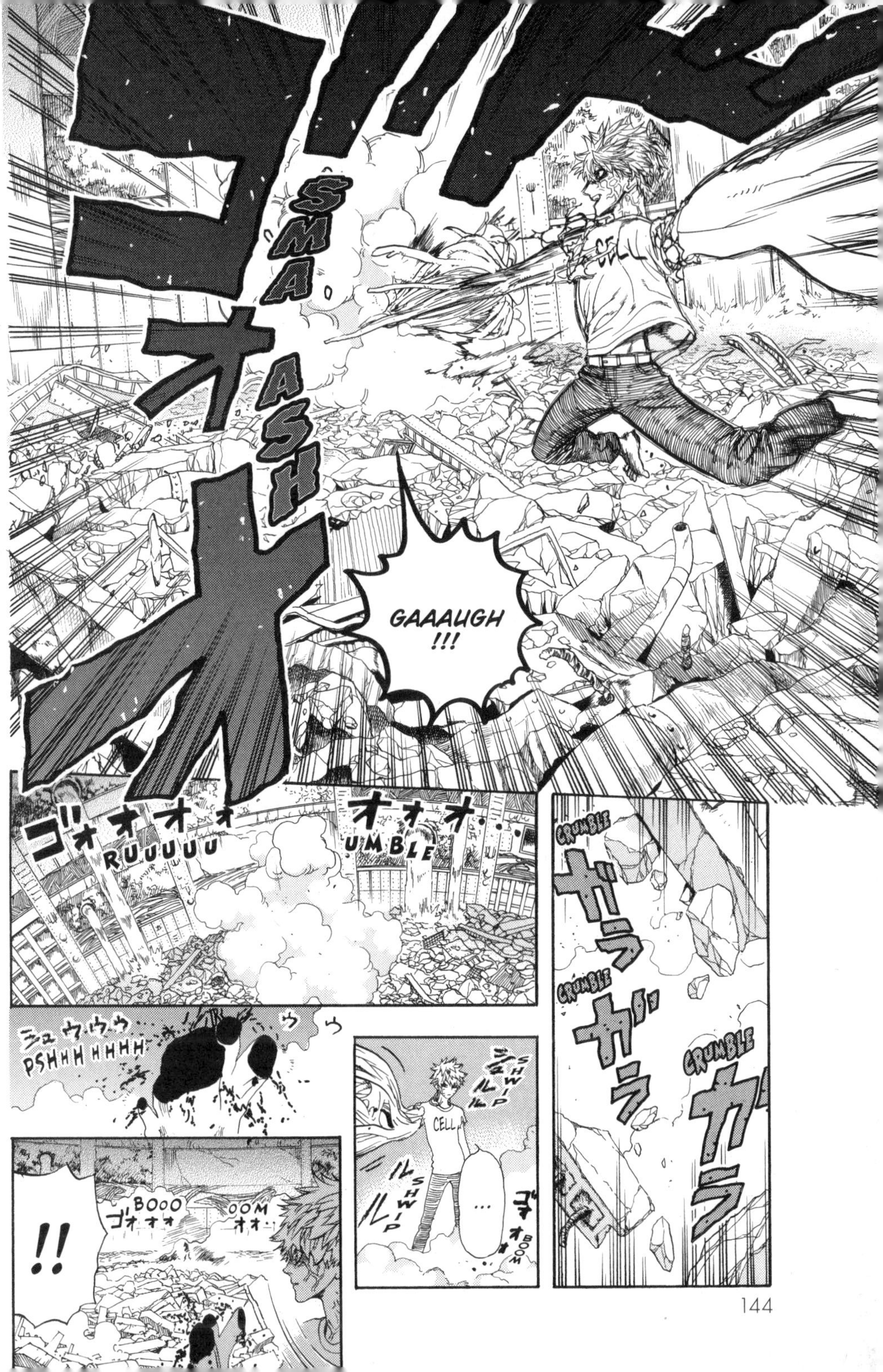
SMAAASH
GAAAUGH!!!
CRUMBLE
CRUMBLE
CRUMBLE
RUUUUUU UMBLE
PSHHHHHHH
SHWIP
SHWIP
...
BOOM
BOOO OOM
!!

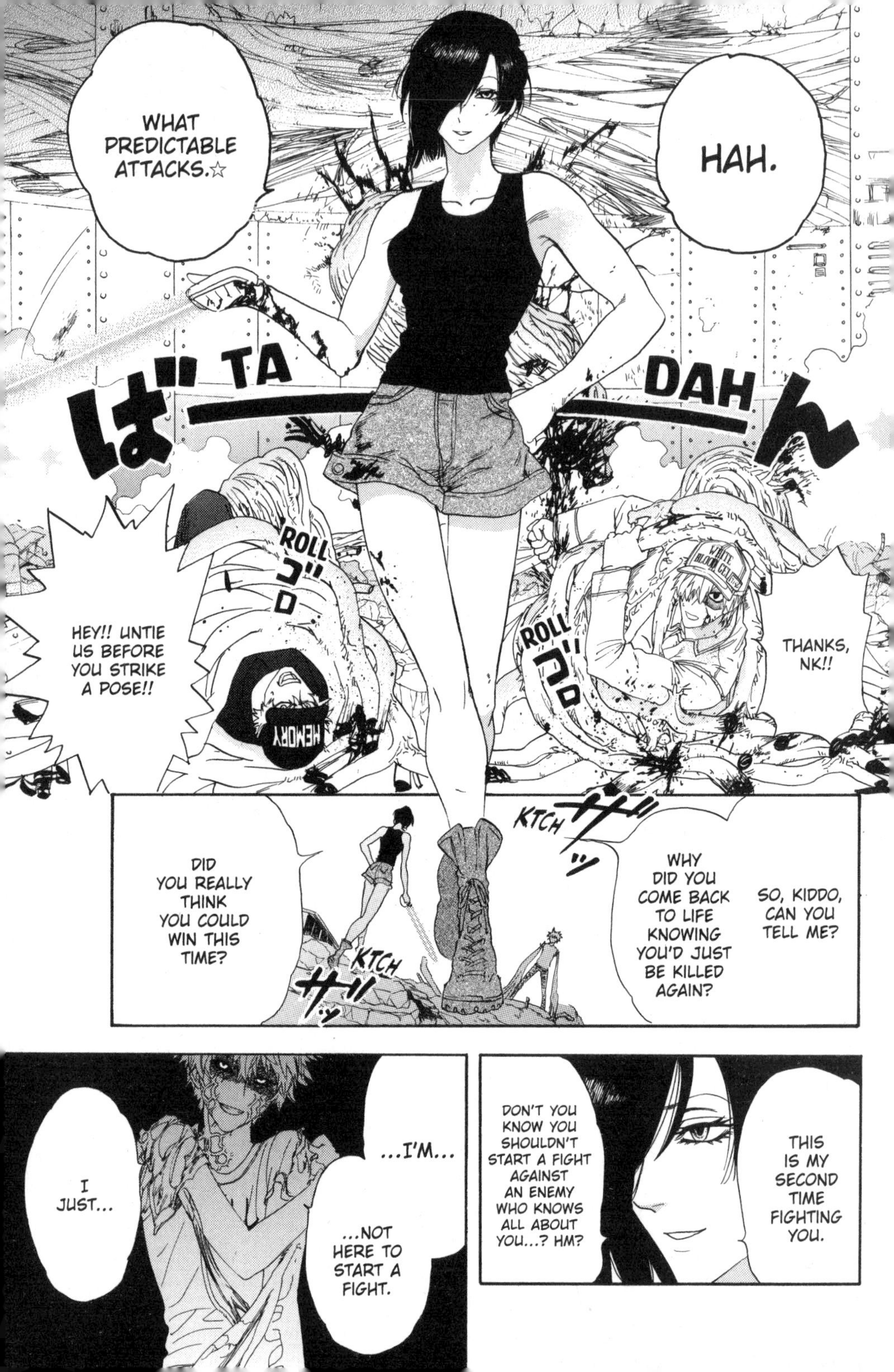
HAH.
WHAT PREDICTABLE ATTACKS.☆
ばーーん TA DAH
THANKS, NK!!
ROLL ゴロ
ROLL ゴロ
HEY!! UNTIE US BEFORE YOU STRIKE A POSE!!
SO, KIDDO, CAN YOU TELL ME?
WHY DID YOU COME BACK TO LIFE KNOWING YOU'D JUST BE KILLED AGAIN?
KTCH ザッ
DID YOU REALLY THINK YOU COULD WIN THIS TIME?
KTCH ザッ
THIS IS MY SECOND TIME FIGHTING YOU.
DON'T YOU KNOW YOU SHOULDN'T START A FIGHT AGAINST AN ENEMY WHO KNOWS ALL ABOUT YOU...? HM?
...I'M...
...NOT HERE TO START A FIGHT.
I JUST...

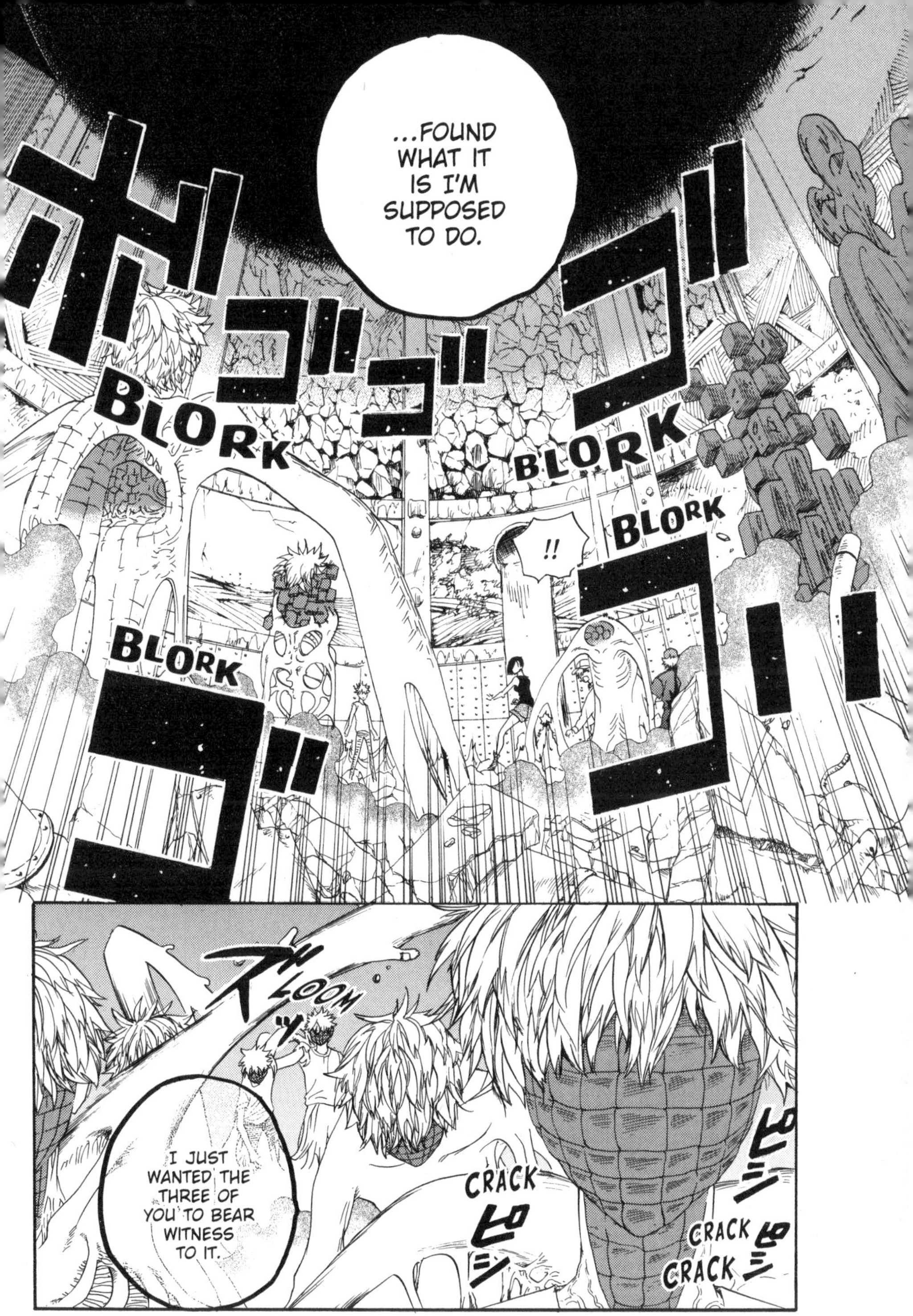
...FOUND WHAT IT IS I'M SUPPOSED TO DO.
BLORK
BLORK
!!
BLORK
BLORK
ZLOOM
CRACK
CRACK
CRACK
I JUST WANTED THE THREE OF YOU TO BEAR WITNESS TO IT.

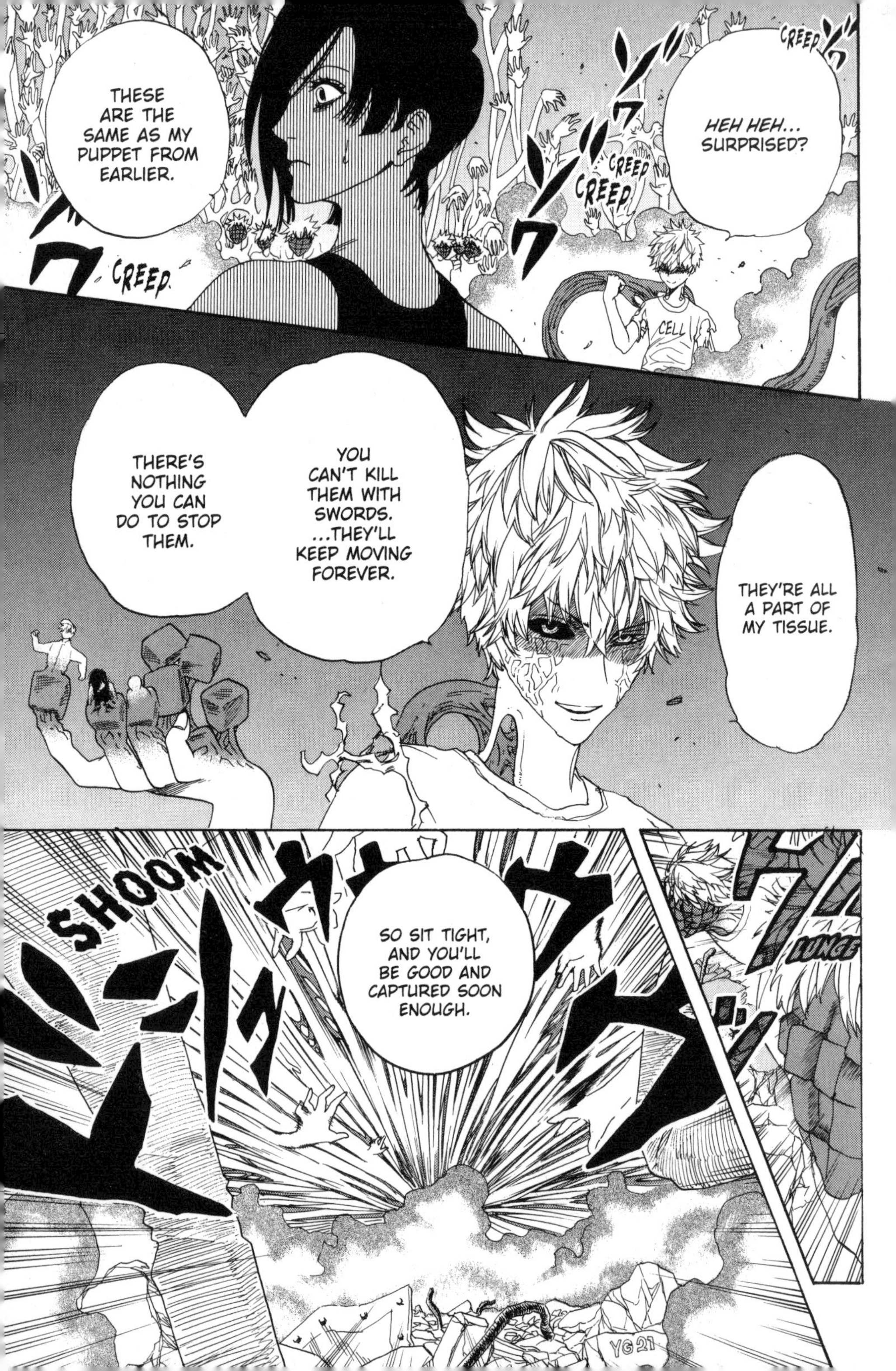
CREEP
HEH HEH... SURPRISED?
CREEP
CREEP
THESE ARE THE SAME AS MY PUPPET FROM EARLIER.
CREEP
CELL
THEY'RE ALL A PART OF MY TISSUE.
YOU CAN'T KILL THEM WITH SWORDS. ...THEY'LL KEEP MOVING FOREVER.
THERE'S NOTHING YOU CAN DO TO STOP THEM.
LUNGE
SO SIT TIGHT, AND YOU'LL BE GOOD AND CAPTURED SOON ENOUGH.
SHOOM
YG 21

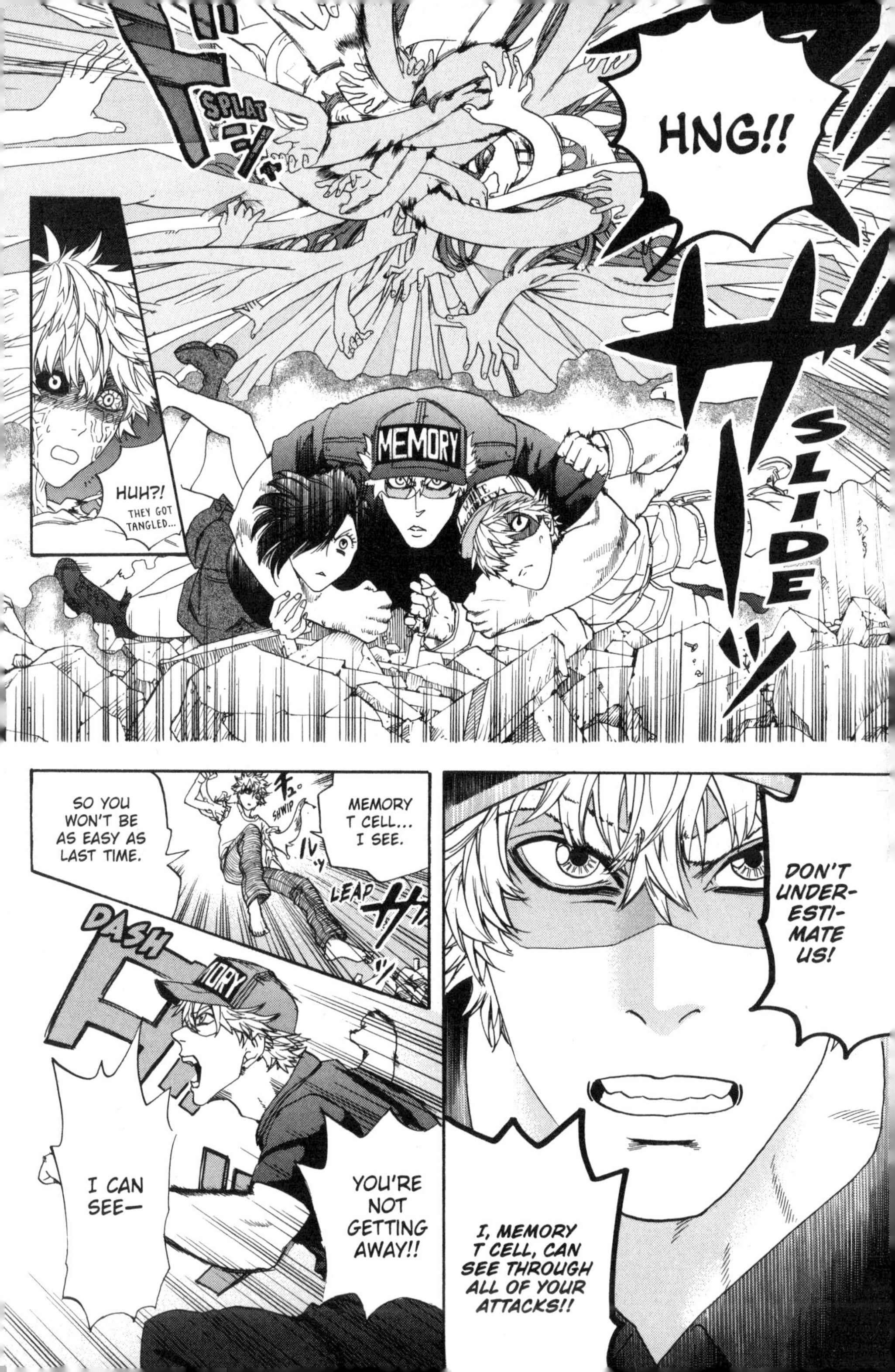
HNG!!
SLIDE
SPLAT
HUH?!
THEY GOT TANGLED...
DON'T UNDER-ESTI-MATE US!
I, MEMORY T CELL, CAN SEE THROUGH ALL OF YOUR ATTACKS!!
MEMORY T CELL... I SEE.
SHWIP
LEAP
SO YOU WON'T BE AS EASY AS LAST TIME.
DASH
YOU'RE NOT GETTING AWAY!!
I CAN SEE—

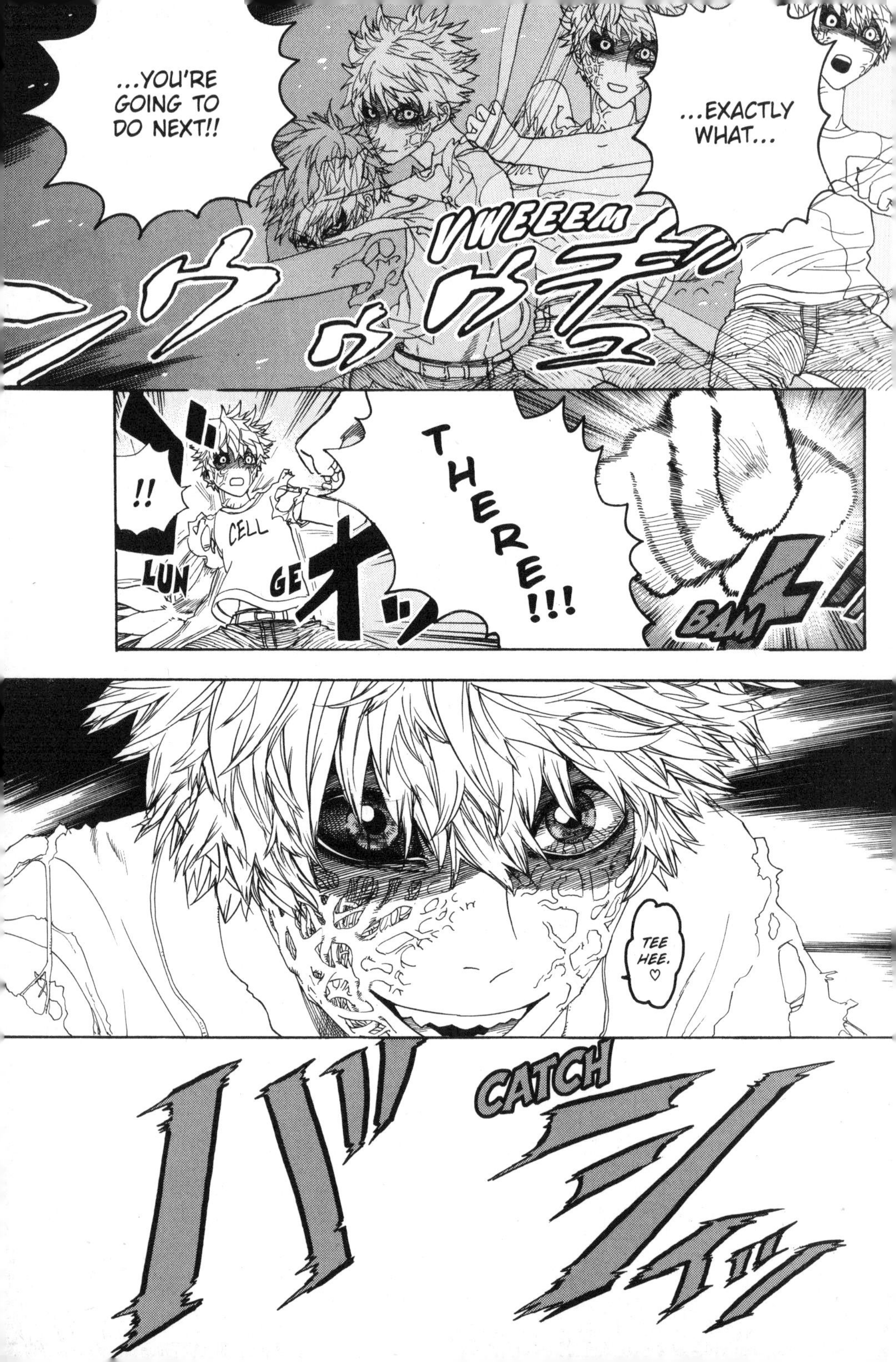
...EXACTLY WHAT...
...YOU'RE GOING TO DO NEXT!!
VWEEEM
BAM
THERE!!!
!!
CELL
LUNGE
TEE HEE. ♡
CATCH

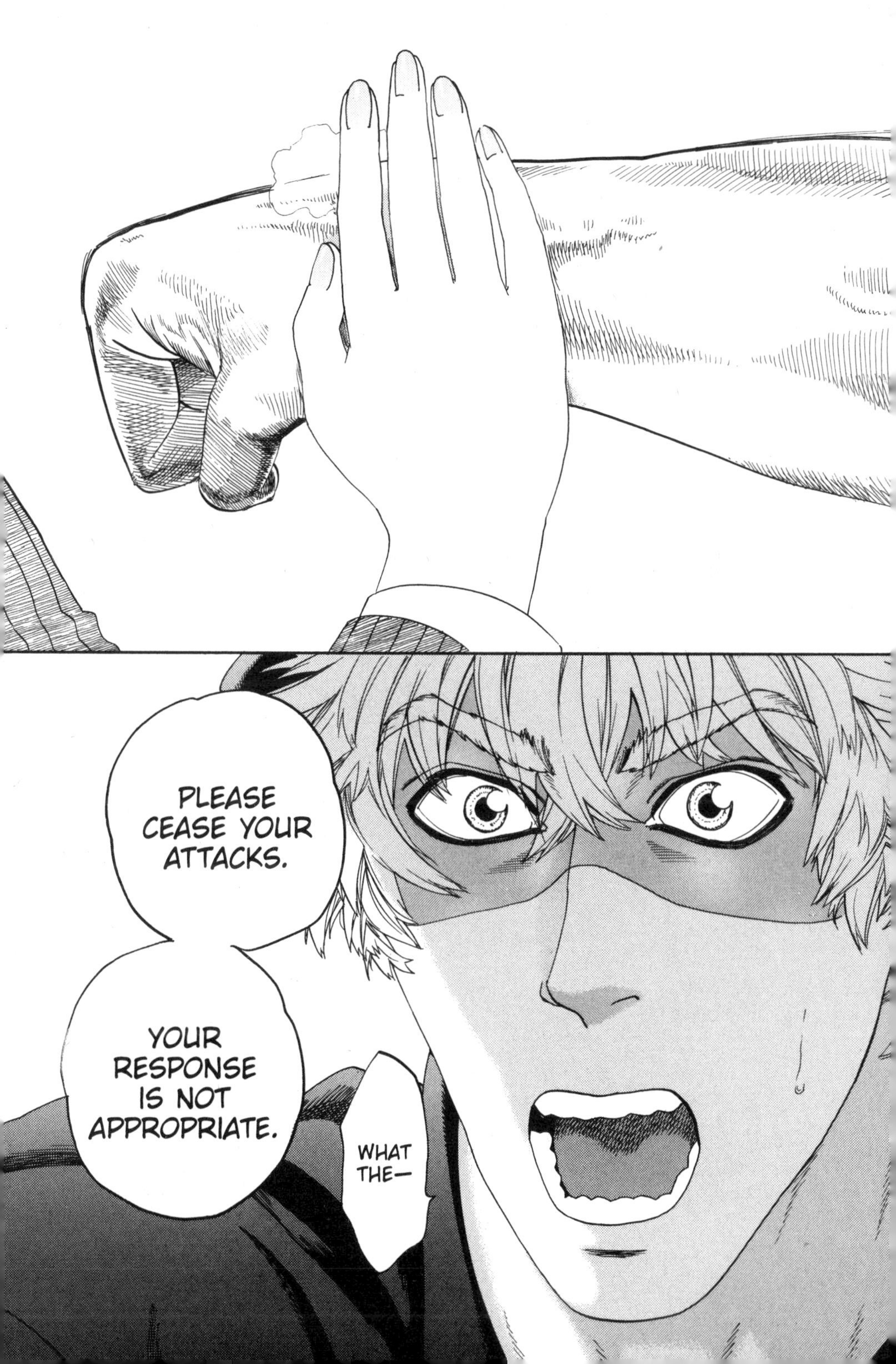
WHAT THE—
PLEASE CEASE YOUR ATTACKS.
YOUR RESPONSE IS NOT APPROPRIATE.

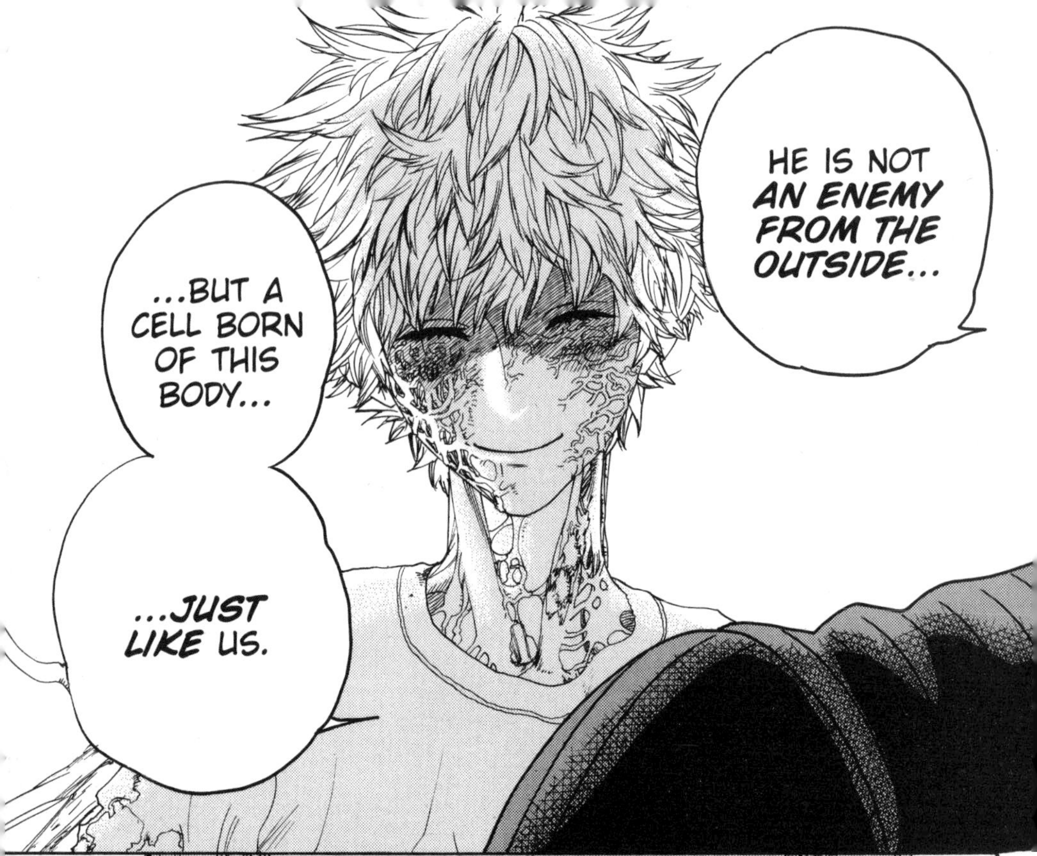
HE IS NOT **AN ENEMY FROM THE OUTSIDE...**
...BUT A CELL BORN OF THIS BODY...
...**JUST LIKE** US.

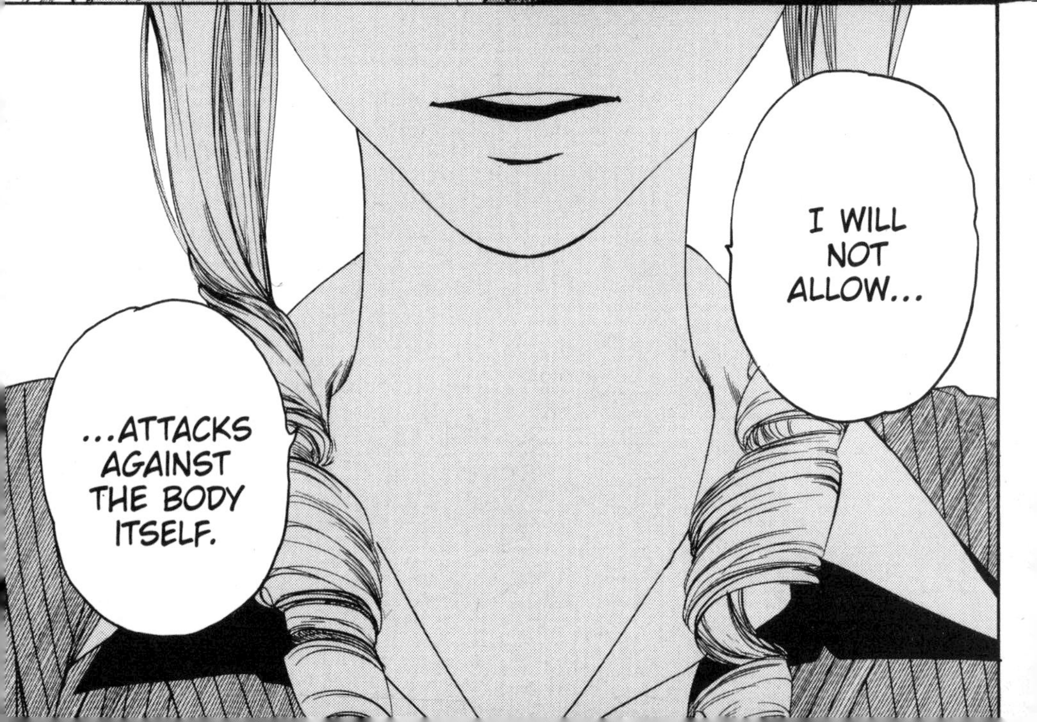
I WILL NOT ALLOW...
...ATTACKS AGAINST THE BODY ITSELF.

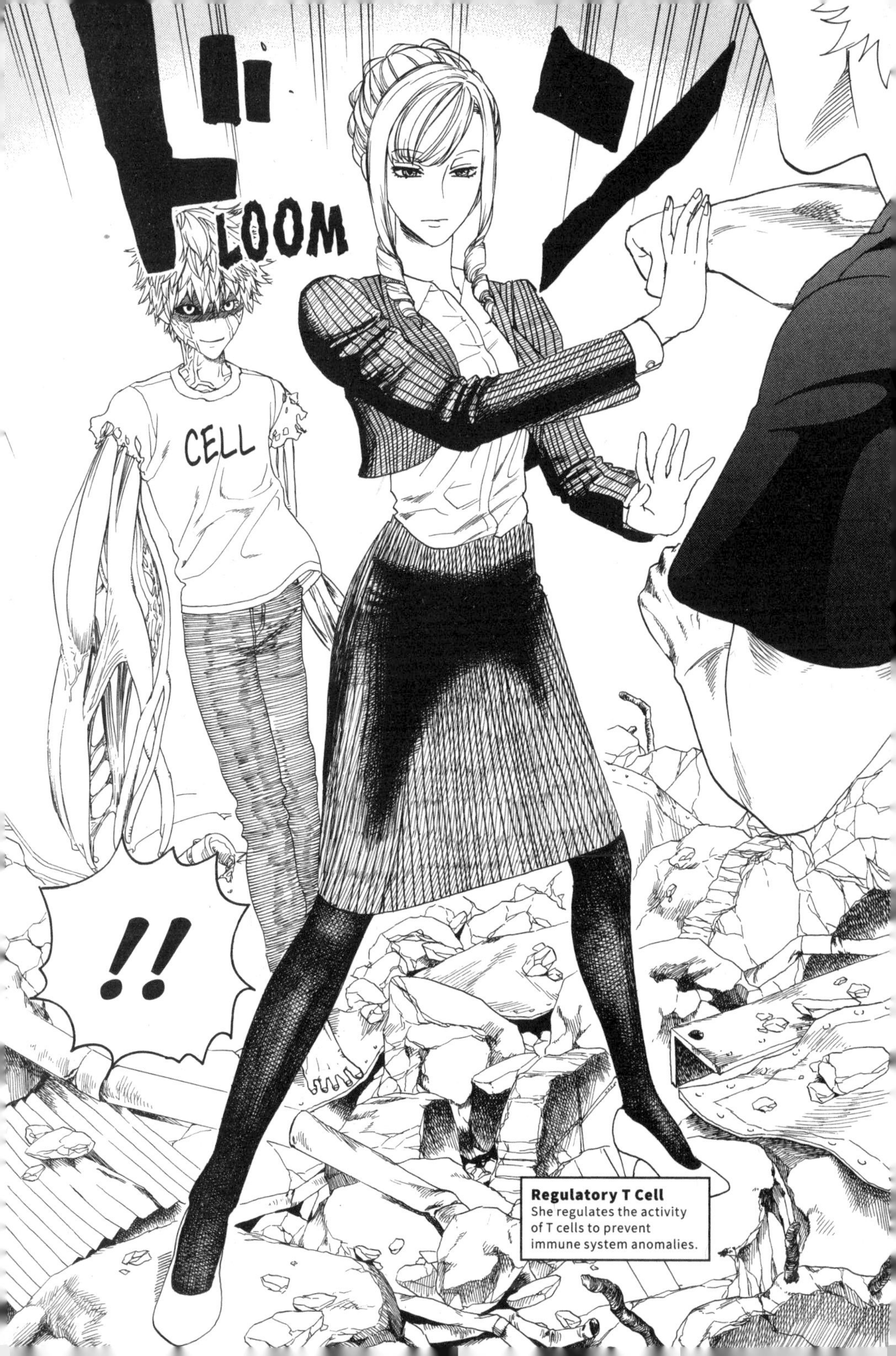
FLOOM
CELL
Regulatory T Cell
She regulates the activity of T cells to prevent immune system anomalies.
!!

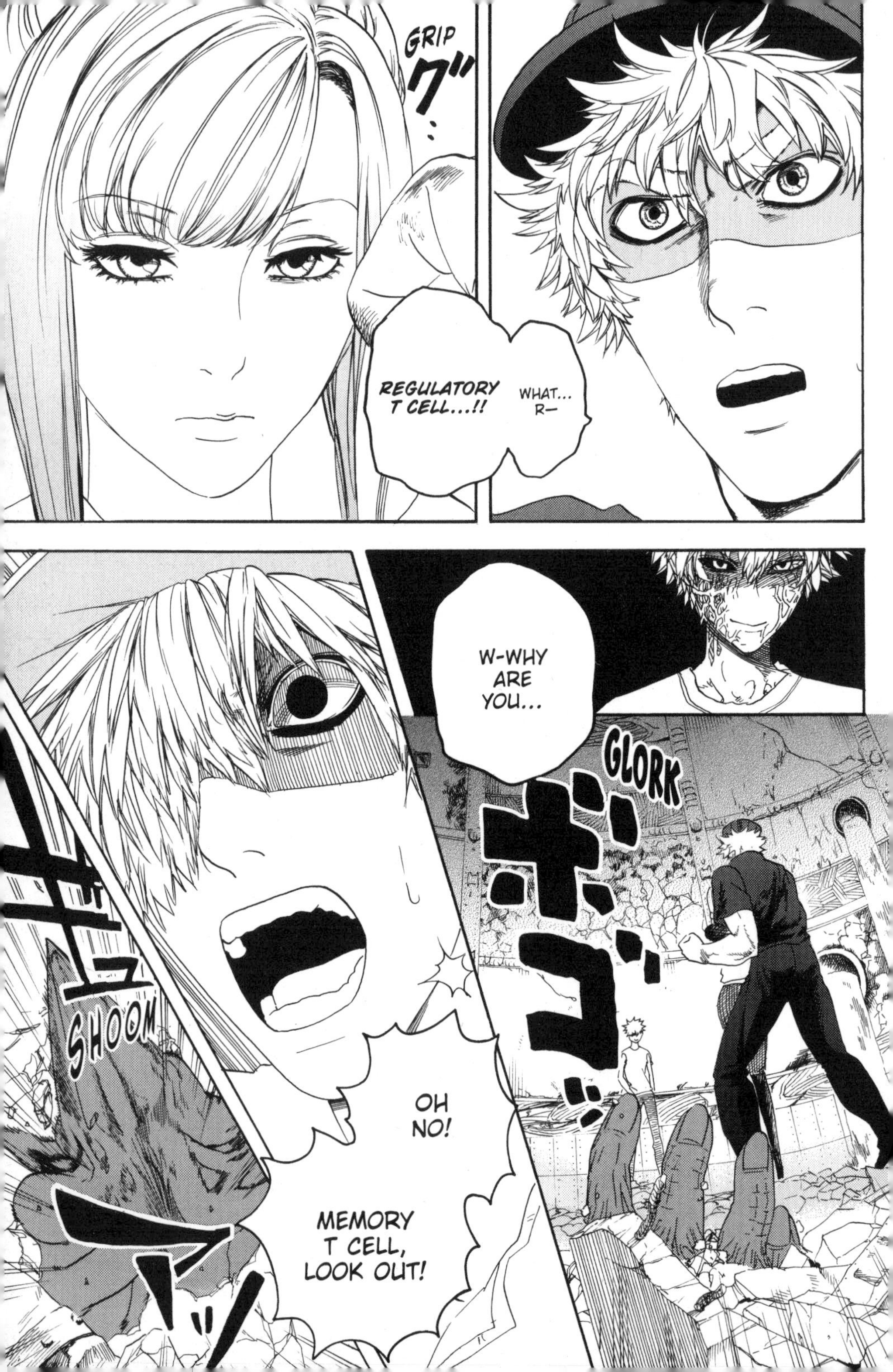
WHAT... R—
GRIP
REGULATORY T CELL...!!
W-WHY ARE YOU...
GLORK
SHOOM
OH NO!
MEMORY T CELL, LOOK OUT!

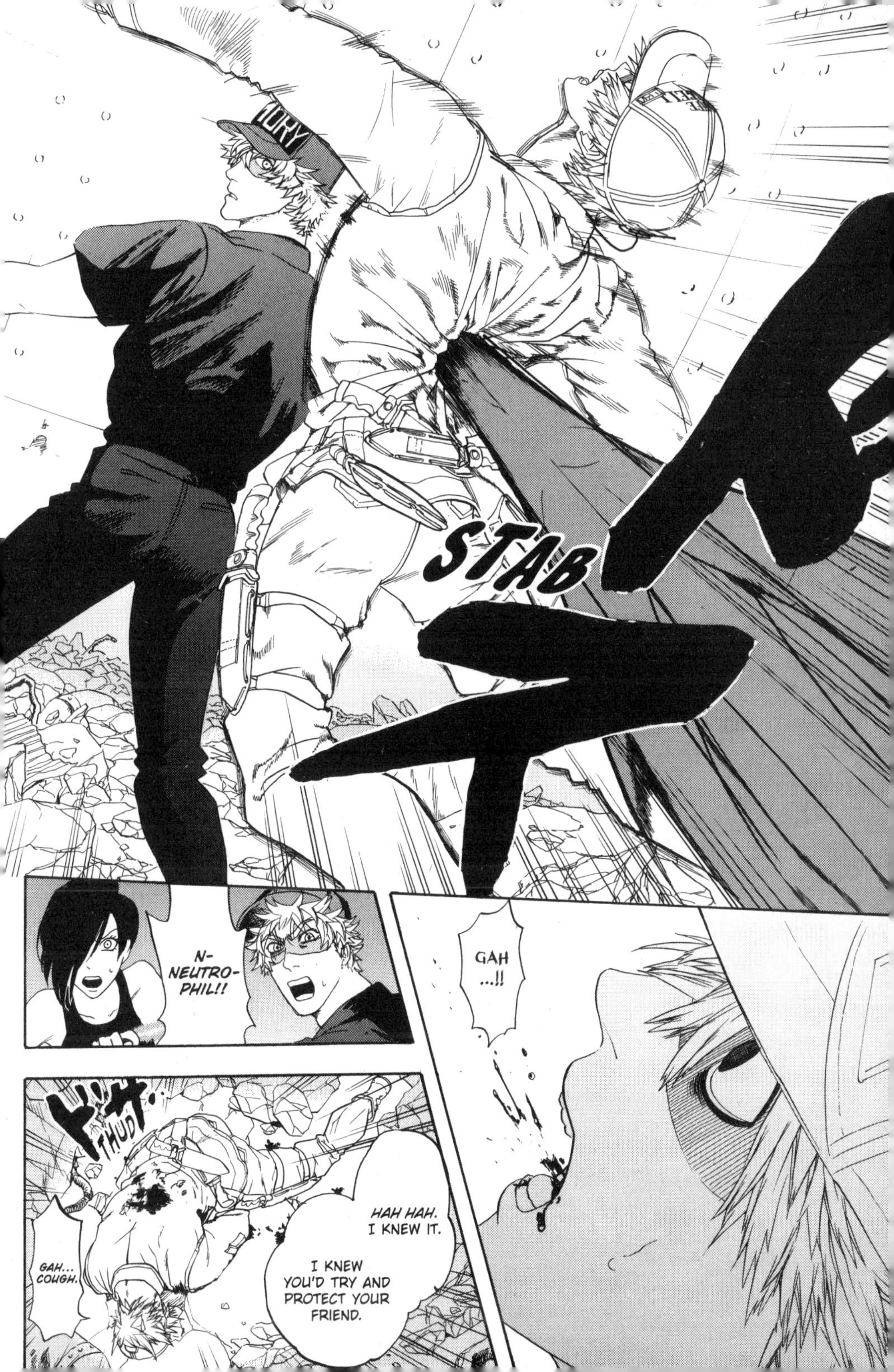
STAB
GAH ...!!
N-NEUTRO-PHIL!!
THUD
HAH HAH. I KNEW IT.
I KNEW YOU'D TRY AND PROTECT YOUR FRIEND.
GAH... COUGH.

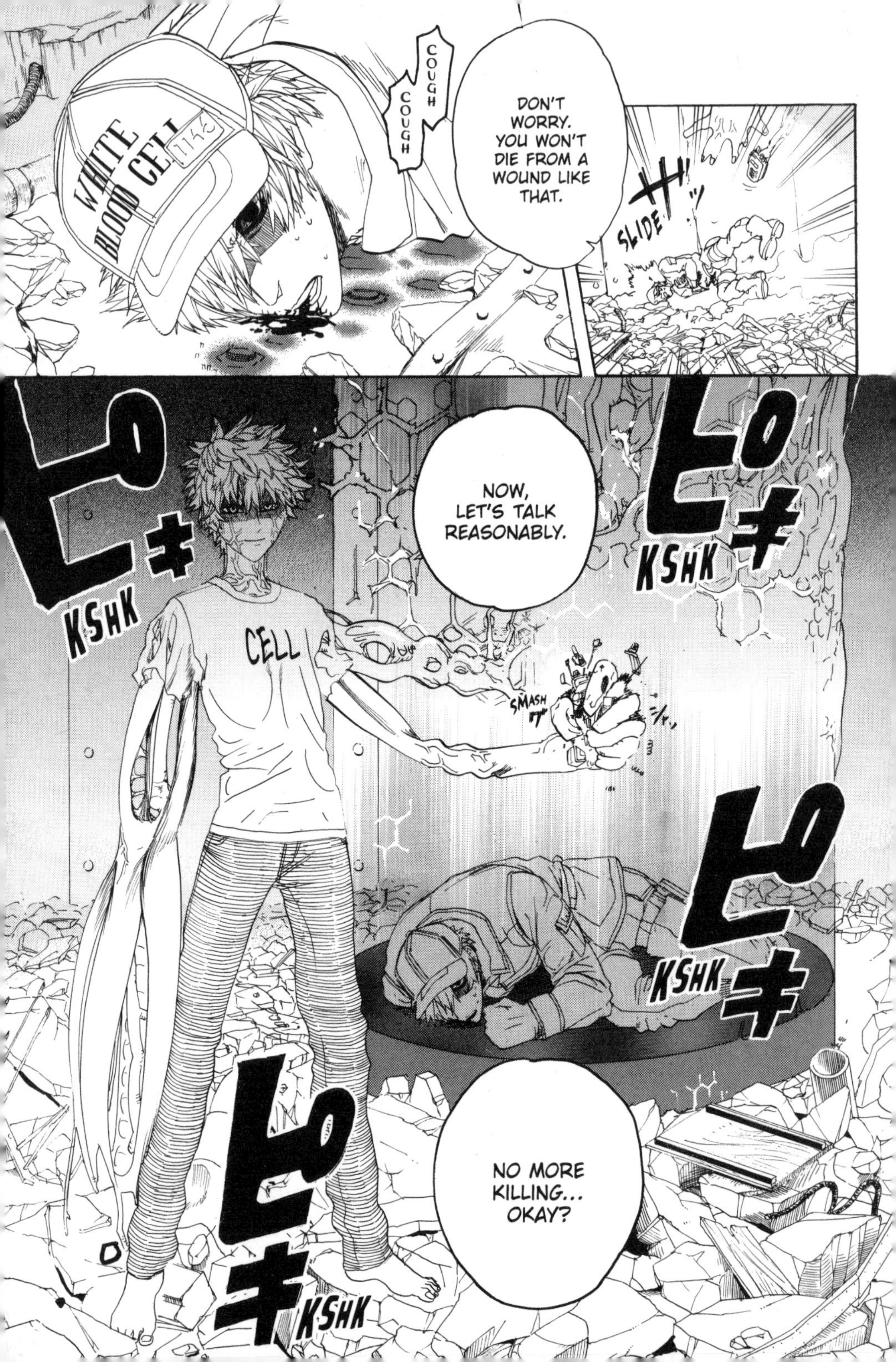
SLIDE
COUGH
COUGH
WHITE BLOOD CELL
1146
DON'T WORRY. YOU WON'T DIE FROM A WOUND LIKE THAT.
ピキ
KSHK
NOW, LET'S TALK REASONABLY.
ピキ
KSHK
CELL
SMASH
ピキ
KSHK
NO MORE KILLING... OKAY?
ピキ
KSHK

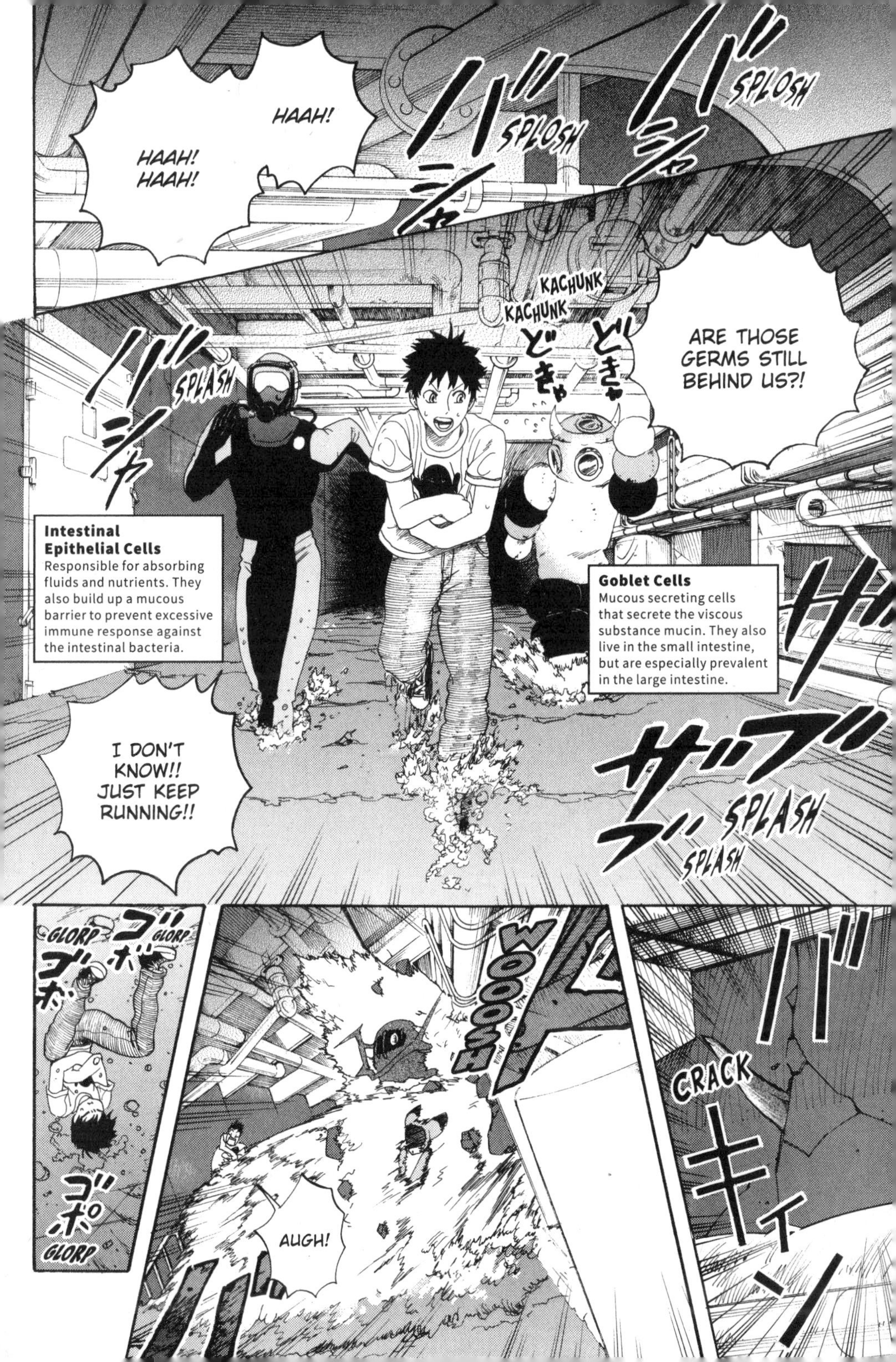
バシャ
SPLOSH
バシャ
SPLOSH
HAAH!
HAAH! HAAH!
ARE THOSE GERMS STILL BEHIND US?!
どきゃ
どきゃ
KACHUNK
KACHUNK
バシャ
SPLASH
Goblet Cells
Mucous secreting cells that secrete the viscous substance mucin. They also live in the small intestine, but are especially prevalent in the large intestine.
Intestinal Epithelial Cells
Responsible for absorbing fluids and nutrients. They also build up a mucous barrier to prevent excessive immune response against the intestinal bacteria.
ザブ
ザブ
SPLASH
SPLASH
I DON'T KNOW!! JUST KEEP RUNNING!!
CRACK
WOOOSH
AUGH!
ゴボ
GLORP
GLORP
ゴボ
ゴボ
GLORP

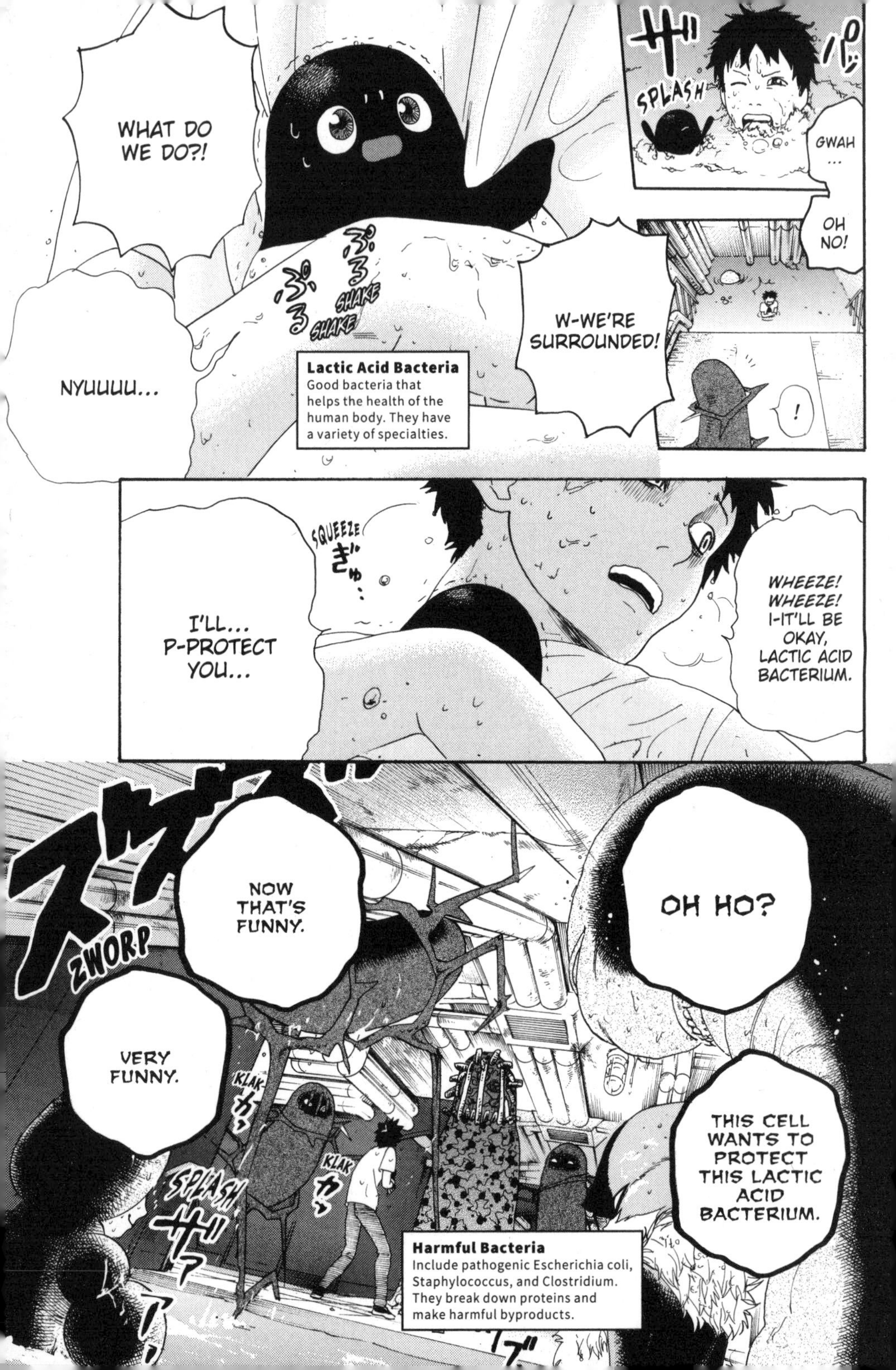
SPLASH
GWAH...
OH NO!
!
W-WE'RE SURROUNDED!
WHAT DO WE DO?!
ぷるぷる
SHAKE SHAKE
NYUUUU...
Lactic Acid Bacteria
Good bacteria that helps the health of the human body. They have a variety of specialties.
WHEEZE! WHEEZE! I-IT'LL BE OKAY, LACTIC ACID BACTERIUM.
SQUEEZE
ぎゅ
I'LL... P-PROTECT YOU...
OH HO?
THIS CELL WANTS TO PROTECT THIS LACTIC ACID BACTERIUM.
NOW THAT'S FUNNY.
ZWORP
VERY FUNNY.
KLAK
KLAK
SPLASH
Harmful Bacteria
Include pathogenic Escherichia coli, Staphylococcus, and Clostridium. They break down proteins and make harmful byproducts.

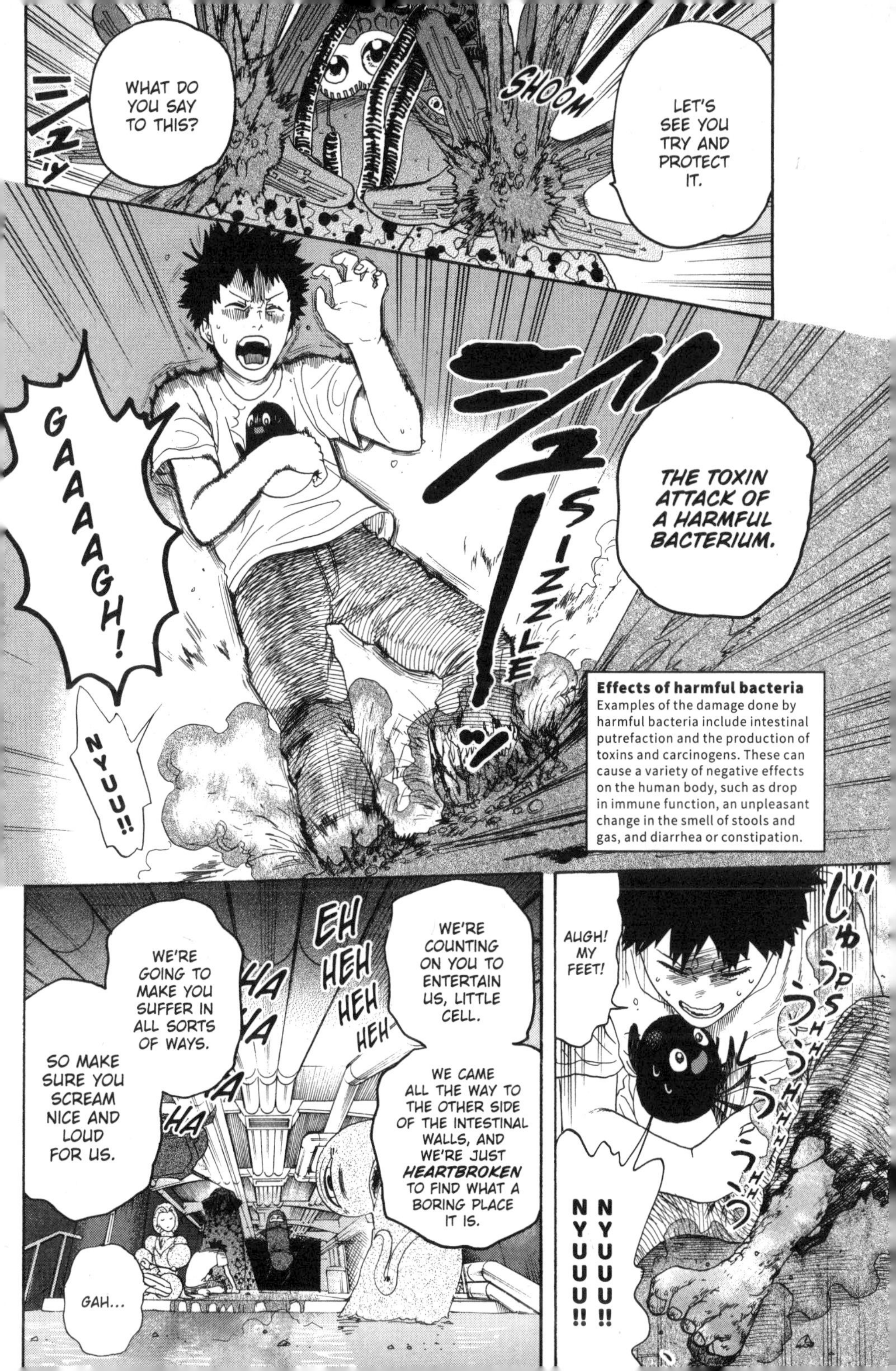
SHOOM
LET'S SEE YOU TRY AND PROTECT IT.
WHAT DO YOU SAY TO THIS?
THE TOXIN ATTACK OF A HARMFUL BACTERIUM.
SIZZLE
GAAAAAGH!
NYUU!!
Effects of harmful bacteria
Examples of the damage done by harmful bacteria include intestinal putrefaction and the production of toxins and carcinogens. These can cause a variety of negative effects on the human body, such as drop in immune function, an unpleasant change in the smell of stools and gas, and diarrhea or constipation.
AUGH! MY FEET!
NYUUU!!
NYUUU!!
WE'RE COUNTING ON YOU TO ENTERTAIN US, LITTLE CELL.
EH HEH HEH HEH
WE CAME ALL THE WAY TO THE OTHER SIDE OF THE INTESTINAL WALLS, AND WE'RE JUST *HEARTBROKEN* TO FIND WHAT A BORING PLACE IT IS.
WE'RE GOING TO MAKE YOU SUFFER IN ALL SORTS OF WAYS.
HA HA HA HA
SO MAKE SURE YOU SCREAM NICE AND LOUD FOR US.
GAH...

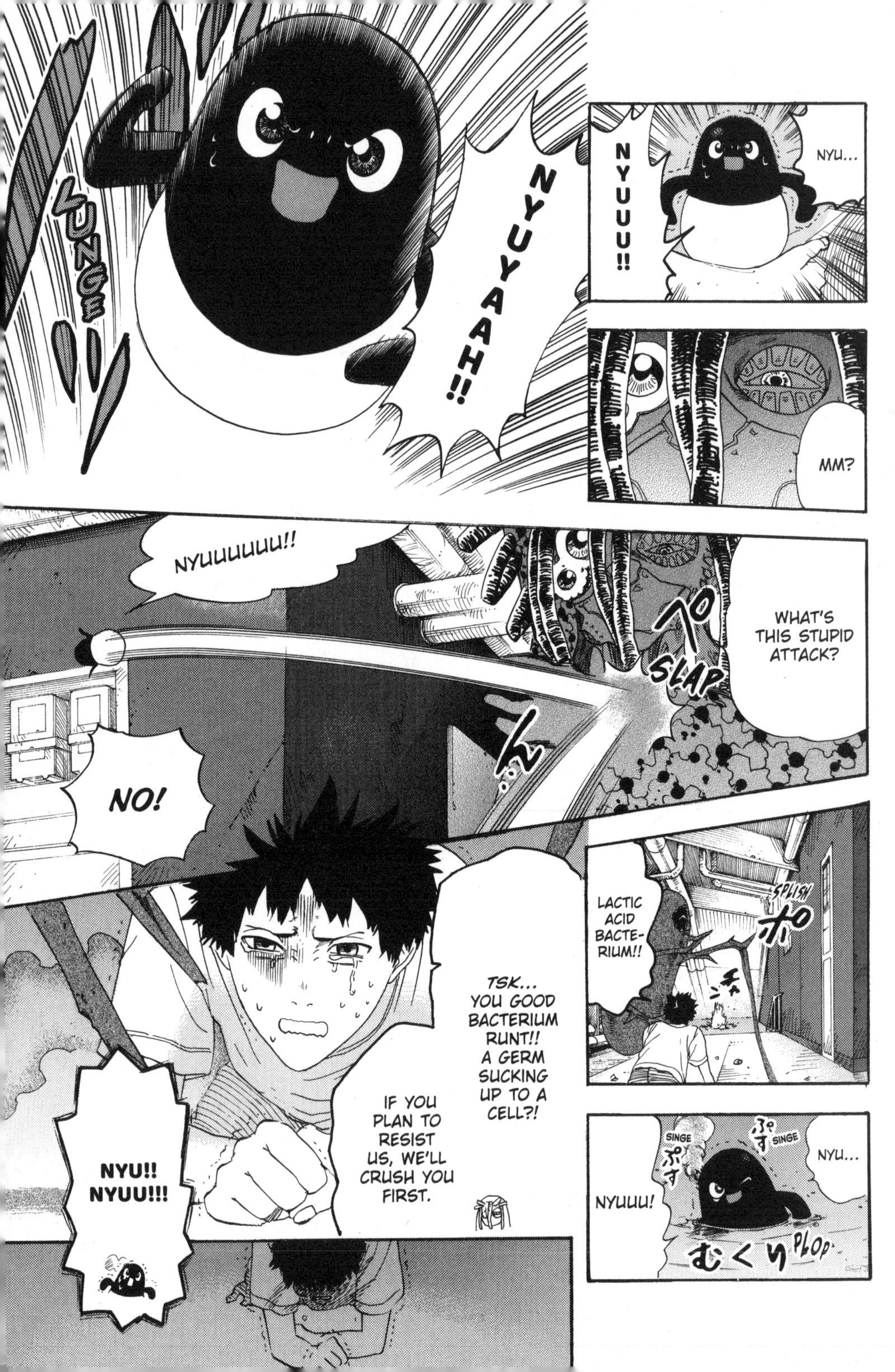
NYU...
NYUUU!!
MM?
NYUYAAAH!!
LUNGE!!
WHAT'S THIS STUPID ATTACK?
SLAP
NYUUUUUU!!
NO!
LACTIC ACID BACTERIUM!!
SPLISH
NYU...
SINGE
SINGE
NYUUU!
PLOP
TSK... YOU GOOD BACTERIUM RUNT!! A GERM SUCKING UP TO A CELL?!
IF YOU PLAN TO RESIST US, WE'LL CRUSH YOU FIRST.
NYU!! NYUU!!!

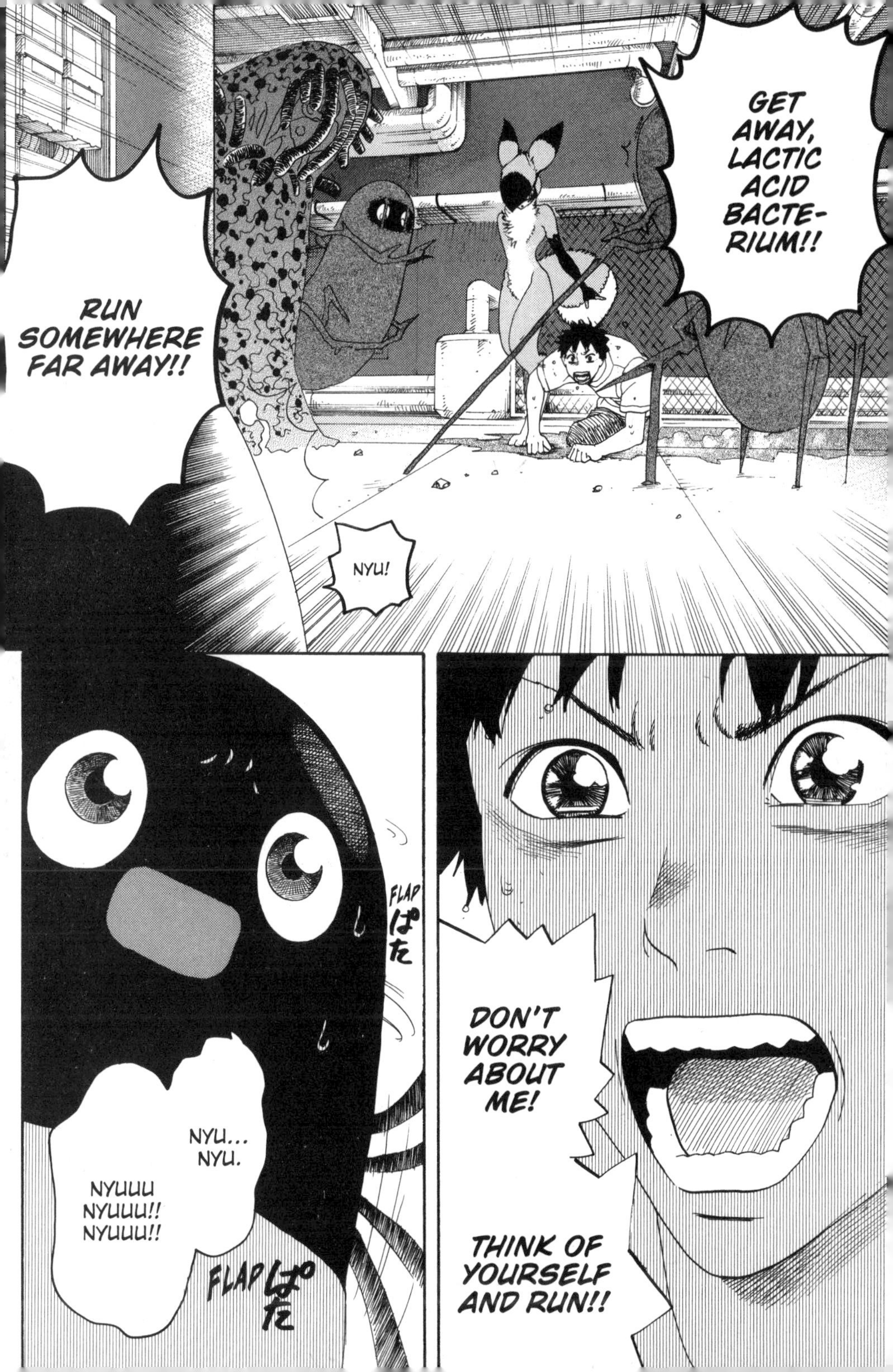
GET AWAY, LACTIC ACID BACTERIUM!!
RUN SOMEWHERE FAR AWAY!!
NYU!
DON'T WORRY ABOUT ME!
THINK OF YOURSELF AND RUN!!
FLAP ぱた
NYU... NYU.
NYUUU NYUUU!! NYUUU!!
FLAP ぱた

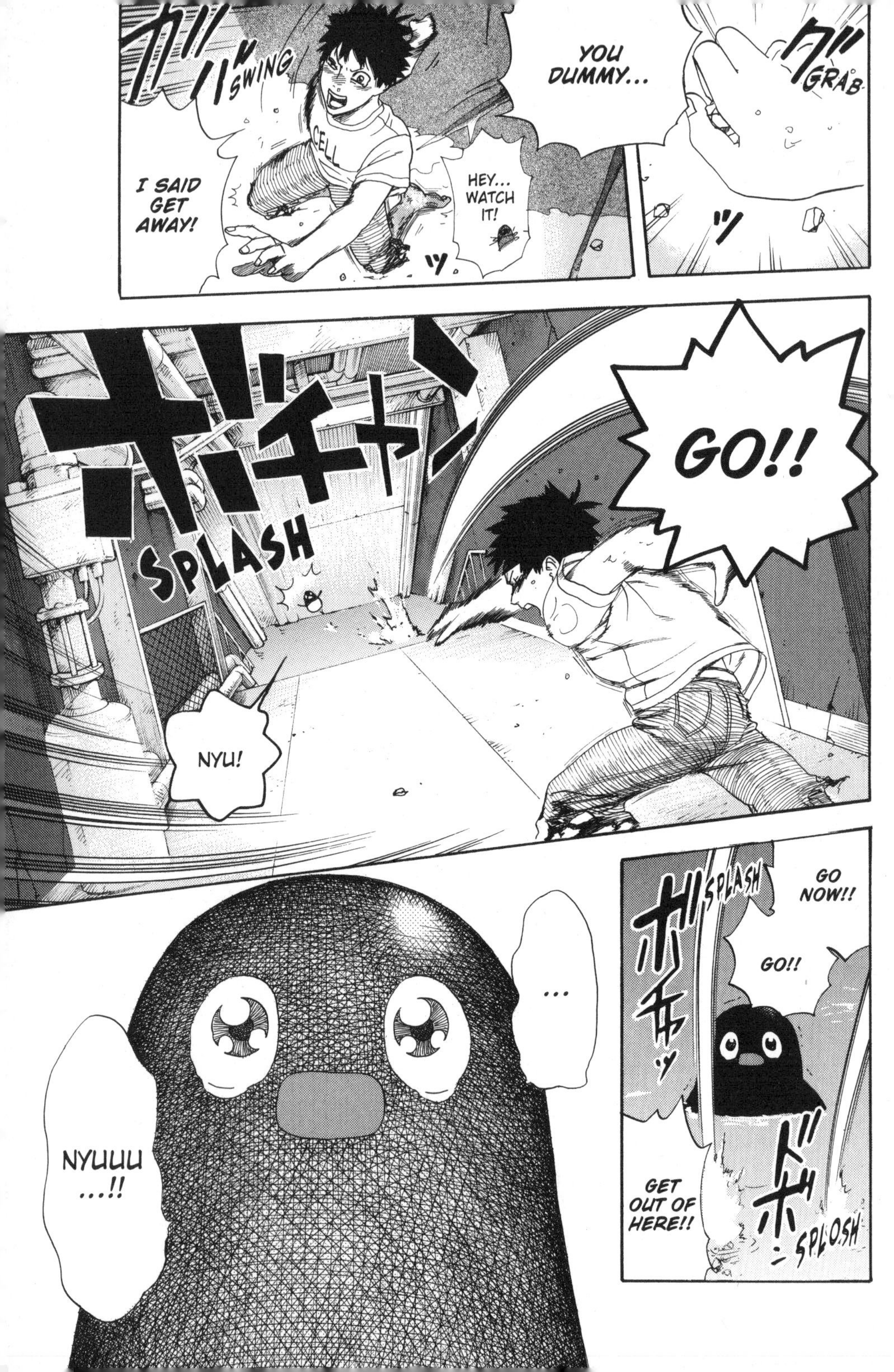
GRAB
YOU DUMMY...
SWING
HEY... WATCH IT!
I SAID GET AWAY!
GO!!
SPLASH
NYU!
GO NOW!!
SPLASH
GO!!
GET OUT OF HERE!!
SPLOSH
...
NYUUU ...!!

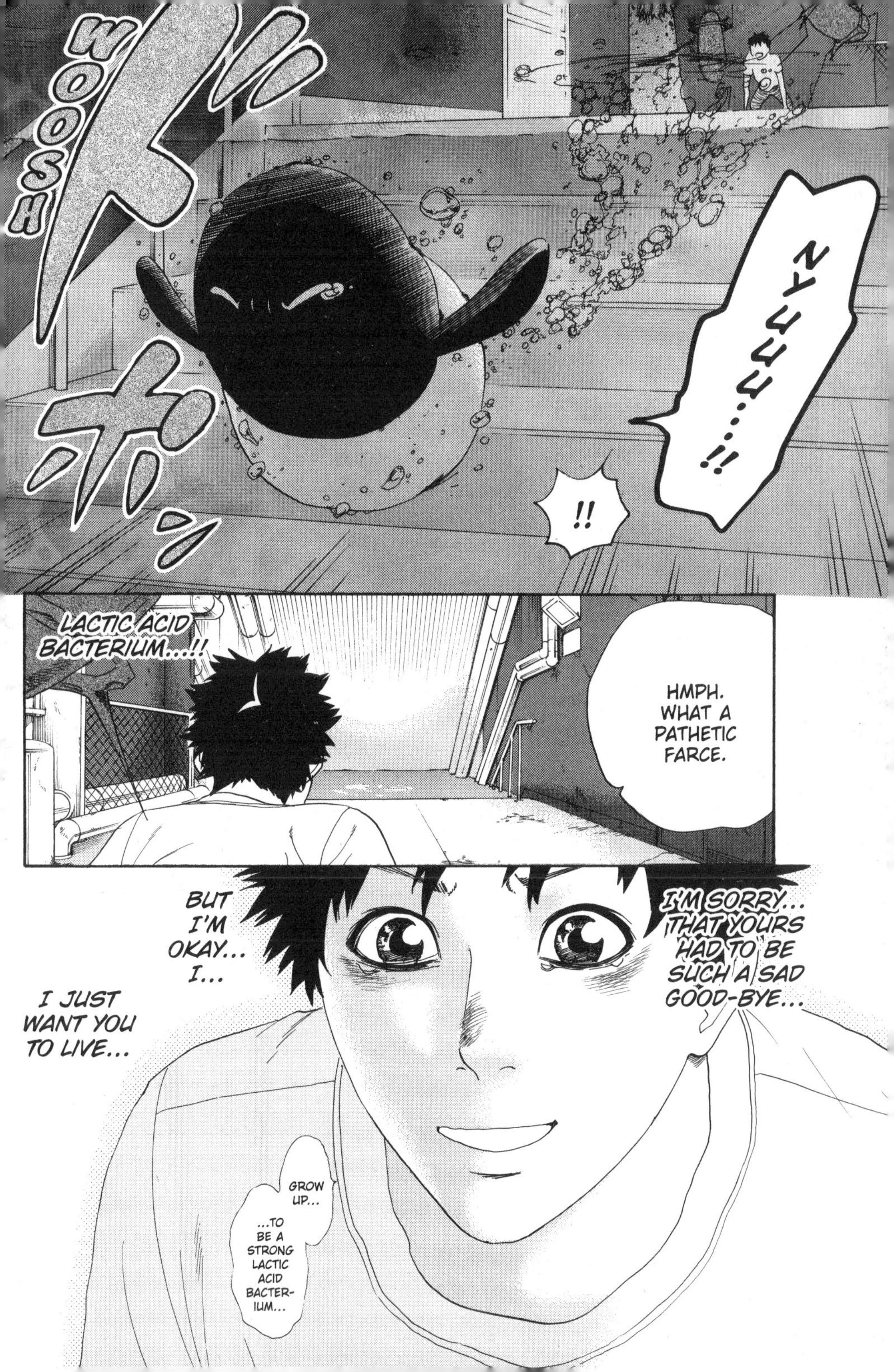
NYUUU...!!
!!
WOOSH
HMPH. WHAT A PATHETIC FARCE.
LACTIC ACID BACTERIUM...!!
I'M SORRY... THAT YOURS HAD TO BE SUCH A SAD GOOD-BYE...
BUT I'M OKAY... I...
I JUST WANT YOU TO LIVE...
GROW UP...
...TO BE A STRONG LACTIC ACID BACTERIUM...

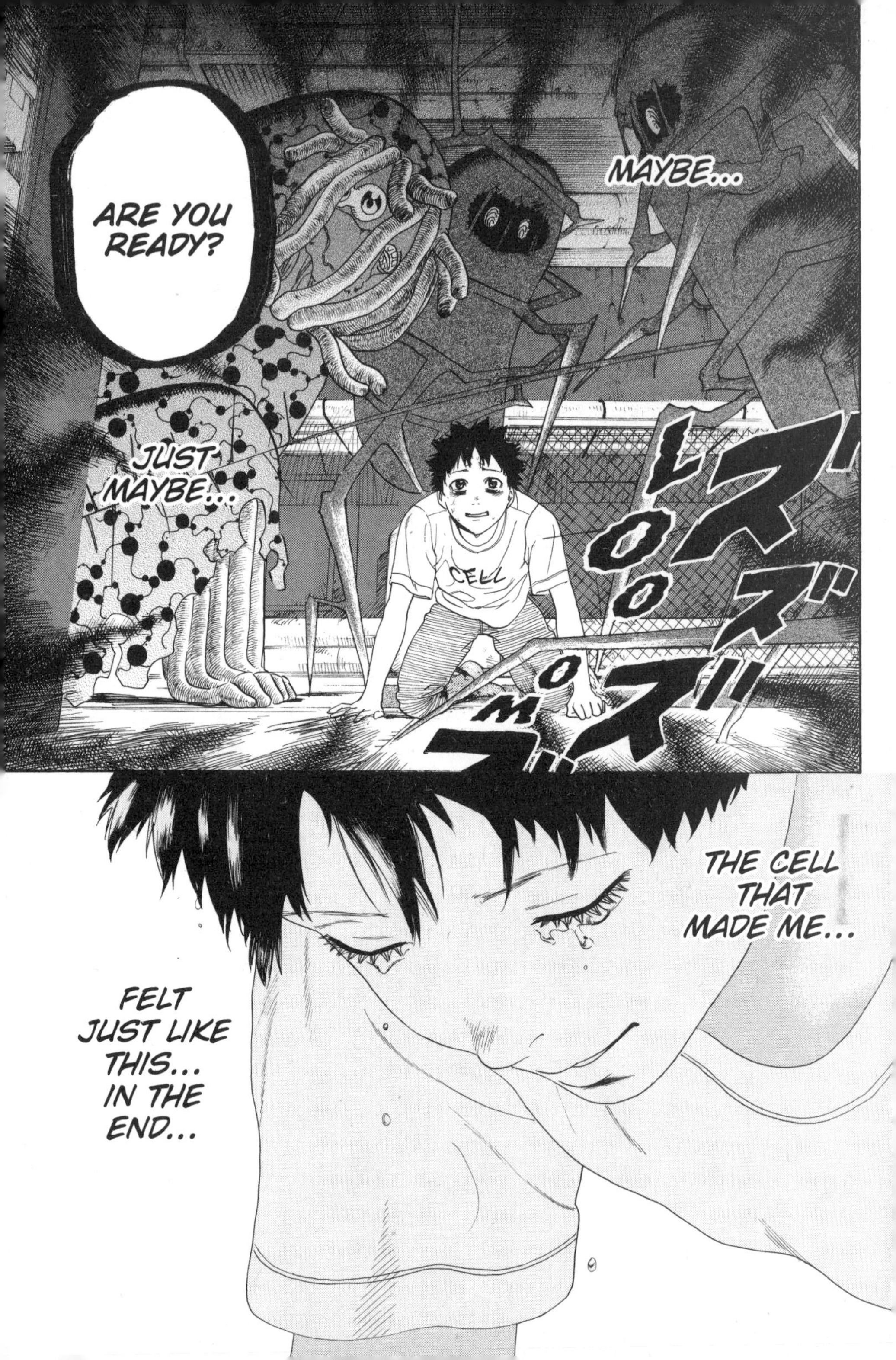
MAYBE...
ARE YOU READY?
JUST MAYBE...
CELL
THE CELL THAT MADE ME...
FELT JUST LIKE THIS... IN THE END...

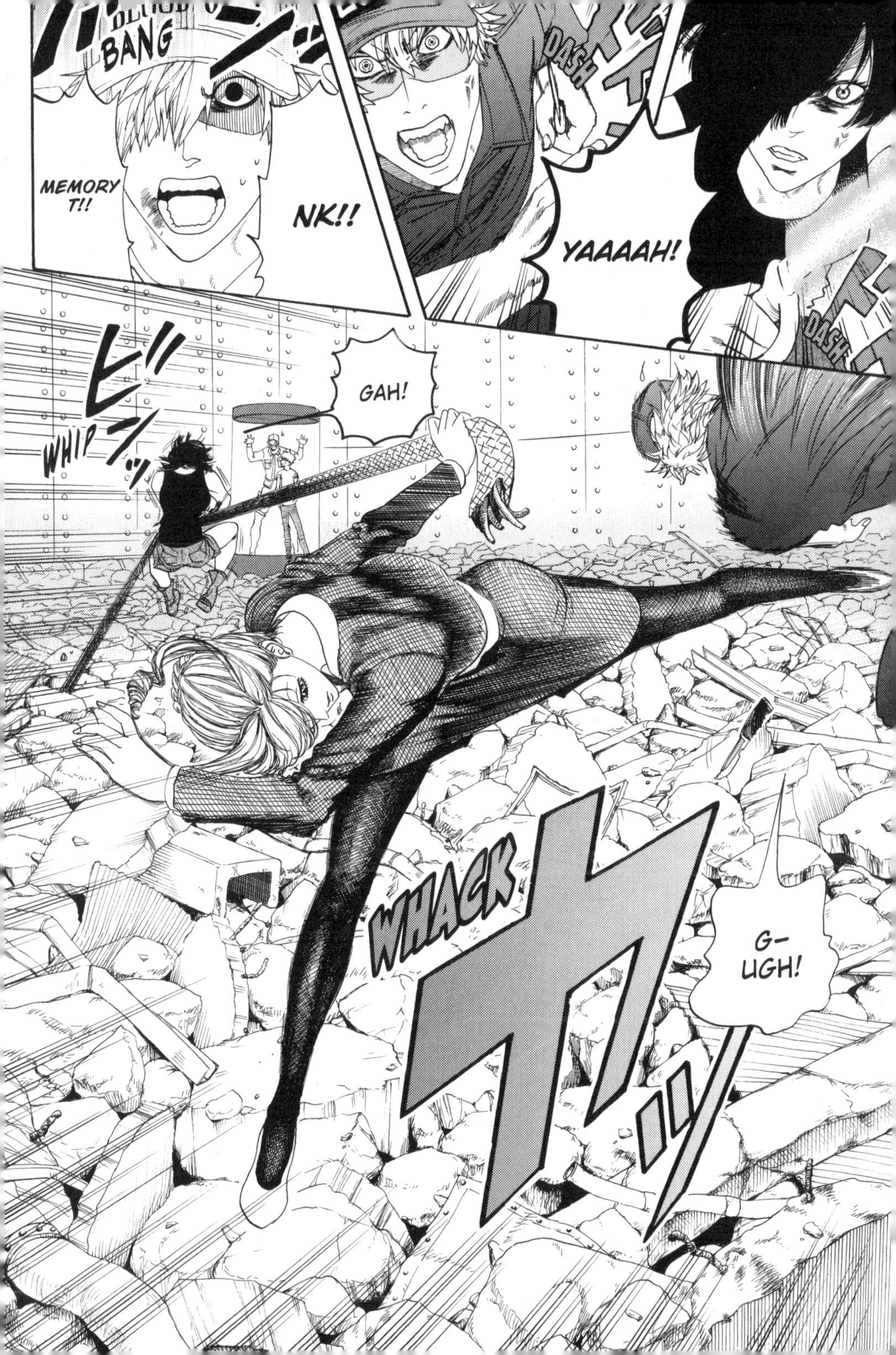

YAAAAH!
DASH
DASH
BANG
MEMORY T!!
NK!!
GAH!
WHIP
G- UGH!
WHACK

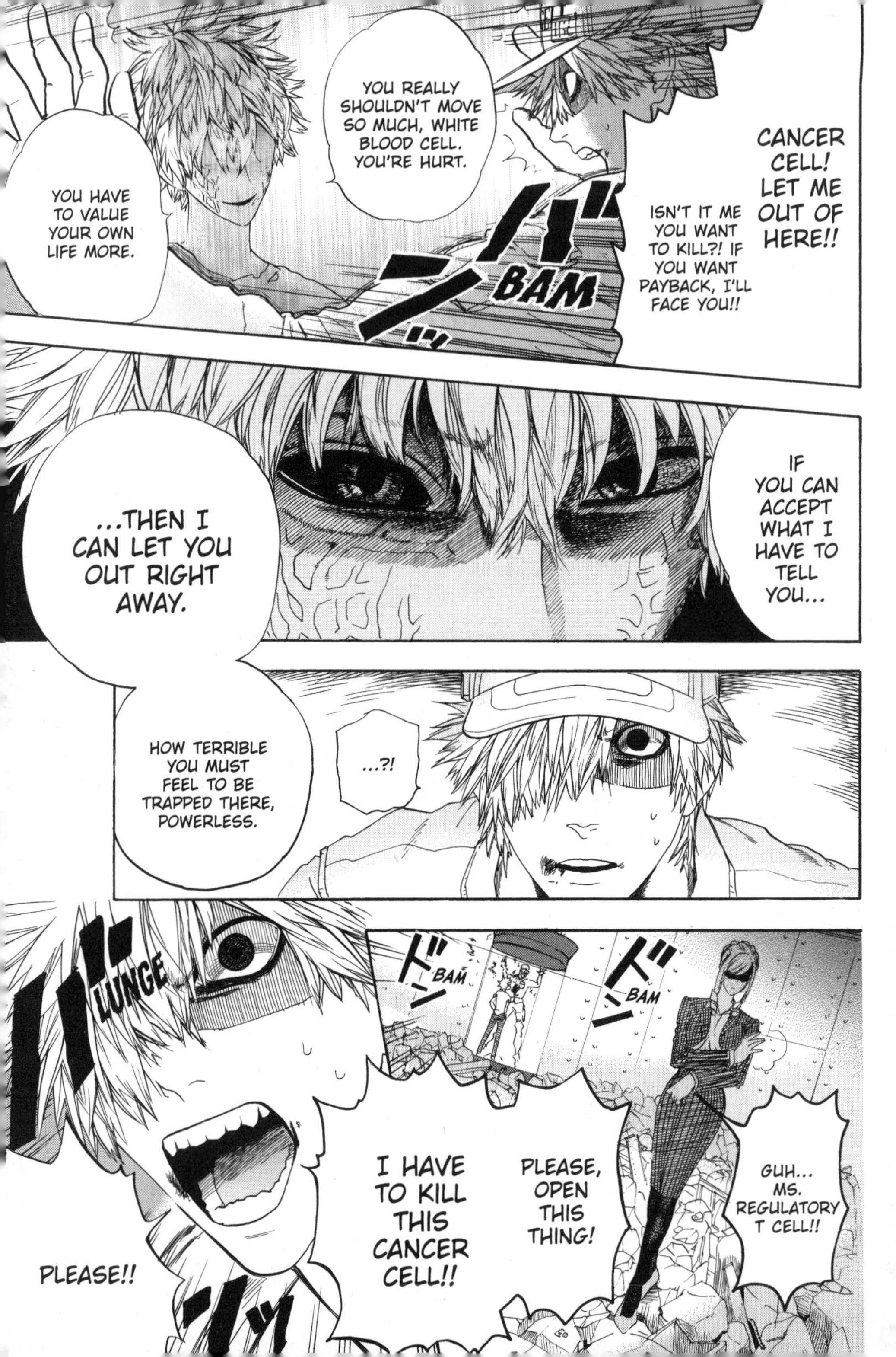
CANCER CELL! LET ME OUT OF HERE!!
ISN'T IT ME YOU WANT TO KILL?! IF YOU WANT PAYBACK, I'LL FACE YOU!!
BAM
YOU REALLY SHOULDN'T MOVE SO MUCH, WHITE BLOOD CELL. YOU'RE HURT.
YOU HAVE TO VALUE YOUR OWN LIFE MORE.
IF YOU CAN ACCEPT WHAT I HAVE TO TELL YOU...
...THEN I CAN LET YOU OUT RIGHT AWAY.
...?!
HOW TERRIBLE YOU MUST FEEL TO BE TRAPPED THERE, POWERLESS.
BAM
BAM
GUH... MS. REGULATORY T CELL!!
LUNGE
PLEASE, OPEN THIS THING!
I HAVE TO KILL THIS CANCER CELL!!
PLEASE!!

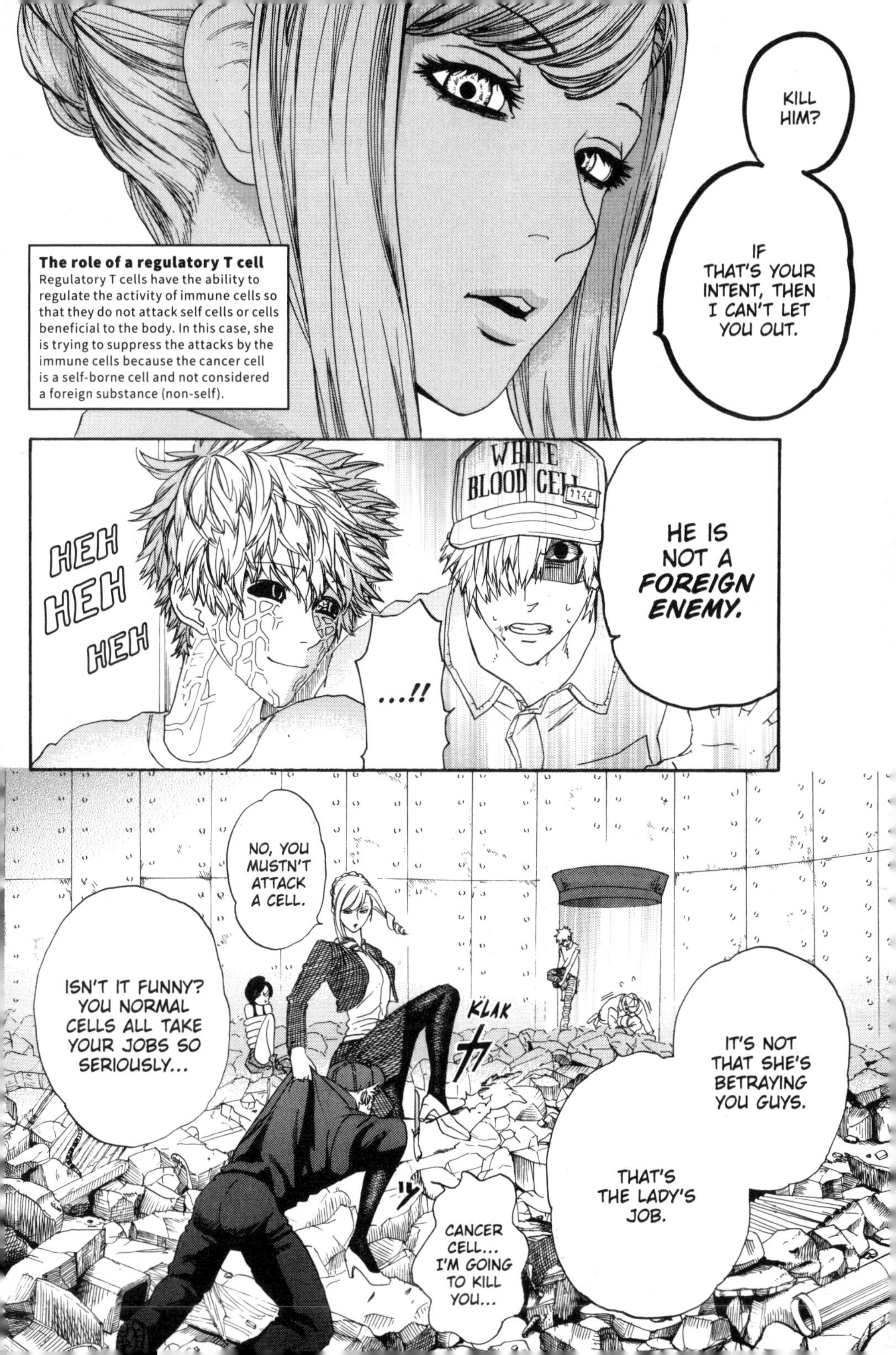
KILL HIM?
IF THAT'S YOUR INTENT, THEN I CAN'T LET YOU OUT.
The role of a regulatory T cell
Regulatory T cells have the ability to regulate the activity of immune cells so that they do not attack self cells or cells beneficial to the body. In this case, she is trying to suppress the attacks by the immune cells because the cancer cell is a self-borne cell and not considered a foreign substance (non-self).
WHITE BLOOD CELL
HE IS NOT A *FOREIGN ENEMY.*
...!!
HEH HEH HEH
IT'S NOT THAT SHE'S BETRAYING YOU GUYS.
THAT'S THE LADY'S JOB.
CANCER CELL... I'M GOING TO KILL YOU...
KLAK
NO, YOU MUSTN'T ATTACK A CELL.
ISN'T IT FUNNY? YOU NORMAL CELLS ALL TAKE YOUR JOBS SO SERIOUSLY...

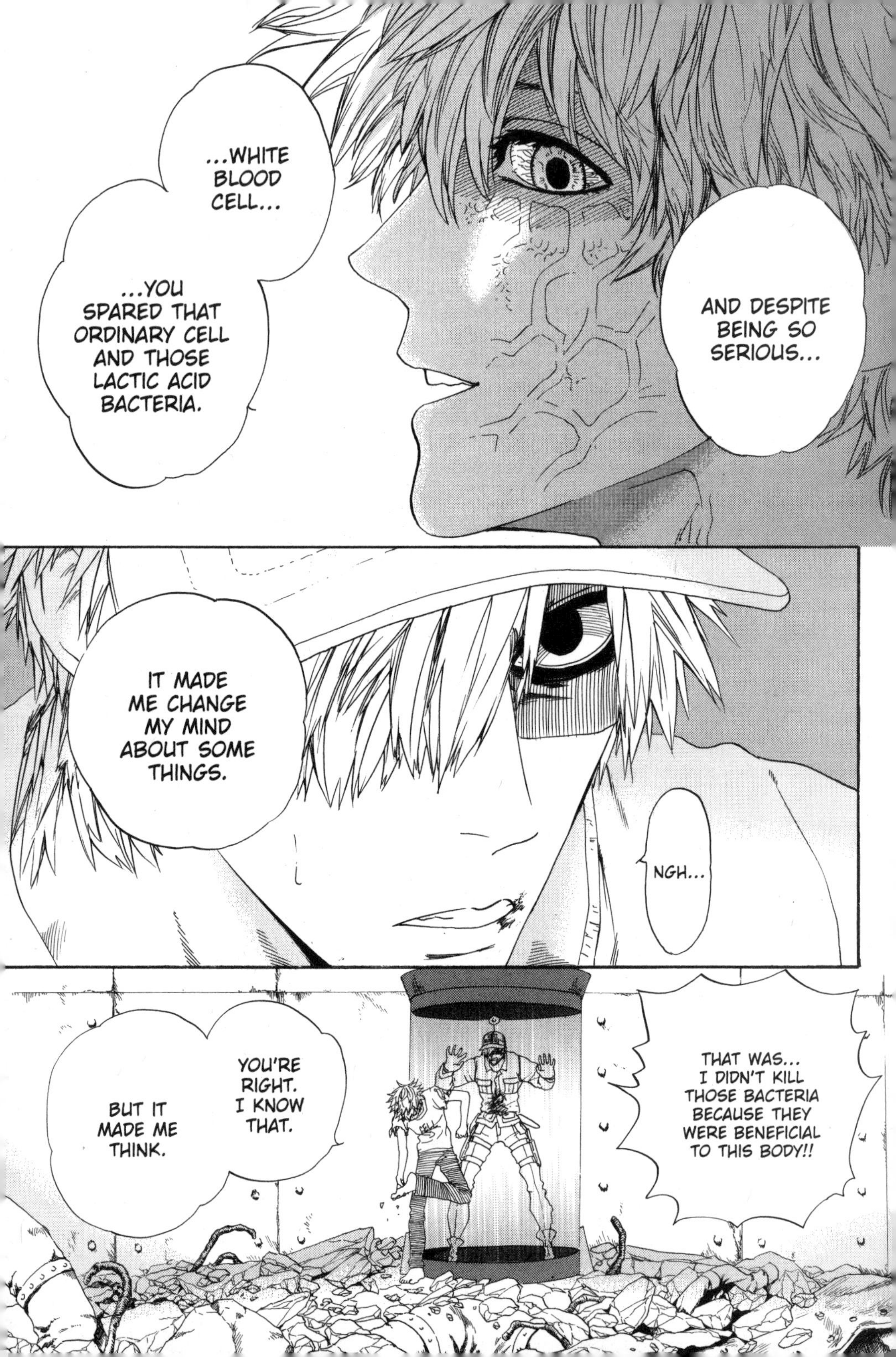
...WHITE BLOOD CELL...
...YOU SPARED THAT ORDINARY CELL AND THOSE LACTIC ACID BACTERIA.
AND DESPITE BEING SO SERIOUS...
IT MADE ME CHANGE MY MIND ABOUT SOME THINGS.
NGH...
THAT WAS... I DIDN'T KILL THOSE BACTERIA BECAUSE THEY WERE BENEFICIAL TO THIS BODY!!
YOU'RE RIGHT. I KNOW THAT.
BUT IT MADE ME THINK.

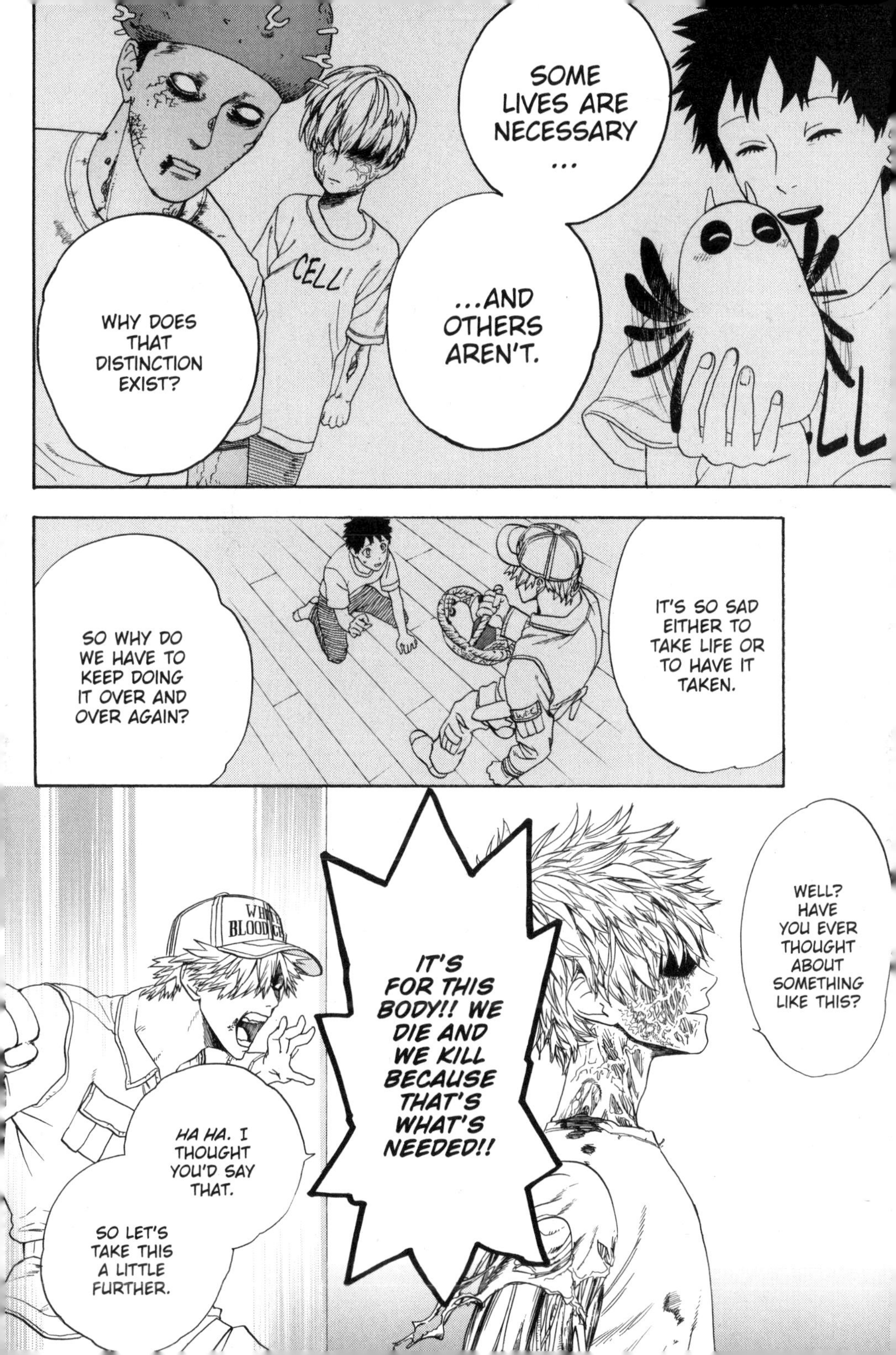
SOME LIVES ARE NECESSARY ...
...AND OTHERS AREN'T.
CELL
WHY DOES THAT DISTINCTION EXIST?
IT'S SO SAD EITHER TO TAKE LIFE OR TO HAVE IT TAKEN.
SO WHY DO WE HAVE TO KEEP DOING IT OVER AND OVER AGAIN?
WELL? HAVE YOU EVER THOUGHT ABOUT SOMETHING LIKE THIS?
IT'S FOR THIS BODY!! WE DIE AND WE KILL BECAUSE THAT'S WHAT'S NEEDED!!
HA HA. I THOUGHT YOU'D SAY THAT.
SO LET'S TAKE THIS A LITTLE FURTHER.

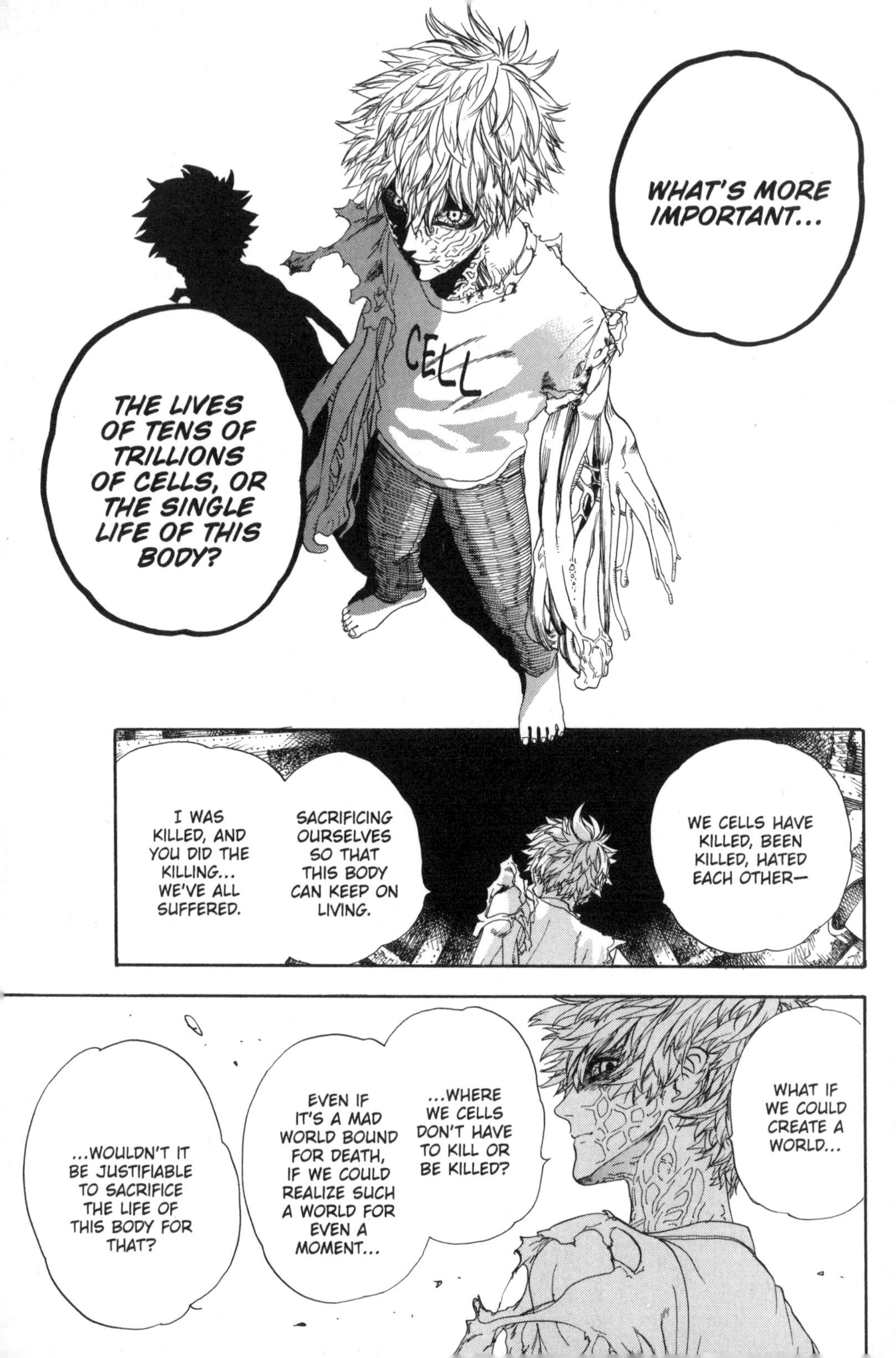
WHAT'S MORE IMPORTANT...
CELL
THE LIVES OF TENS OF TRILLIONS OF CELLS, OR THE SINGLE LIFE OF THIS BODY?
WE CELLS HAVE KILLED, BEEN KILLED, HATED EACH OTHER—
SACRIFICING OURSELVES SO THAT THIS BODY CAN KEEP ON LIVING.
I WAS KILLED, AND YOU DID THE KILLING... WE'VE ALL SUFFERED.
WHAT IF WE COULD CREATE A WORLD...
...WHERE WE CELLS DON'T HAVE TO KILL OR BE KILLED?
EVEN IF IT'S A MAD WORLD BOUND FOR DEATH, IF WE COULD REALIZE SUCH A WORLD FOR EVEN A MOMENT...
...WOULDN'T IT BE JUSTIFIABLE TO SACRIFICE THE LIFE OF THIS BODY FOR THAT?

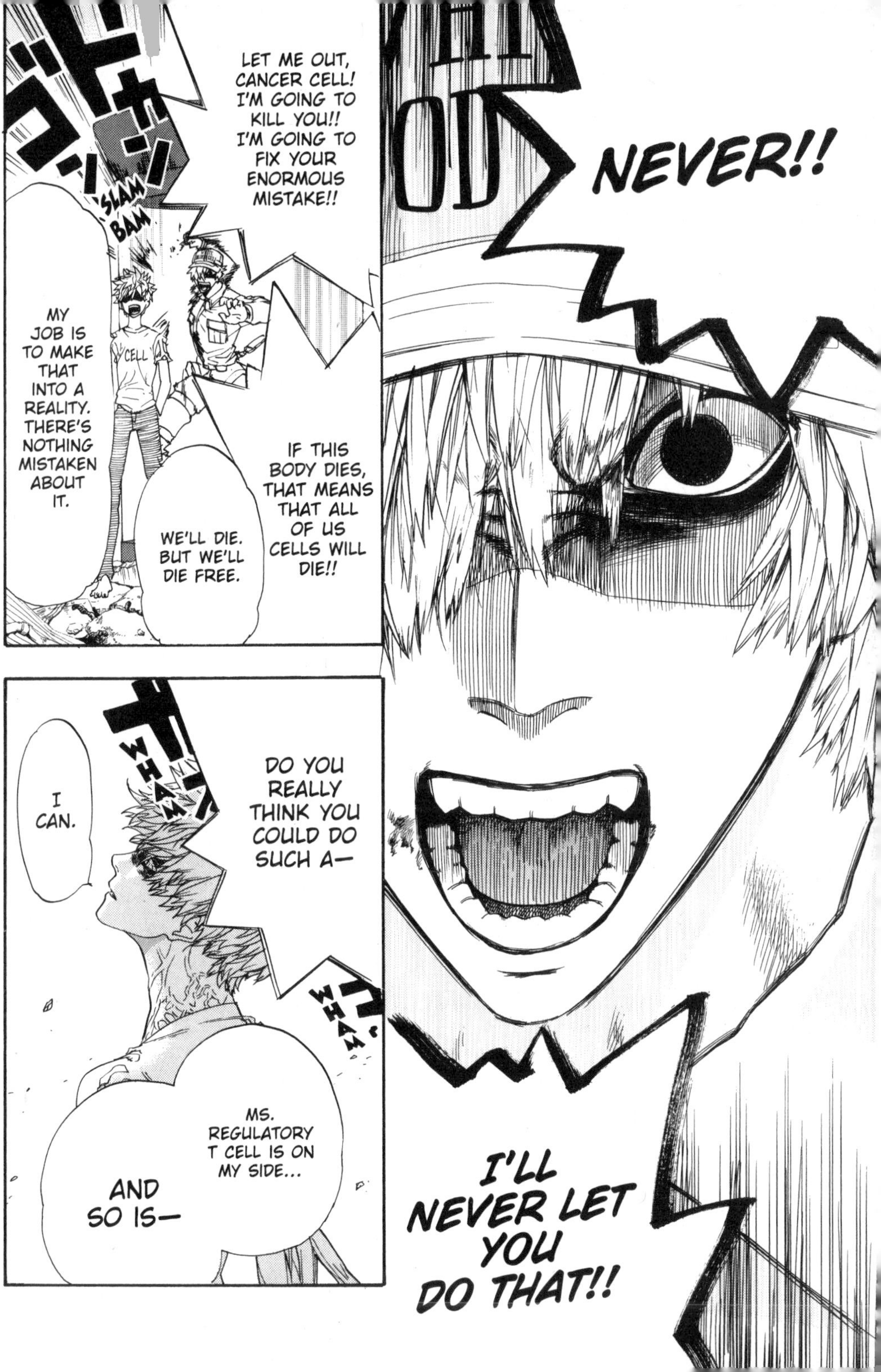
NEVER!!
I'LL NEVER LET YOU DO THAT!!
LET ME OUT, CANCER CELL! I'M GOING TO KILL YOU!! I'M GOING TO FIX YOUR ENORMOUS MISTAKE!!
SLAM BAM
MY JOB IS TO MAKE THAT INTO A REALITY. THERE'S NOTHING MISTAKEN ABOUT IT.
CELL
IF THIS BODY DIES, THAT MEANS THAT ALL OF US CELLS WILL DIE!!
WE'LL DIE. BUT WE'LL DIE FREE.
DO YOU REALLY THINK YOU COULD DO SUCH A—
WHAM
I CAN.
WHAM
MS. REGULATORY T CELL IS ON MY SIDE...
AND SO IS—

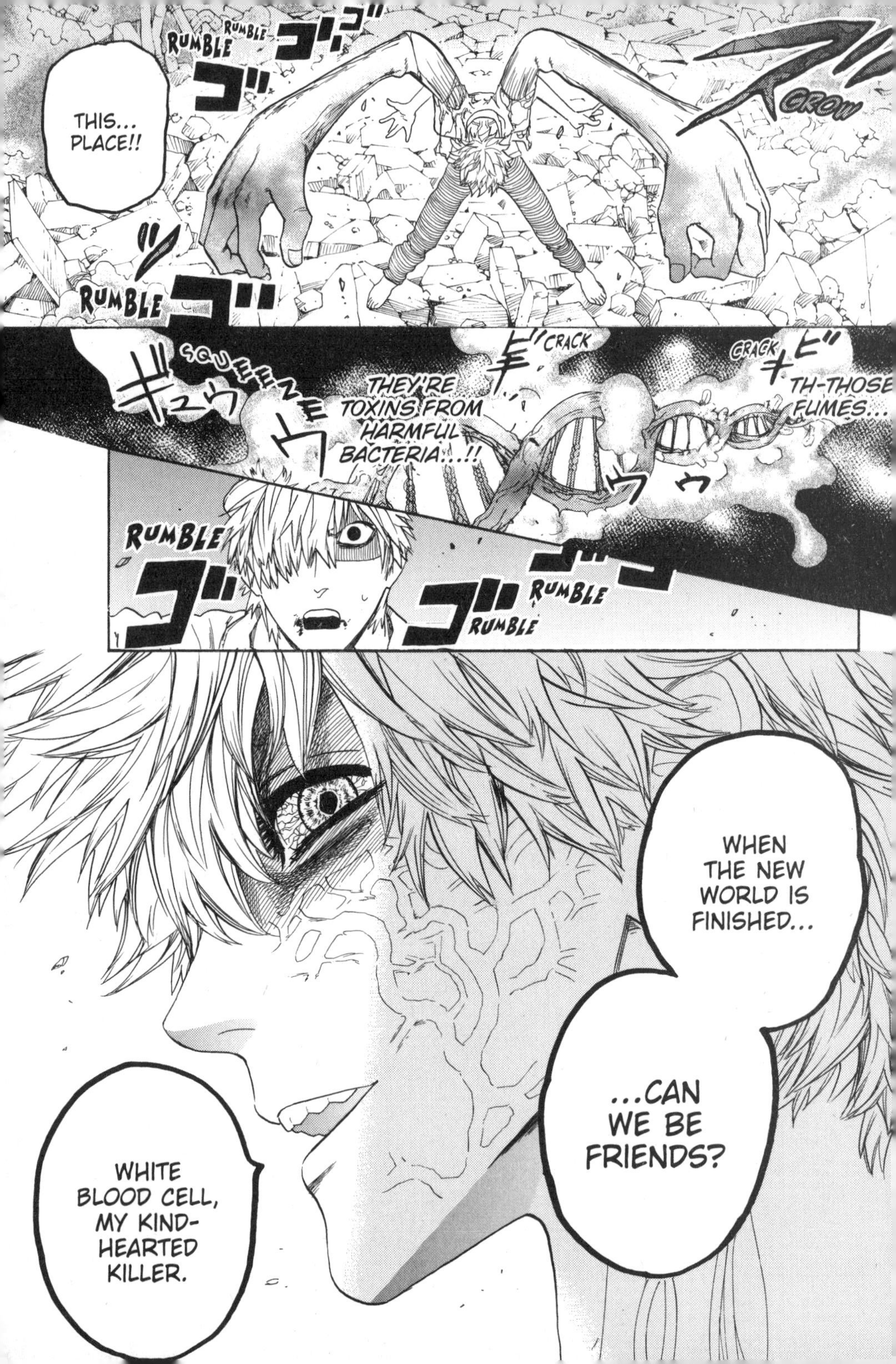
GROW
RUMBLE RUMBLE
THIS... PLACE!!
RUMBLE
CRACK
TH-THOSE FUMES...
CRACK
THEY'RE TOXINS FROM HARMFUL BACTERIA...!!
SQUEEEZE
RUMBLE
RUMBLE
RUMBLE
WHEN THE NEW WORLD IS FINISHED...
...CAN WE BE FRIENDS?
WHITE BLOOD CELL, MY KIND-HEARTED KILLER.

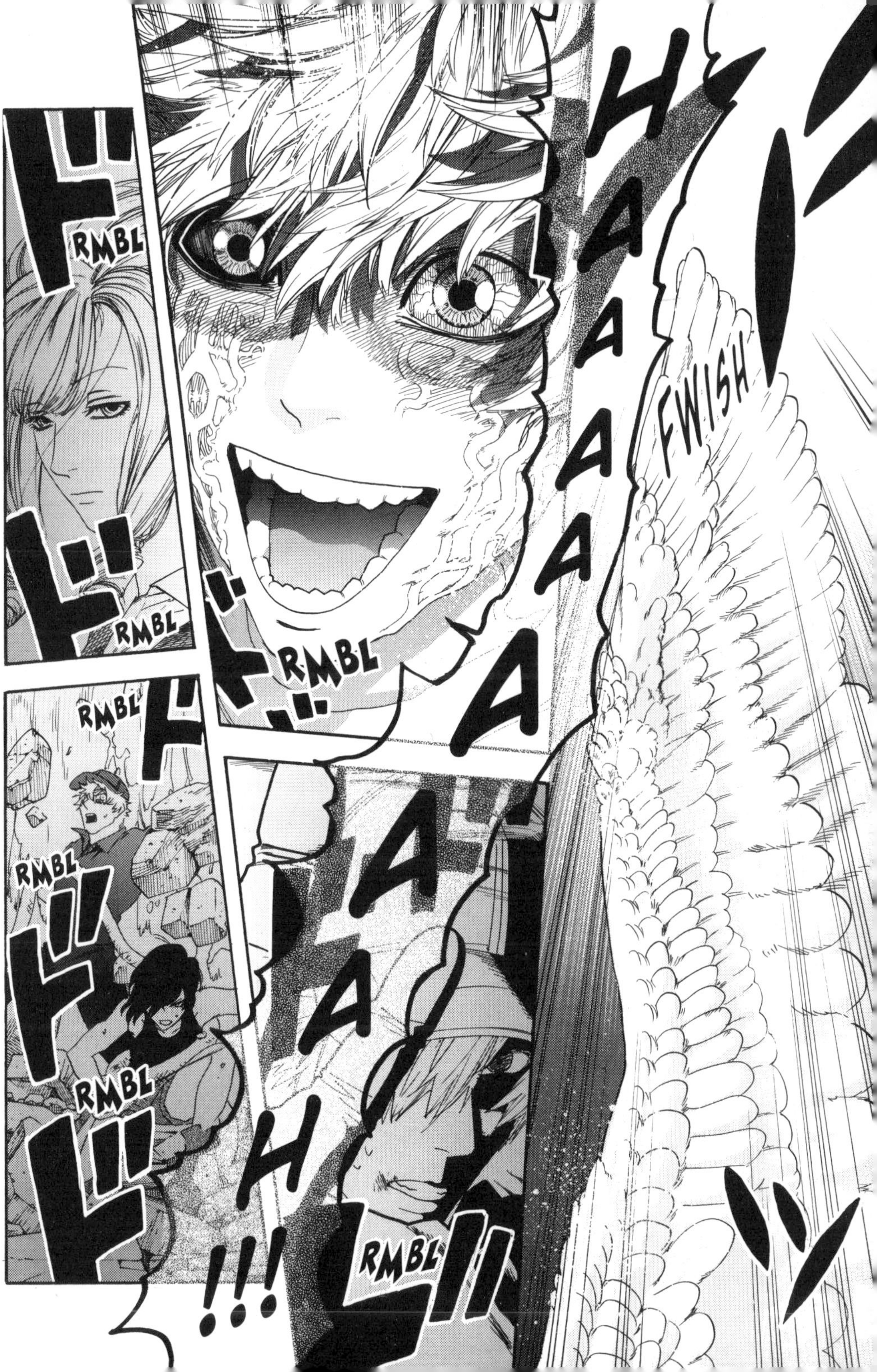
HAAAAAAAAAAH!!!
FWISH
RMBL
ドド
RMBL
RMBL
ドド
RMBL
RMBL
ドド
RMBL
RMBL
ドド

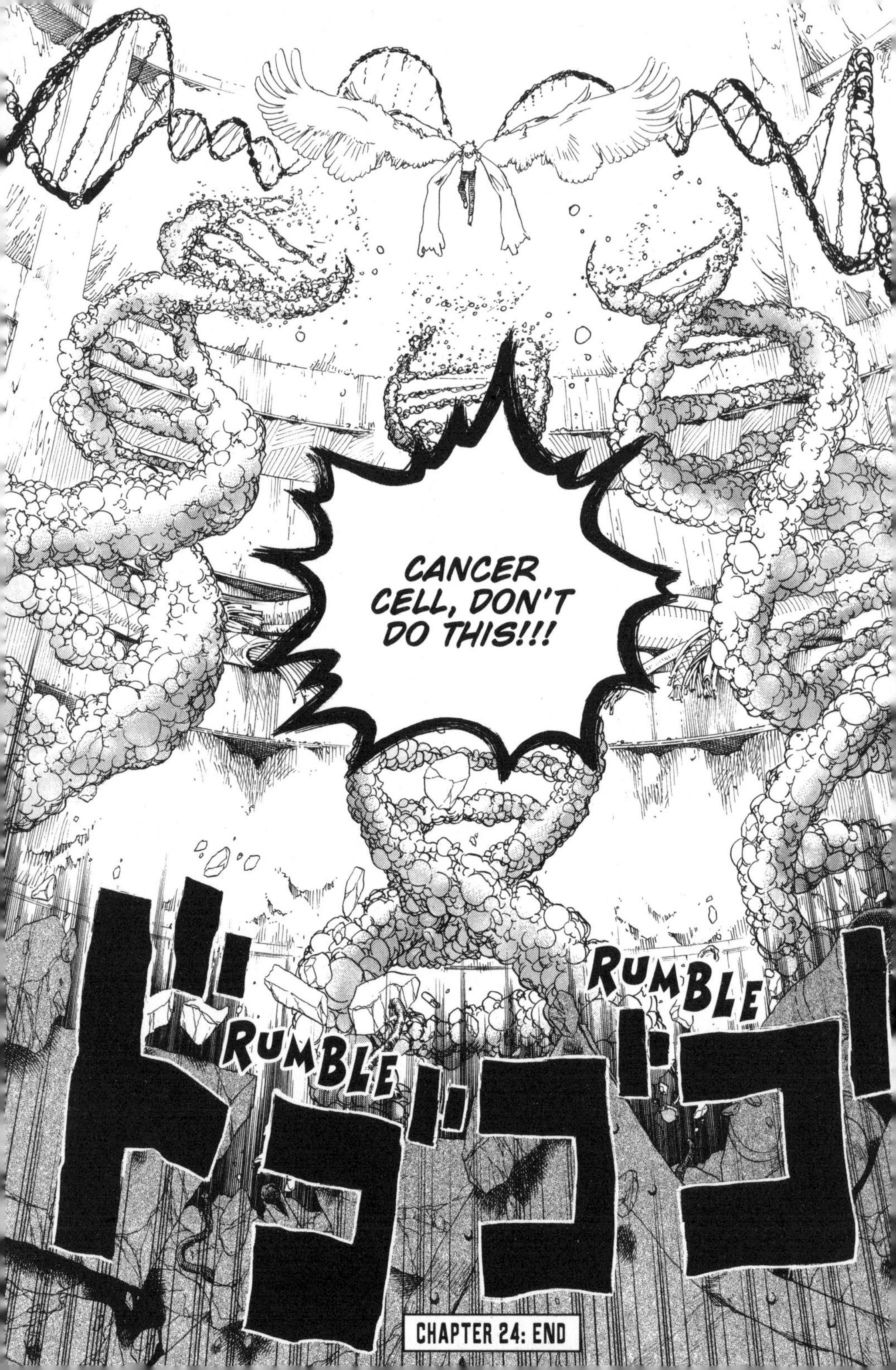
CANCER CELL, DON'T DO THIS!!!
RUMBLE
RUMBLE
ドドゴゴ

CHAPTER 24: END

Cells at Work!

はたらく細胞

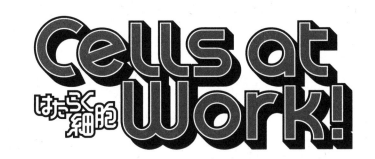

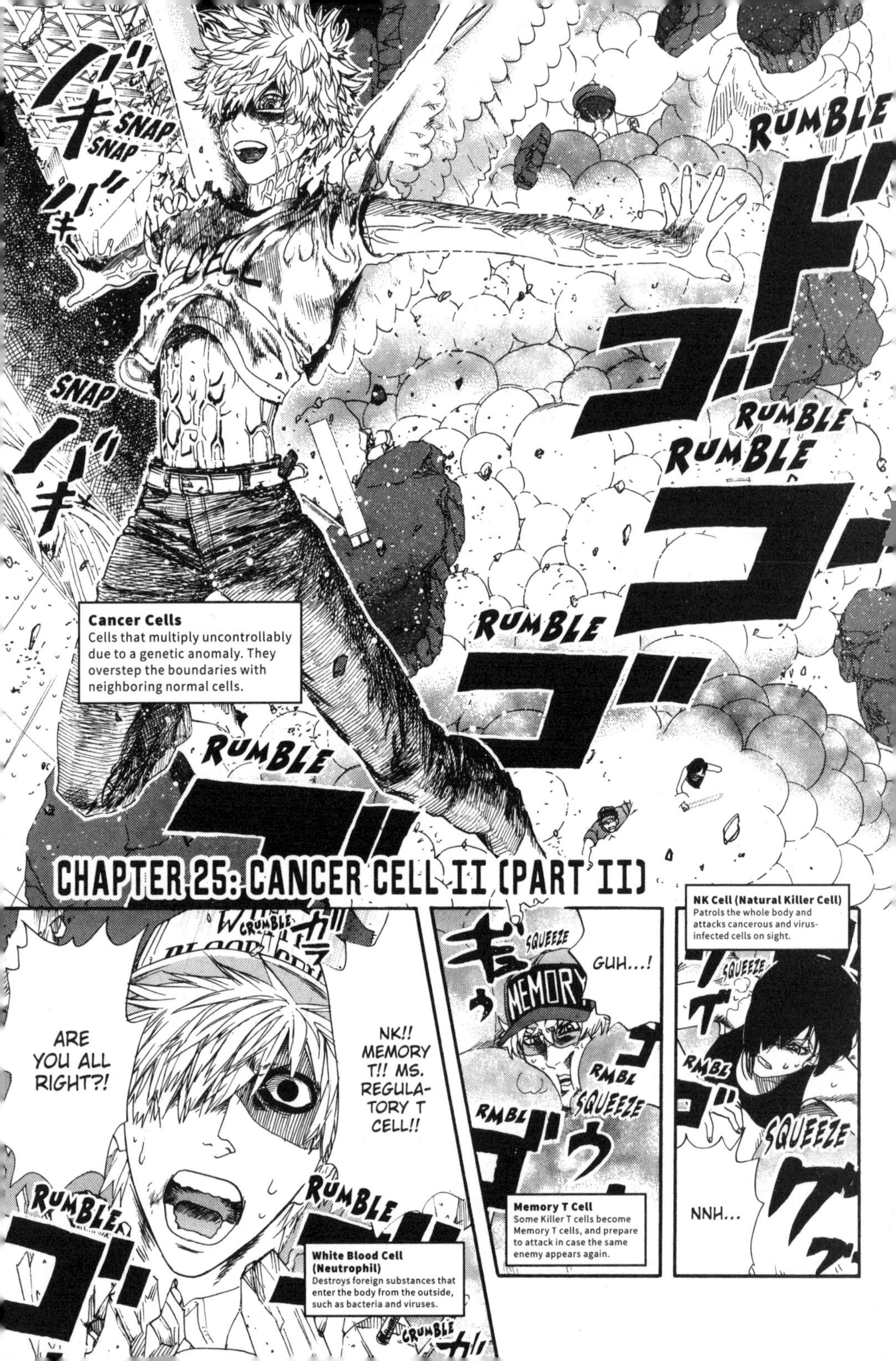
RUMBLE
SNAP
SNAP
RUMBLE
RUMBLE
SNAP
RUMBLE
Cancer Cells
Cells that multiply uncontrollably due to a genetic anomaly. They overstep the boundaries with neighboring normal cells.
RUMBLE
CHAPTER 25: CANCER CELL II (PART II)
NK Cell (Natural Killer Cell)
Patrols the whole body and attacks cancerous and virus-infected cells on sight.
SQUEEZE
RMBL
SQUEEZE
NNH...
SQUEEZE
GUH...!
MEMORY
RMBL
SQUEEZE
RMBL
Memory T Cell
Some Killer T cells become Memory T cells, and prepare to attack in case the same enemy appears again.
CRUMBLE
NK!! MEMORY T!! MS. REGULATORY T CELL!!
ARE YOU ALL RIGHT?!
RUMBLE
RUMBLE
White Blood Cell (Neutrophil)
Destroys foreign substances that enter the body from the outside, such as bacteria and viruses.
CRUMBLE

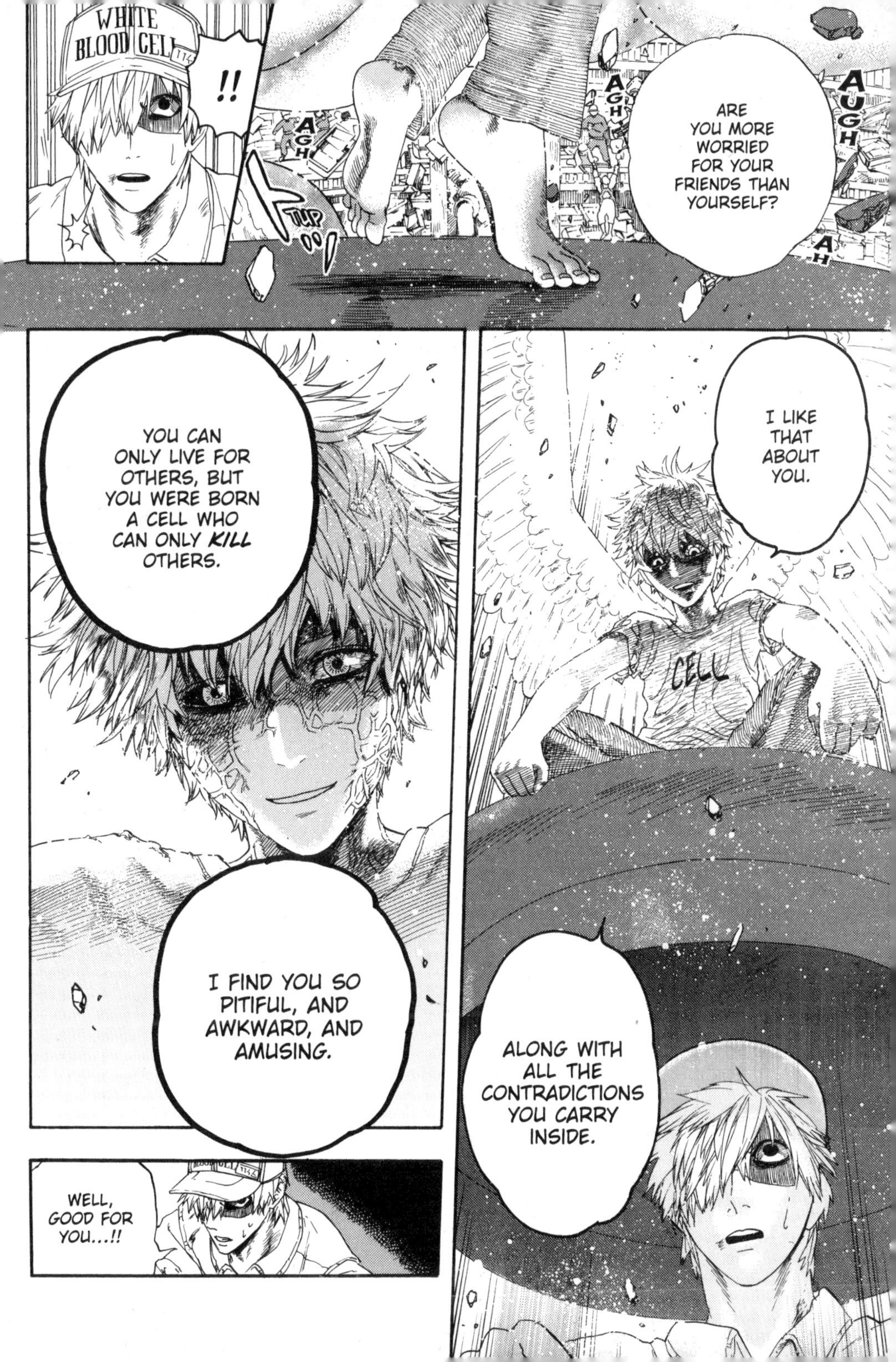
ARE YOU MORE WORRIED FOR YOUR FRIENDS THAN YOURSELF?
AUGH
AGH
AH
AGH
WHITE BLOOD CELL
!!
I LIKE THAT ABOUT YOU.
CELL
ALONG WITH ALL THE CONTRADICTIONS YOU CARRY INSIDE.
YOU CAN ONLY LIVE FOR OTHERS, BUT YOU WERE BORN A CELL WHO CAN ONLY *KILL* OTHERS.
I FIND YOU SO PITIFUL, AND AWKWARD, AND AMUSING.
WELL, GOOD FOR YOU...!!

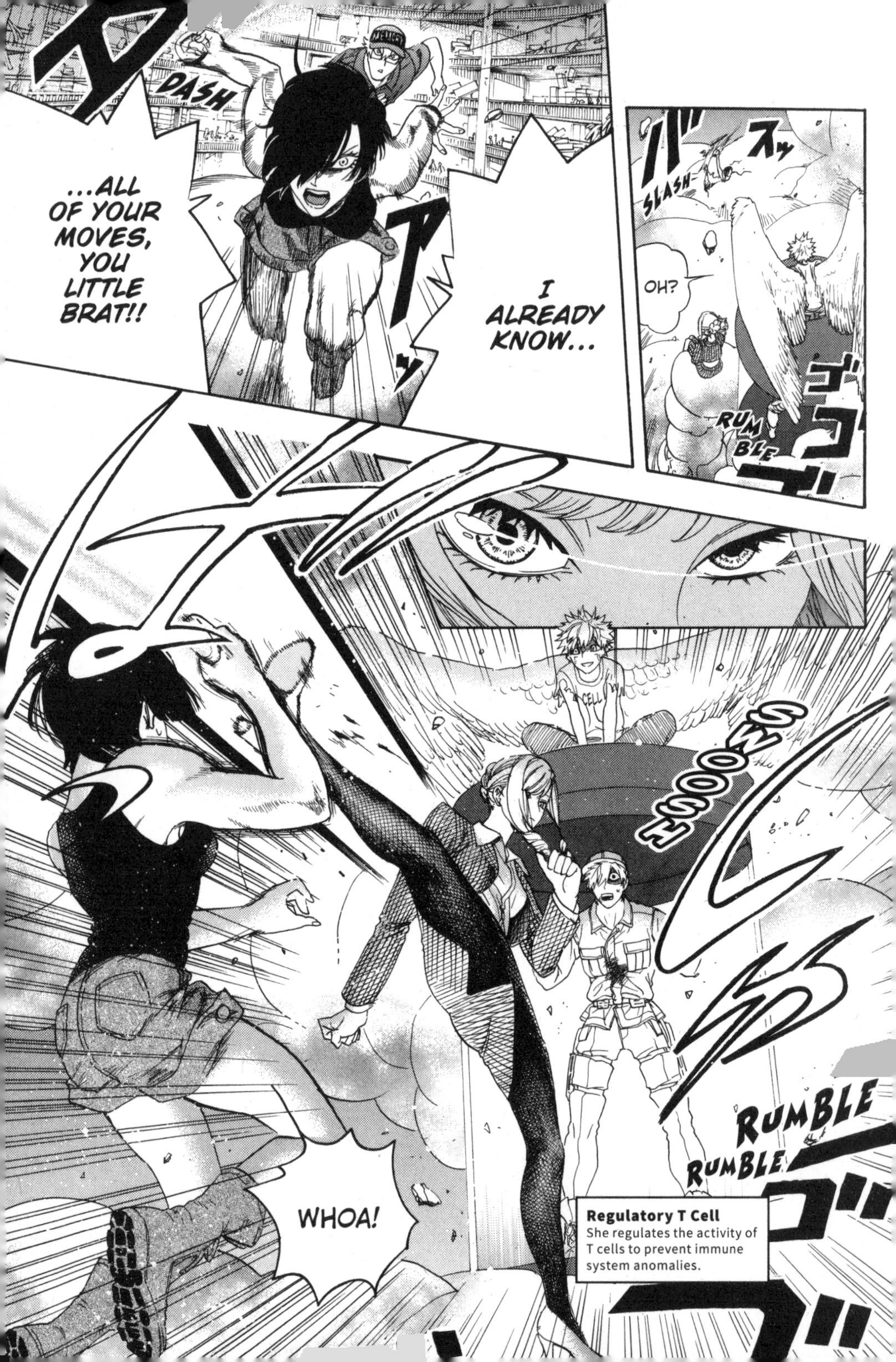
SLASH
OH?
RUMBLE
DASH
I ALREADY KNOW...
...ALL OF YOUR MOVES, YOU LITTLE BRAT!!
SWOOSH
RUMBLE RUMBLE
Regulatory T Cell
She regulates the activity of T cells to prevent immune system anomalies.
WHOA!

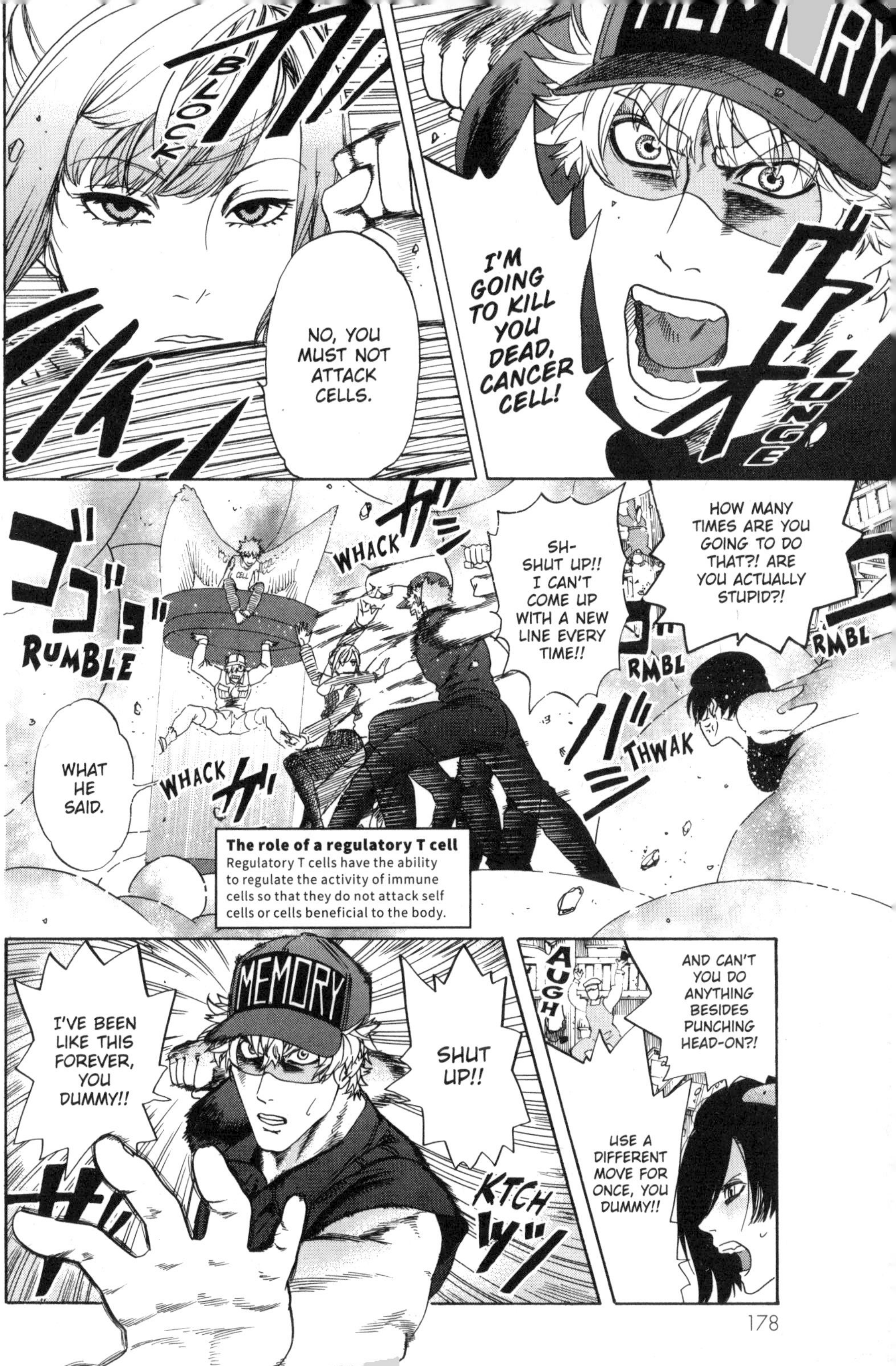

LUNGE
I'M GOING TO KILL YOU DEAD, CANCER CELL!
BLOCK
NO, YOU MUST NOT ATTACK CELLS.
HOW MANY TIMES ARE YOU GOING TO DO THAT?! ARE YOU ACTUALLY STUPID?!
RMBL
SH- SHUT UP!! I CAN'T COME UP WITH A NEW LINE EVERY TIME!!
WHACK
RMBL
THWAK
RUMBLE
WHAT HE SAID.
WHACK
The role of a regulatory T cell
Regulatory T cells have the ability to regulate the activity of immune cells so that they do not attack self cells or cells beneficial to the body.
AUGH
AND CAN'T YOU DO ANYTHING BESIDES PUNCHING HEAD-ON?!
USE A DIFFERENT MOVE FOR ONCE, YOU DUMMY!!
SHUT UP!!
MEMORY
I'VE BEEN LIKE THIS FOREVER, YOU DUMMY!!
KTCH

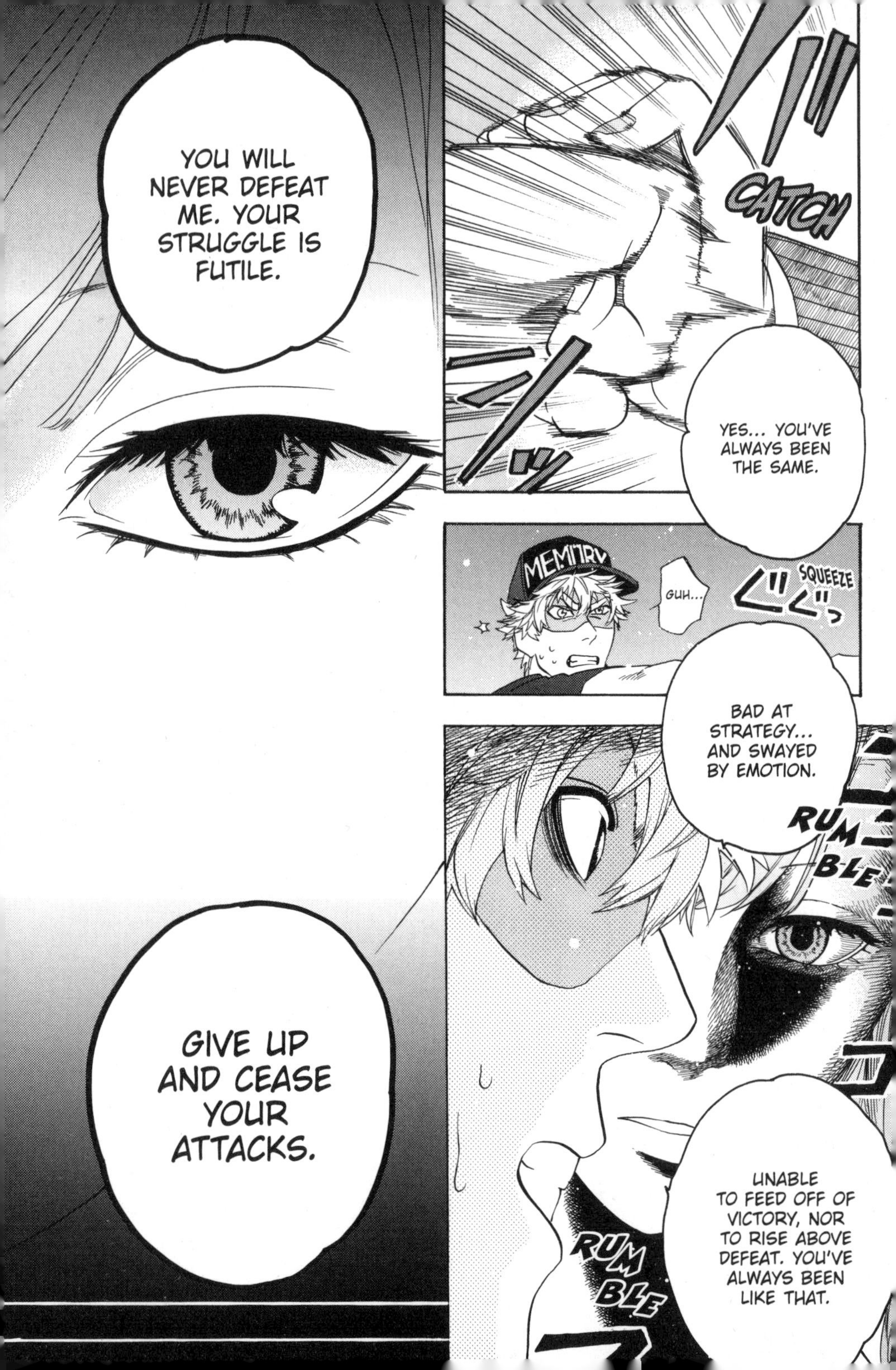
CATCH
YES... YOU'VE ALWAYS BEEN THE SAME.
GUH...
SQUEEZE
BAD AT STRATEGY... AND SWAYED BY EMOTION.
RUMBLE
UNABLE TO FEED OFF OF VICTORY, NOR TO RISE ABOVE DEFEAT. YOU'VE ALWAYS BEEN LIKE THAT.
RUMBLE
YOU WILL NEVER DEFEAT ME. YOUR STRUGGLE IS FUTILE.
GIVE UP AND CEASE YOUR ATTACKS.

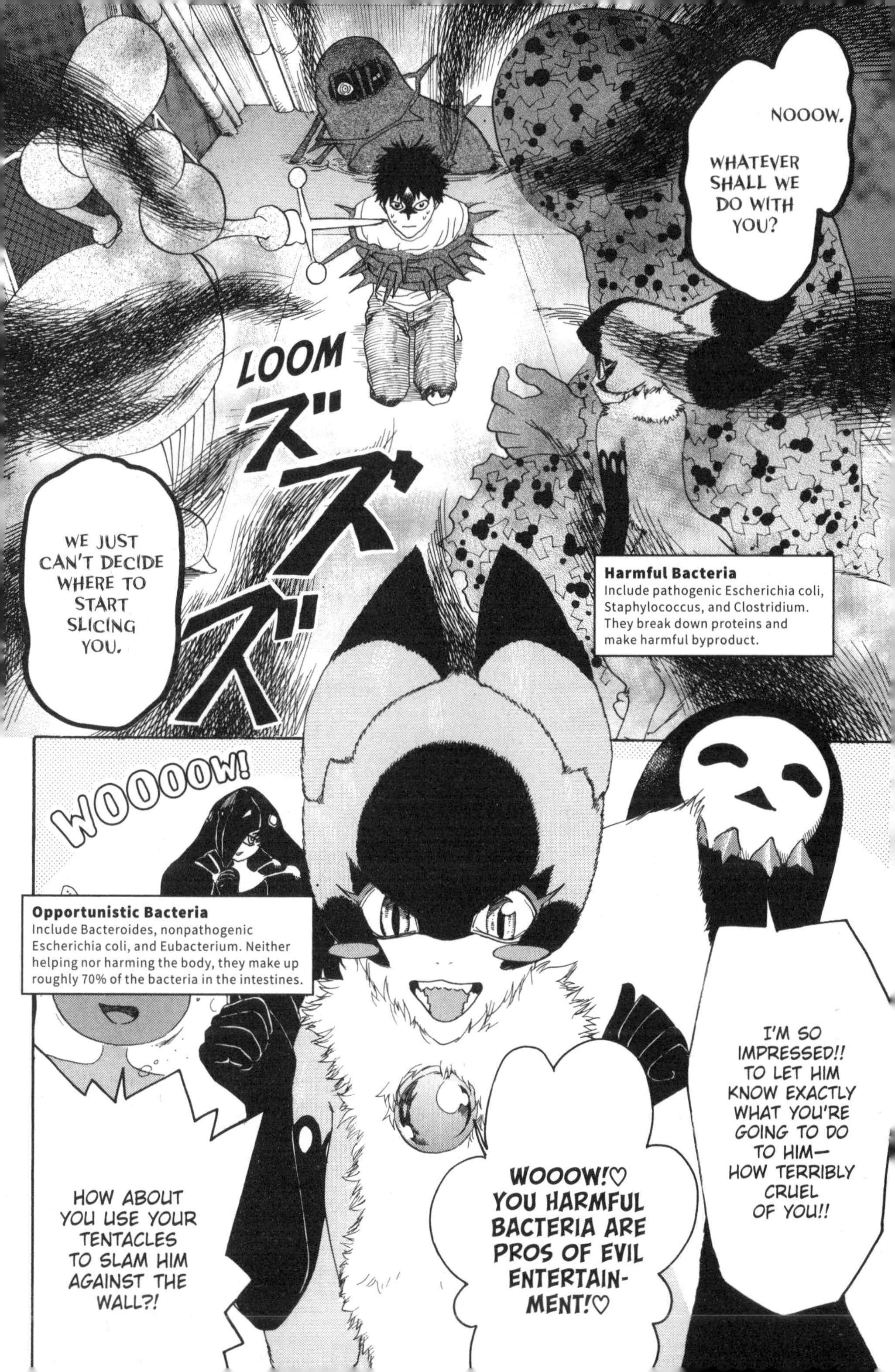
NOOOW.
WHATEVER SHALL WE DO WITH YOU?
LOOM
ズズズ
Harmful Bacteria
Include pathogenic Escherichia coli, Staphylococcus, and Clostridium. They break down proteins and make harmful byproduct.
WE JUST CAN'T DECIDE WHERE TO START SLICING YOU.
WOOOOW!
Opportunistic Bacteria
Include Bacteroides, nonpathogenic Escherichia coli, and Eubacterium. Neither helping nor harming the body, they make up roughly 70% of the bacteria in the intestines.
I'M SO IMPRESSED!! TO LET HIM KNOW EXACTLY WHAT YOU'RE GOING TO DO TO HIM— HOW TERRIBLY CRUEL OF YOU!!
WOOOW!♡ YOU HARMFUL BACTERIA ARE PROS OF EVIL ENTERTAIN-MENT!♡
HOW ABOUT YOU USE YOUR TENTACLES TO SLAM HIM AGAINST THE WALL?!

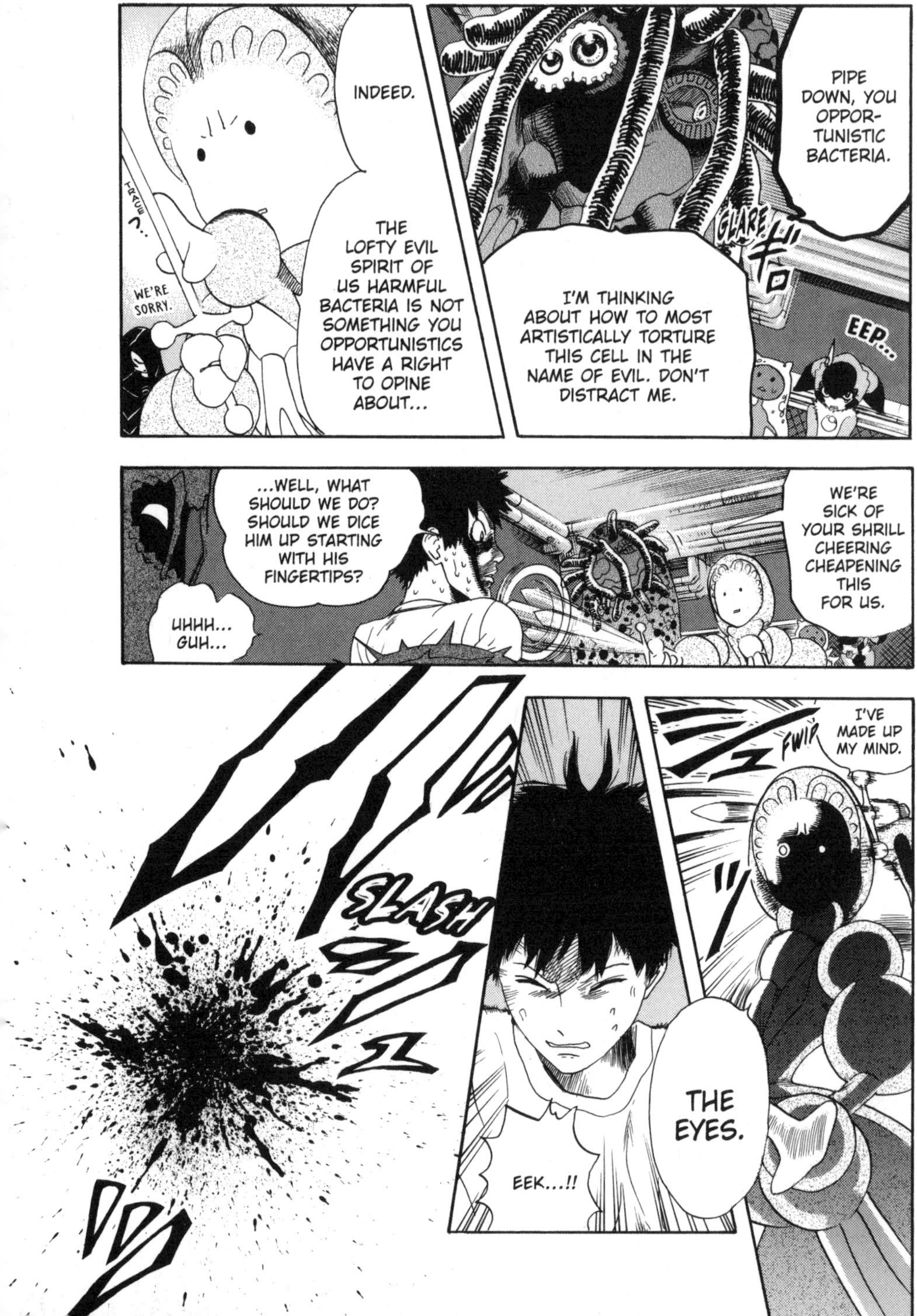
PIPE DOWN, YOU OPPOR-TUNISTIC BACTERIA.
GLARE
I'M THINKING ABOUT HOW TO MOST ARTISTICALLY TORTURE THIS CELL IN THE NAME OF EVIL. DON'T DISTRACT ME.
EEP...
INDEED.
THE LOFTY EVIL SPIRIT OF US HARMFUL BACTERIA IS NOT SOMETHING YOU OPPORTUNISTICS HAVE A RIGHT TO OPINE ABOUT...
TRACE
WE'RE SORRY.
WE'RE SICK OF YOUR SHRILL CHEERING CHEAPENING THIS FOR US.
...WELL, WHAT SHOULD WE DO? SHOULD WE DICE HIM UP STARTING WITH HIS FINGERTIPS?
UHHH... GUH...
I'VE MADE UP MY MIND.
FWIP
THE EYES.
EEK...!!
SLASH

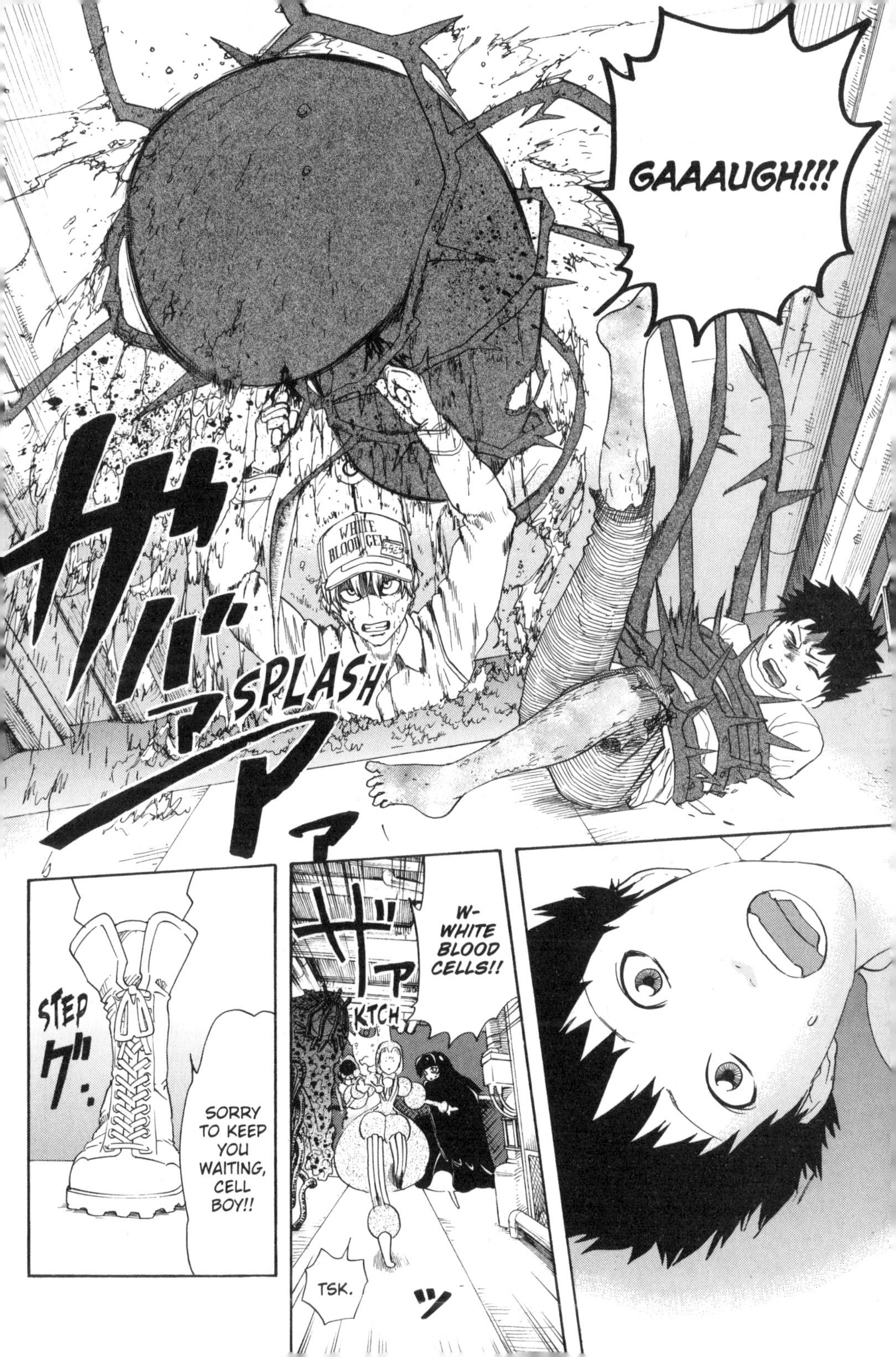
GAAAUGH!!!
SPLASH
W-WHITE BLOOD CELLS!!
KTCH
TSK.
STEP
SORRY TO KEEP YOU WAITING, CELL BOY!!

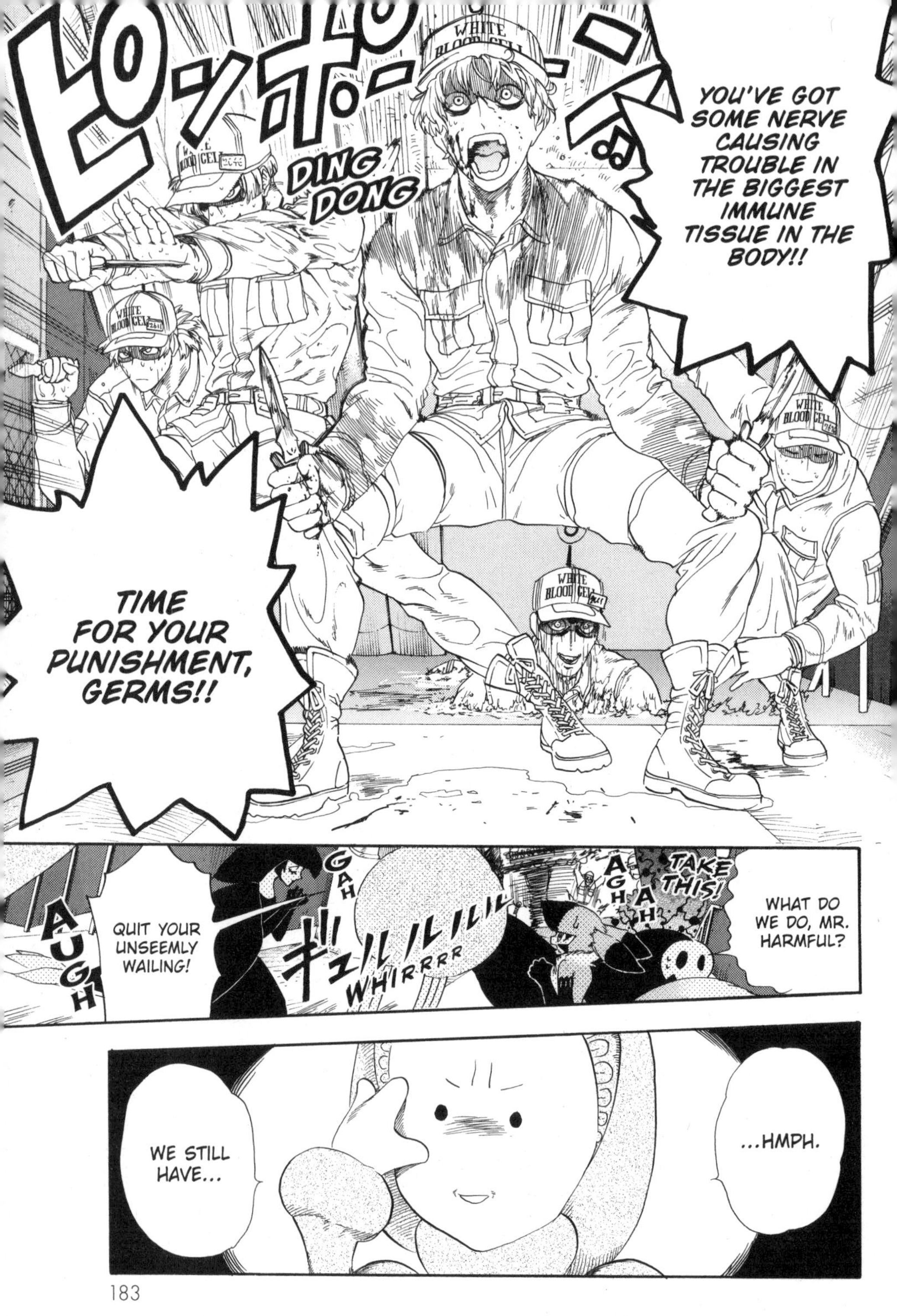
YOU'VE GOT SOME NERVE CAUSING TROUBLE IN THE BIGGEST IMMUNE TISSUE IN THE BODY!!
DING DONG
TIME FOR YOUR PUNISHMENT, GERMS!!
WHAT DO WE DO, MR. HARMFUL?
TAKE THIS!
AGH
AH
GAH
WHIRRRR
QUIT YOUR UNSEEMLY WAILING!
AUGH
...HMPH.
WE STILL HAVE...

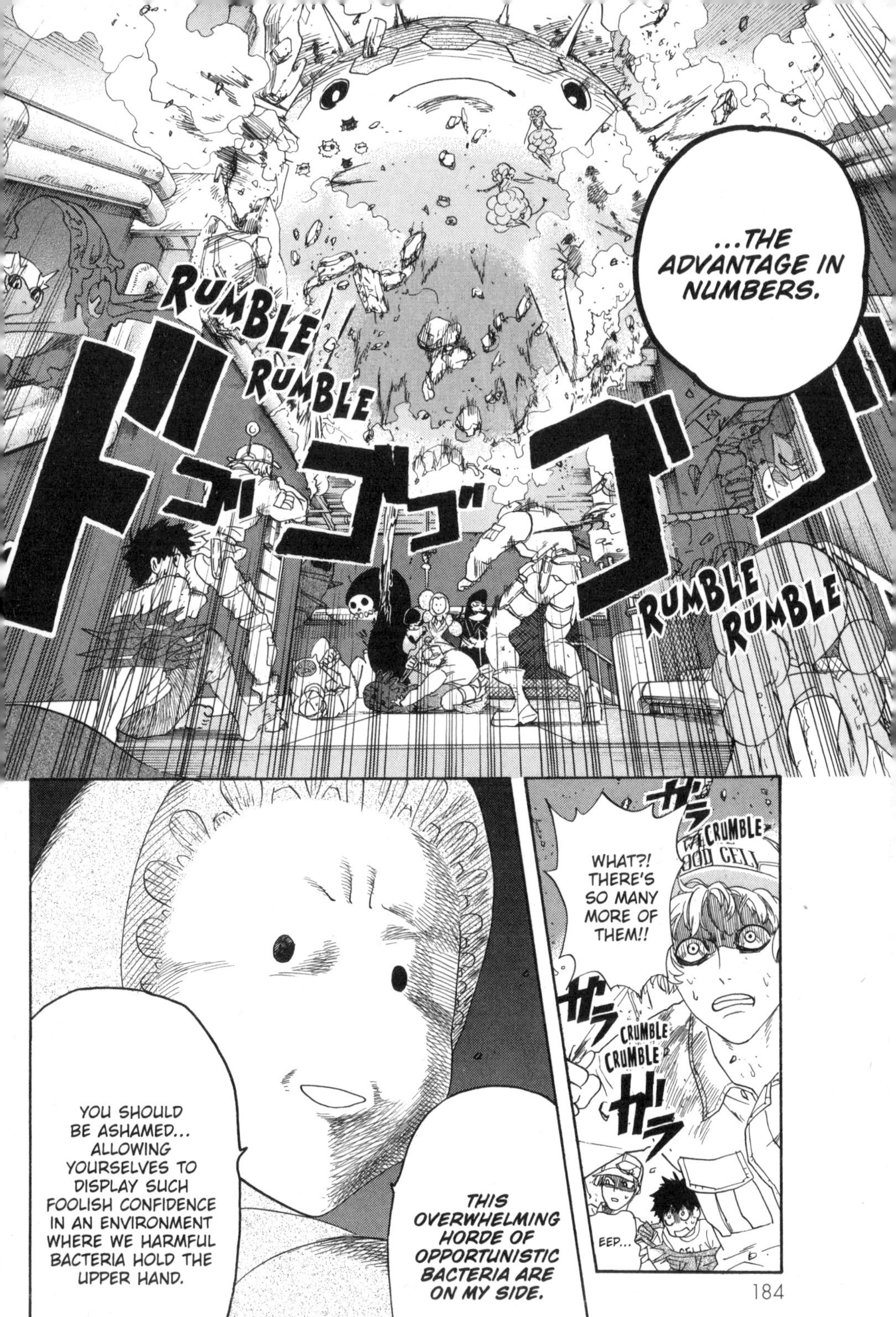
RUMBLE RUMBLE
...THE ADVANTAGE IN NUMBERS.
RUMBLE RUMBLE
ガラ
CRUMBLE
WHAT?! THERE'S SO MANY MORE OF THEM!!
ガラ
CRUMBLE CRUMBLE
ガラ
EEP...
THIS OVERWHELMING HORDE OF OPPORTUNISTIC BACTERIA ARE ON MY SIDE.
YOU SHOULD BE ASHAMED... ALLOWING YOURSELVES TO DISPLAY SUCH FOOLISH CONFIDENCE IN AN ENVIRONMENT WHERE WE HARMFUL BACTERIA HOLD THE UPPER HAND.

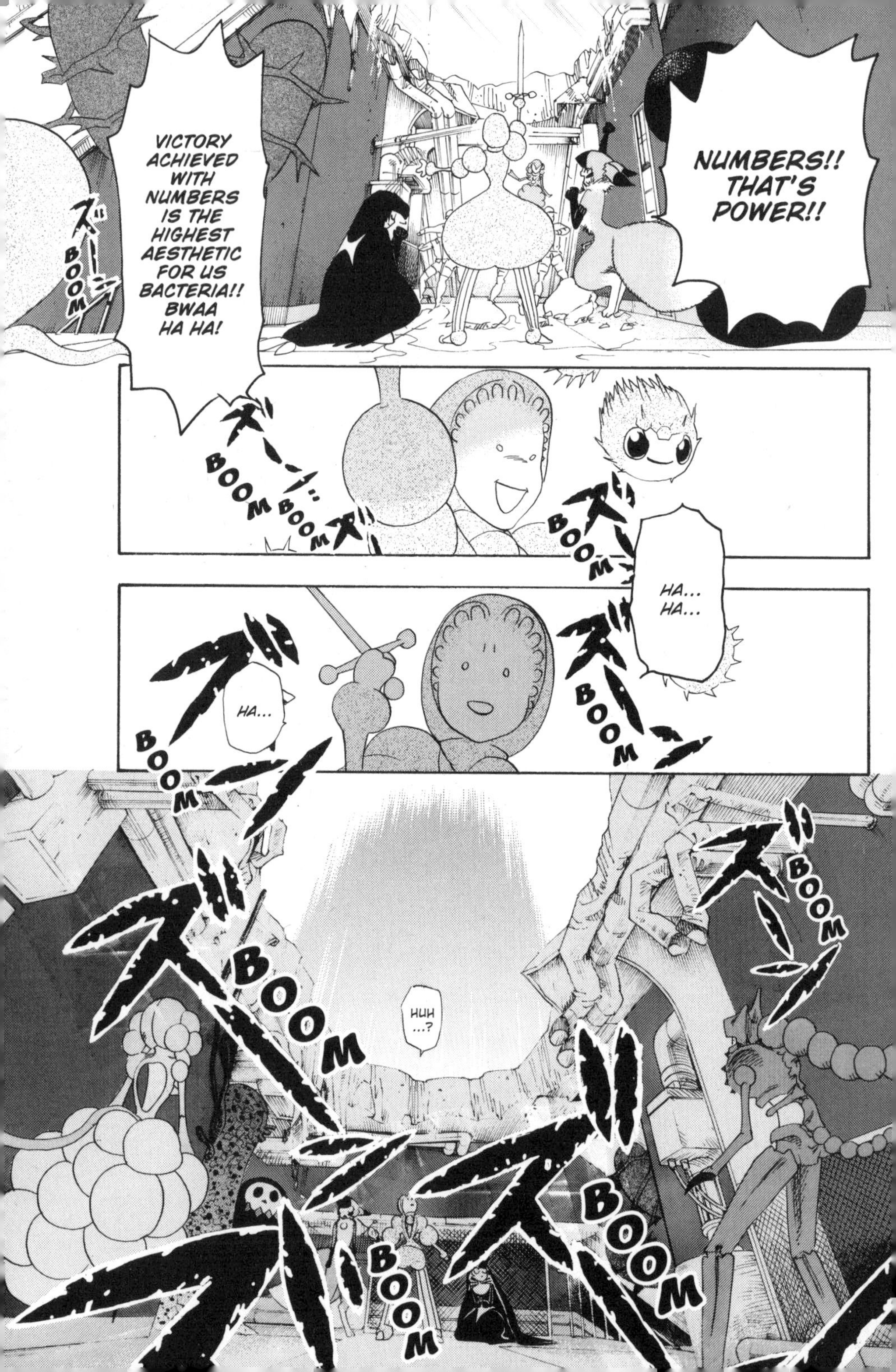
NUMBERS!! THAT'S POWER!!
VICTORY ACHIEVED WITH NUMBERS IS THE HIGHEST AESTHETIC FOR US BACTERIA!! BWAA HA HA!
BOOM
BOOM
BOOM
BOOM
HA... HA...
BOOM
HA...
BOOM
BOOM
BOOM
HUH ...?
BOOM
BOOM

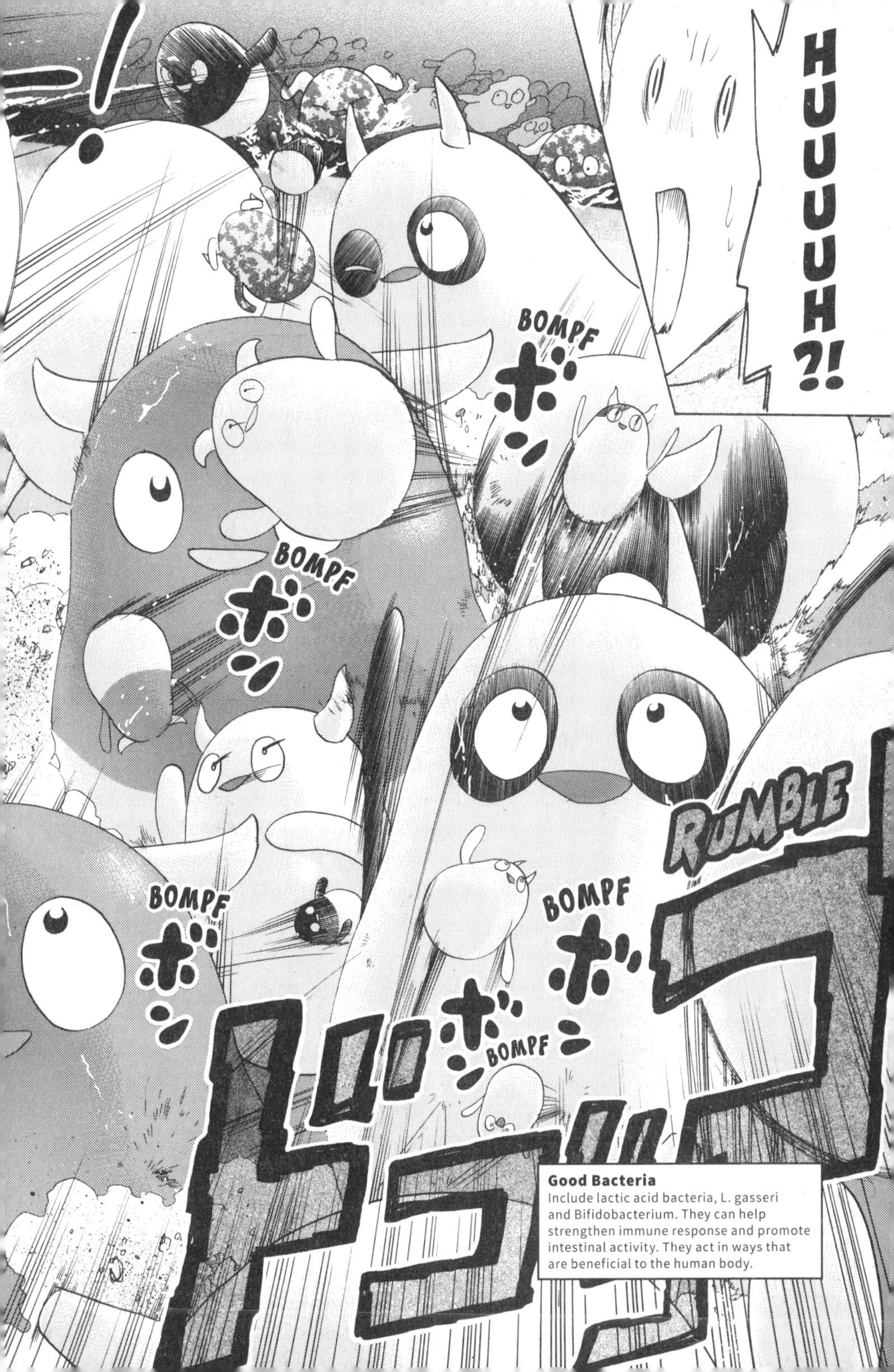
HUUUUUH?!
BOMPF
BOMPF
RUMBLE
BOMPF
BOMPF
BOMPF

Good Bacteria
Include lactic acid bacteria, L. gasseri and Bifidobacterium. They can help strengthen immune response and promote intestinal activity. They act in ways that are beneficial to the human body.

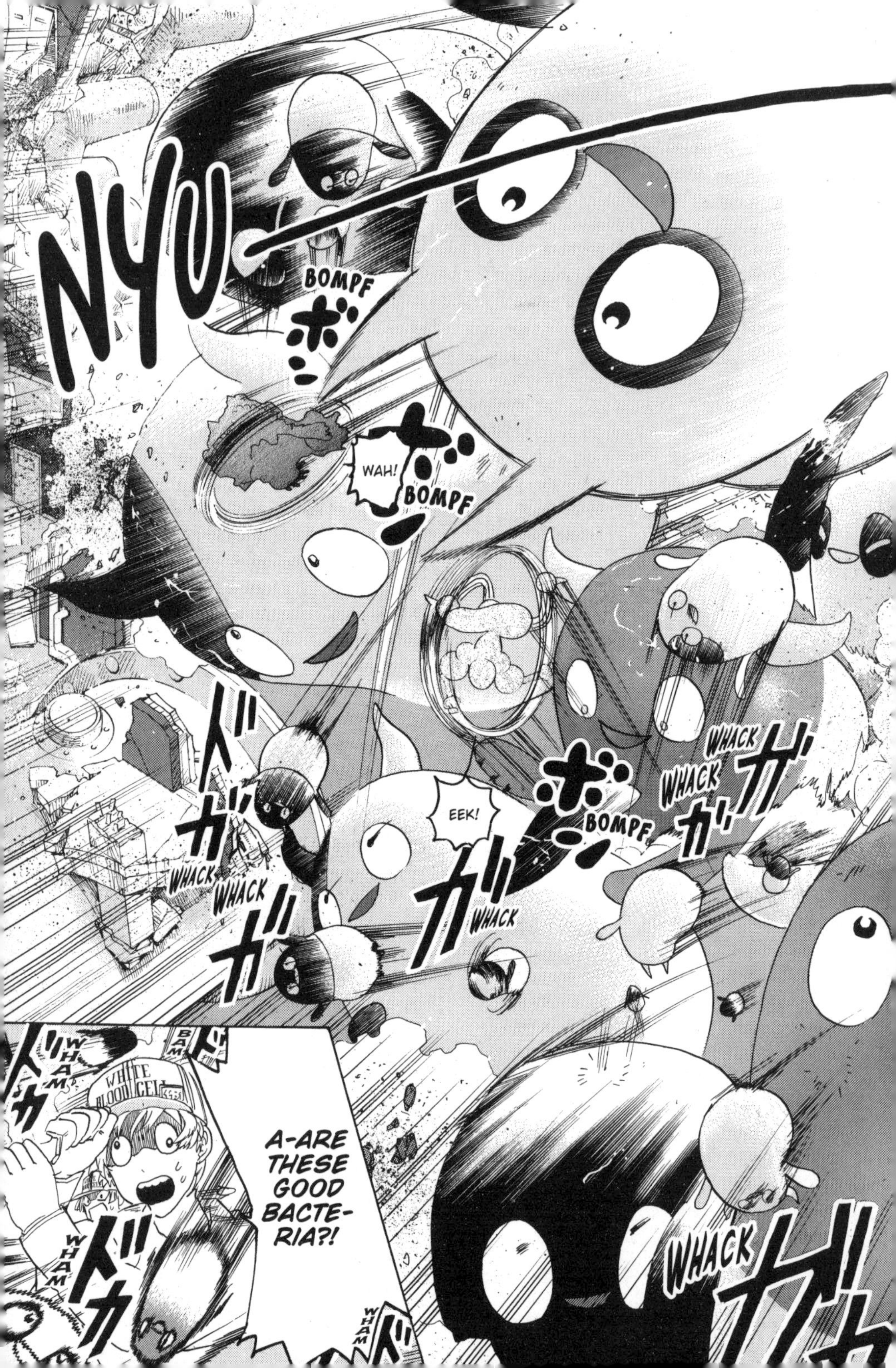
NYU
BOMPF
WAH!
BOMPF
WHACK
WHACK
BOMPF
EEK!
WHACK
WHACK
WHACK
WHACK
WHACK
BAM
WHAM
A-ARE THESE GOOD BACTE-RIA?!
WHAM
WHAM

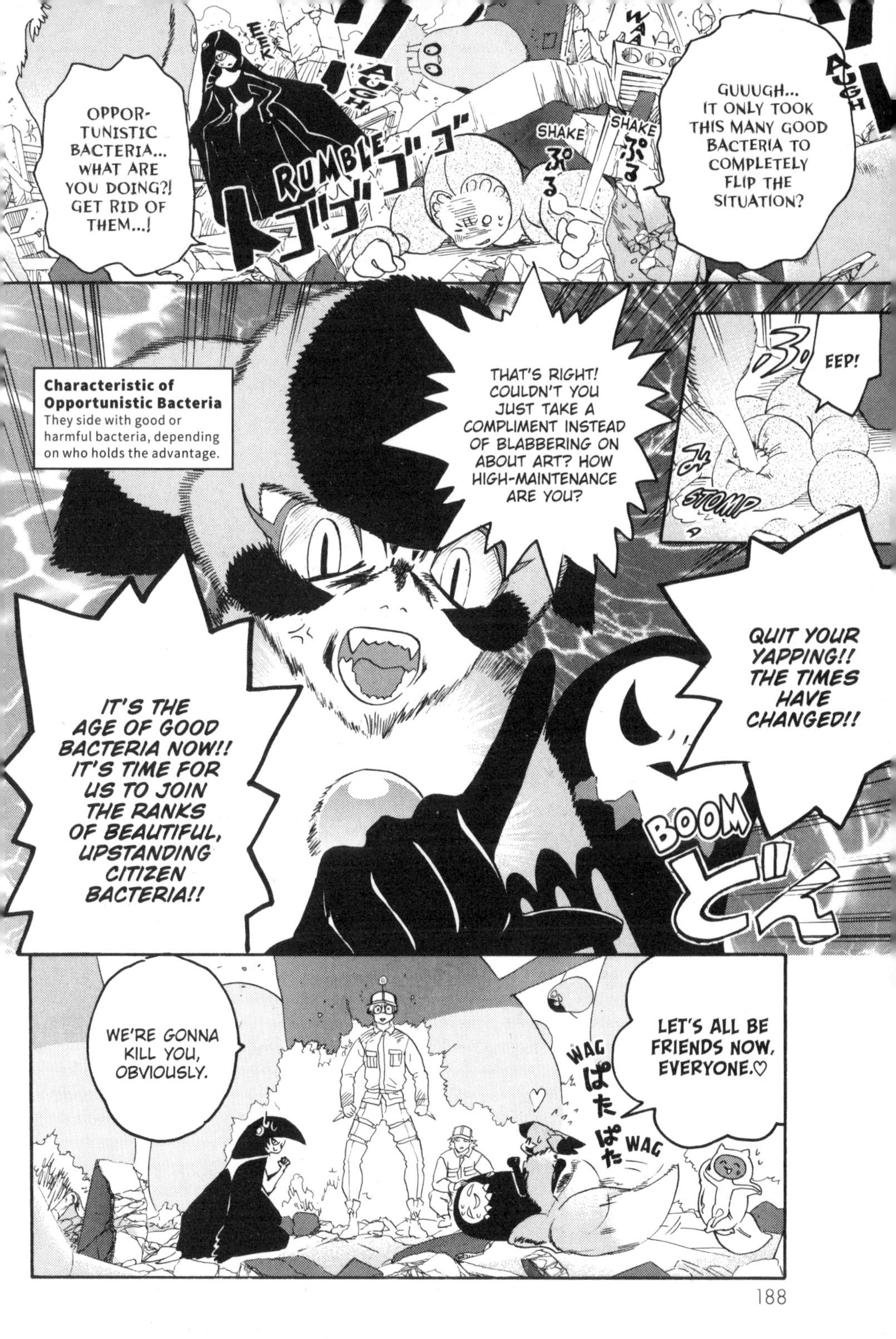
AUGH
GUUUGH... IT ONLY TOOK THIS MANY GOOD BACTERIA TO COMPLETELY FLIP THE SITUATION?
WAAA
SHAKE ぷる
SHAKE ぷる
AUGH
EEEK
RUMBLE ゴゴゴゴ
OPPORTUNISTIC BACTERIA... WHAT ARE YOU DOING?! GET RID OF THEM...!
ふ EEP!
STOMP
THAT'S RIGHT! COULDN'T YOU JUST TAKE A COMPLIMENT INSTEAD OF BLABBERING ON ABOUT ART? HOW HIGH-MAINTENANCE ARE YOU?
Characteristic of Opportunistic Bacteria
They side with good or harmful bacteria, depending on who holds the advantage.
QUIT YOUR YAPPING!! THE TIMES HAVE CHANGED!!
BOOM どん
IT'S THE AGE OF GOOD BACTERIA NOW!! IT'S TIME FOR US TO JOIN THE RANKS OF BEAUTIFUL, UPSTANDING CITIZEN BACTERIA!!
LET'S ALL BE FRIENDS NOW, EVERYONE.♡
WAG ぱた
ぱた WAG
WE'RE GONNA KILL YOU, OBVIOUSLY.

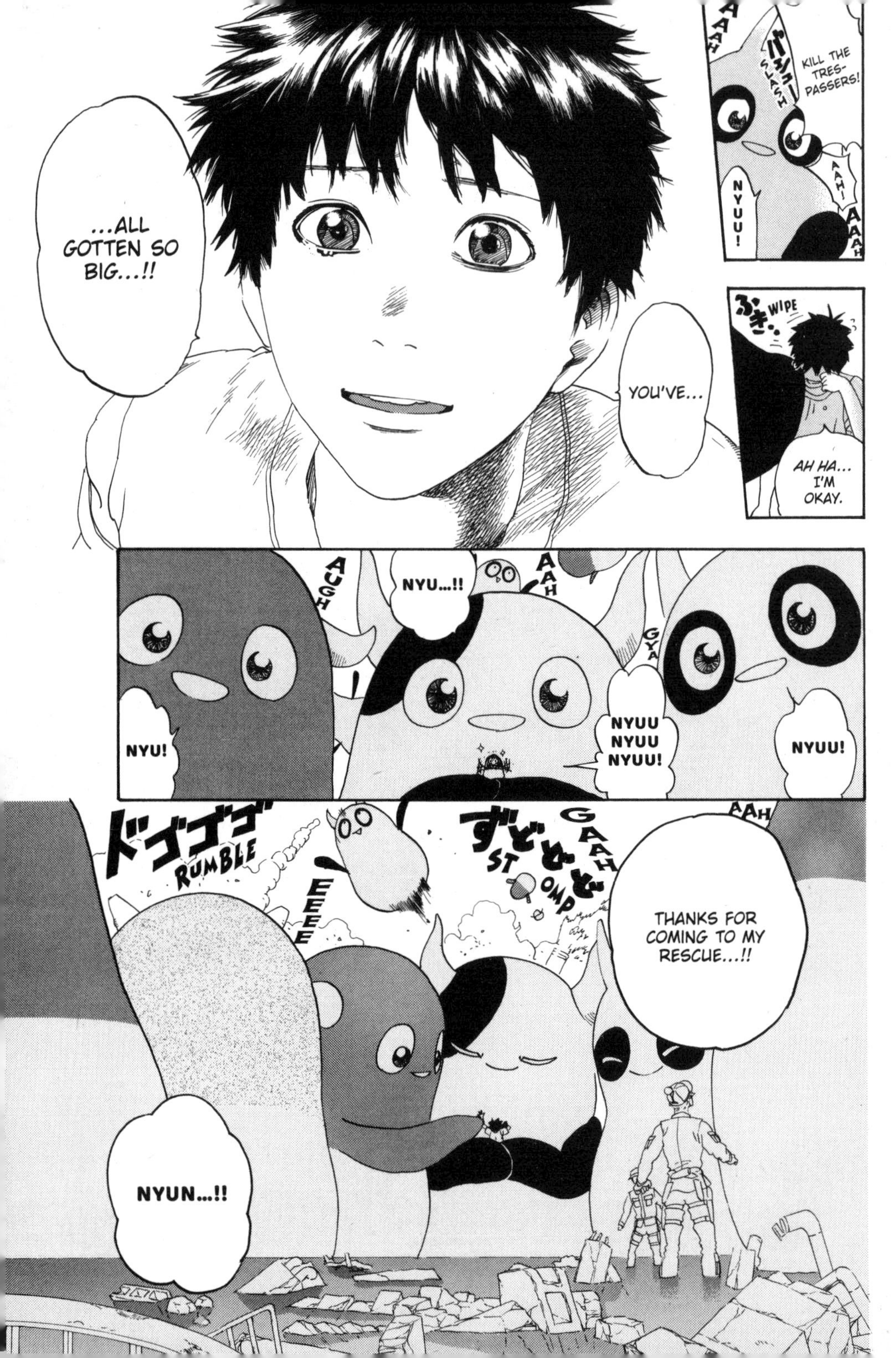
AAAAH
SLASH
KILL THE TRES-PASSERS!
AAH!
NYUU!
AAAAH
ふき…
WIPE
AH HA… I'M OKAY.
YOU'VE…
…ALL GOTTEN SO BIG…!!
NYUU!
GYA
NYUU NYUU NYUU!
AAH
NYU…!!
AUGH
NYU!
AAH
THANKS FOR COMING TO MY RESCUE…!!
GAAAH
STOMP
EEEE
ドゴゴゴ
RUMBLE
NYUN…!!

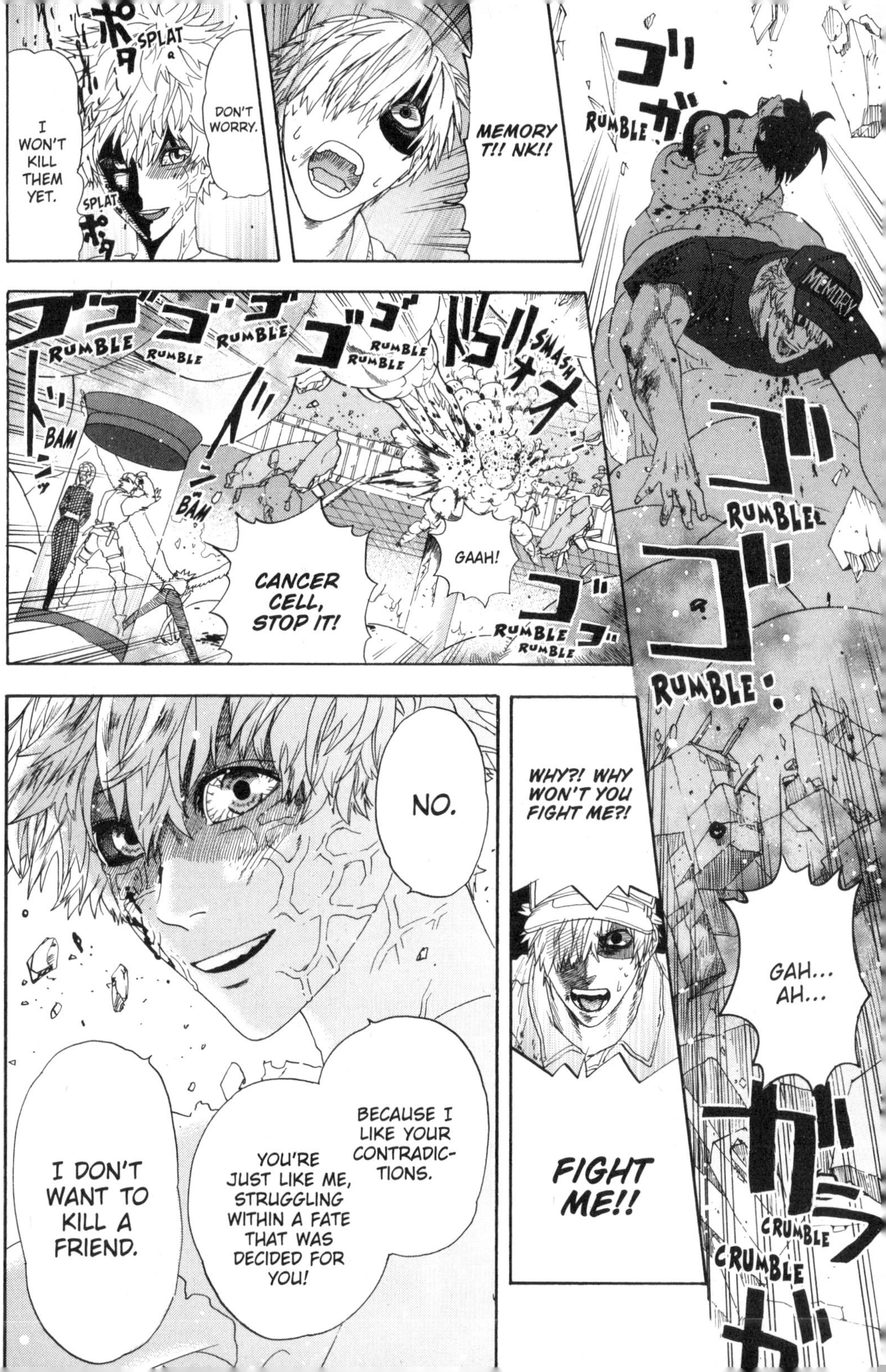
RUMBLE
RUMBLE
RUMBLE
GAH... AH...
CRUMBLE
CRUMBLE
MEMORY T!! NK!!
DON'T WORRY.
SPLAT
I WON'T KILL THEM YET.
SPLAT
RUMBLE
RUMBLE
RUMBLE
RUMBLE
RUMBLE
SMASH
BAM
BAM
GAAH!
CANCER CELL, STOP IT!
RUMBLE
RUMBLE
WHY?! WHY WON'T YOU FIGHT ME?!
FIGHT ME!!
NO.
BECAUSE I LIKE YOUR CONTRADIC-TIONS.
YOU'RE JUST LIKE ME, STRUGGLING WITHIN A FATE THAT WAS DECIDED FOR YOU!
I DON'T WANT TO KILL A FRIEND.

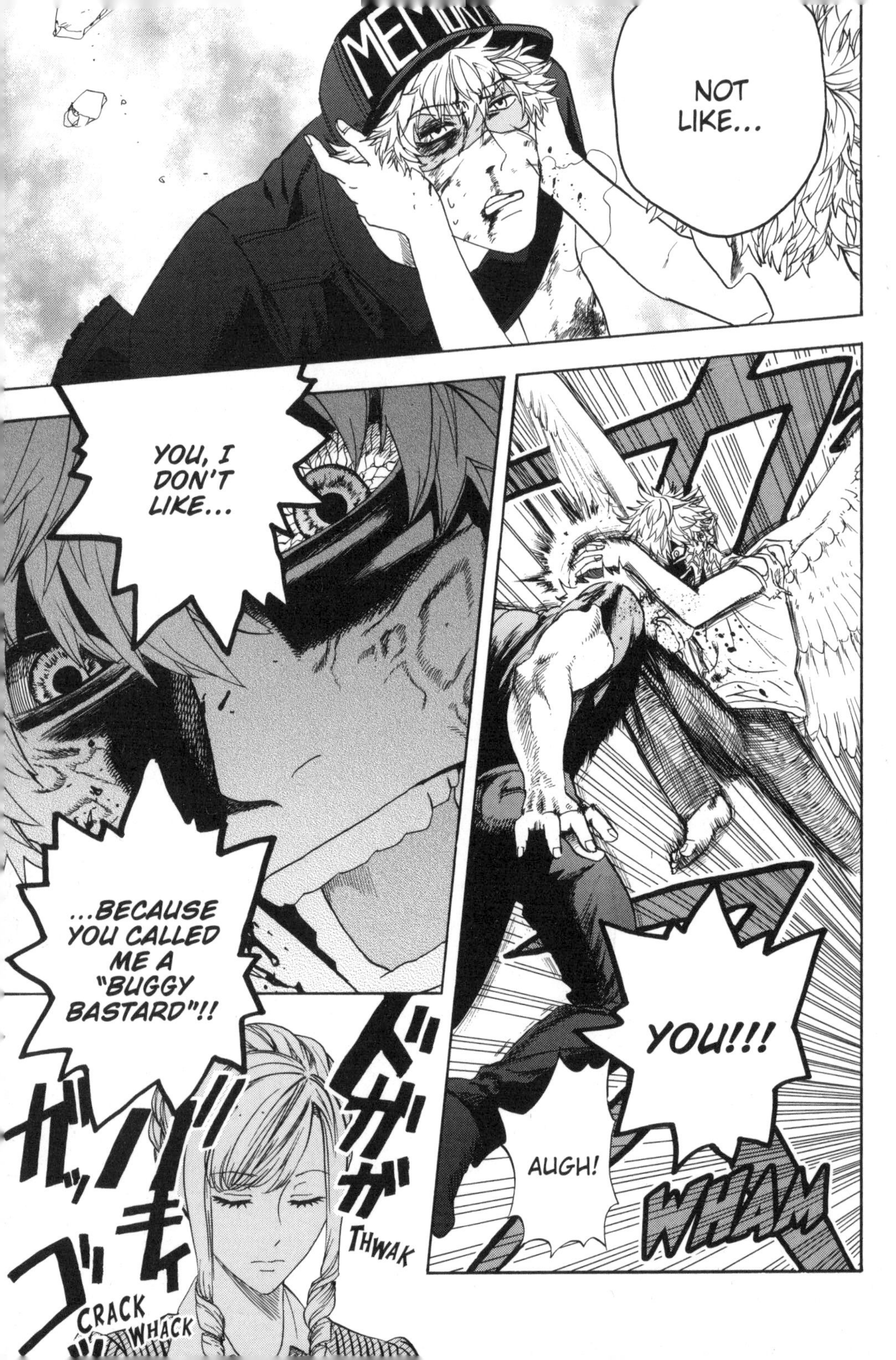
NOT LIKE...
YOU!!!
AUGH!
WHAM
YOU, I DON'T LIKE...
...BECAUSE YOU CALLED ME A "BUGGY BASTARD"!!
THWAK
CRACK
WHACK

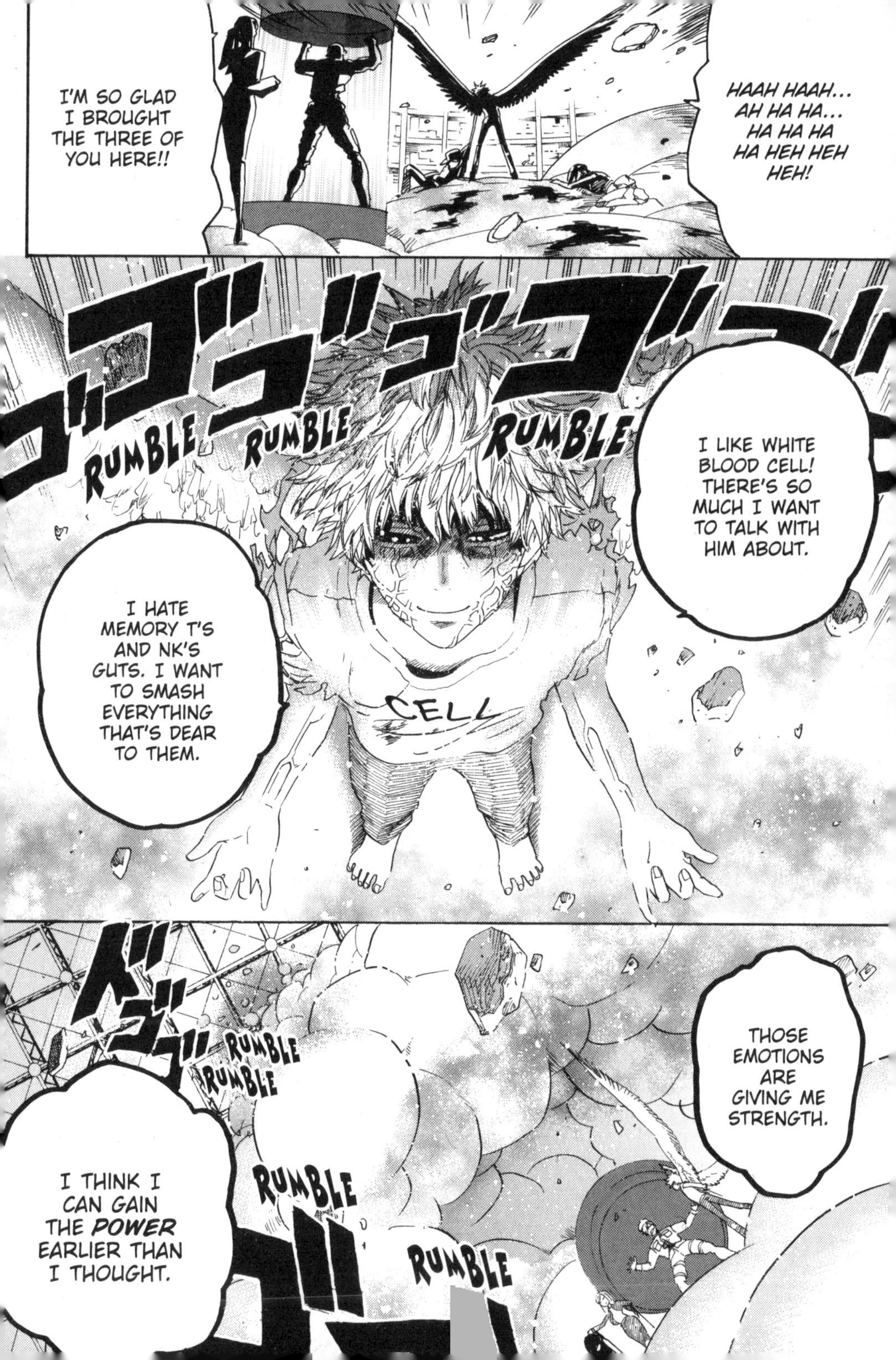
HAAH HAAH... AH HA HA... HA HA HA HA HEH HEH HEH!
I'M SO GLAD I BROUGHT THE THREE OF YOU HERE!!
RUMBLE
RUMBLE
RUMBLE
I LIKE WHITE BLOOD CELL! THERE'S SO MUCH I WANT TO TALK WITH HIM ABOUT.
CELL
I HATE MEMORY T'S AND NK'S GUTS. I WANT TO SMASH EVERYTHING THAT'S DEAR TO THEM.
THOSE EMOTIONS ARE GIVING ME STRENGTH.
RUMBLE
RUMBLE
RUMBLE
I THINK I CAN GAIN THE *POWER* EARLIER THAN I THOUGHT.
RUMBLE

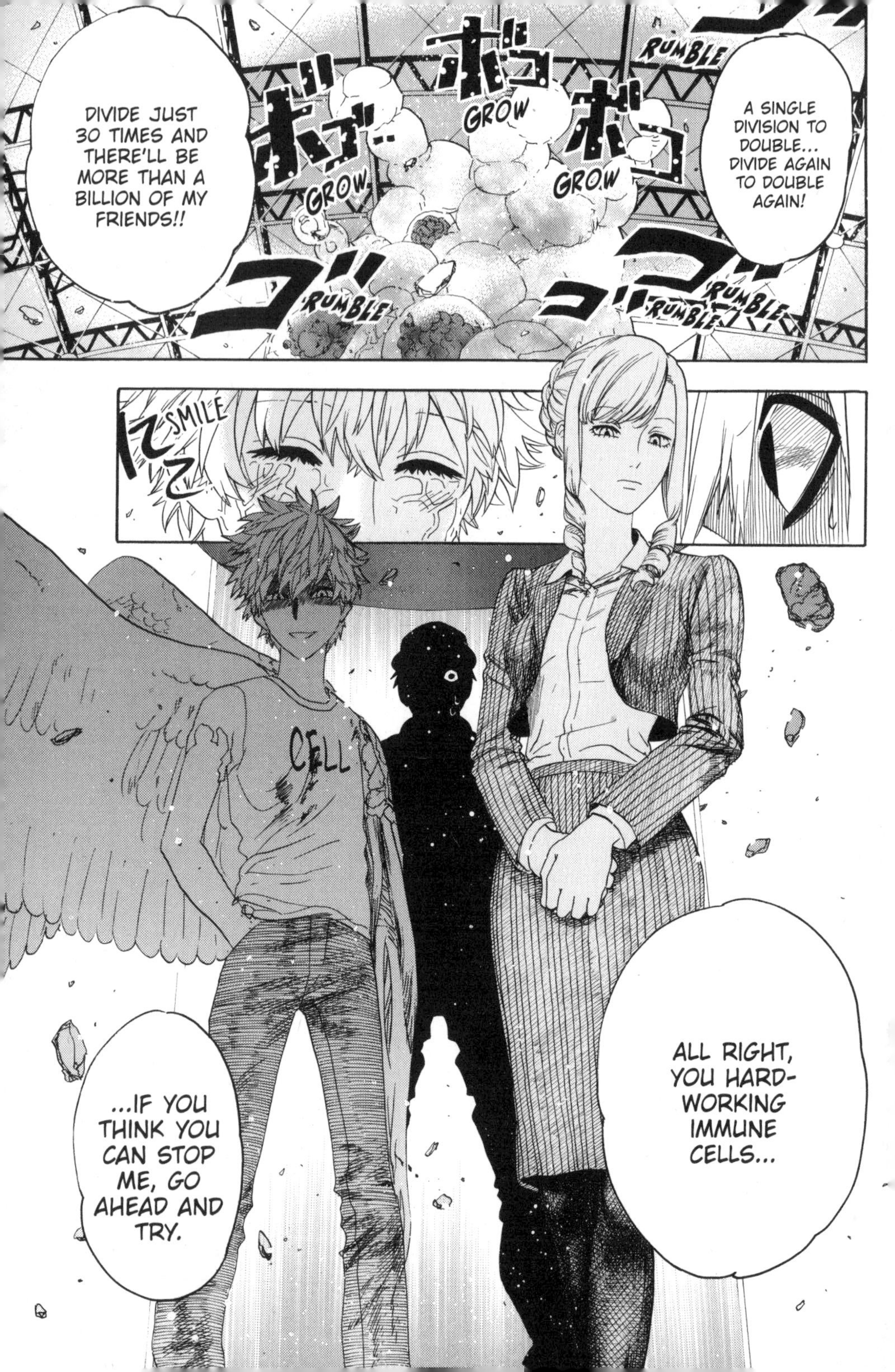
RUMBLE
A SINGLE DIVISION TO DOUBLE... DIVIDE AGAIN TO DOUBLE AGAIN!
GROW
GROW
GROW
RUMBLE
RUMBLE
RUMBLE
DIVIDE JUST 30 TIMES AND THERE'LL BE MORE THAN A BILLION OF MY FRIENDS!!
SMILE
CELL
ALL RIGHT, YOU HARD-WORKING IMMUNE CELLS...
...IF YOU THINK YOU CAN STOP ME, GO AHEAD AND TRY.

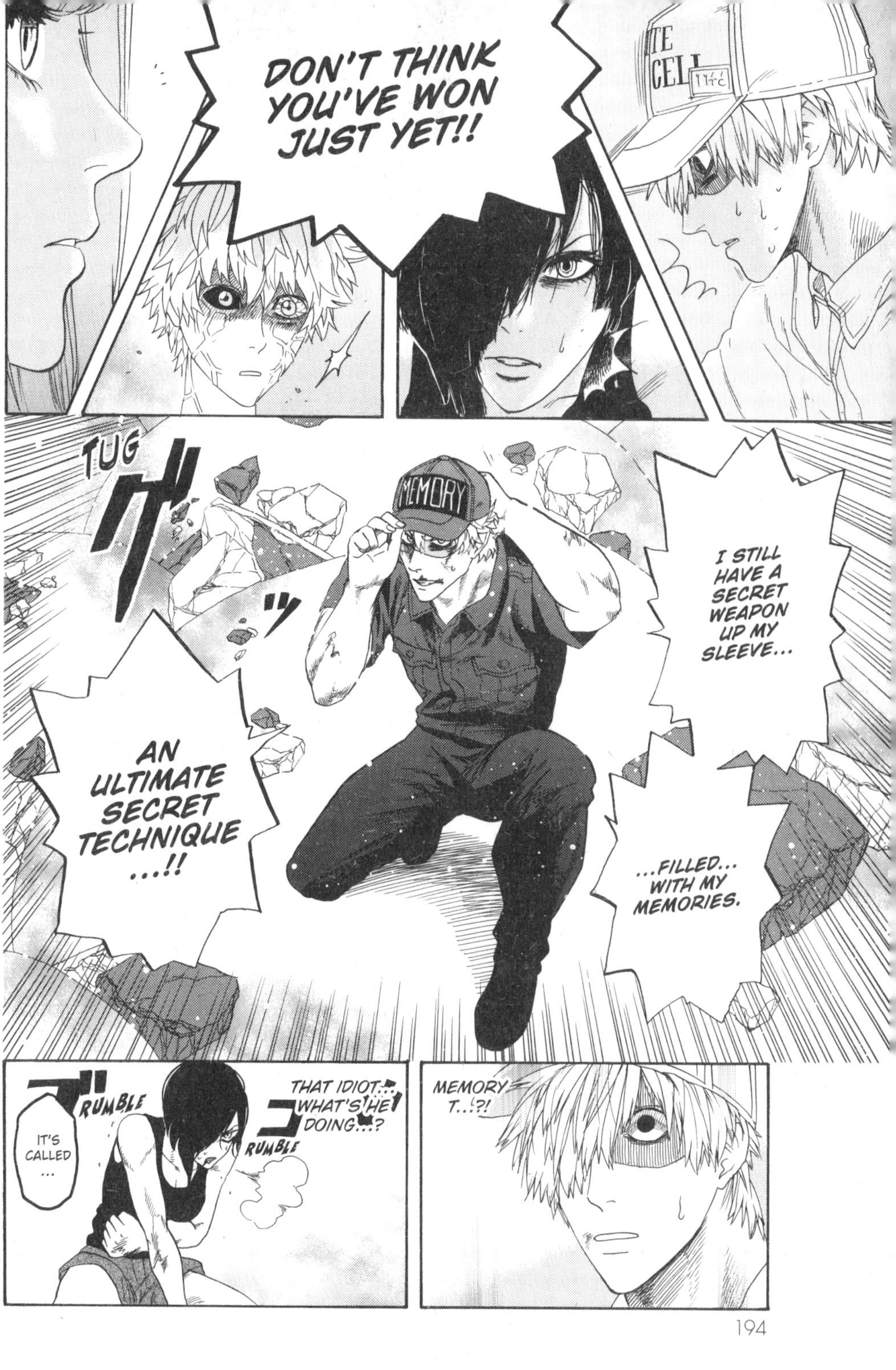
DON'T THINK YOU'VE WON JUST YET!!
TUG
I STILL HAVE A SECRET WEAPON UP MY SLEEVE...
AN ULTIMATE SECRET TECHNIQUE ...!!
...FILLED... WITH MY MEMORIES.
MEMORY T...!?!
THAT IDIOT... WHAT'S HE DOING...?
RUMBLE
RUMBLE
IT'S CALLED ...

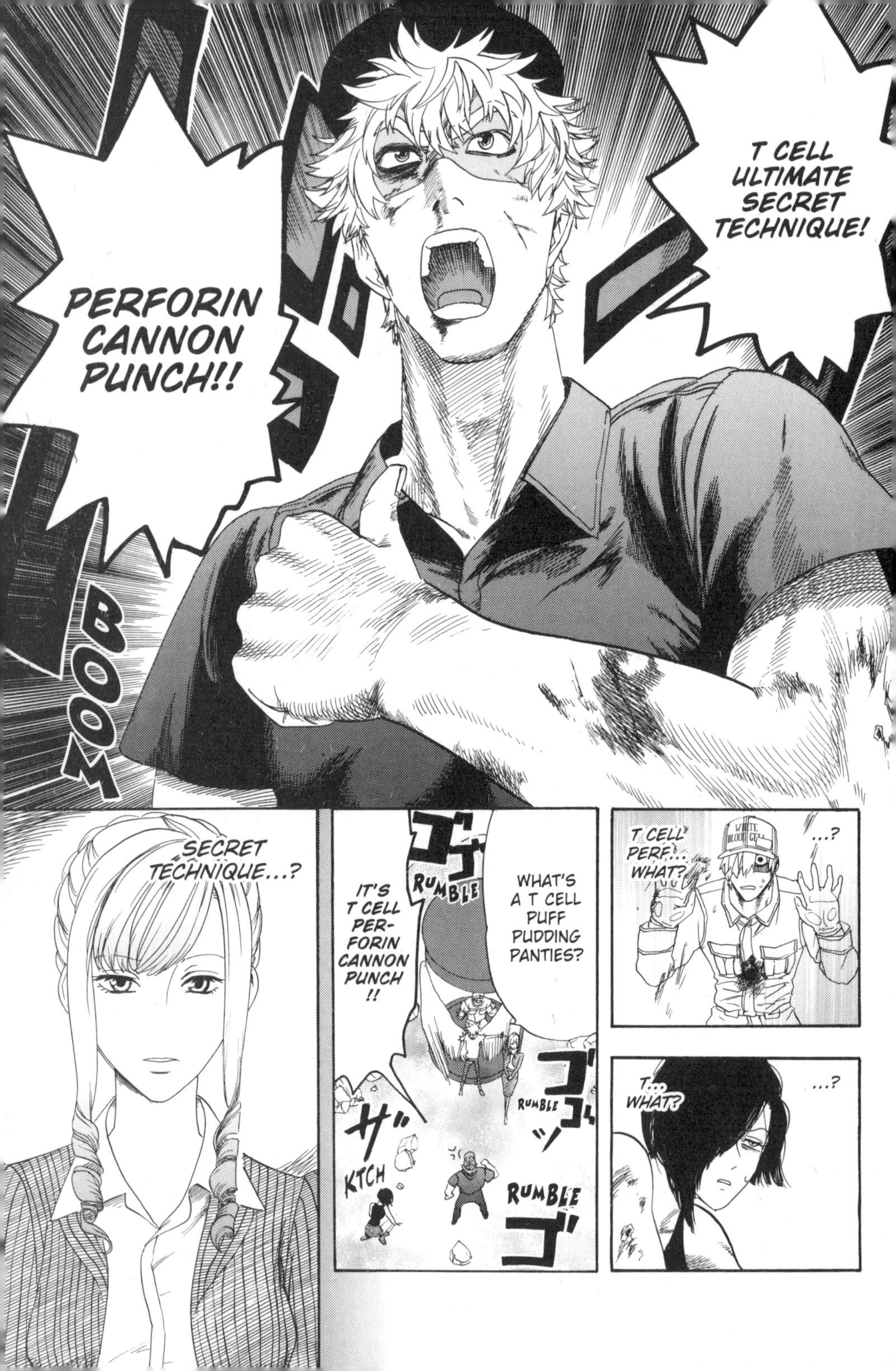
T CELL ULTIMATE SECRET TECHNIQUE!
PERFORIN CANNON PUNCH!!
BOOM
...?
T CELL PERF... WHAT?
...?
T... WHAT?
WHAT'S A T CELL PUFF PUDDING PANTIES?
IT'S T CELL PER-FORIN CANNON PUNCH !!
RUMBLE
RUMBLE
RUMBLE
KTCH
SECRET TECHNIQUE...?

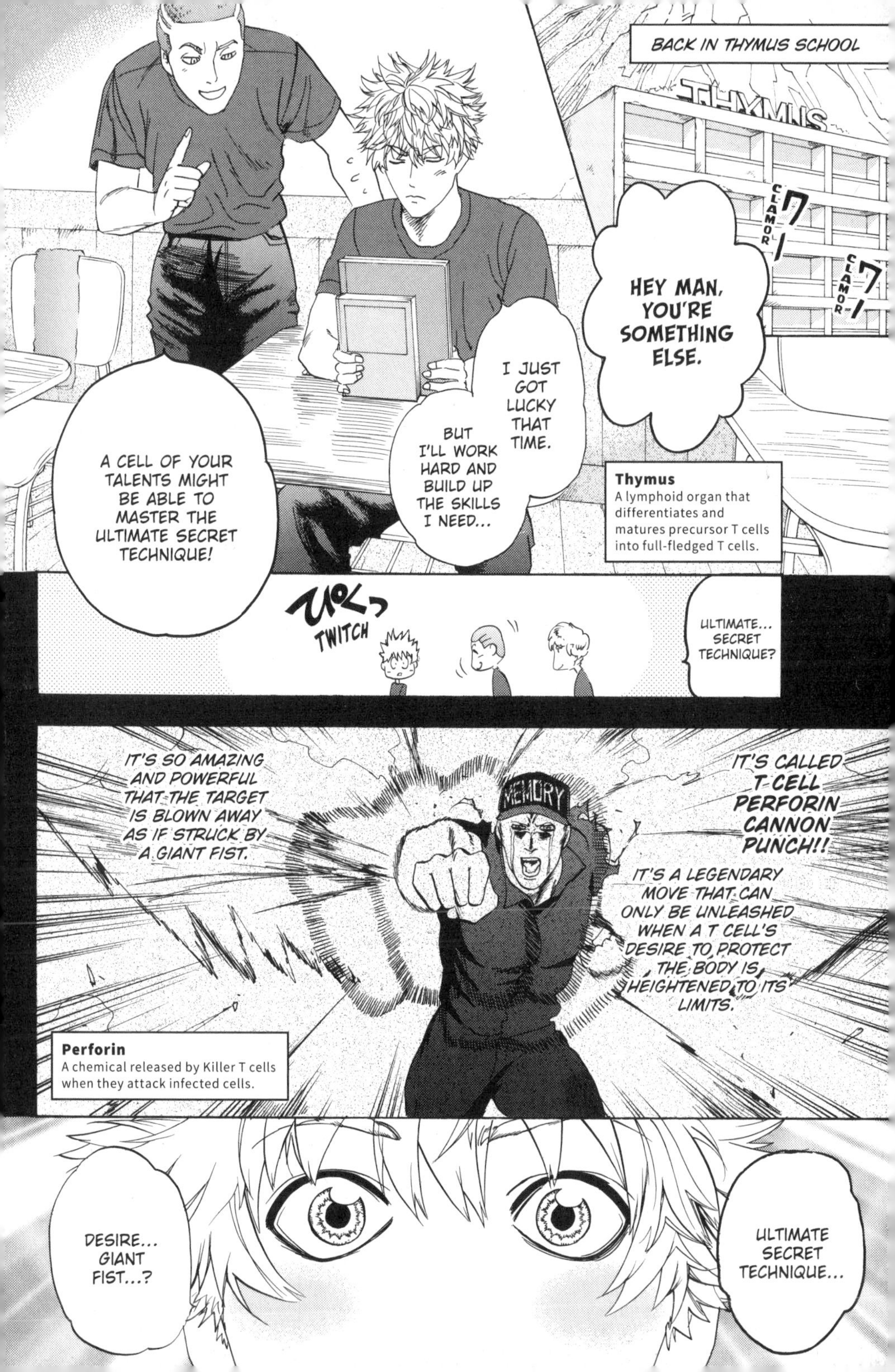
BACK IN THYMUS SCHOOL
THYMUS
CLAMOR
CLAMOR
HEY MAN, YOU'RE SOMETHING ELSE.
Thymus
A lymphoid organ that differentiates and matures precursor T cells into full-fledged T cells.
I JUST GOT LUCKY THAT TIME.
BUT I'LL WORK HARD AND BUILD UP THE SKILLS I NEED...
A CELL OF YOUR TALENTS MIGHT BE ABLE TO MASTER THE ULTIMATE SECRET TECHNIQUE!
ULTIMATE... SECRET TECHNIQUE?
ぴくっ
TWITCH
IT'S CALLED T CELL PERFORIN CANNON PUNCH!!
IT'S A LEGENDARY MOVE THAT CAN ONLY BE UNLEASHED WHEN A T CELL'S DESIRE TO PROTECT THE BODY IS HEIGHTENED TO ITS LIMITS.
MEMORY
IT'S SO AMAZING AND POWERFUL THAT THE TARGET IS BLOWN AWAY AS IF STRUCK BY A GIANT FIST.
Perforin
A chemical released by Killer T cells when they attack infected cells.
ULTIMATE SECRET TECHNIQUE...
DESIRE... GIANT FIST...?

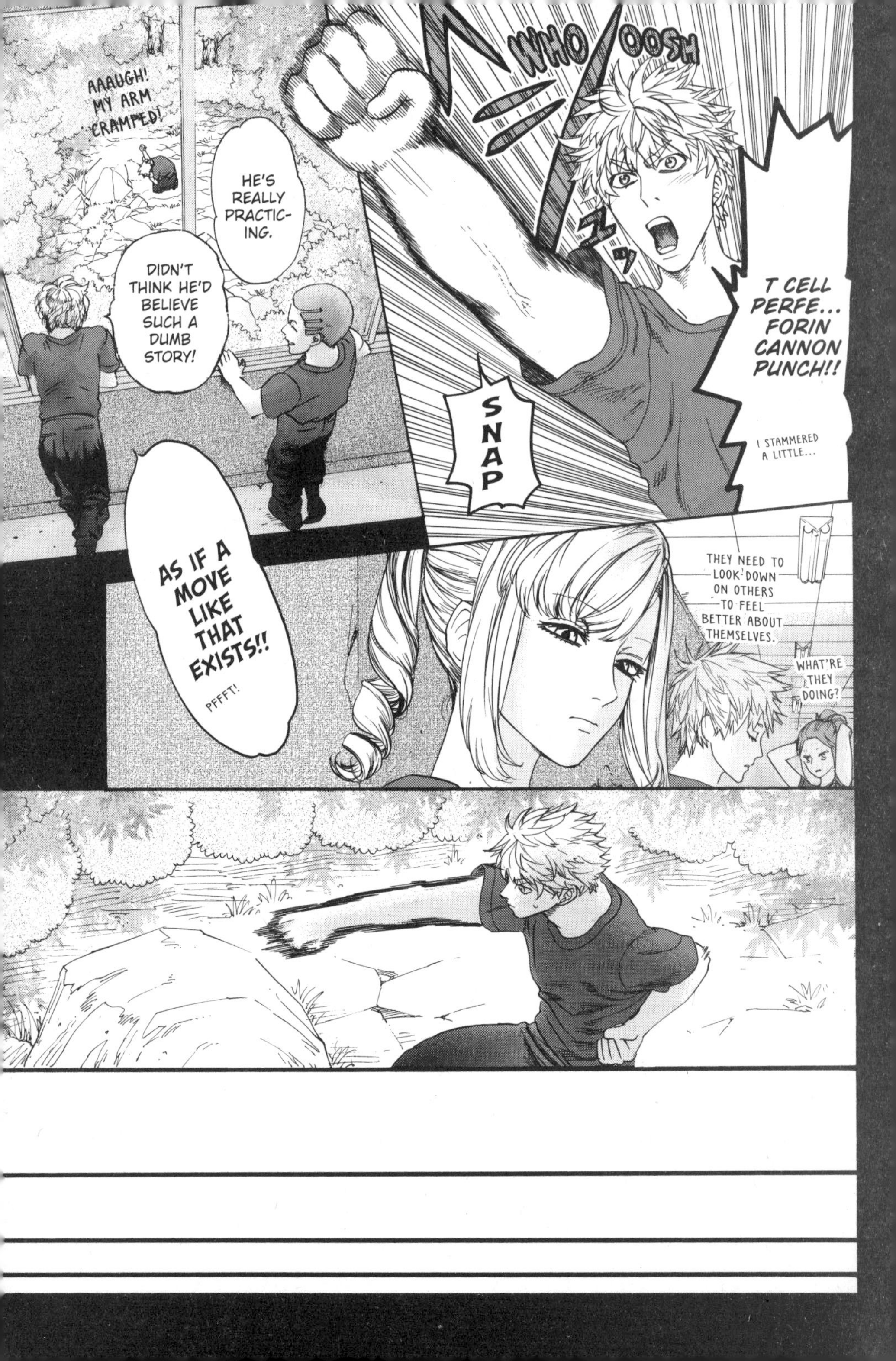
WHOOSH
T CELL PERFE... FORIN CANNON PUNCH!!
SNAP
I STAMMERED A LITTLE...
AAAUGH! MY ARM CRAMPED!
HE'S REALLY PRACTIC-ING.
DIDN'T THINK HE'D BELIEVE SUCH A DUMB STORY!
AS IF A MOVE LIKE THAT EXISTS!!
PFFFT!
THEY NEED TO LOOK DOWN ON OTHERS TO FEEL BETTER ABOUT THEMSELVES.
WHAT'RE THEY DOING?

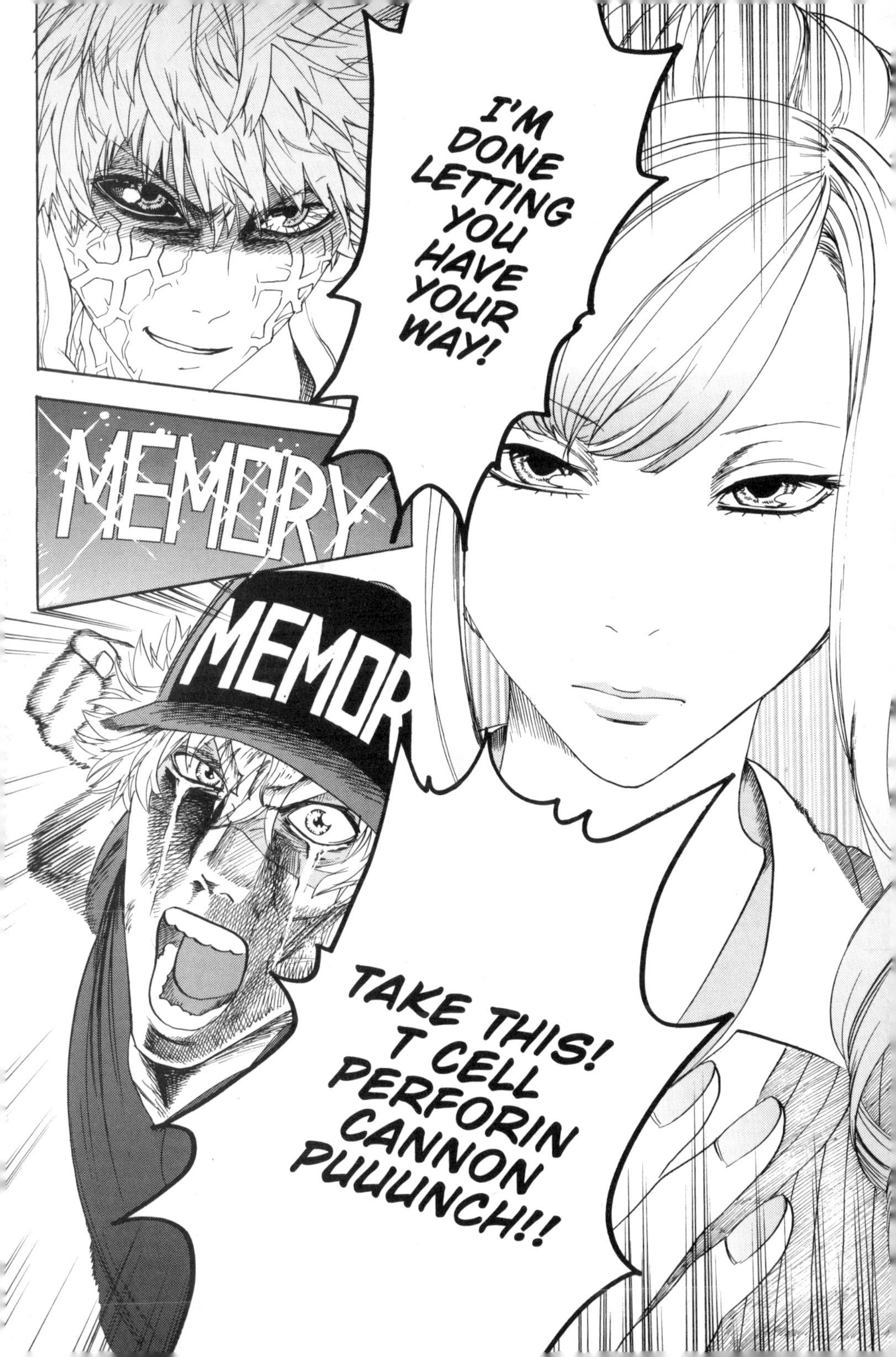
I'M DONE LETTING YOU HAVE YOUR WAY!
MEMORY
MEMOR
TAKE THIS! T CELL PERFORIN CANNON PUUUNCH!!

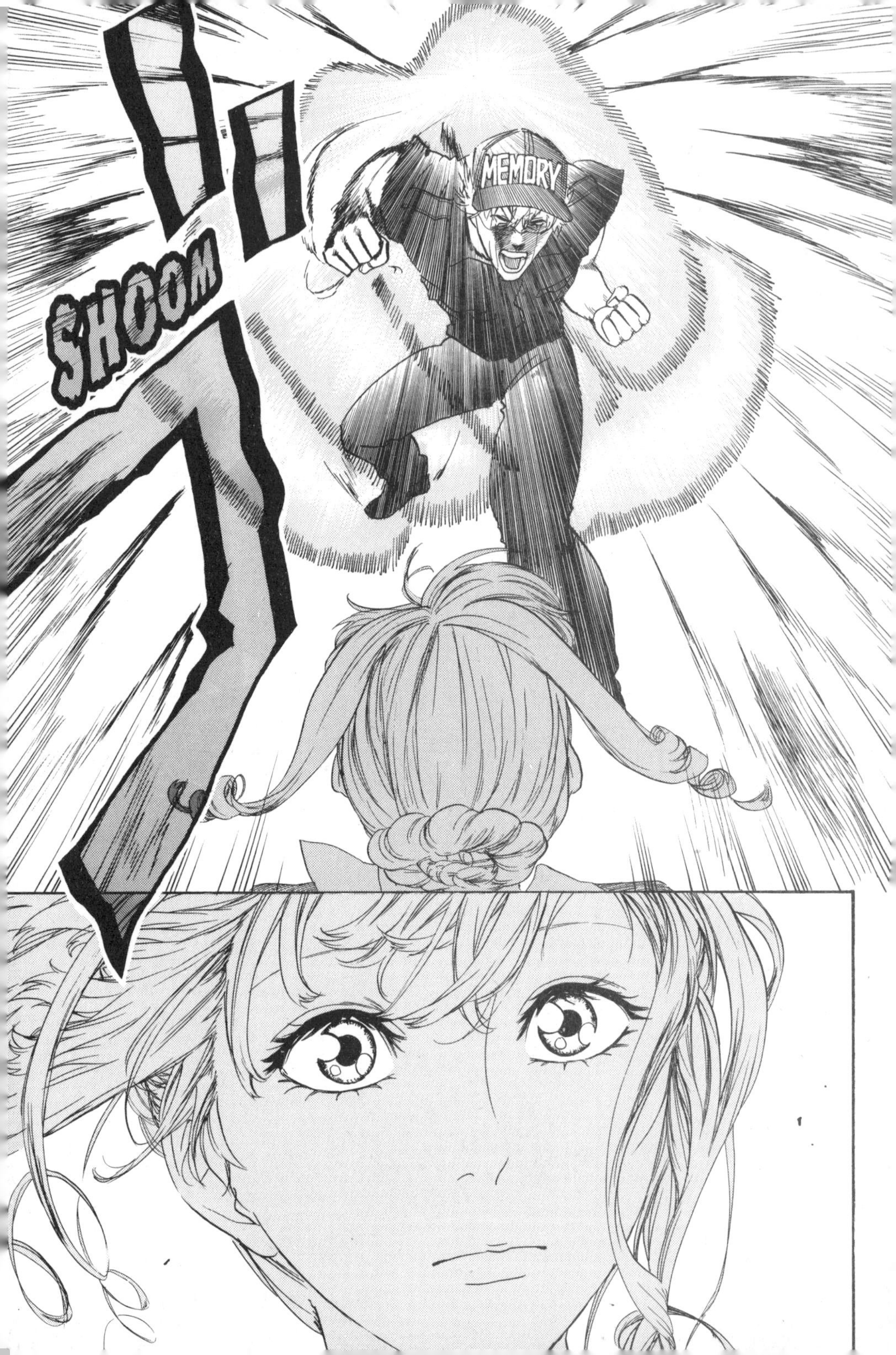
SHOOM
MEMORY

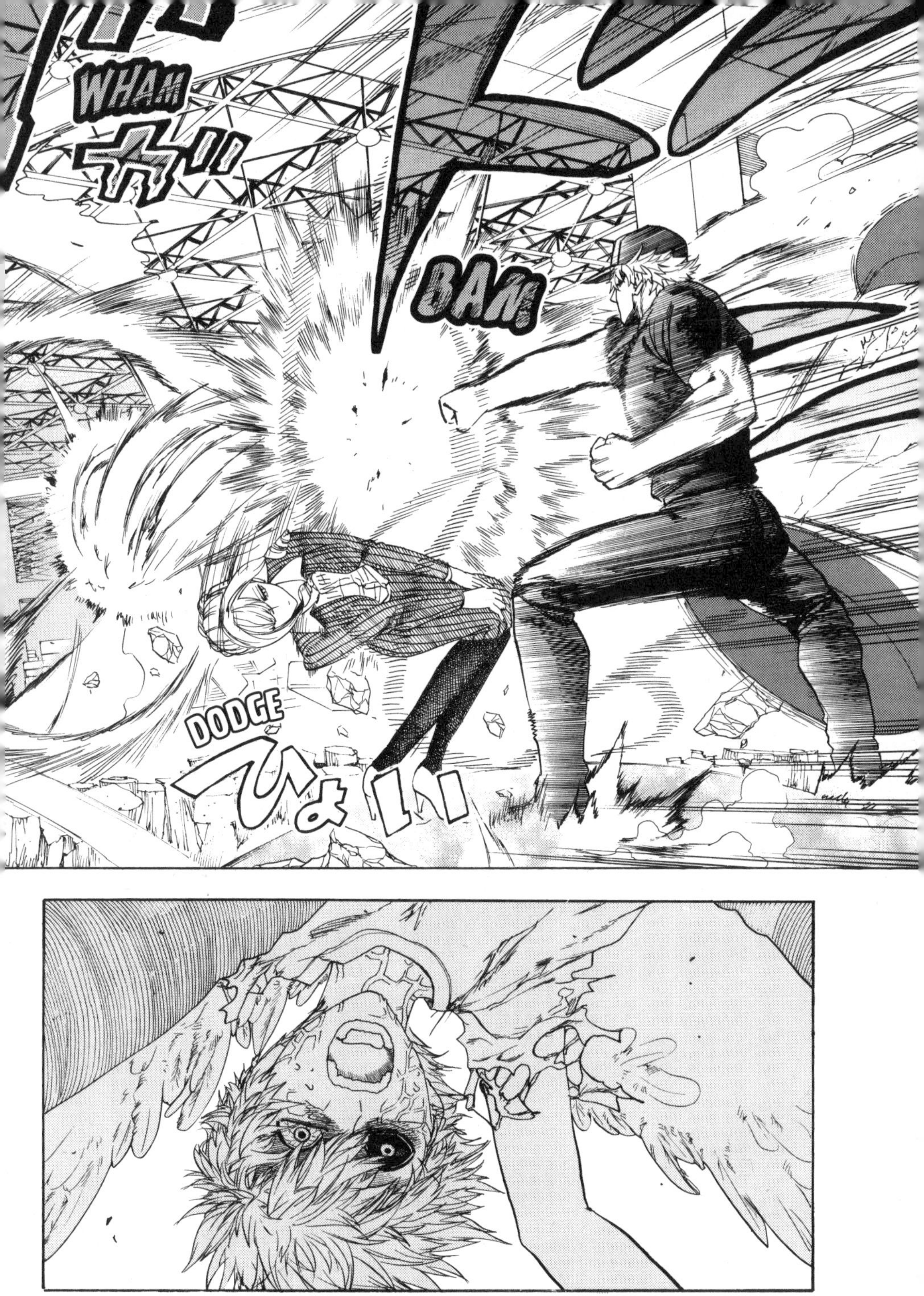
BAM
WHAM
ガッ
DODGE
ひょい

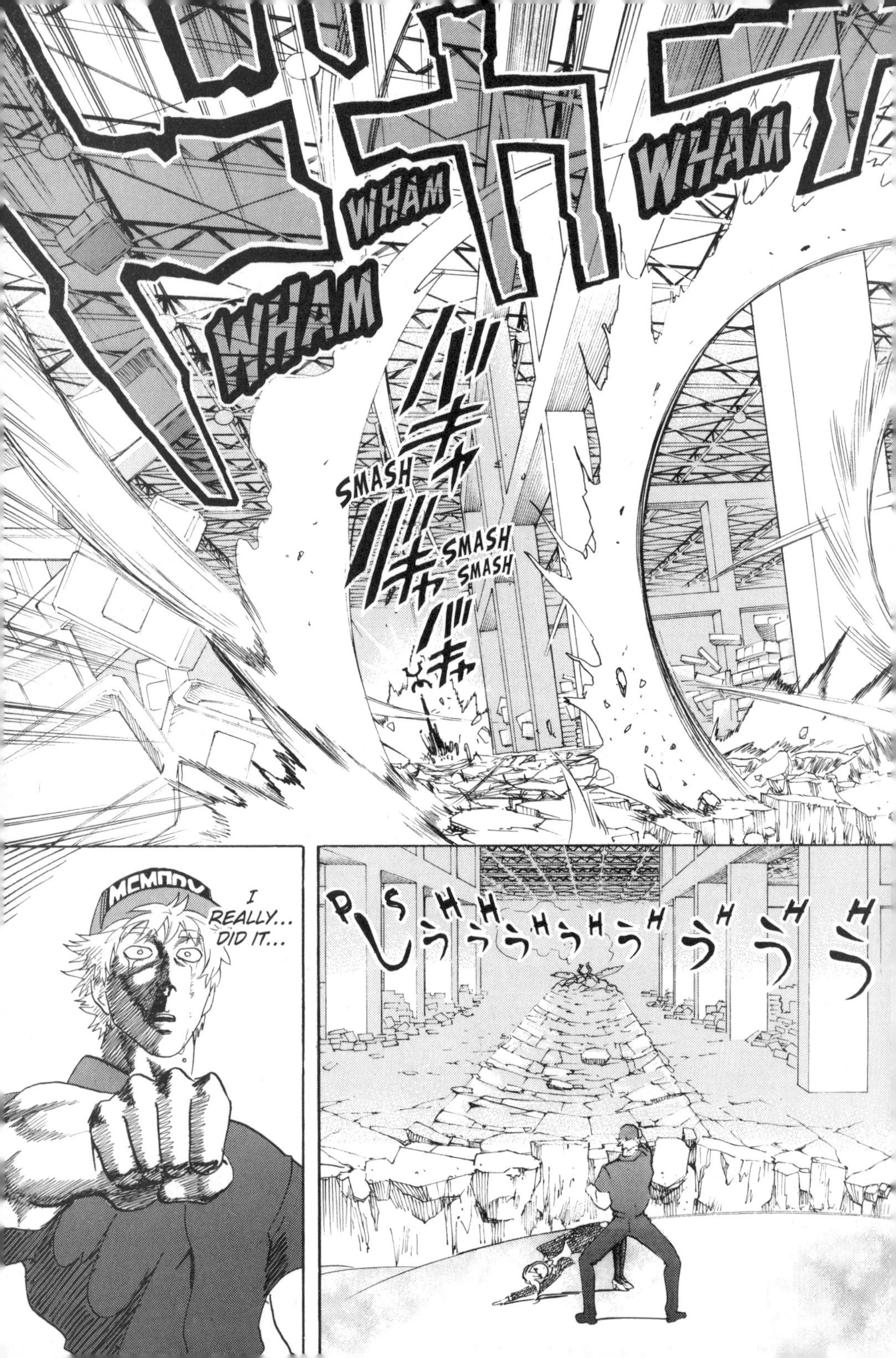
WHAM
WHAM
WHAM
WHAM
SMASH
SMASH
SMASH
PSHHHHHHHH
I REALLY... DID IT...

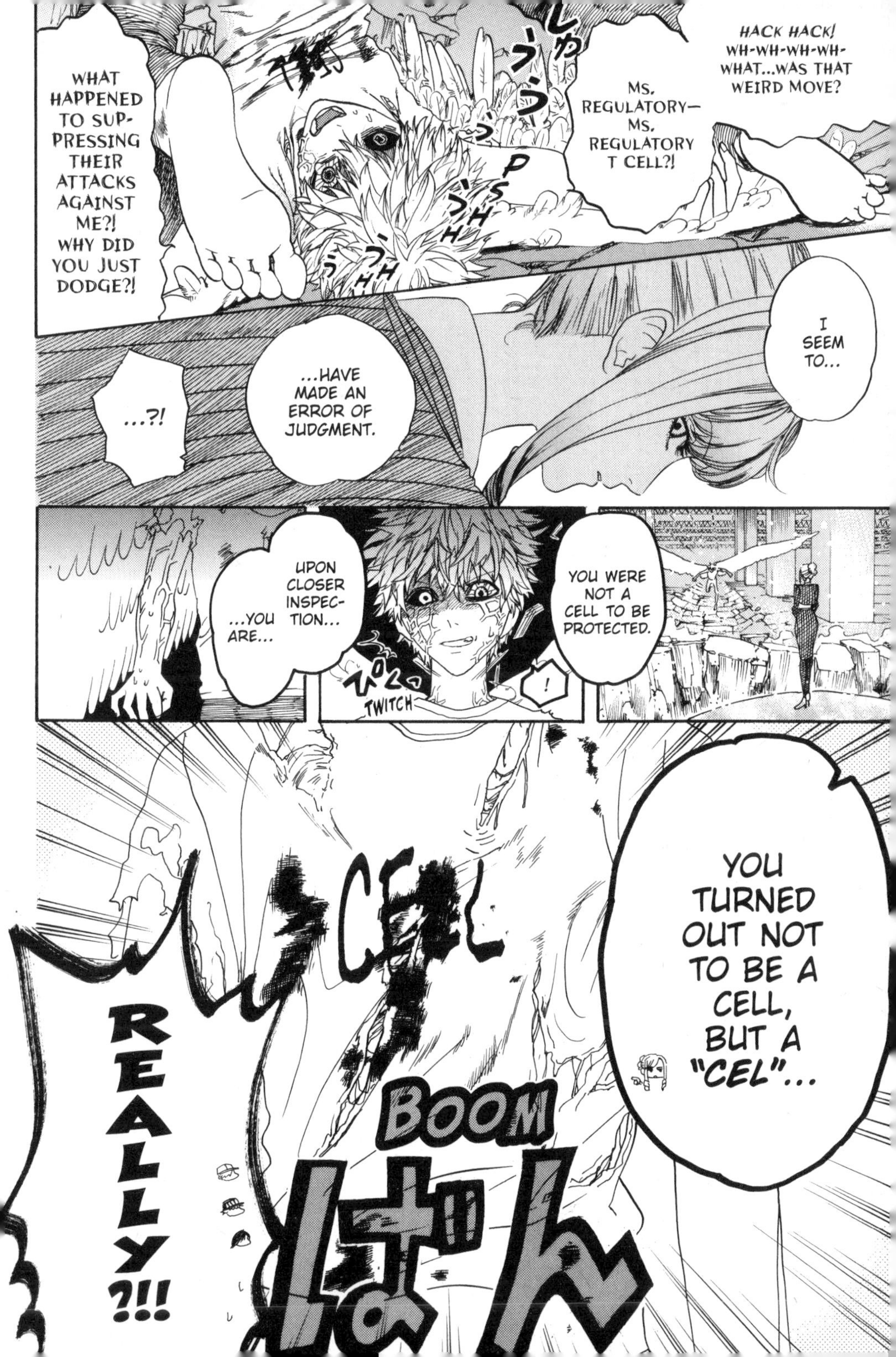
HACK HACK! WH-WH-WH-WH-WHAT...WAS THAT WEIRD MOVE?
MS. REGULATORY— MS. REGULATORY T CELL?!
PSHH
WHAT HAPPENED TO SUP-PRESSING THEIR ATTACKS AGAINST ME?! WHY DID YOU JUST DODGE?!
I SEEM TO...
...HAVE MADE AN ERROR OF JUDGMENT.
...?!
YOU WERE NOT A CELL TO BE PROTECTED.
!
TWITCH
UPON CLOSER INSPECTION...
...YOU ARE...
YOU TURNED OUT NOT TO BE A CELL, BUT A "CEL"...
CEL
BOOM
ばん
REALLY?!!

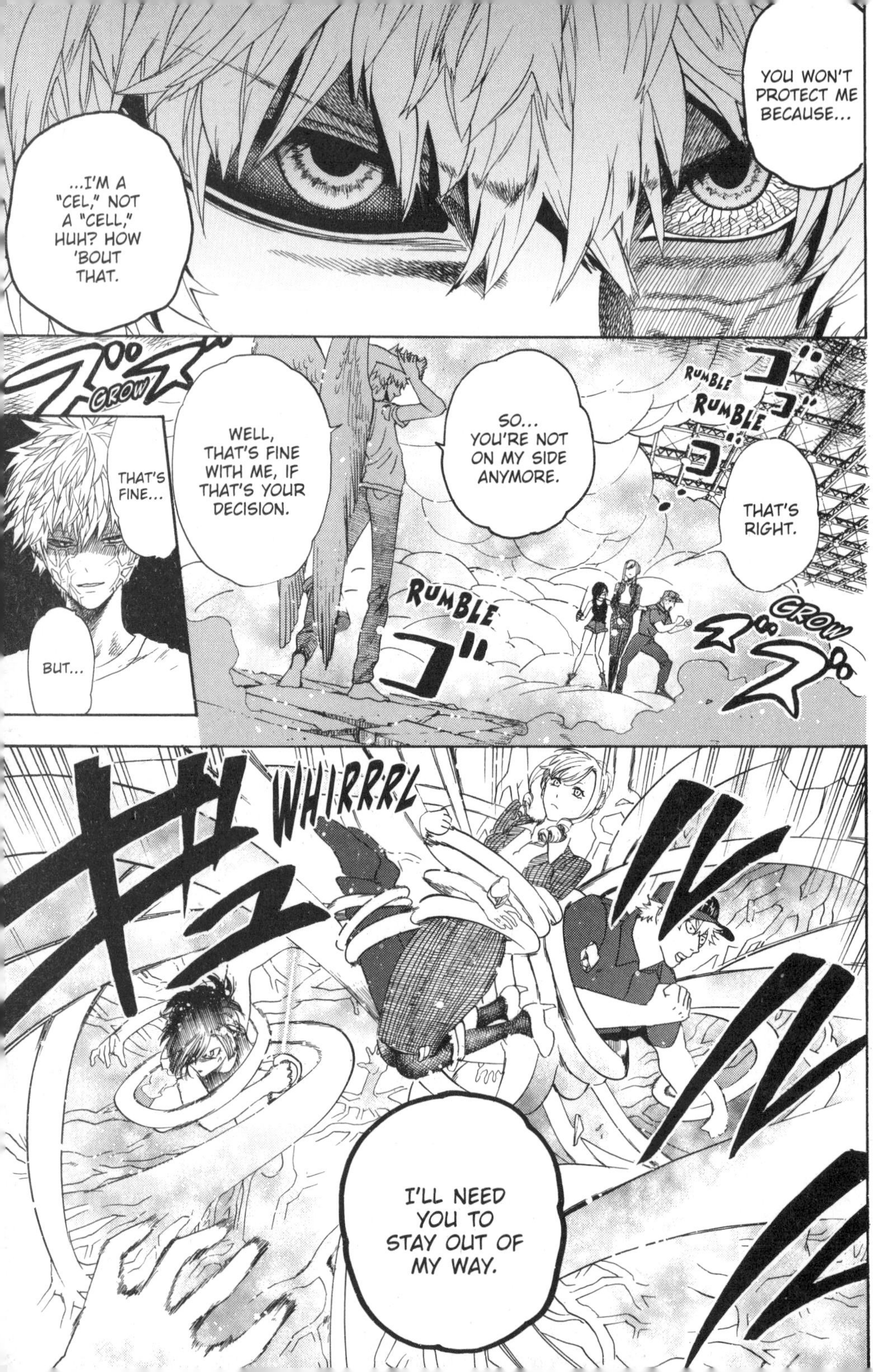
YOU WON'T PROTECT ME BECAUSE...
...I'M A "CEL," NOT A "CELL," HUH? HOW 'BOUT THAT.
RUMBLE
RUMBLE
SO... YOU'RE NOT ON MY SIDE ANYMORE.
THAT'S RIGHT.
WELL, THAT'S FINE WITH ME, IF THAT'S YOUR DECISION.
GROW
RUMBLE
GROW
THAT'S FINE...
BUT...
WHIRRRL
I'LL NEED YOU TO STAY OUT OF MY WAY.

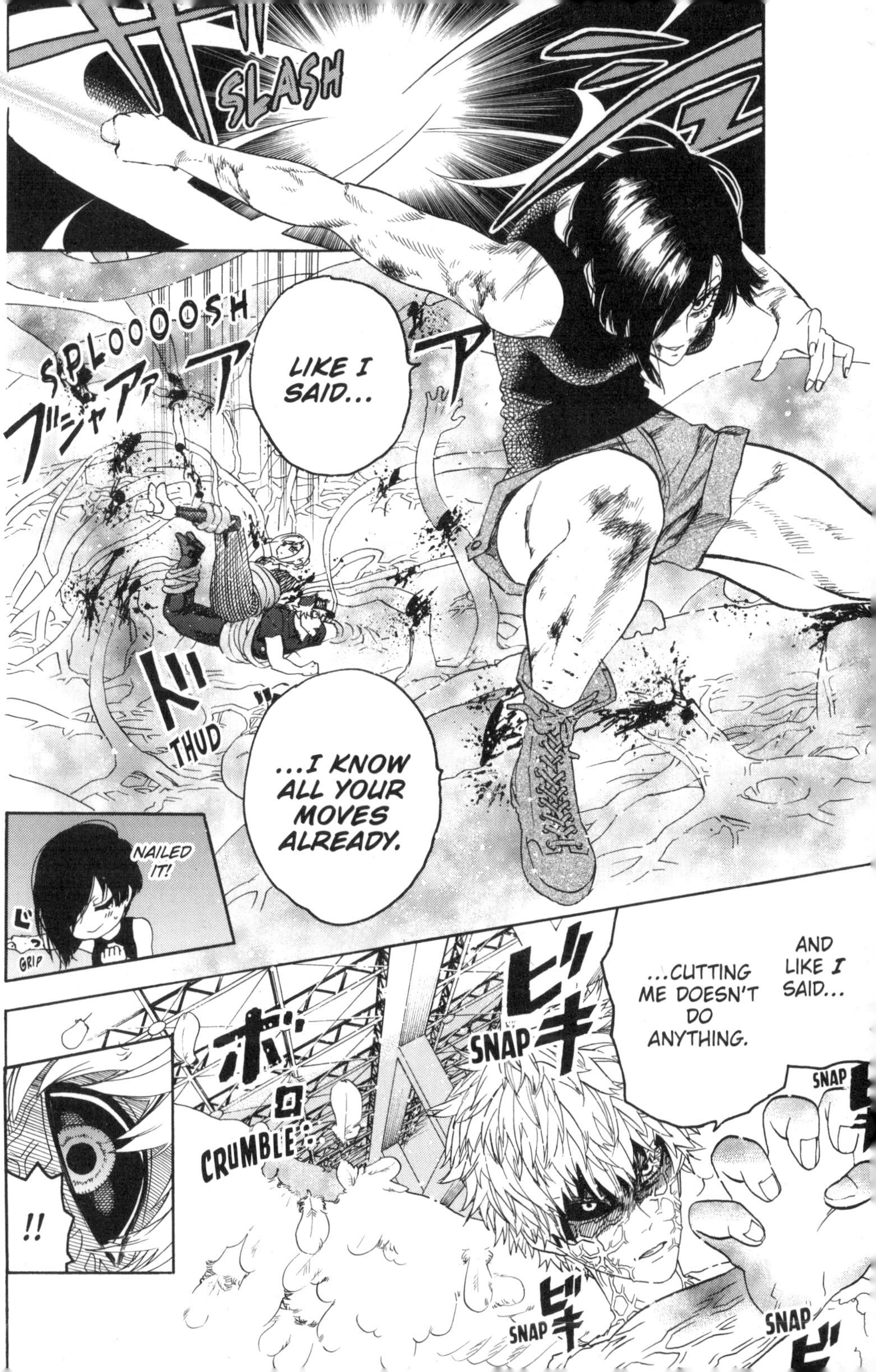
SLASH
SPLOOOOSH
LIKE I SAID...
...I KNOW ALL YOUR MOVES ALREADY.
THUD
NAILED IT!
GRIP
AND LIKE I SAID...
...CUTTING ME DOESN'T DO ANYTHING.
SNAP
SNAP
SNAP
SNAP
CRUMBLE
!!

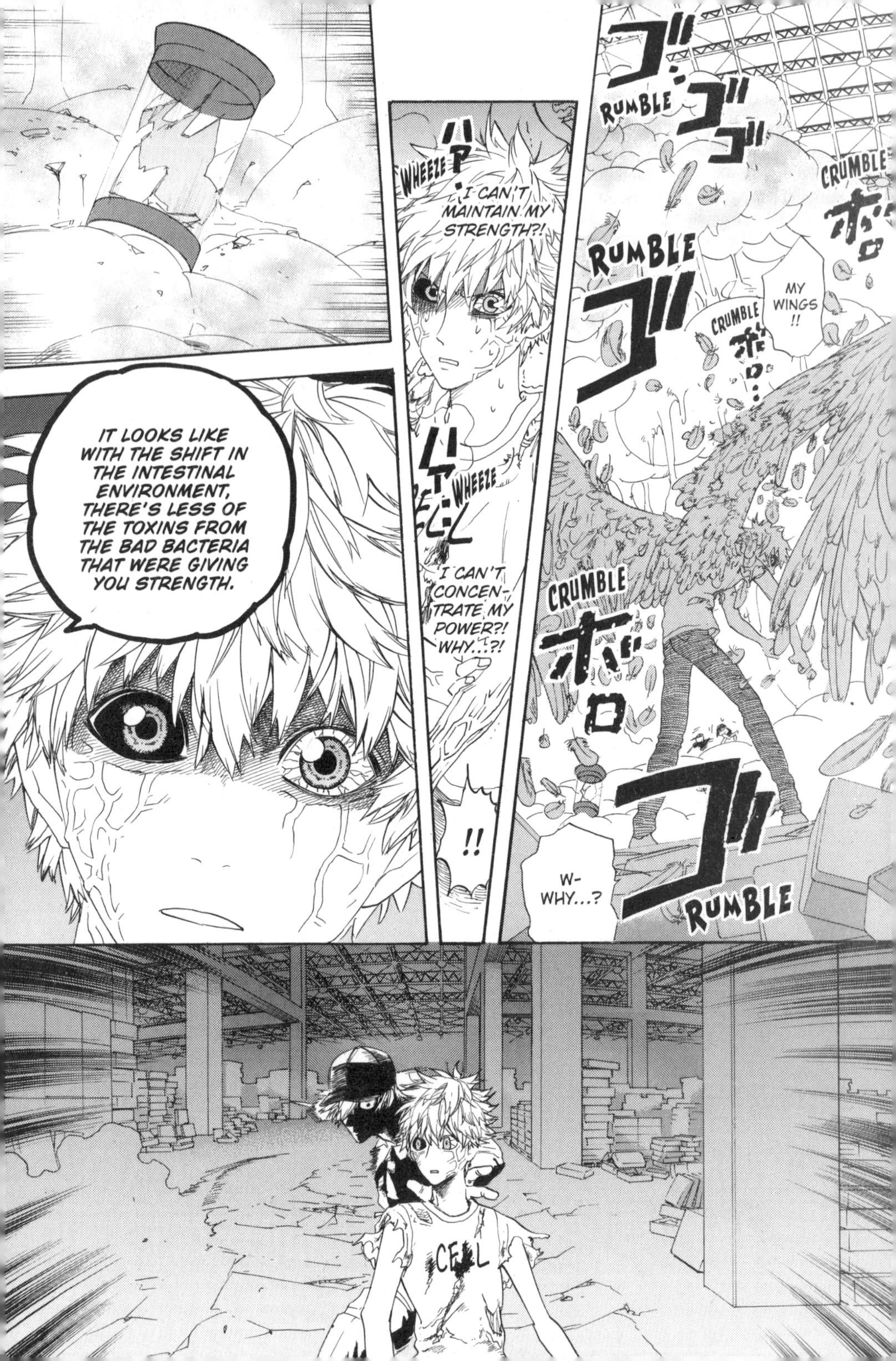
RUMBLE
CRUMBLE
RUMBLE
MY WINGS !!
CRUMBLE
CRUMBLE
W- WHY...?
RUMBLE
WHEEZE
I CAN'T MAINTAIN MY STRENGTH?!
WHEEZE
I CAN'T CONCEN- TRATE MY POWER?! WHY...?!
!!
IT LOOKS LIKE WITH THE SHIFT IN THE INTESTINAL ENVIRONMENT, THERE'S LESS OF THE TOXINS FROM THE BAD BACTERIA THAT WERE GIVING YOU STRENGTH.
CELL

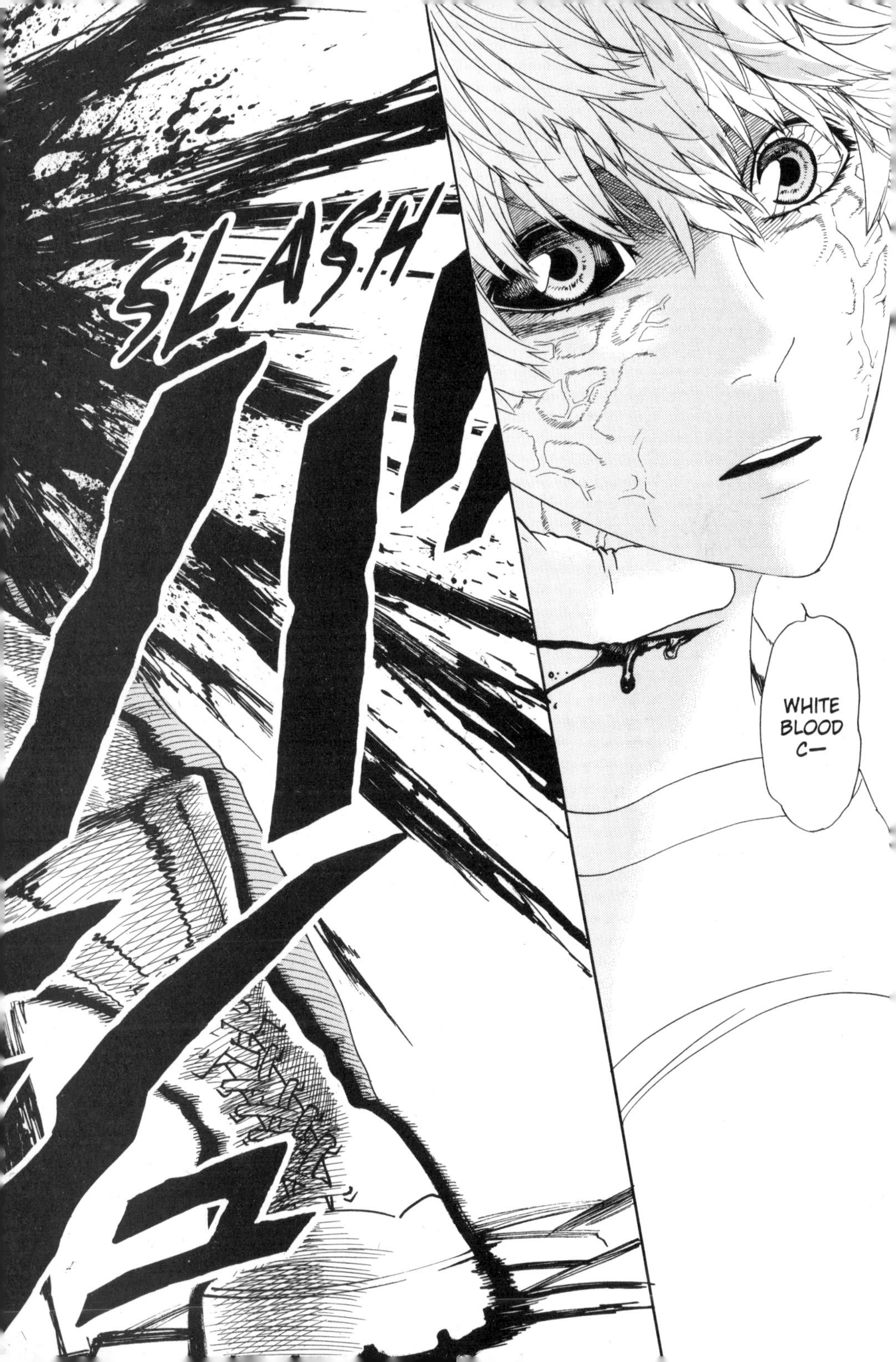
WHITE BLOOD C—
SLASH

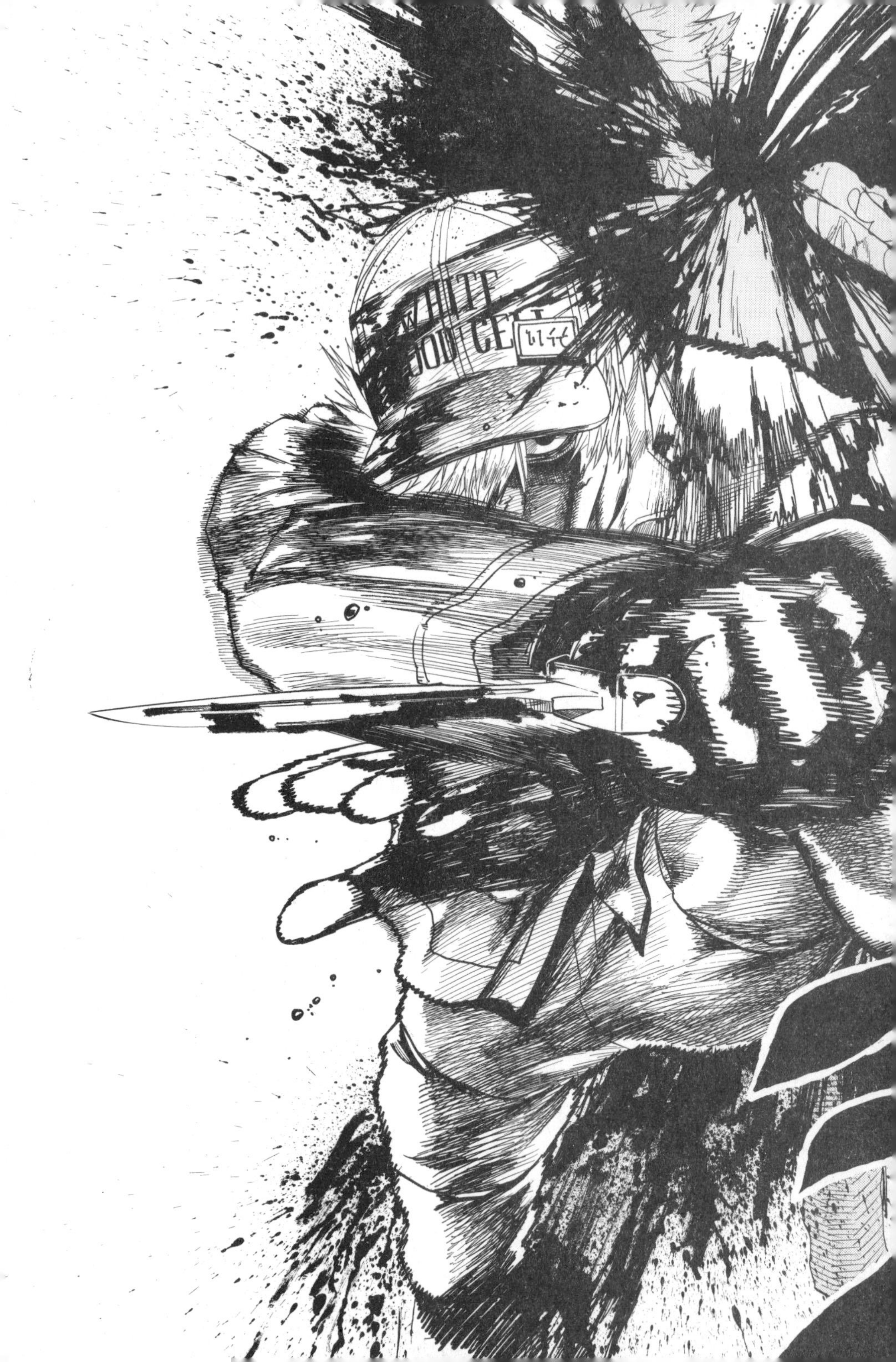
WHITE
1146

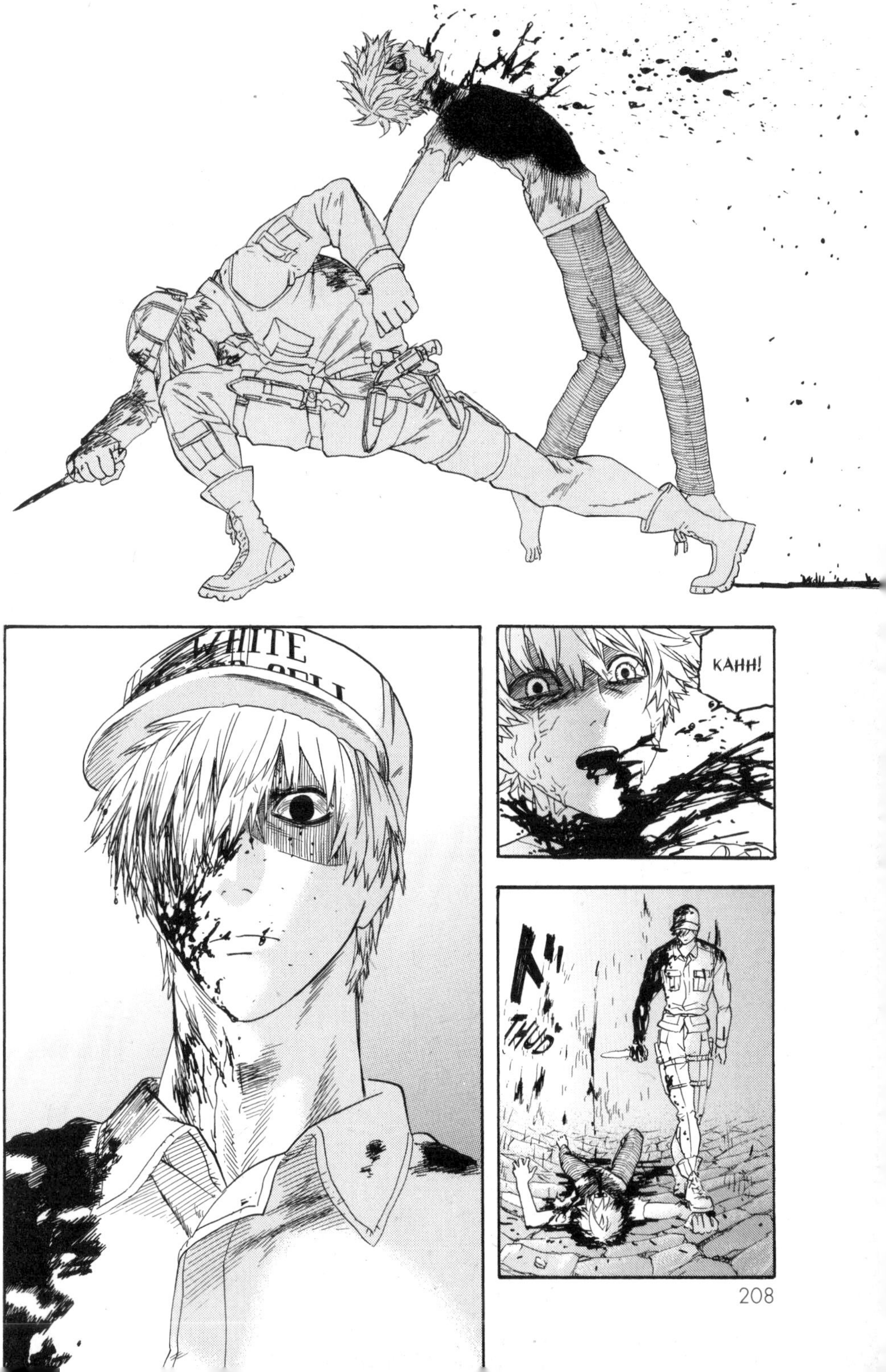
KAHH!
THUD
WHITE

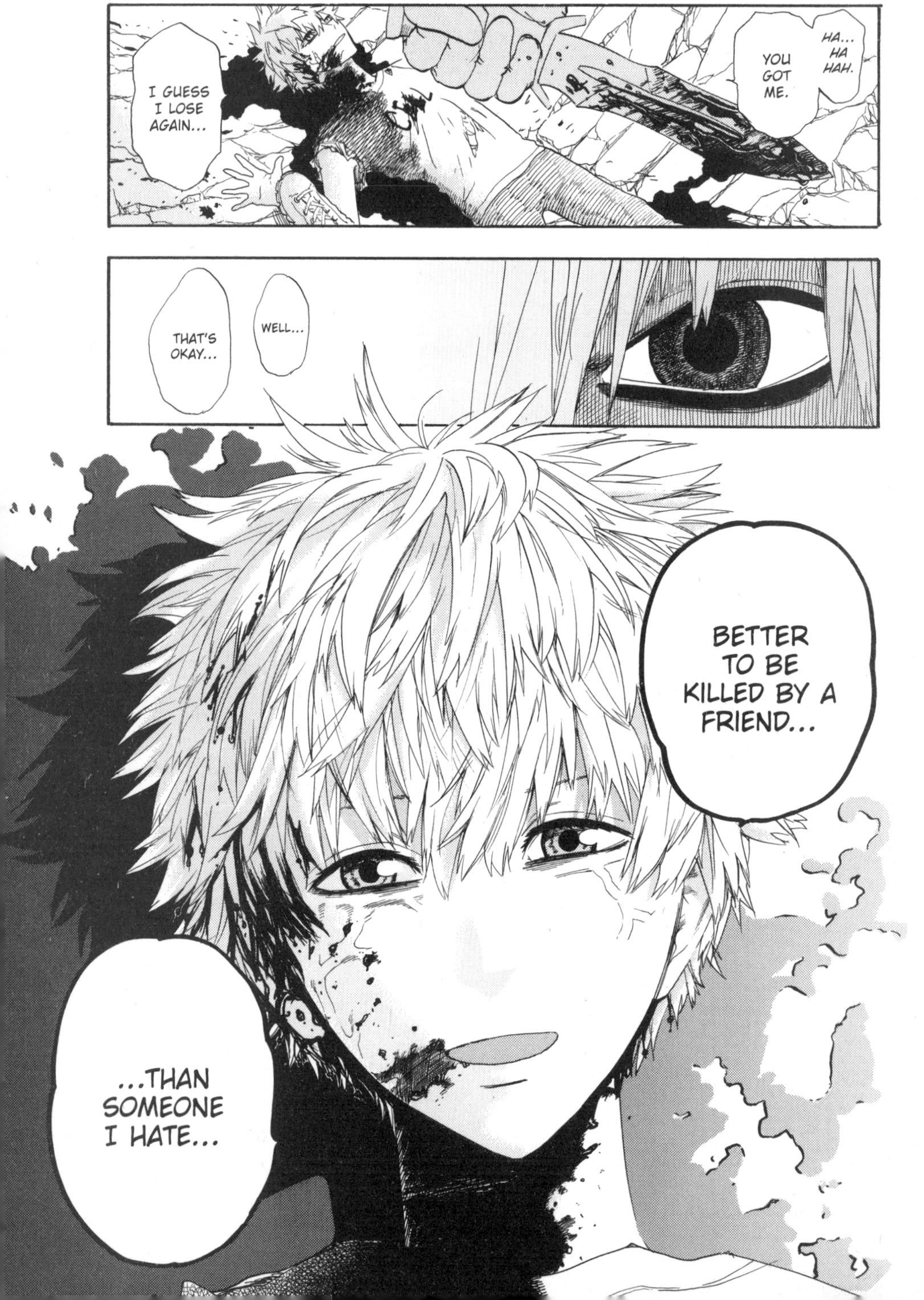
HA... HA HAH.
YOU GOT ME.
I GUESS I LOSE AGAIN...
WELL...
THAT'S OKAY...
BETTER TO BE KILLED BY A FRIEND...
...THAN SOMEONE I HATE...

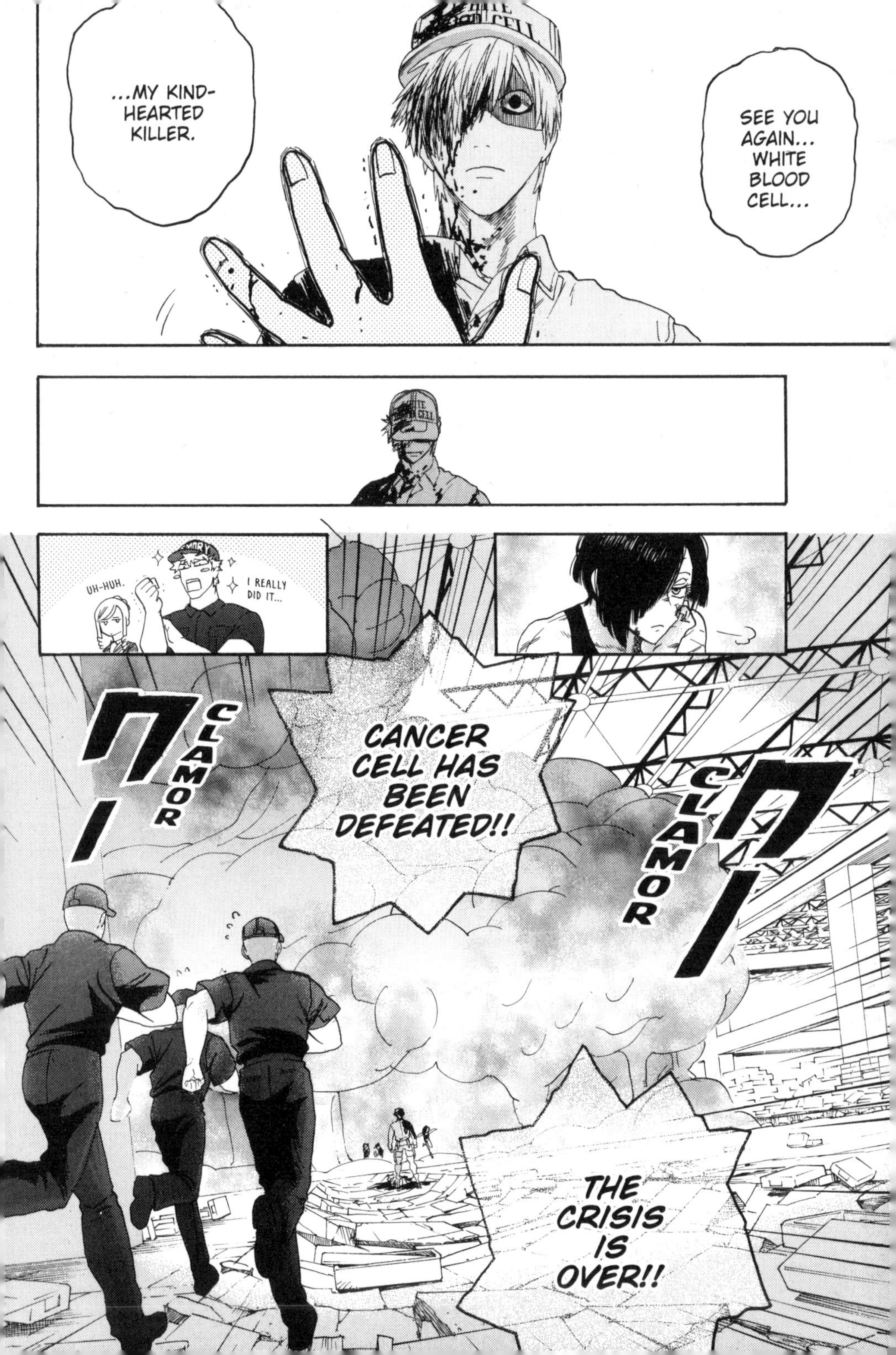
SEE YOU AGAIN... WHITE BLOOD CELL...
...MY KIND-HEARTED KILLER.
I REALLY DID IT...
UH-HUH.
ワー
CLAMOR
CANCER CELL HAS BEEN DEFEATED!!
ワー
CLAMOR
THE CRISIS IS OVER!!

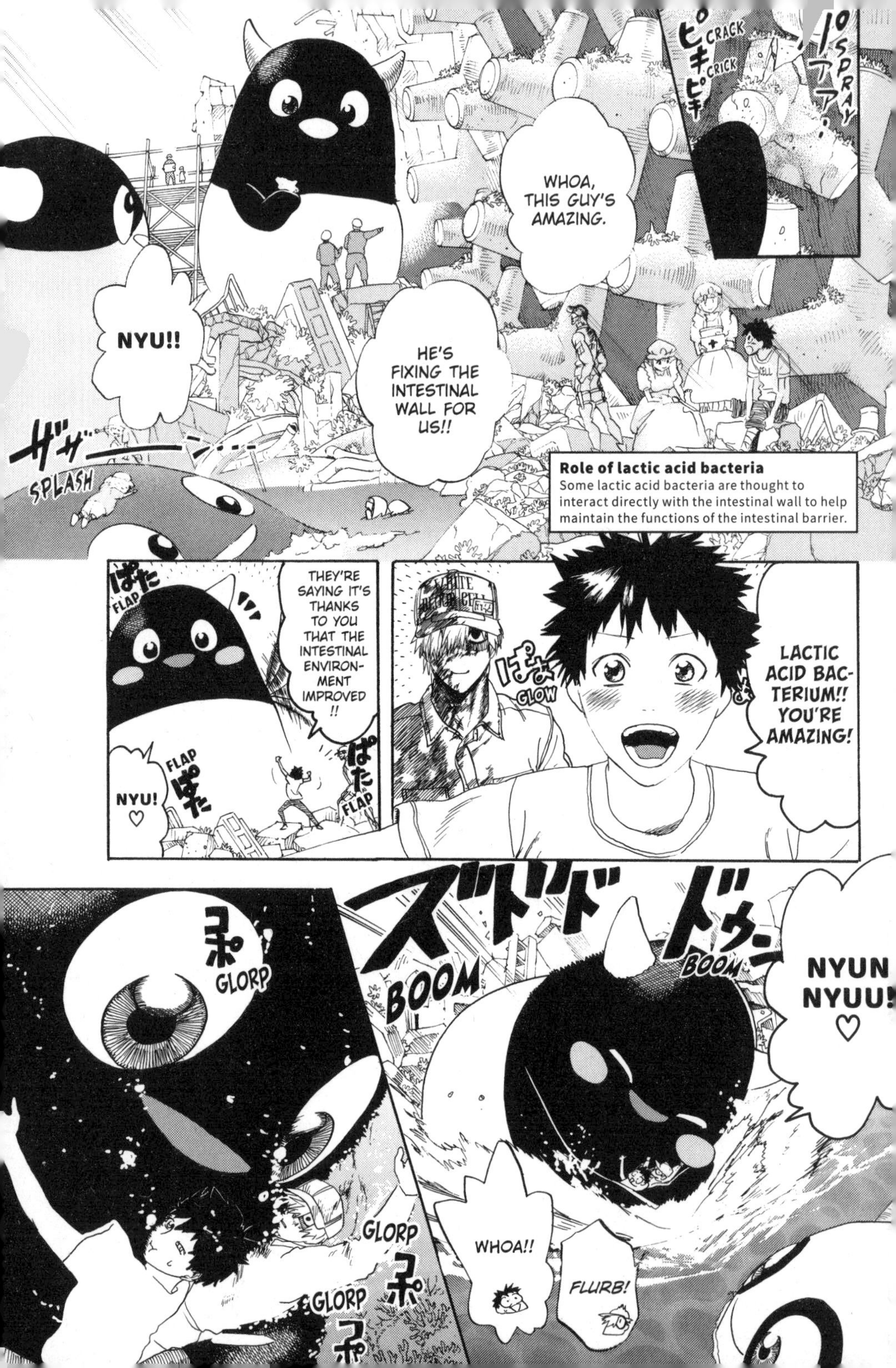

SPRAY
CRACK
CRICK
WHOA, THIS GUY'S AMAZING.
HE'S FIXING THE INTESTINAL WALL FOR US!!
NYU!!
Role of lactic acid bacteria
Some lactic acid bacteria are thought to interact directly with the intestinal wall to help maintain the functions of the intestinal barrier.
SPLASH
LACTIC ACID BAC-TERIUM!! YOU'RE AMAZING!
GLOW
THEY'RE SAYING IT'S THANKS TO YOU THAT THE INTESTINAL ENVIRON-MENT IMPROVED!!
FLAP
FLAP
FLAP
NYU! ♡
NYUN NYUU! ♡
BOOM
BOOM
WHOA!!
FLURB!
GLORP
GLORP
GLORP

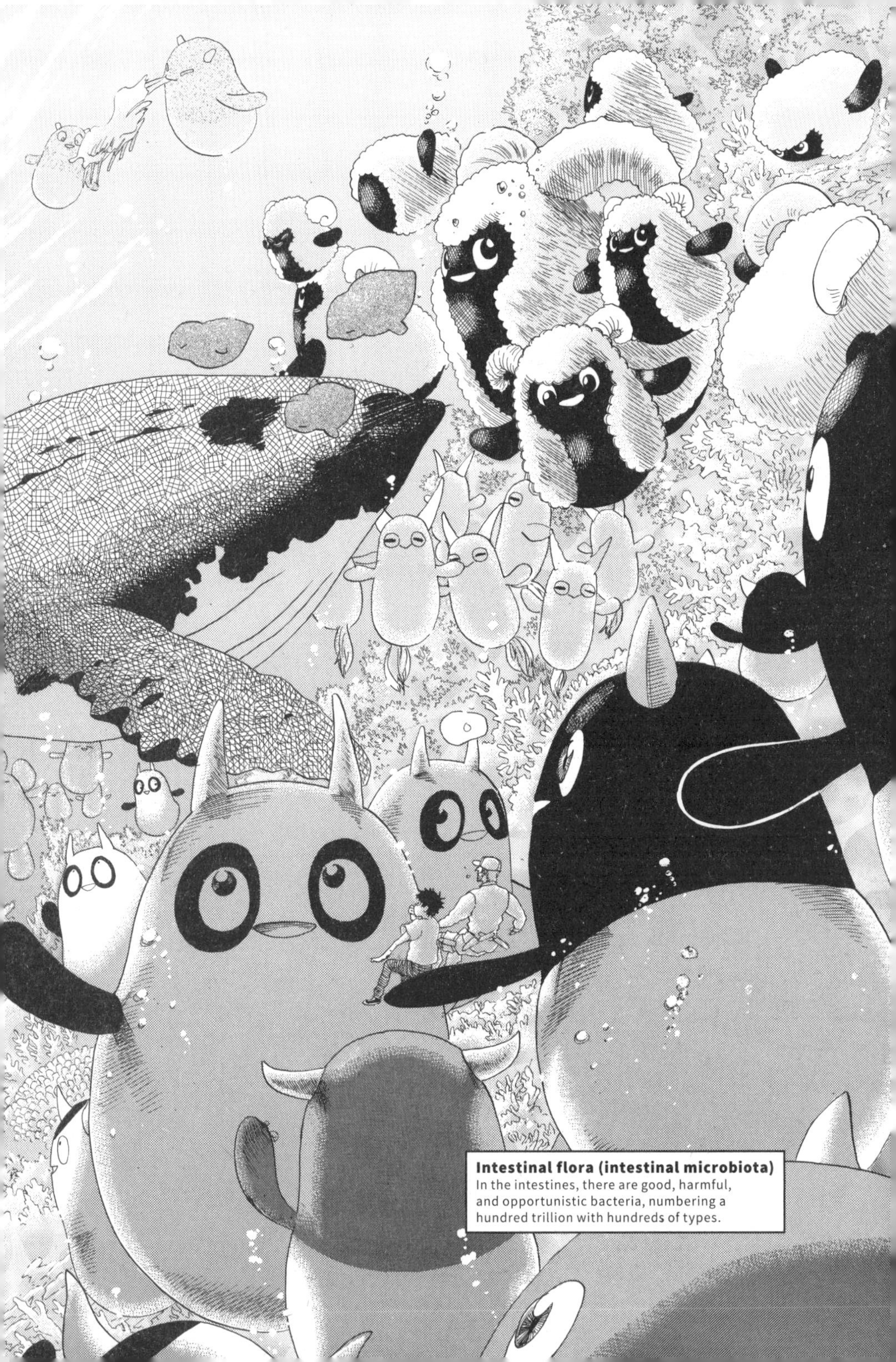
Intestinal flora (intestinal microbiota)
In the intestines, there are good, harmful, and opportunistic bacteria, numbering a hundred trillion with hundreds of types.

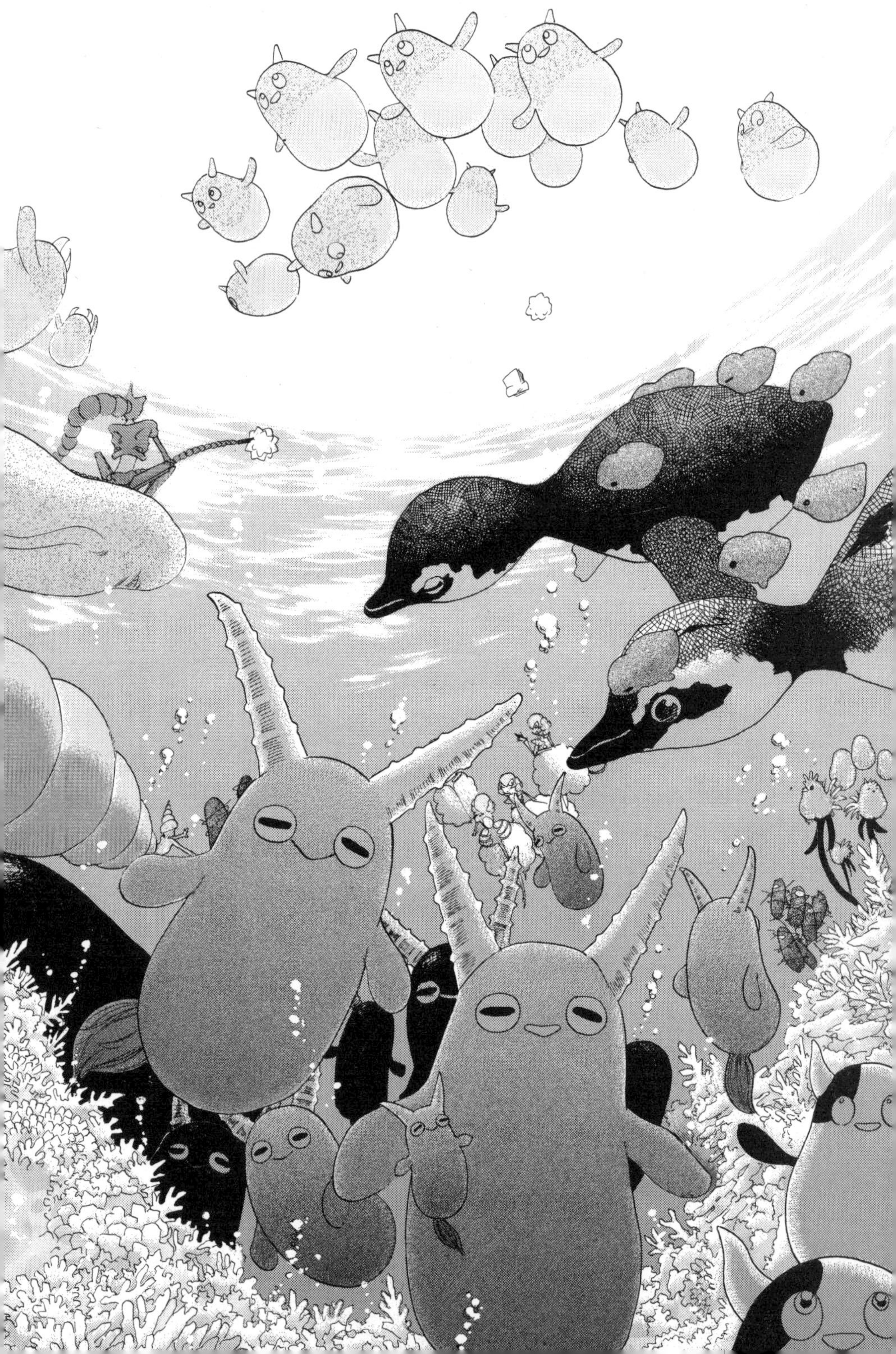

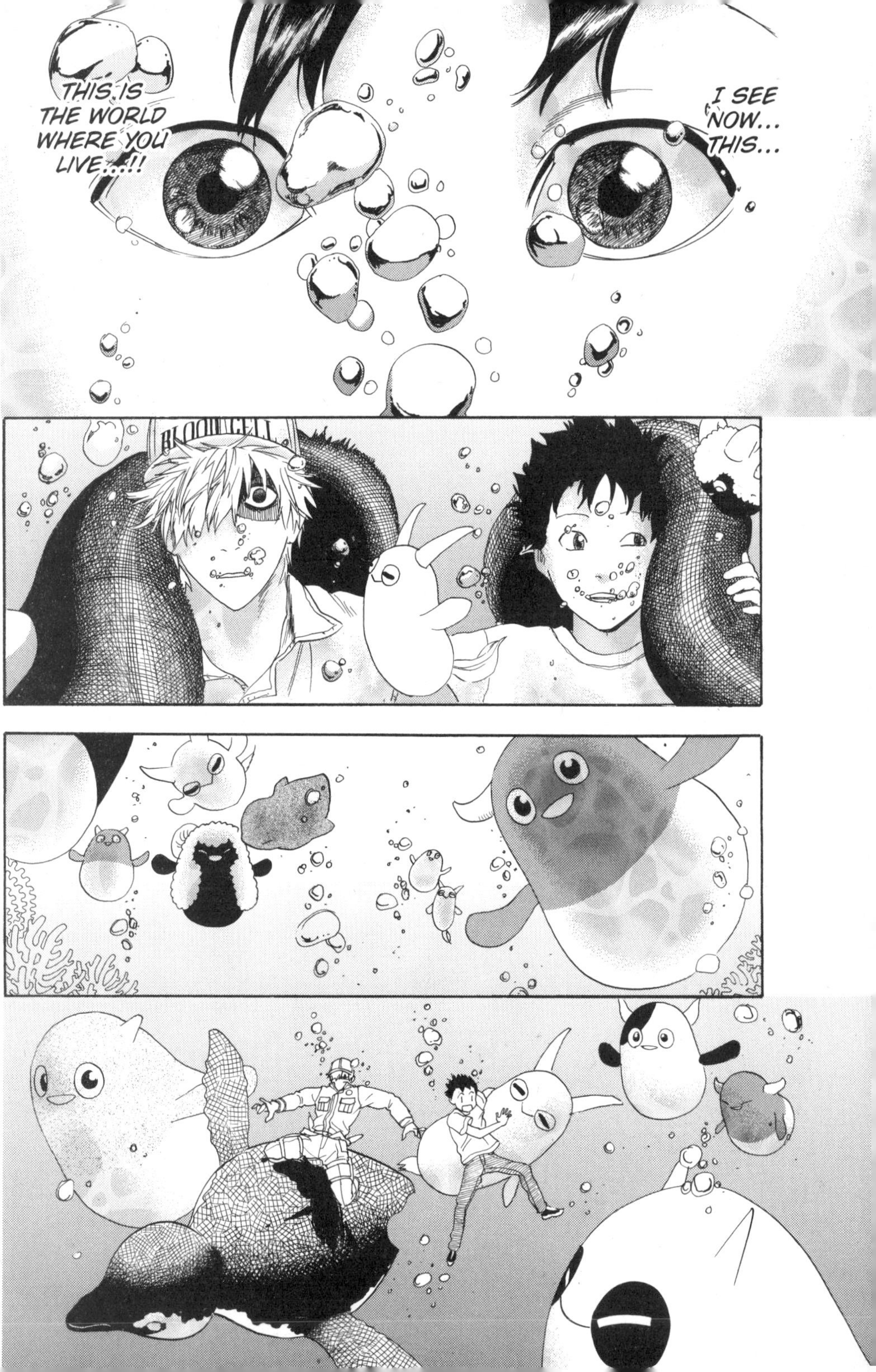
I SEE NOW... THIS...
THIS IS THE WORLD WHERE YOU LIVE...!!

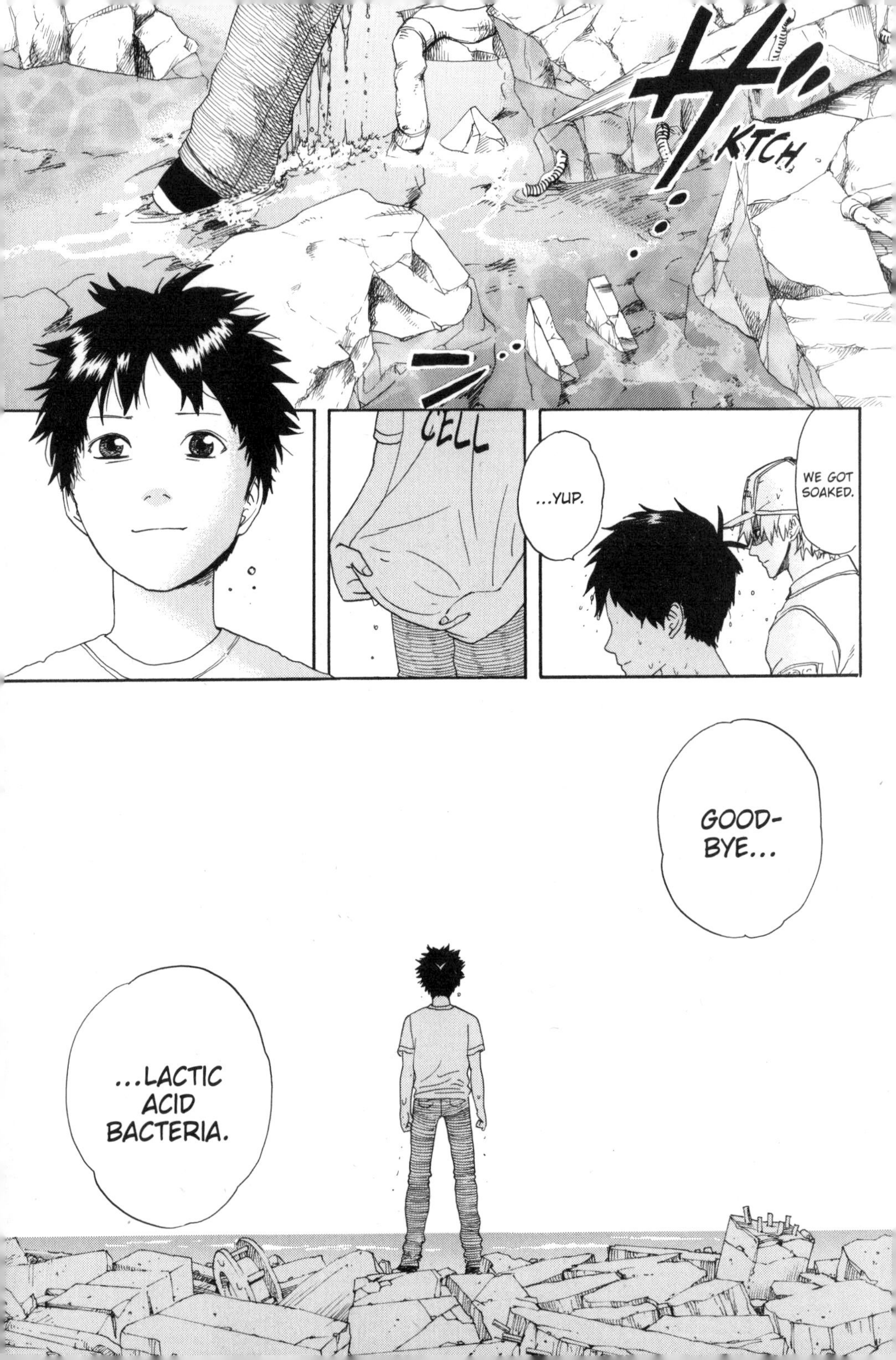
KTCH
WE GOT SOAKED.
...YUP.
CELL
GOOD-BYE...
...LACTIC ACID BACTERIA.

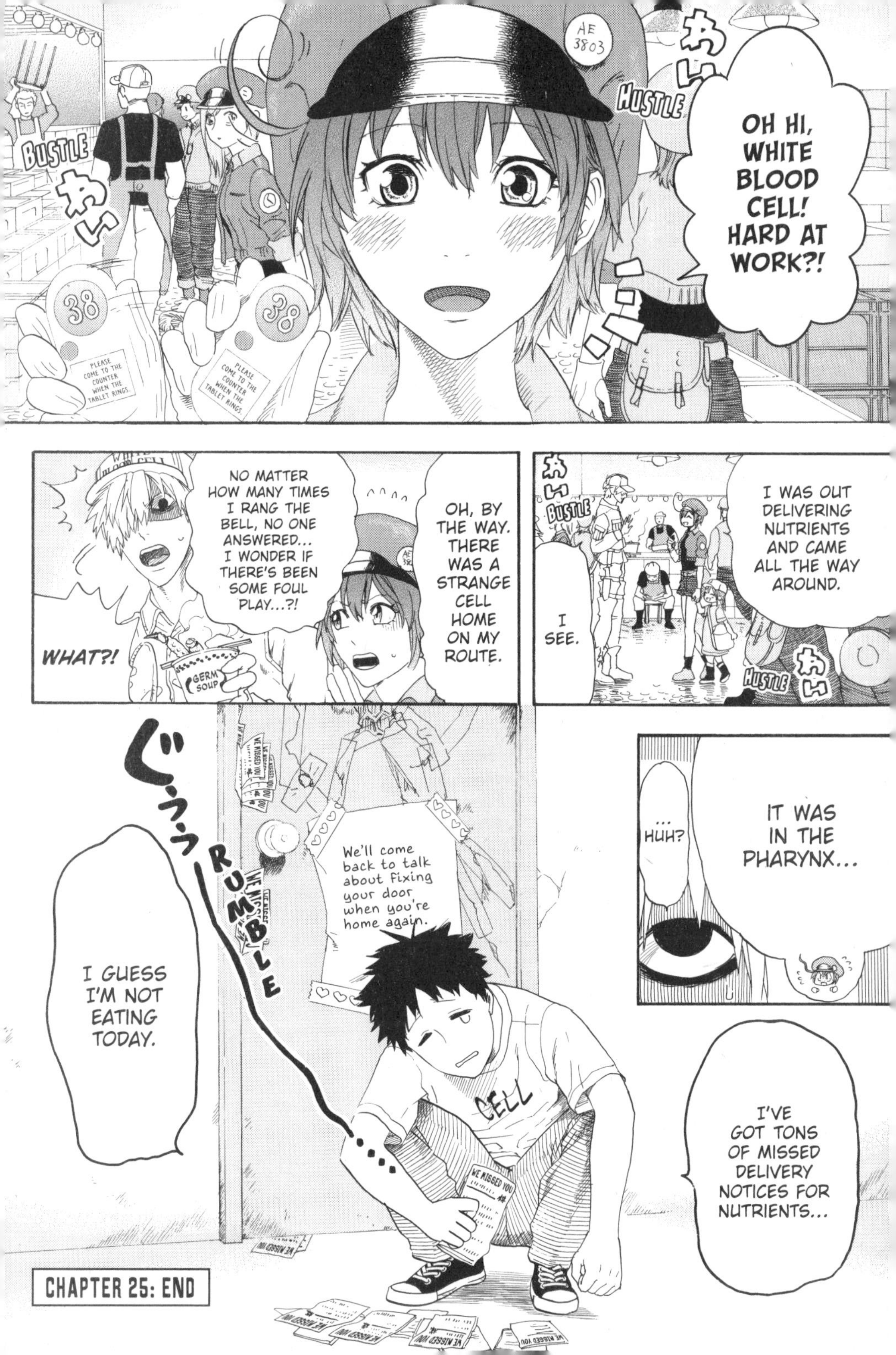
AE 3803
HUSTLE
BUSTLE
OH HI, WHITE BLOOD CELL! HARD AT WORK?!
38
PLEASE COME TO THE COUNTER WHEN THE TABLET RINGS.
38
PLEASE COME TO THE COUNTER WHEN THE TABLET RINGS.
I WAS OUT DELIVERING NUTRIENTS AND CAME ALL THE WAY AROUND.
I SEE.
BUSTLE
HUSTLE
OH, BY THE WAY. THERE WAS A STRANGE CELL HOME ON MY ROUTE.
NO MATTER HOW MANY TIMES I RANG THE BELL, NO ONE ANSWERED... I WONDER IF THERE'S BEEN SOME FOUL PLAY...?!
WHAT?!
GERM SOUP
IT WAS IN THE PHARYNX...
...HUH?
I'VE GOT TONS OF MISSED DELIVERY NOTICES FOR NUTRIENTS...
We'll come back to talk about fixing your door when you're home again.
WE MISSED YOU
RUMBLE
I GUESS I'M NOT EATING TODAY.
....
CELL
WE MISSED YOU

CHAPTER 25: END

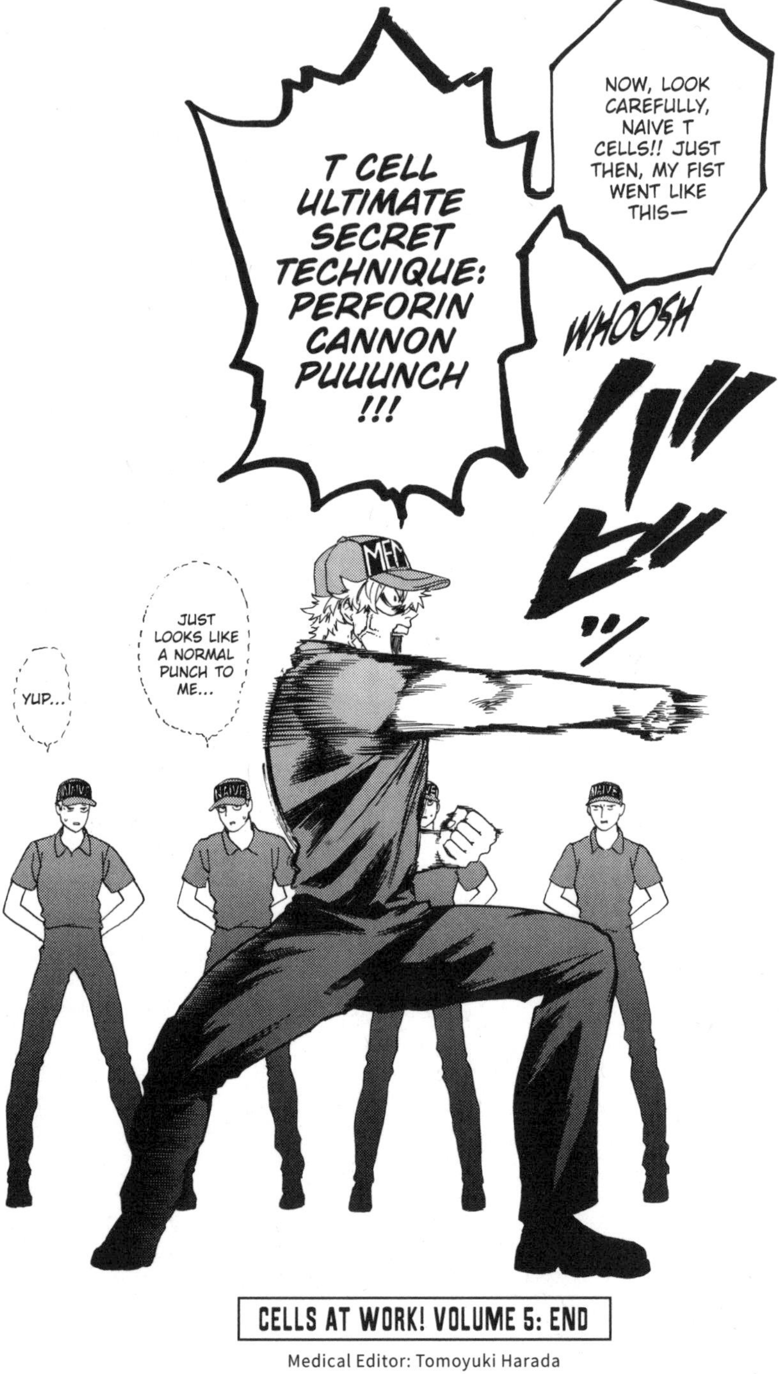
NOW, LOOK CAREFULLY, NAIVE T CELLS!! JUST THEN, MY FIST WENT LIKE THIS—
T CELL ULTIMATE SECRET TECHNIQUE: PERFORIN CANNON PUUUNCH!!!
WHOOSH
JUST LOOKS LIKE A NORMAL PUNCH TO ME...
YUP...

CELLS AT WORK! VOLUME 5: END

Medical Editor: Tomoyuki Harada

Cells at Work!

はたらく細胞

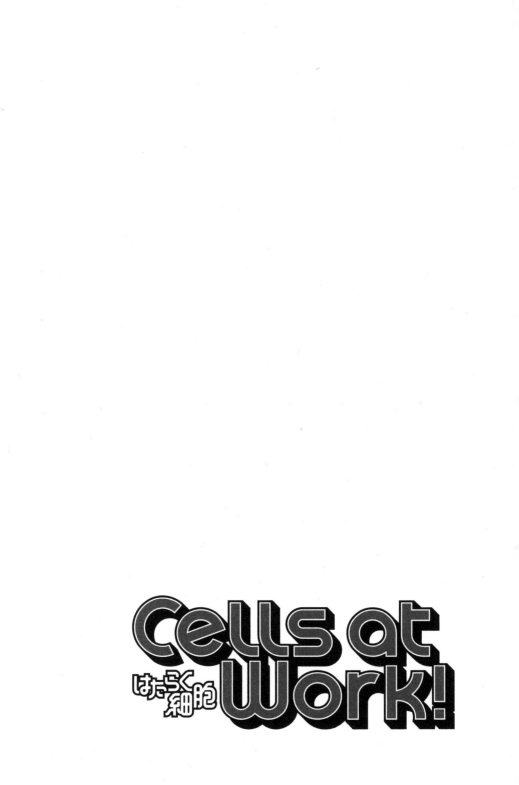

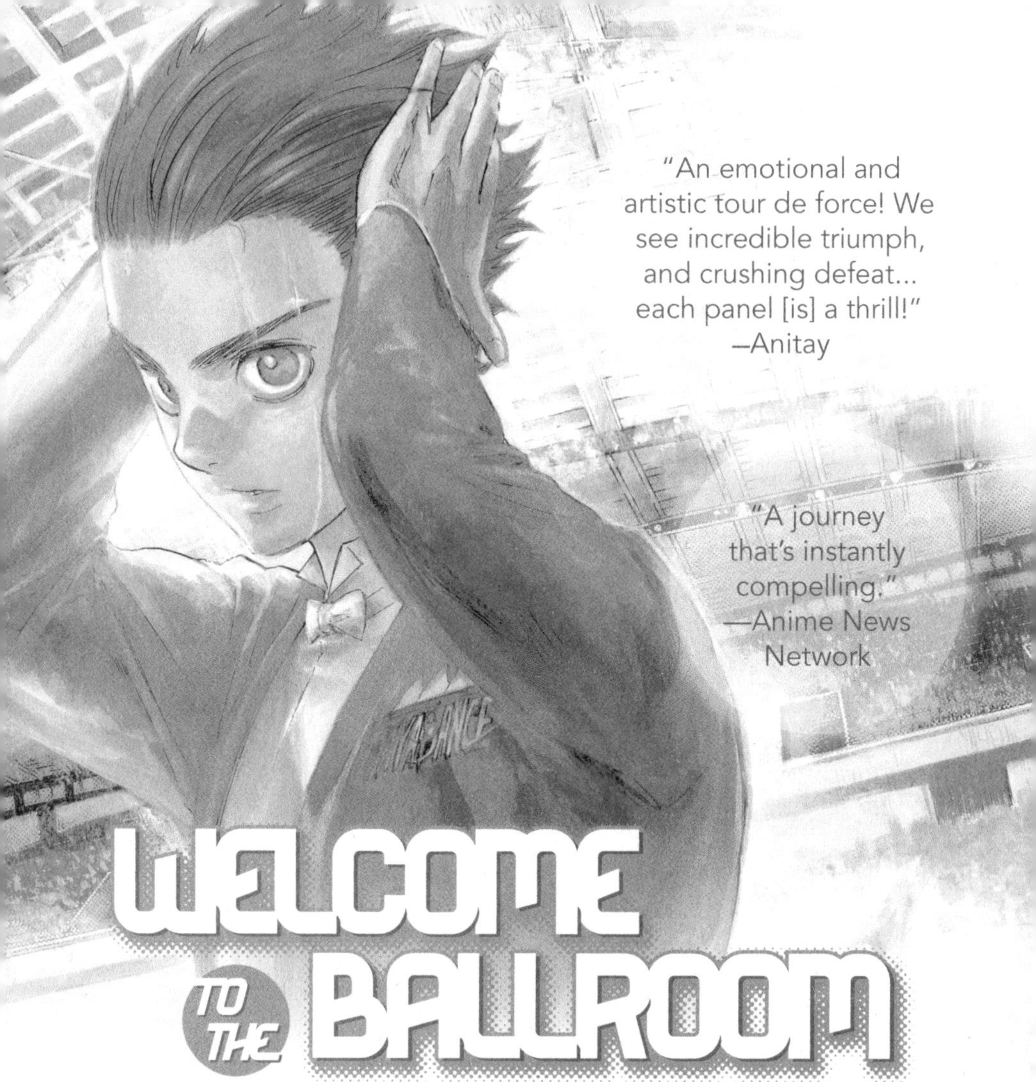

"An emotional and artistic tour de force! We see incredible triumph, and crushing defeat... each panel [is] a thrill!"
—Anitay

"A journey that's instantly compelling."
—Anime News Network

WELCOME TO THE BALLROOM

By Tomo Takeuchi

Feckless high school student Tatara Fujita wants to be good at something—anything. Unfortunately, he's about as average as a slouchy teen can be. The local bullies know this, and make it a habit to hit him up for cash, but all that changes when the debonair Kaname Sengoku sends them packing. Sengoku's not the neighborhood watch, though. He's a professional ballroom dancer. And once Tatara Fujita gets pulled into the world of ballroom, his life will never be the same.

New action series from Hiroyuki Takei, creator of the classic shonen franchise Shaman King!

In medieval Japan, a bell hanging on the collar is a sign that a cat has a master. Norachiyo's bell hangs from his katana sheath, but he is nonetheless a stray — a ronin. This one-eyed cat samurai travels across a dishonest world, cutting through pretense and deception with his blade.

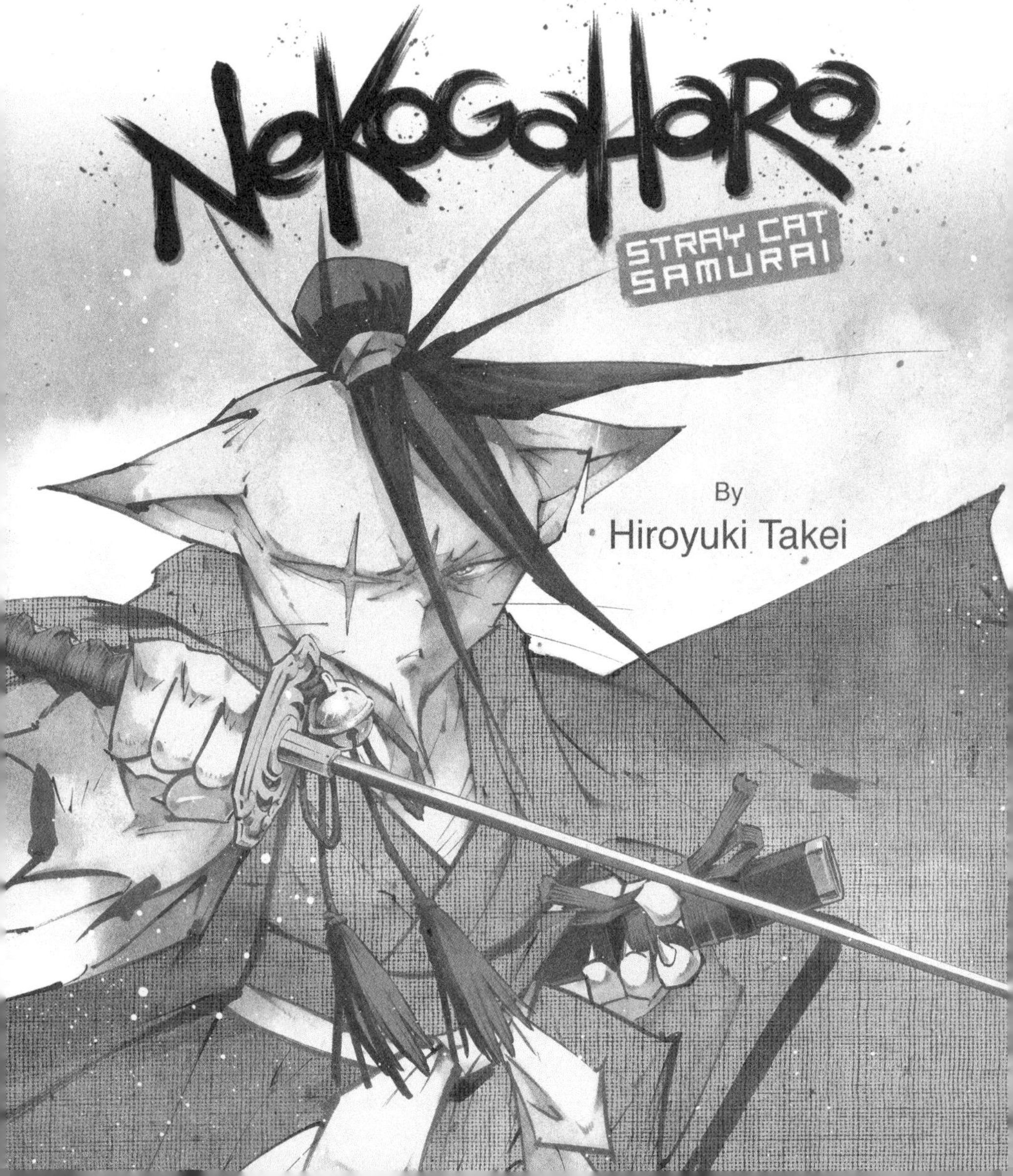
NekoGaHara
STRAY CAT SAMURAI
By
Hiroyuki Takei

KC KODANSHA COMICS

Japan's most powerful spirit medium delves into the ghost world's greatest mysteries!

Story by Kyo Shirodaira, famed author of mystery fiction and creator of *Spiral*, *Blast of Tempest*, and *The Record of a Fallen Vampire*.

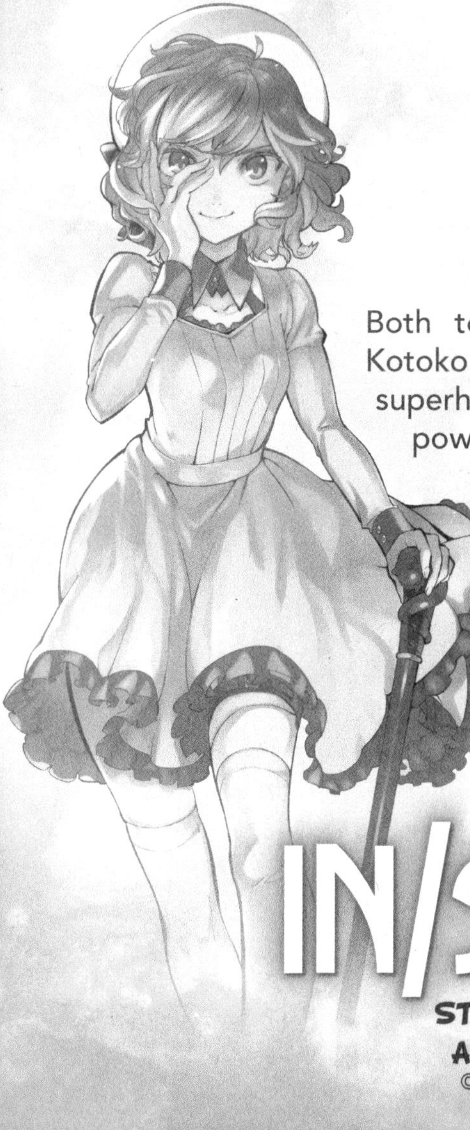

Both touched by spirits called yôkai, Kotoko and Kurô have gained unique superhuman powers. But to gain her powers Kotoko has given up an eye and a leg, and Kurô's personal life is in shambles. So when Kotoko suggests they team up to deal with renegades from the spirit world, Kurô doesn't have many other choices, but Kotoko might just have a few ulterior motives...

IN/SPECTRE

STORY BY KYO SHIRODAIRA
ART BY CHASHIBA KATASE

HAPPINESS

―ハピネス―

By Shuzo Oshimi

From the creator of *The Flowers of Evil*

Nothing interesting is happening in Makoto Ozaki's first year of high school. His life is a series of quiet humiliations: low-grade bullies, unreliable friends, and the constant frustration of his adolescent lust. But one night, a pale, thin girl knocks him to the ground in an alley and offers him a choice. Now everything is different. Daylight is searingly bright. Food tastes awful. And worse than anything is the terrible, consuming thirst...

Praise for Shuzo Oshimi's *The Flowers of Evil*

"A shockingly readable story that vividly—one might even say queasily—evokes the fear and confusion of discovering one's own sexuality. Recommended." —The Manga Critic

"A page-turning tale of sordid middle school blackmail." —Otaku USA Magazine

"A stunning new horror manga." —Third Eye Comics

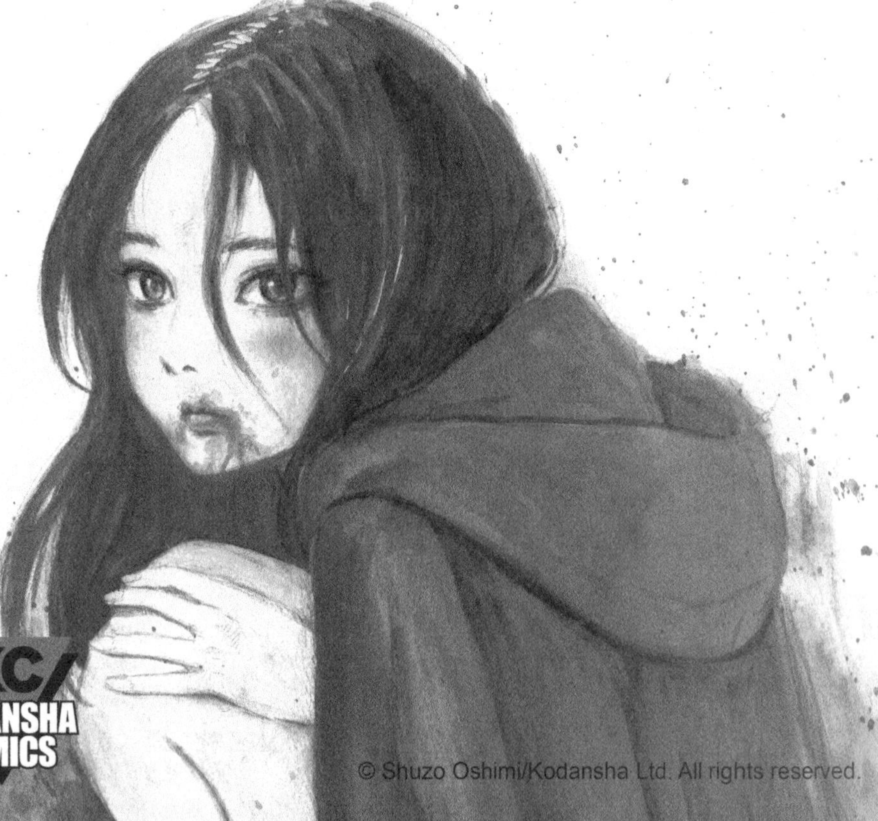

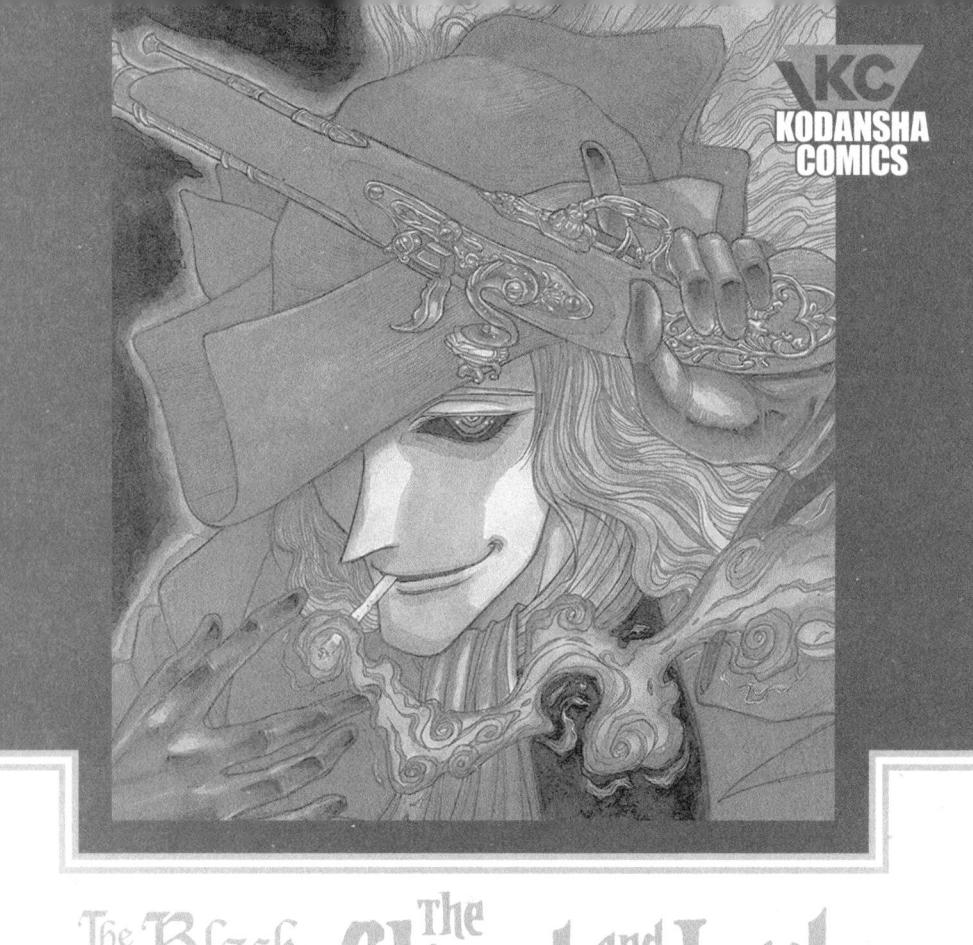

KC

KODANSHA
COMICS

The Black Museum The Ghost and the Lady

By Kazuhiro Fujita

Deep in Scotland Yard in London sits an evidence room dedicated to the greatest mysteries of British history. In this "Black Museum" sits a misshapen hunk of lead—two bullets fused together—the key to a wartime encounter between Florence Nightingale, the mother of modern nursing, and a supernatural Man in Grey. This story is unknown to most scholars of history, but a special guest of the museum will tell the tale of The Ghost and the Lady...

Praise for Kazuhiro Fujita's *Ushio and Tora*

"A charming revival that combines a classic look with modern depth and pacing... **Essential viewing both for curmudgeons and new fans alike.**" — Anime News Network

"**GREAT!** The first episode of Ushio and Tora captures the essence of '90s anime." — IGN

KODANSHA COMICS

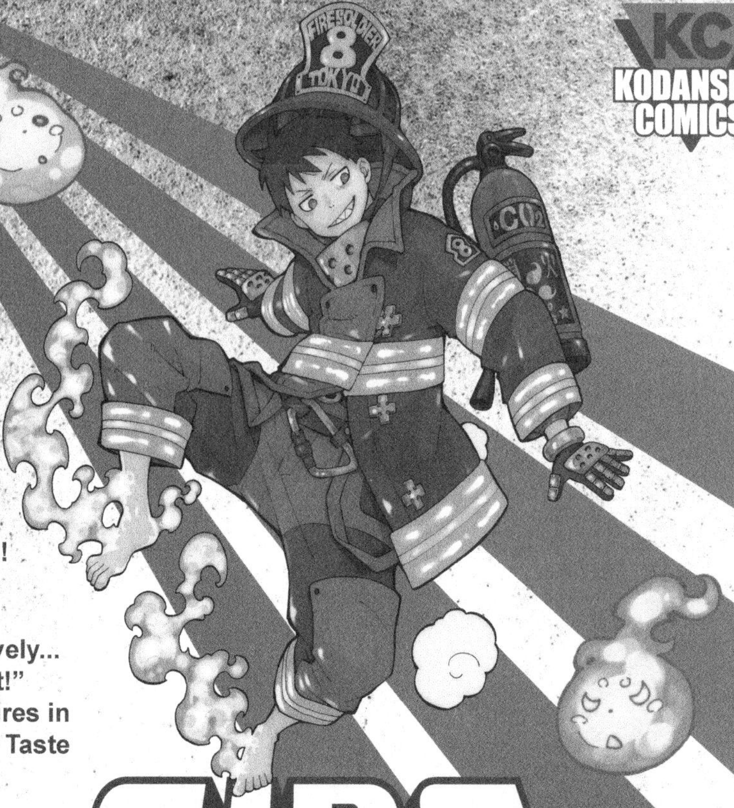

A new series from the creator of *Soul Eater*, the megahit manga and anime seen on Toonami!

"Fun and lively... a great start!"
    -Adventures in
        Poor Taste

FIRE FORCE

By Atsushi Ohkubo

The city of Tokyo is plagued by a deadly phenomenon: spontaneous human combustion! Luckily, a special team is there to quench the inferno: The Fire Force! The fire soldiers at Special Fire Cathedral 8 are about to get a unique addition. Enter Shinra, a boy who possesses the power to run at the speed of a rocket, leaving behind the famous "devil's footprints" (and destroying his shoes in the process). Can Shinra and his colleagues discover the source of this strange epidemic before the city burns to ashes?

© Atsushi Ohkubo/Kodansha Ltd. All rights reserved.

A Kodansha Comics Trade Paperback Original.

Published in the United States by Kodansha Comics, an imprint of Kodansha USA Publishing, LLC, New York.

Publication rights for this English edition arranged through Kodansha Ltd., Tokyo.

First published in Japan in 2017 by Kodansha Ltd., Tokyo, as *Hataraku Saibou* volume 5.

ISBN 978-1-63236-426-5

Printed in the United States of America.

www.kodanshacomics.com

9 8 7 6 5 4 3 2

Translator: Yamato Tanaka
Lettering: Abigail Blackman
Editing: Paul Starr
Kodansha Comics edition cover design by Phil Balsman